THEOLOGICAL AESTHETICS

Theological Aesthetics

A READER

Edited by

Gesa Elsbeth Thiessen

WILLIAM B. EERDMANS PUBLISHING COMPANY

GRAND RAPIDS, MICHIGAN / CAMBRIDGE, U.K.

First published 2004 in the U.K. by
SCM Press, 9–17 St Albans Place, London N1 0NX

© Gesa Elsbeth Thiessen 2004
All rights reserved

This edition published 2005 in the United States of America by
Wm. B. Eerdmans Publishing Co.
255 Jefferson Ave. S.E., Grand Rapids, Michigan 49503 /
P.O. Box 163, Cambridge CB3 9PU U.K.

Printed in the United States of America

09 08 07 06 05   7 6 5 4 3 2 1

ISBN 0-8028-2888-4

www.eerdmans.com

Contents

And the Word became flesh and lived among us,
and we have seen His glory.

John 1.14

Trusting in your goodness, I have ventured to surrender myself to rapture in order to see you, who are invisible, and the unrevealable vision revealed.

Nicholas of Cusa

Yes, would to God that I could persuade the rich and the mighty that they would permit the whole Bible to be painted on houses, on the inside and outside, so that all can see it. That would be a Christian work . . . If it is not a sin but good to have the image of Christ in my heart, why should it be a sin to have it in my eyes? This is especially true since the heart is more important than the eyes, and should be less stained by sin because it is the true abode and dwelling place of God.

Martin Luther

Meinen Freunden und Kollegen
am Milltown Institute of Theology and Philosophy
mit Dank

Preface

— —

'Another reader?' the exhausted student or lecturer might exclaim, and quietly add, 'Does this subject deserve an anthology, is there actually enough material to be gleaned from theology, past and present?'

A few years ago when I was engaged in doctoral research on the relationship between theology and the visual arts, especially with regard to modern Irish painting, the search for sources related to (theological) aesthetics took much time and effort. Naturally, here and there I came across relevant texts, yet no work was available which provided a collection of original texts or an overview of the history of aesthetics in a Christian context. The theme for another venture thus became clear, a reader on theological aesthetics as a source book for scholars and students.

Through the process of assembling, editing, writing and proofreading I have enjoyed, and am grateful for, the assistance of colleagues and friends at Milltown Institute and from further afar, in particular, Una Agnew, Finbarr Clancy, James Corkery, Bernadette Flanagan, David Kelly, Peter de Mey (Leuven) Patrick Mullins, Kevin O'Higgnis, Thomas O'Loughlin (Lampeter), Kieran O'Mahony, Patricia Quigley and all the Milltown Institute library staff, Ruth Sheehy and Margarita Synnott.

My sincere thanks go to Brian Grogan, President of Milltown Institute, whose generous support made it possible for me to continue my work on the Reader. My very special thanks are due to George Pattison (Oxford) for his many comments on the form and contents of the Reader. I appreciate his invaluable help and encouragement in bringing the Reader to a conclusion. I thank Patrick Sherry (Lancaster) for helpful comments. My thanks to Thomas Dalzell for his thorough reading of, and commenting on, the introductions. I also valued the assistance and courtesy from both Anna Hardman and Barbara Laing at SCM Press in the process.

A delightful Easter of 2002 in the windswept Heinrich Böll Cottage on Achill Island in County Mayo, Ireland, provided an occasion for concentrated work in the former living room of the writer; my thanks to the Heinrich Böll Committee on Achill Island, Mayo County Council and the Arts Council of Ireland for their affording me this opportunity.

Personal support, encouragement and humour I received along from my family and friends. Declan Marmion re-read the introductions, provided many helpful comments and cheerfully encouraged me when the task seemed unending; ihm mein herzlicher Dank.

General Introduction

About three decades ago, the need for a Reader on the subject of theological aesthetics would hardly have been a priority for any theologian. Scholars were aware, of course, that theologians past and present had written on themes relating to aesthetics in the context of a theology of God and Christian faith. Yet, it is only in the last twenty years that the field of theological aesthetics, including the dialogue between theology and the arts, has become a major focus in theology.

The aestheticization of everyday life in postmodern society through the powerful impact of images in mass media, the arts and culture, the constant presence of music, mostly of the popular variety, and the cult of the body and of youth, are now ever-present features in our lives. The hunger for instant gratification, be it through exotic food, travel, films, music, body-cult, as well as the desire for religious or quasi-religious experiences, ranging from crystal-gazing to traditional forms of Christian worship, are all based in aesthetic, i.e. sensuous, experience and phenomena.

On a more academic level, in philosophy and theology, the aesthetic dimension is also receiving growing attention. Not only is this obvious in the numerous publications on the theme, but whole conferences and even sub-departments are now devoted to the dialogue between theology and the arts in Europe and in the United States. Indeed, a quick glance at the bibliography for further reading at the end of this book makes apparent the rapid growth of study in this field.

First of all, then, one might ask what is theological aesthetics? Naturally, various authors will offer various definitions. While it is neither possible nor necessary to supply a 'once and for all' definition, I suggest, to paraphrase Richard Viladesau, that theological aesthetics is concerned with questions about God and issues in theology in the light of and perceived through sense knowledge (sensation, feeling, imagination), through beauty, and the arts. This is a wide 'definition' which hints at the multi-faceted contents and methods in theological aesthetics. For example, any issue of a contemporary journal in this field will comprise critical writings on aesthetic theories and commentaries on current projects in visual art, music, literature and church architecture. There are also articles on theoretical and practical aspects of the relationship between theology and the arts written by theologians, pastors, musicians and artists, reviews and

Beauty is not an extra, it is essential to all existence. Truth or goodness without beauty become dull, lifeless, boring, formalistic and cold. It is beauty – sensuous and spiritual, spiritual in the sensuous, and sensuous in the spiritual – which excites and nourishes human feeling, desire, thought and imagination. It is the splendour of beauty that makes the true and the good whole. The magnitude of beauty in nature and in all human creation, wherever it is experienced, gives us a glimpse of the beauty of God, therein lies its saving power. In this way beauty becomes a way to God and a manifestation of God at the same time. God's beauty is what draws us to God, and this includes the mystery and glory of Christ on the cross, the utter distortion of divine-human beauty and yet its complete fulfilment. This paradox is the basis of Christian faith and cannot be overlooked, not even and especially in a theological aesthetics.

Ultimately, the vision of God is eschatological. If in some sense all theology is eschatology, this certainly applies to theological aesthetics. The vision of God is a future hope, it is dimly perceived now and in all its unimaginable splendour in the life to come. While on earth we aspire to that vision, it is only in the eschaton that the unbearable white light of Christ will be fully manifest. Art, too, has an eschatological dimension since in art we can imagine and express the world as it could or should be. Indeed, one might claim that real art points us in the most diverse ways to a reality that could be and is not yet, whether in the Gothic cathedral or Rembrandt's 'Prodigal Son', Gauguin's visions of a lost paradise, Bach's cello suites, a small country chapel, or Picasso's 'Guernica'. Why 'Guernica', why a picture by a self-proclaimed atheist like Picasso?, one might object. Precisely because in 'Guernica' Picasso showed his protest against war by confronting the viewer with its horror, thereby pointing to a world that should be other than it is!

A world in need of redemption is a world in which the vision of God is not an optional extra. The vision of God constitutes the eschatological hope, the destination and goal of all followers of Christ and ultimately maybe of all human beings, as they are made in the image of God. The vision of God still attracts and awes people. Art, faith, theology, and doing the good, can provide paths to such glimpses of the transcendent.

Theologians have noted not only the eschatological dimension intrinsic to all theology, but also its doxological aspect. No doubt, even the most painful questions in theology, such as theodicy, are ultimately struggled with in the light of faith, a faith that may be weak and torn, but which still desires to live, express its vision, and thereby witness to the reality of God. Given the concern in theological aesthetics with the image, beauty and vision of God, with sensuous knowledge and the arts, doxology, like eschatology, plays a special role in this field. In fact, one might claim that both the eschatological and doxological dimensions are truly central in theological aesthetics with its appreciation of revelation in the beauty of art and nature and of the ever-transcendent beauty of God. The element of praise is palpable especially in the Church fathers and in the mystics when they write in systematic-conceptual terms on God and then suddenly burst into poetic words and song, addressing God directly as Thou and confessing their love of God *to* God and to us. Perhaps it is time to reclaim something of this wholesome systematic-poetic way of doing theology, an aesthetic theology and a theological aesthetics.

Part 1

The Early Church

— —

Introduction

The themes in patristic writing relating to a theological aesthetics span the years from c.160 to c.650 AD, beginning with Justin Martyr and culminating in the remarkably developed ideas on the beautiful in Pseudo-Dionysius. In what follows the main topics will be introduced, and divergences and connections between the early theologians and their ideas will be noted.

The vision of God or of God's glory, the image of God in Christ and in us, and the concern with idol worship are the most prevalent themes in the early Christian thinkers. For numerous theologians – not only in the early Church, but throughout medieval history and even to this day, who have referred to the vision of God – the eye appears to have had a certain pre-eminence over the other senses. Justin Martyr was the first to make the vision of God a theme in his theology. For him God is glory, for God 'sometimes appears in visions', and he likens God's power to the light of the sun. Irenaeus asserts that by the vision of God humans will become immortal; we desire to see God so as to live, and to live eternally. Origen, like John's Gospel, reminds us that the glory of the invisible Godhead is seen through the incarnate Son. Basil and Gregory of Nyssa emphasize that only the purified mind will see the beauty of God, of Christ. Purification means purification of the eye of the soul. This purification enables the contemplation of beauty. Augustine similarly exclaims that that soul which in itself has become purified and therefore beautiful will see God and that the vision of beauty is promised to Christians. God is the 'intelligible light' that we can see only if our hearts are cleansed. If the eye or seeing has a certain pre-eminence it is thus not so much in a literal sense but somewhat metaphorical. It does not merely refer to the physical act of seeing, but to seeing in a spiritualized sense of grasping with a pure heart and soul. Seeing God then is aesthetic, spiritual, intellectual, ethical and even ascetical and achieved only in the context of faith and through contemplation.

What essentially shaped the early theologians' thought were relevant New Testament passages (e.g. John 1.18; 2 Cor. 4.18; 1 John 1–3) and the Platonist and Neo-Platonist thinking of their time. For Plato the contemplation of the forms, i.e. their structures and their way of being, through true knowledge is always something whereby we have a glimpse of the beautiful (*kalon*). All being is beautiful, but being is understood as a complex of differentiated, ordered forms under the ever-transcendent ultimate good (cf. Farley, 2001, p. 20). At the end of the *Symposium*, Plato asserts that from an ascent of knowledge of sensuous beauty in forms, in virtues, in various kinds of knowledge, one reaches the knowledge of the beautiful. The ultimate, uniquely beautiful is that which we desire to contemplate and with which we want to be connected, because it is pure and touches truth and creates true virtue. Those who reach this contemplation deserve immortality and to be loved by the Gods.

Plotinus, the most important Neo-Platonist and hugely influential in patristic writing, expands on Plato in the *Enneads* by asserting that beauty is not simply the order of the forms but is also present and alive in the soul, in its wisdom and its desire to see the forms (cf. Farley, 2001, p. 20). The soul by purifying itself becomes good and beautiful and thus like the One or the Good who is 'beauty above beauty'. Plotinus, like Plato, holds that true being is beautiful; being which is not true is ugly. He juxtaposes light and darkness; those who see the light see beauty, and he asserts that only those whose soul has become like God, i.e. beautiful, will see the beautiful and God. In both Plato and Plotinus the vision of the beautiful is an intellectual act, the aesthetic act being ancillary, so to speak, as the vision of exterior beauty is only a first step before one perceives the ideas, which are the source of the mind and the cause for all being and beauty. Given what has been said about Justin Martyr et al above, it becomes clear how much they were influenced in their thought on the vision of God by these philosophers. This includes ideas about the purification of heart and soul as a requirement to see God, the vision of God or of the beautiful through the intellect, the union with the divine by purified seeing, and the recurrent symbolism of light.

However, there is, of course, an essential change concerning the vision of the divine in Christianity, i.e. the development of the dogma of the revelation of God in the incarnate Son, and of the dogma of the Trinity, both central in the emerging theology of the first centuries after Christ. Those who believe in Jesus see in him the perfect image of God, the prototype. In the early Christian writers this theme of the vision of the visible image of God, through whom we, as images of the divine, shall be assimilated to the invisible Father, appears repeatedly, e.g. in Irenaeus and also in Origen, who describes the Son as the light through whom we know the Father. A recurring metaphor employed for Christ is the sun, which again indicates the Platonist influence. This symbol appears too in Christian art, both in relation to Christ and to Mary. The sun implies light and light means truth, the truth of God in Christ. Lactantius, Hilary, Ambrose and Augustine likewise use the symbolism of light and describe and praise Christ as the light of truth, the true glorious image of the invisible God.

The Holy Spirit plays the mediating role in the vision of God and the presence of (divine) beauty in the world. Irenaeus appears to have been the first Christian theologian who dwelled on the Spirit's function. Clement of Alexandria refers to the Spirit in sensuous terms as the 'holy myrrh' with which women and men shall be anointed. Hilary speaks of the Trinity as Father, Image and Gift, and attributes beauty to the Son. Ambrose, in his work *The Holy Spirit*, also considers the biblical metaphors and analogies regarding the Spirit as the 'ointment of Christ', 'the oil of gladness', and as light and fire. God's Spirit – no longer the ideas or forms – is the one through whom God's beauty is communicated in natural creation and who inspires artistic creation, and therewith anticipates the eternal beauty of the eschaton (cf. Sherry, 2002, p. 160). Although the Spirit and its creative, life-giving power features less often as a theme in the early writers than Christ as image of God, the Spirit's role as the one who communicates God's beauty, goodness and truth in the world is an element in Christian thought right from the beginning.

In stark, although not surprising, contrast to Christ as the image of God is the deep and consistent concern with idolatry. This issue remained prominent up to the Reformation. It recedes into the background in the contexts of Post-Enlightenment secular modernity and postmodernity. In the ancient world, idol worship and the worship of many gods was, of course, very much a fact of everyday life. Whether Greek or Roman deities or the Baals in Canaan, the early Christian writers were constantly faced with the need to address this problem and juxtapose the truth of the one God whose only perfect image – or *eikon* – is that of Christ with the misguided, naive and dangerous worship of idols. Not only did they mention non-Christian gods, but they elaborated in great detail that images of Christ or of any holy Christian figures should be prohibited. Otherwise one would be prone to worship the sculptures or images made of matter rather than what remains always transcendent – the invisible God. Justin and Irenaeus vigorously attacked idol worship, along with Lactantius, who simply declared that 'there is no religion wherever there is a statue or image'. Later, the extreme Byzantine iconoclasts of the seventh and eighth centuries and the Reformers in the sixteenth century would again dispute this issue. (The theme is discussed in more detail in the Introduction to Part 3.)

The dualistic view of being, originating with Plato and his contemporaries – i.e. the continuously asserted superiority and purity of spiritual life, soul, and intellect in contrast to the suspicion and even denigration of material, sensuous existence – is not only reflected in the fear of idolatry but it essentially shaped Christian anthropology, faith and theology. This is most obvious in three spheres: the perception of the senses, the role of the body, and the view of women. The comments differ in tone and degree; sometimes the senses are even praised, yet a dualism prevails in patristic literature and beyond. Tertullian, on the one hand, passionately, and in what one might call remarkably 'holistic', 'postmodern' fashion, defends sense knowledge in his work *On the Soul*. On the other hand, in his *On the Apparel of Women*, he viciously attacks women, 'the devil's gateway', as those who brought sin into the world; thus they must at all times dress modestly so as not to lead men into temptation through sensuous apparel. Clement of Alexandria allows for certain 'useful' oils, yet they must not be erotic lest they lead to 'lustful desires' and 'sexual relations'. For him, as for others, the spiritual 'odour of Christ' is the one with which Christians shall clad themselves. Ambrose and John Chrysostom in the same way attack women for using cosmetics, which results in 'ugliness' and 'deceit', rather than in beauty. Augustine makes use of many metaphors from the realm of the senses and of feeling, especially in his doxologies; 'Thou didst shine forth and glow . . . Thou didst send forth Thy fragrance, and I drew in my breath, and now I pant for thee; I have tasted, and now I hunger and thirst; Thou didst touch me, and I was inflamed with desire for Thy peace.' Still, he laments, there remain the eye's pleasures of his flesh, the 'lower kind of beauties', which disturb his search for the true spiritual beauty of God.

Despite this dualism and ambiguity, it needs to be pointed out that the language of the early Christian writers is interspersed with a great variety of – sometimes markedly sensuous – metaphors and symbols. Theological language naturally cannot be and has never been anything but analogical, as we are always limited to the confines of human language in talking of what lies utterly beyond – the invisible, 'unnameable' God. Only in our perception of the incarnate Son through the Christian Testament do we leave, but only to some extent, the realm of analogy. Jesus himself chose symbolism, imagery and metaphors in his telling of parables and stories. It is this analogical language which founds, limits and enriches theology, and in itself pertains profoundly to a theological aesthetics due to its often sensuous, emotional, aesthetic and, at times, erotic content. This is especially noticeable in Origen, in Ephrem's poems, in Ambrose and in Augustine. It is thus both ironic and significant that while these thinkers were obsessed with a 'pure' spiritual way of life, and frequently suspicious of the sensuous bodily realm, their mode of communicating the truths of faith was often emphatically sensuous, imaginative, emotional, intimate, and expressive of desire and yearning. If one looks at the 'detached', quasi-scientific, theological language of later times, then this way of speaking to and about God at the same time had a more holistic, i.e. emotional, sensuous and intellectual, ring to it. The retrieval and development of a theological aesthetics and the interest in mystical theology in recent decades may also be seen as an acknowledgement of a 'poetic poverty' in much (modern) theology.

In this context of language, God as the one who is supremely imaginative and creates, and likewise our task of being creative and imaginative, should be mentioned. The patristic writings speak of God not only as creator, but, more concretely, they refer to God in biblical and artistic terms as supreme artist (Ambrose, Augustine), as musician and craftsman (Paulinus of Nola, Augustine), and to Christ being the prototype, the perfect image, whom we have to learn to imitate by becoming painters of our own lives by applying as perfectly as possible the colours of the pure virtues of the model (Gregory).

This brings us finally to the idea of beauty, referred to by the various writers. As was noted above, Plato and Plotinus both made important contributions to this issue. For the early Christians beauty, truth, unity and goodness in the world are always seen as signs of divine revelation, of God's beauty, truth, unity and goodness. Beauty is objective, and always also has to do with spiritual and moral purification. The good, the true and the beautiful cannot be thought of apart from one another, as God in Godself is supreme beauty, goodness and truth. Augustine, in particular, emphasizes in Platonic fashion how beauty includes symmetry, proportion and order. Chaos cannot be beautiful. Beauty relates to the cosmos. The individual parts of the cosmos are beautiful and make up its total beauty. Beauty is something that attracts and something we love. Augustine wrote a specific work on the beautiful but he admits in the *Confessions* that it got lost. Certainly, in the patristic period, it was Pseudo-Dionysius who, in his *The Divine Names*, had the most developed aesthetics on beauty. Influenced to a great extent by Neo-Platonism and also by Gnosticism, his apophatic, mystical theology develops the symbolism of light, whereby the supreme light is the Good itself that radiates in every mind. This light of beauty unites those who possess reason and mind, perfecting them and turning them back to the truly real and to true knowledge. Beauty is the source of everything that is beautiful and it unites everything. And in turn all creatures must yearn for that God who is Beauty and Goodness. Pseudo-Dionysius thus achieved a certain synthesis in his ideas on beauty as he integrated (Neo-)Platonist, biblical and patristic thought, which would be taken up later by medieval theologians.

I

Divine Beauty, Purification and the Vision of God

— —

1.1 Justin Martyr, from *Dialogue with Trypho*

Justin Martyr (c.100–165) was a Christian apologist and the first Christian thinker who sought to reconcile the claims of faith and of reason. Here he emphasizes the glory of God, which at times appears in visions. He makes an analogy between the image of the light of Christ, indivisible from the Father, and the light of the sun of the skies, indivisible from the light of the sun on the earth.

I have taken great care to prove at length that Christ is the Lord and God the Son, that in times gone He appeared by His power as man and angel, and in the glory of fire as in the bush, and that He was present to execute the judgment against Sodom. Then I repeated all that I had already quoted from the Book of Exodus concerning the vision in the bush, and the imposition of the name Jesus [Josue], and continued, 'Gentlemen, please do not accuse me of being verbose or repetitious in my explanations. My remarks are rather lengthy because I know that some of you are about to anticipate them, and to declare that the power which was sent from the Universal Father and appeared to Moses, Abraham, or Jacob, was called Angel because He came to men (since by that power the Father's messages are communicated to men); is called Glory, because He sometimes appears in visions that cannot be contained; is called a man and human being, because He appears arrayed in such forms as please the Father; and they call Him the Word, because He reveals to men the discourses of the Father. But some teach that this power is indivisible and inseparable from the Father, just as the light of the sun on earth is indivisible and inseparable from the sun in the skies; for, when the sun sets, its light disappears from the earth. So, they claim, the Father by His will can cause His power to go forth and, whenever He wishes, to return again.' (Ch. 128, pp. 346–7)

Source: *The Fathers of the Church, Saint Justin Martyr*, ed. Thomas B. Falls, Washington, The Catholic University of America Press in assoc. with Consortium Books, 1948

1.2 Irenaeus, from *Against Heresies*

Irenaeus (c.130–c.200), Bishop of Lyons, was the first great Christian theologian. In particular, he wrote against Gnosticism. In this extract he rejects the Gnostics' claim of possessing and displaying a portrait of Christ along with images of Greek philosophers. He points out the visible and audible dimension of God, being all eye, all light, and he commends the Gnostics to learn the arts. He insists that humans, by their vision of God, will become immortal and that God, in becoming the incarnate, visible Son, reassimilated humans to the invisible God.

Some of them brand their disciples on the back part of the right ear lobe. One of them named Marcellina came to Rome under Anicetus and caused the destruction of many. They call themselves Gnostics. They have images, some painted, others made of various materials, for, they say, a portrait of Christ was made by Pilate in the time when Jesus was with men. They put crowns on these and show them forth with images of the worldly philosophers, that is, Pythagoras, Plato, Aristotle, and others, and pay them the same honours as among pagans. (Book 1, Ch. 25, para. 6, p. 94)

If they had known the scriptures and had been taught by the truth, they would know that God is not like men (Num 23.19) and that God's thoughts are not like men's thoughts (Is 55.8–9). For the Father of all is at a great remove from human emotions and passions; He is unified, not composite, without diversity of members, completely similar and equal to himself, since he is all Mind, all Spirit, all Mentality, all Thought, all Word, all Hearing, all Eye, all Light, and entirely the source of every good thing – as religious and pious men rightly say of God.

But he is still above this and therefore ineffable. For he is rightly called all-embracing Mind, but unlike the human mind; and most justly called Light, but Light in no way resembling the light we know. Thus also in regard to all the other appellations the Father of all in no way resembles the weakness of humanity, and while he is given these names because of his love he is considered above them because of his greatness.

Just as it is right to say that he is all Seeing and all Hearing – for as he sees he hears, and as he hears he sees – so it is also right to say that he is all Mind and all Logos, and in that he is Mind he is Logos, and his Mind is this Logos. (Book 2, Ch. 13, para. 3, 4, 8, p. 109)

Further, when they call themselves bound to accomplish all deeds and all actions so as to achieve them all in one life, if possible, and thus reach perfection, they are never found even trying to do what relates to virtue and involves labour and glorious deeds and efforts in the arts, approved as good by all. For if they ought to experience every work and activity, first they ought to learn all the arts, whether theoretical or practical or learned through labour and meditation and perseverance – for example, every form of music and arithmetic and geometry and astronomy, and all the other theoretical disciplines. They should also study the whole of medicine and the science of pharmacy and all the disciplines developed for human health, and painting and sculpture and working in bronze and marble and other arts like these, as well as every form of agriculture and the care of horses and of flocks and herds, and the mechanical arts, which are said to involve all the others; and navigation, gymnastics, hunting, military science, kingship – without counting all the others. If they worked their entire lives they could not learn a ten-thousandth part of them. (Book 2, Ch. 32, para. 2, p. 121)

Therefore men will see God in order to live, becoming immortal by the vision and attaining to God. That is what, as I have said, was figuratively shown through the prophets, that God will be seen by the men who bear his Spirit and always await his coming, as Moses said in Deuteronomy (5.24), 'In that day we shall see, because God will speak to a man and he will live.' Some of them saw the prophetic Spirit and its work in all kinds of gifts poured forth; others saw the coming of the Lord and his ministry from the beginning, by which he achieved the will of the Father as in heaven, so on earth (Matt 6.10); still others saw the Father's glories adapted in various times to men who saw and then heard, and to those who would hear subsequently. Thus, then, God was manifested; for through all these things God the Father is shown forth, as the Spirit works and the Son administers and the Father approves, and man is made perfect for his salvation. (Book 4, Ch. 20, para. 6, p. 152)

And thus was the hand of God plainly shown forth, by which Adam was fashioned, and we too have been formed; and since there is one and the same Father, whose voice from the beginning even to the end is present with His handiwork, and the substance from which we were formed is plainly declared through the Gospel, we should therefore not seek after another Father besides Him, nor [look for] another substance from which we have been formed, besides what was mentioned beforehand, and shown forth by the Lord; nor another hand of God besides that which, from the beginning even to the end, forms us and prepares us for life, and is present with His handiwork, and perfects it after the image and likeness of God.

And then, again, this Word was manifested when the Word of God was made man, assimilating Himself to man, and man to Himself, so that by means of his resemblance to the Son, man might become precious to the Father. For in times long past, it was *said* that man was created after the image of God, but it was not [actually] *shown*; for the Word was as yet invisible, after whose image man was created. Wherefore also he did easily lose the similitude. When, however, the Word of God became flesh, He confirmed both these: for He both showed forth the image truly, since He became Himself what was His image; and He re-established the similitude after a sure manner, by assimilating man to the invisible Father through means of the visible Word. (*Book 5, Ch. 16, para. 1 and 2, p. 544)

Source: *The Early Church Fathers, Irenaeus of Lyons*, ed. Robert Grant, London, New York, Routledge, 1997; and *The Ante-Nicene Christian Library*, vol. 9, eds James Donaldson and Alexander Roberts, Edinburgh, T. & T. Clark, 1869.

1.3 Origen, from *De Principiis*

Origen (c.185–254), who lived in Alexandria and Caesarea, was a major patristic theologian. He engaged especially in biblical criticism. In this passage he explores central metaphors and analogies used in our speaking of Christ, such as light, glory and the express image of God.

For we must of necessity hold that there is something exceptional and worthy of God which does not admit of any comparison at all, not merely in things, but which cannot even be conceived by thought or discovered by perception, so that a human mind should be able to apprehend how the unbegotten God is made the Father of the only-begotten Son. Because His generation is as eternal and ever-lasting as the brilliancy which is produced from the sun. For it is not by receiving the breath of life that He is made a Son, by *any outward act,* but by His own nature.

Let us now ascertain how those statements which we have advanced are supported by the authority of holy Scripture. The Apostle Paul says, that the only-begotten Son is the 'image of the invisible God', and 'the first-born of every creature'. And when writing to the Hebrews, he says of Him that He is 'the brightness of His glory, and the express image of His person'. Now, we find in the treatise called the Wisdom of Solomon the following description of the wisdom of God: 'For she is the breath of the power of God, and the purest efflux of the glory of the Almighty.' Nothing that is polluted can therefore come upon her. For she is the splendour of the eternal light, and the stainless mirror of God's working, and the image of His goodness. Now we say, as before, that Wisdom has her existence nowhere else save in Him who is the beginning of all things: from whom also is derived everything that is wise, because He Himself is the only one who is by nature a Son, and is therefore termed the Only-begotten. (Book 1, Ch. 2, para. 4–5, p. 22)

Rather, therefore, as an act of the will proceeds from the understanding, and neither cuts off any part nor is separated or divided from it, so after some such fashion is the Father to be supposed as having begotten the Son, His own image; namely, so that, as He is Himself invisible by nature, He also begat an image that was invisible. For the Son is the Word, and therefore we are not to understand that anything in Him is cognisable by the senses. He is wisdom, and in wisdom there can be no suspicion of anything corporeal. He is the true light, which enlightens every man that cometh into this world; but He has nothing in common with the light of this sun. Our Saviour, therefore, is the image of the invisible God, inasmuch as compared with the Father Himself He is the truth: and as compared with us, to whom He reveals the Father, He is the image by which we come to the knowledge of the Father, whom no one knows save the Son, and he to whom the Son is pleased to reveal Him. And the method of revealing Him is through the understanding. For He by whom the Son Himself is understood, understands, as a consequence, the Father also, according to His own words: 'He that hath seen me, hath seen the Father also.'

But since we quoted the language of Paul regarding Christ, where he says of Him that He is 'the brightness of the glory of God, and the express figure of his person', let us see what idea we are to form of this. According to John, 'God is light'. The only-begotten Son, therefore, is the glory of this light, proceeding inseparably from [God] Himself, as brightness does from light, and illuminating the whole of creation. For, agreeably to what we have already explained as to the manner in which He is the Way, and conducts to the Father; and in which He is the Word, interpreting the secrets of wisdom, and the mysteries of knowledge, making them known to the rational creation; and is also the Truth, and the Life, and the Resurrection, – in the same way ought we to understand also the meaning of His being the brightness: for it is by its splendour that we understand and feel what light itself is. And this splendour, presenting itself gently and softly to the frail and weak eyes of mortals, and gradually training, as it were, and accustoming them to bear the brightness of the light, when it has put away from them every hindrance and obstruction to vision, according to the Lord's own precept, 'Cast forth the beam out of thine eye', renders them capable of enduring the splendour of the light, being made in this respect also a sort of mediator between men and the light.

In order, however, to arrive at a fuller understanding of the manner in which the Saviour is the figure of the person or subsistence of God, let us take an instance, which, although it does not describe the subject of which we are treating either fully or appropriately, may nevertheless be seen to be employed for this purpose only, to show that the Son of God, who was in the form of God, divesting Himself [of His glory], makes it His object, by this very divesting of Himself, to demonstrate to us the fulness of His deity. For instance, suppose that there were a statue of so enormous a size as to fill the whole world, and which on that account could be seen by no one; and that another statue were formed altogether resembling it in the shape of the limbs, and in the features of the countenance, and in form and material, but without the same immensity of size, so that those who were unable to behold the one of enormous proportions, should, on seeing the latter, acknowledge that they had seen the former, because it preserved all the features of its limbs and countenance, and even the very form and material, so closely, as to be altogether undistinguishable from it; by some such similitude, the Son of God, divesting Himself of His equality with the Father, and showing to us the way to the knowledge of Him, is made the express image of His person: so that we, who were unable to look upon the glory of that marvellous light when placed in the greatness of His Godhead, may, by His being made to us brightness, obtain the means of beholding the divine light by looking upon the brightness. This comparison, of course, of statues, as belonging to material things, is employed for no other purpose than to show that the Son of God, though placed in the very insignificant form of a human body, in consequence of the resemblance of His works and power to the Father, showed that there was in Him an immense and invisible greatness, inasmuch as He said to His disciples, 'He who sees me, sees the Father also'; and, 'I and the Father are one.' And to these belong also the similar expression, 'The Father is in me, and I in the Father.' (Book 1, Ch. 2, para. 6–8, pp. 24–6)

Source: *The Ante-Nicene Christian Library, vol. 10, The Writings of Origin*, eds James Donaldson and Alexander Roberts, Edinburgh, T. & T. Clark, 1869.

1.4 Hilary of Poitiers, from *The Trinity*

Hilary (c.315–67) was Bishop of Poitiers and a highly respected theologian. He is especially remembered for his writings on the Trinity. Like his predecessors, Hilary here raises the central issue, whether the infinity and invisibility of God can be revealed in finite form, and how we are 'made conformable to the glory of the body of Christ'.

There is no danger of the one faith not being the one faith because it teaches many things. The Evangelist had reported that the Lord has said: 'He who has seen me has seen also the Father.' But, has Paul, the teacher of the Gentiles, been unaware of or silent about the meaning of these words, when he said: 'Who is the image of the invisible God?' I ask whether there is a visible image of the invisible God, and whether the infinite God can be brought together in an image so that He is visible through the image of a limited form? An image must express the form of Him whose image it is. Let those who wish the Son to have a different kind of nature decide upon what kind of an image they wish the Son to be of the invisible Father. Do they desire it to be bodily and visible, one that wanders from place to place by its movement and walking? Let them bear in mind that Christ is a Spirit and God is a Spirit, according to the Gospels and the Prophets. And if they will circumscribe this Spirit Christ within the bounds of that which may be formed and is corporeal, then the Incarnate One will not be the image of the invisible God and a finite limitation will not be the form of Him who is infinite. (Book 8, para. 48, p. 313)

It will therefore be a gain for our assumption that God will be all in all. We must again confess that He who was found in the form of a slave when He was in the form of God is in the glory of God the Father in order that it may be clearly understood that He possesses His form in whose glory He shares. Hence, it is only a dispensation, not a change, for He possesses that which He had possessed. But, since that which had a beginning is in the middle, that is to say, the born man, so everything is acquired for that nature which previously was not God, since God is revealed as being all in all after the mystery of the dispensation. Accordingly, these things are for our benefit and our advancement, that is, we are to be made conformable to the glory of the body of God. Furthermore, although the only-begotten God was also born as man, He is nothing else than God, the all in all. That subjection of the body whereby what is carnal in Him vanishes into the nature of the spirit will bring it about that He who, besides being God, is also man will be God, the all in all, but that man of ours advances toward it. Moreover, we shall press forward to a glory similar to that of our man, and we who have been renewed unto the knowledge of God shall be again formed into the image of the Creator, according to the words of the Apostle: 'Having stripped off the old man with his deeds and put on the new, one that is being renewed unto the knowledge of God, according to the image of him who created him.' Hence, man is made perfect as the image of God. When he has been made conformable to the glory of God's body he will be raised to the image of his Creator, according to the exemplar of the first man that has been placed before him. And after the sin and the old man, the new man who has been made unto the knowledge of God receives the perfection of his nature, while he recognizes his God and thereby becomes His image, and while he advances toward eternity through the true worship of God he will remain throughout the image of his Creator. (Book 11, para. 49, pp. 499–500)

Source: *The Fathers of the Church, Saint Hilary of Poitiers, The Trinity*, trans. Stephen McKenna, CSSR, Washington, The Catholic University of America Press, 1954.

1.5 Ephrem the Syrian, from *Letter to Publius*

The biblical exegete Ephrem (c.306–73) worked in Edessa and wrote most of his work in verse. In this passage he uses the imagery of the mirror of the Gospel; although in itself it does not change, it changes appearance before different colours and things. It faces believers with their own sins, and it anticipates the redemptive, eschatological beauty of heaven.

You would do well not to let fall from your hands the polished mirror of the holy Gospel of your Lord, which reproduces the image of everyone who gazes at it and the likeness of everyone who peers into it. While it keeps its own natural quality, undergoes no change, is devoid of any spots, and is free of any soiling, it changes its appearance before colours although it itself is not changed.

Before white things it becomes [white] like them.
Before black things, it becomes dark like them.
Before red things, [it becomes] red like them.
Before beautiful things, it becomes beautiful like them and
    before ugly things, it becomes hideous like them.

It paints every detail on itself. It rebukes the ugly ones for their defects so that they might heal themselves and remove the foulness from their faces. It exhorts the beautiful to be watchful over their beauty and even to increase their natural beauty with whatever ornaments they wish, lest they become sullied with dirt.

Although it is silent, it speaks.
Although it is mute, it cries out.
Although it is reckoned as dead, it makes proclamation.
Although it is still, it dances.
Although it has no belly, its womb is of great expanse.

And there in those hidden inner chambers every limb is painted and every body is framed in a bare fraction of a second. Within it they are created with undetectable quickness.

For this mirror is a foreshadowing of the holy tidings of the outer Gospel, within which is depicted the beauty of the beautiful ones who gaze at it. Also within it the blemishes of the ugly ones who are despised are put to shame. And just as this natural mirror is a foreshadowing of the Gospel, so also is the Gospel a foreshadowing of that heavenly unfading beauty by which all the sins of Creation are reproved and by which reward is given to all those who have preserved their beauty from being defiled with filth. To everyone who peers into this mirror, his sins are visible in it. And everyone who takes careful notice will see in it that portion which is reserved for him, whether good or evil.

There the kingdom of heaven is depicted and can be seen by those who have a
    pure eye.
There the exalted ranks of the good ones can be seen.
There the high ranks of the middle ones can be discerned.
There the lowly ranks of the evil ones are delineated.
There the beautiful places, which have been prepared for those worthy of
    them, are evident.
There Paradise can be seen rejoicing in its flowers.

Source: *The Fathers of the Church, Ephrem the Syrian, Selected Prose Works*, ed. Kathleen McVey, trans. Edward G. Mathews Jr. and Joseph P. Amar, Washington, The Catholic University of America Press, 1994.

1.6 Basil, from *On Psalm 29 (Homily 14)*

Basil the Great (c.330–79) was a hermit before he became Bishop of Caesarea in 370. One of the Cappadocian Fathers, he wrote against various heresies, defending the deity of the Holy Spirit. Here he speaks about the virtue of beauty which evolves from contemplation and wisdom. Only the purified mind can see divine beauty and thus share in it through grace.

'O Lord, in thy favour, thou gavest strength to my beauty.' They who are engaged in the examination of the reason for virtues, have said that some of the virtues spring from contemplation and some are noncontemplative; as for instance, prudence springs from contemplation in the sphere of things good and evil, but self-control from the contemplation of things to be chosen or avoided, justice, of things to be assigned or not to be assigned, and valor, of those that are dangerous or not dangerous; but beauty and strength are noncontemplative virtues, since they follow from the contemplative. From the fitness and harmony of the contemplations of the soul, some wise men have perceived beauty; and from the effectiveness of the suggestions from the contemplative virtues, they have become aware of strength. But, for this, namely, that beauty may exist in the soul, and also the power for the fulfillment of what is proper, we need divine grace. As, therefore, he said above: 'Life is in his good will,' so, now, he extols God through his thanksgiving, saying: 'In thy favour, thou gavest strength to my beauty.' For, I was beautiful according to nature, but weak, because I was dead by sin through the treachery of the serpent. To my beauty, then, which I received from You at the beginning of my creation, You added a strength which is appropriate for what is proper. Every soul is beautiful, which is considered by the standard of its own virtues. But beauty, true and most lovely, which can be contemplated by him alone who has purified his mind, is that of the divine and blessed nature. He who gazes steadfastly at the splendour and graces of it, receives some share from it, as if from an immersion, tingeing his own face with a sort of brilliant radiance. Whence Moses also was made resplendent in face by receiving some share of beauty when he held converse with God. Therefore, he who is conscious of his own beauty utters this act of thanksgiving: 'O Lord, in thy favour, thou gavest strength to my beauty.' Just as the noncontemplative virtues, both beauty and strength, follow from the contemplative virtues, so there are certain noncontemplative vices, shameful conduct and weakness. In fact, what is more unbecoming and uglier than a passionate soul? Observe, I beg you, the wrathful man and his fierceness. Look at the man who is distressed, his abasement and dejection of soul. Who could endure to look at him who is sunk in sensuality and gluttony or who is alarmed by fears? For, the feelings of the soul affect even the extremities of the body, just as also the traces of the beauty of the soul shine through in the state of the saint. Accordingly, we must have regard for beauty, in order that the Bridegroom, the Word, receiving us, may say: 'Thou art all fair, O my love, and there is not a spot in thee.'

'Thou turnedst away thy face from me, and I became troubled.' 'As long as the rays of the sun of Your watchfulness shone upon me,' he says, 'I lived in a calm and untroubled state, but, when You turned Your face away, the agitation and confusion of my soul was exposed.' God is said to turn away His face when in times of troubles He permits us to be delivered up to trials, in order that the strength of him who is struggling may be known, Therefore, 'if the peace which surpasses all understanding will guard our hearts,' we shall be able to escape the tumult and confusion of the passions. Since perversion is opposed to the will of God, and disorder to beauty and grace and strength, the disorder would be a deformity and weakness of the soul, present in it because of its estrangement from God. We pray always for the face of God to shine upon us, in order that we may be in a state becoming to a holy person, gentle and untroubled in every way, because of our readiness for the good, 'I am ready,' he says, 'and am not troubled.' (para. 5 and 6, p. 220–2)

Source: *The Fathers of the Church, Saint Basil, Exegetic Homilies*, trans. Agnes Clare Way, CDP, Washington, The Catholic University of America Press, 1963.

1.7 Gregory of Nyssa, from *On Virginity*

Gregory (c.330–c.395), one of the Cappadocian Fathers and Bishop of Nyssa, was an original thinker who wrote on major Christian doctrines. In this extract, the impossibility of saying anything about the incomprehensible beauty of God is raised. Still we need to strive for heavenly beauty. By purifying ourselves we approach beauty, are illumined by it, and participate in the true light.

What is truly desirable. What treatise could possibly describe how great the penalty is for falling away from the truly beautiful? What kind of extravagant language could one use? How could the ineffable and the incomprehensible be presented and delineated? If anyone has such purity of mental vision that he is able to see, to some degree, what is promised by the Lord in His beatitudes, he will despise every human voice as having no power to set forth what is meant by them. On the other hand, if anyone still immersed in material matters has the clear vision of his soul blurred by some bleary-eyed condition, so to speak, any treatise will be futile as far as he is concerned. For, in the case of the insensitive, minimizing wonders and exaggerating them in discourse will amount to the same thing, just as in the case of the rays of the sun. Any verbal explanation of light is useless and idle for a person blind from birth, because it is not possible to visualise the brilliance of the sun through the ear. In the same way, each individual needs his own eyes to see the beauty of the true and the intelligible light. The one who does see it through some divine gift and unexplainable inspiration is astonished in the depths of his consciousness; the one who cannot see will not realise what he has missed. For how can anyone confront him with the very good he has run away from? How can anyone bring the ineffable into his line of vision? We have not devised the particular verbal expressions for that beauty. There are no verbal tokens of what we are seeking. It is even difficult to make it clear by comparison. For who likens the sun to a little spark, or who compares a tiny drop with the boundless sea? The relation of the drop to the sea and the spark to the beam of the sun is similar to the relation between all the beauteous wonders in the world of men and that beauty which is seen with reference to the first Good and to what is beyond every good. So what power of mind can possibly indicate the enormity of the penalty for those who incur it? The great David seems to me to have illustrated this impossibility well. When he was once lifted up in thought by the power of the Spirit, he was, as it were, divorced from himself and saw that incredible and incomprehensible beauty in a blessed ecstasy. But he did see it as far as it is possible for a man to do so when he is released from the limitations of the flesh and comes to the contemplation of the incorporeal and intelligible through thought alone. When he wanted to say something worthy of what he had seen, he sang out that song which all men sing: 'Every man is a liar.' That is, as our treatise shows, that every man who commits his interpretation of the ineffable light to words is really a liar, not because of any hatred of the truth, but because of the weakness of his description. Perceptible beauty as far as it dwells here below in our life, fancied because of some charm in inanimate matter or living bodies, is within our power to admire and to describe and make known to others in treatises, just as such beauty is also painted on an icon. But how could a treatise, even if it explored every means of description, bring into view that whose archetype eludes comprehension, being without colour or form or size or shape or any such foolishness? How could anyone by means of those things which we grasp by perception alone come to know that which is the altogether invisible, the formless, the sizeless, as far as bodily perception goes? And yet one should not, for this reason, despair of his desire simply because these things seem to be beyond his grasp. Indeed, the treatise has shown that, in proportion to the greatness of what is sought after, it is necessary to elevate the mind in thought and to lift it to the level of what we are seeking, so that we are not excluded entirely from participation in the good. For when we try to observe what we are unacquainted with, there is no small risk that we may slip away entirely from the thought of it. (para. 10, pp. 36–8)

How one could gain an understanding of the really beautiful. On account of this weakness of knowing things through the senses, it is necessary for us to direct our mind to the unseen. But can one achieve such a thing? Some people, looking at matters superficially and thoughtlessly, when they see a man or whatever they happen upon, are interested in nothing more than what they see. It is enough for them having seen the size of the body to think that the whole concept of the man has been grasped. But the clear-sighted person, who has educated his soul, does not entrust his consideration of things to his eyes alone, nor does he stop at appearances, or reason that what he has not seen does not exist; he shrewdly contrives a nature of a soul; he examines the qualities appearing in the body, both in general and separately; and, after considering each quality for its own merits, he again looks at the general relationship and whole in connection with the underlying plan of composition. Accordingly, in the seeking of the beautiful, the person who is superficial in his thought, when he sees something in which fantasy is mixed with some beauty, will think that the thing itself is beautiful because of its own nature, his attention being attracted to it because of pleasure, and he will be concerned with nothing beyond this. But the man who has purified the eye of his soul is able to look at such things and forget the matter in which the beauty is encased, and he uses what he sees as a kind of basis for his contemplation of intelligible beauty. By a participation in this beauty, the other beautiful things come into being and are identified. . . . Indeed, the person who removes himself from all hatred and fleshly odour and rises above all low and earthbound things, having ascended higher than the whole earth in his aforementioned flight, will find the only thing that is worth longing for, and, having come close to beauty, will become beautiful himself. Through his participation in the true light, he will himself be in a state of brightness and illumination. . . . I refer to the person who has purified all the powers of his soul from every form of evil, and I dare say that it is clear that the only thing which is beautiful by nature is that which is the cause of all beauty and all goodness. For, just as the eye cleansed from rheum sees objects shining brightly in the distance in the air, so also the soul through incorruptibility acquires the power to perceive the Light. The goal of true virginity and zeal for incorruptibility is the ability to see God, for the chief and first and only beautiful and good and pure is the God of all, and no one is so blind in mind as not to perceive that even by himself. (para. 11, pp. 38–40, 41)

Source: *The Fathers of the Church, Gregory of Nyssa, Ascetical Works*, trans. Virginia Woods Callahan, Washington, The Catholic University of America Press, 1967.

1.8 Ambrose, from *The Holy Spirit*

Ambrose (c.339–97), a doctor of the Church and Bishop of Milan, concerned himself especially with ethics. He was a strong defender of orthodoxy and also wrote a number of Latin hymns. In his writing on the Holy Spirit, Ambrose explores the metaphors of ointment and fire for the Holy Spirit, and of light for both the Spirit and Christ.

Now many have thought that the Holy Spirit is the ointment of Christ. And well is He ointment, because He is called the oil of gladness, the joining together of many graces giving forth a fragrance. But God the Almighty Father anointed

Him the chief of the priests, who was anointed not as others in a type under the law, but was both anointed according to the law in the body, and in truth was full of the virtue of the Holy Spirit from the Father above the law.

This is the oil of gladness, of which the Prophet says: 'God, thy God hath anointed thee with the oil of gladness above thy fellows.' Finally, Peter speaks of Jesus as anointed with the Spirit, as you have it: 'You know the word which hath been published through all Judea; for it began from Galilee, after the baptism which John preached, Jesus of Nazareth, how God anointed him with the Holy Ghost.' So the Holy Spirit is the oil of gladness.

And well did he say oil of gladness, lest you might think Him a creature, for the nature of the oil is such that it by no means mingles with the moisture of another nature. Gladness also does not anoint the body, but illumines the recesses of the heart, as the Prophet has said: 'Thou hast given gladness in my heart.' So since he wastes his time who wishes to mingle oil with moister material, because, since the nature of oil is lighter than others, while other materials settle, it rises and is separated, how do those meanest of hucksters think that the oil of gladness can be fraudulently mingled with other creatures, when surely corporeal things cannot be mixed with the incorporeal, nor created things with the uncreated?

And well is that called the oil of gladness with which Christ was anointed, for no customary and common oil was to be sought for Him with which either wounds are 'refreshed or fever relieved', since the salvation of the world did not seek the alleviation of His wounds, nor did eternal might demand the refreshment of a tired body. (para. 100–102A, pp. 72–3)

But why should I add that just as the Father is light, so, too, the Son is light, and the Holy Spirit is light? This surely belongs to divine power. For God is light, as John said: 'That God is light; and that in Him there is no darkness.'

But the Son also is Light, because 'Life was the Light of men.' And the Evangelist, that he might show that he spoke of the Son of God, says of John the Baptist: 'He was not the light, but was to bear witness to the light, that he was the true light, which enlighteneth every man that cometh into this world.' Therefore, since God is the Light, and the Son of God is the true Light, without doubt the Son of God is true God. (para. 140 and 141, p. 86)

Moreover, who will doubt that the Father Himself is light, when it is read of His Son that He is the splendour of eternal light? For of whom if not of the eternal Father is the Son the splendour, who both is always with the Father and always shines not with a dissimilar but with the same light?

And Isaias points out that the Holy Spirit is not only light but is also fire, when he says: 'And the light of Israel shall be as fire.' Thus the Prophets called Him a burning fire, because in those three points we notice more readily the majesty of the Godhead, for to sanctify is of the Godhead, and to illuminate is proper to fire and light, and to be expressed and to be seen in the appearance of fire is customary with the Godhead; 'for God is a consuming fire,' as Moses said. (para. 143 and 144, pp. 86–7)

What, then, is that fire? Surely not fire made of common twigs, or roaring by the burning of the stubble of the forests, but that fire which, like gold, improves good deeds, and consumes sins like stubble. This surely is the Holy Spirit, who is called both the fire and the light of the Lord's countenance; the light, as we have said above: 'The light of thy countenance, O Lord, is signed upon us.' What then is the light that is sealed, if not the light of that spiritual seal 'in whom believing,' he says, 'you were sealed with the holy Spirit of promise'? (para. 149, p. 88)

Source: *The Fathers of the Church, Saint Ambrose, Theological and Dogmatic Works*, trans. Roy J. Deferrari, Washington, The Catholic University of America Press in association with Consortium Books, 1963.

1.9 John Chrysostom, from *On the Incomprehensible Nature of God (Homily 12)*

Chrysostom (c.347–407) was Bishop of Constantinople. His works on Genesis and several New Testament books made him a great expositor of Christian faith. Like his theological predecessors, the author here juxtaposes physical and spiritual beauty. While the former vanishes, the latter is permanent and is achieved by a life of virtue, with love of neighbour and faith in God.

When a man goes home from church, his wife sees him as a more worthy husband. When a woman goes home from here, her husband sees her as a more desirable wife. For physical beauty does not make a wife more lovable, but the virtue of her soul does. Cosmetics, eye shadow, gold ornaments, and expensive clothes cannot do this. But chastity and sobriety, goodness and virtue, and a firm fear of God can win and keep her husband's love.

Spiritual beauty cannot be developed perfectly anywhere else except in this marvellous and divine stronghold of the church. Here the apostles and prophets wipe clean and beautify the face, they strip away the marks of senility left by sin, they apply the bloom of youth, they get rid of every wrinkle, stain, and blemish from our souls. Therefore, let us all, men and women, be eager to implant this beauty in ourselves.

Sickness withers physical beauty, length of years destroys it, old age drains it dry, death comes and takes it all away. But beauty of the soul cannot be marred by time, disease, old age, death, or any other such thing. It stays constantly in bloom. But many a time physical beauty provokes to licentious deeds those who look upon it. When the beauty is beauty of the soul, it draws God himself to love it. It is just as the prophet said when he was addressing the Church: 'Hear, O daughter, and see; turn your ear, forget your people and your father's house, and the King shall desire your beauty.'

Therefore, beloved, let us develop this beauty every day and so become dear to God. Let us wipe away every stain by reading the Scriptures, by prayer and alms-giving, by peace and concord with one another. Let us do this so that the King may come to love the beauty in our souls and deem us worthy of the kingdom of heaven. May it come to pass that we all gain this through the grace and loving-kindness of our Lord Jesus Christ, with whom be glory to the Father together with the Holy Spirit, now and forever, world without end. Amen. (para. 56–9, pp. 306–7)

Source: *The Fathers of the Church, St John Chrysostom, On the Incomprehensible Nature of God*, trans. Paul W. Harkins, Washington, The Catholic University of America Press, 1984.

1.10.1 Augustine, from *Divine Providence and the Problem of Evil*

Augustine (354–430) was Bishop of Hippo, doctor of the Church and one of the most influential writers in the history of Christian theology. He notably contributed to the doctrines of grace, the Trinity, ecclesiology and sacraments. In this passage he exclaims how the soul and the purified eye will see God, who is beauty and truth.

But, when the soul has properly adjusted and disposed itself, and has rendered itself harmonious and beautiful, then will it venture to see God, the very source of all truth and the very Father of Truth. O great God, what kind of eyes shall those be! How pure! How beautiful! How powerful! How constant! How serene! How blessed! And what is that which they can see! What is it? I ask. What should we surmise? What should we believe? What should we say? Everyday expressions present themselves, but they have been rendered sordid by things of least worth. I shall say no more, except that to us is promised a vision of beauty – the beauty through whose imitation all other things are beautiful, and by comparison with which all other things are unsightly. Whosoever will have glimpsed this beauty – and he will see it who lives well, prays well, studies well – when will it ever trouble him why one man, desiring to have children, has them not, while another man casts out his own offspring as being unduly numerous; why one man hates children before they are born, and another man loves them after birth; or how is it not absurd that nothing will come to pass which is not with God – and, therefore, it is inevitable that all things come into being in accordance with order – and nevertheless God is not petitioned in vain? (para. 51, p. 328)

Source: *The Fathers of the Church, Saint Augustine, The Divine Providence and the Problem of Evil*, trans. Robert P. Russell, OSA, and *Soliloquies*, trans. Thomas F. Gilligan, OSA, New York, CIMA Publishing Co. Inc., 1948.

1.10.2 Augustine, from *Soliloquies*

In semi-poetic language Augustine praises God by using rich imagery, including the metaphors of 'beauty', 'happiness', 'wisdom' and 'light'.

O God, who from nothing hast created this world which every eye sees to be most beautiful. . . . O God, the Father of Truth, the Father of Wisdom, Father of True and Supreme Life, Father of Happiness, Father of the Good and the Beautiful, Father of Intelligible Light, Father of our watching and our enlightenment, Father of the covenant by which we are admonished to return to Thee.

I call upon Thee, O God the Truth, in whom and by whom and through whom all those things are true which are true. O God, Wisdom, in whom and by whom and through whom all those are wise who are wise. O God, True and Supreme Life, in whom and by whom and through whom all those things live which truly and perfectly live. O God, Happiness, in whom and by whom and through whom all those things are happy which are happy. O God, the Good and the Beautiful, in whom and by whom and through whom all those things are good and beautiful which are good and beautiful. O God, Intelligible Light, in whom and by whom and through whom all those things which have intelligible light have their intelligible light. (para. 2 and 3, pp. 344–5)

Source: *The Fathers of the Church, Saint Augustine, The Divine Providence and the Problem of Evil*, trans. Robert P. Russell, OSA, and *Soliloquies*, trans. Thomas F. Gilligan, OSA, New York, CIMA Publishing Co. Inc., 1948.

1.10.3 Augustine, from *Expositions on The Book of Psalms*

Augustine contemplates the beauty of the incarnate Word, the infant Jesus, the eternal Christ and, especially, the crucified Saviour on the cross.

(On Psalm XLV) To us, however, now that we are believers, let the Bridegroom, wheresoever He is, appear beautiful. He is 'beautiful' as God, *the Word with*

God; beautiful in the womb of the Virgin, where without losing His Divinity, He assumed the Manhood: Beautiful when born, the Infant Word: for when He was as yet but an Infant, whilst He was hanging at the breast, and was yet borne in arms, the Heavens spoke; the Angels gave forth praises; a Star directed the wise men; He was adored in the manger, He that is the food of gentle ones. He then is 'beautiful' in Heaven, beautiful on earth; beautiful in the womb; beautiful in His parents' hands: beautiful in His miracles; beautiful under the scourge: beautiful when inviting to life; beautiful also when not regarding death: beautiful in 'laying down His life'; beautiful in 'taking it again': beautiful on the Cross; beautiful in the Sepulchre; beautiful in Heaven. Listen then to the song unto 'understanding'; and let not the weakness of the flesh turn away your eyes from the splendour of His beauty! The highest beauty, the real beauty, is that of righteousness: there where you find Him unrighteous, you will see Him not beautiful. If He is righteous every whit, He is also 'beautiful' every whit. (p. 230)

Source: *Expositions on The Book of Psalms by Augustine, Bishop of Hippo, vol.* 2, trans. by members of the English Church, A Library of Fathers of the Holy Catholic Church, Oxford, John Henry Parker, F. and J. Rivington, 1848.

1.10.4 Augustine, from *Letter to Paulina (The Book of the Vision of God)*

The vision of God, Augustine reiterates, is only possible through purification of heart.

God causes those visions in which He appears, as He wills, to whom He wills and when He wills, while His substance remains hidden and unchangeable in itself. If our will, remaining in itself, and without any change in itself, expresses words through which it manifests itself, after a fashion, how much more easily can the omnipotent God, maintaining His nature hidden and unchangeable, appear under any form He wills and to whom He wills, since He made all things out of nothing, and remaining in Himself, 'reneweth all things'. (Ch. 47, p. 216)

But, in order to attain that vision by which we see God as He is, He has warned us that our hearts must be cleansed. As then objects are called visible in our fashion of speaking, so God is called invisible lest He be thought to be a material body, yet He will not deprive pure hearts of the contemplation of His substance, since this great and sublime reward is promised, on the Lord's own word, to those who worship and love God. At the time when He appeared visibly to bodily eyes, He promised that His invisible being also would be seen by the clean of heart: 'He that loveth me shall be loved of my Father, and I will love him, and will manifest myself to him.' It is certain that this nature of His, which He shares with the Father, is equally invisible as it is equally incorruptible, which, as was said above, the Apostle at once set forth as the divine substance, commending it to men with what words he could. But, if bodily eyes behold it, in virtue of the changed nature of bodies at the resurrection, let those who can assert this look to it; for my part, I am more impressed by the statement of him who attributes this to clean hearts, not to bodily eyes, even at the resurrection. (Ch. 48, p. 216–17)

Source: *The Fathers of the Church, Saint Augustine, Letters, vol. 3*, trans. Wilfrid Parsons, SND, Washington, The Catholic University of America Press, 1953.

1.10.5 Augustine, from *Confessions*

Augustine here asks what constitutes beauty. In his poetic, doxological approach, he enthuses about his love for divine beauty by way of analogies from the realm of sense perception. He knows full well that his words are always limited, and while he admits being drawn by external physical beauty, he longs to concentrate solely on the beauty of God.

I did not know these things at the time. I loved the lower kind of beauties and I wandered into the depths, saying to my friends: 'Do we love anything but the beautiful? What, then, is the beautiful? And what is beauty? What is it that attracts us and draws us to things we love? For, unless grace and beauty of form were in them, they certainly would not draw us to themselves.' And I took notice and saw in these bodies that it was one thing to be whole, as it were, and so beautiful, and quite another thing for something to be attractive because aptly suited to another thing, as a part of a body is to its whole, or as a shoe fits a foot, and the like. And this consideration gushed forth in my mind from the depths of my heart, so I wrote some books *On the Beautiful and the Fitting*, two or three, I think. Thou knowest, O God, for the fact has escaped me. We do not have these books now; they have strayed away from us – how, I do not know. (Book 4, Ch. 13, para. 20, pp. 90–1)

But, what do I love, when I love Thee? Not the prettiness of a body, not the gracefulness of temporal rhythm, not the brightness of light (that friend of these eyes), not the sweet melodies of songs in every style, not the fragrance of flowers and ointments and spices, not manna and honey, not limbs which can be grasped in fleshly embraces – these I do not love, when I love my God. Yet, I do love something like a light, a voice, an odour, food, an embrace, when I love my God – the light, voice, odour, food, embrace of my inner man, wherein for my soul a light shines, and place does not encompass it, where there is a sound which time does not sweep away, where there is a fragrance which the breeze does not disperse, where there is a flavour which eating does not diminish, and where there is a clinging which satiety does not disentwine. This is what I love when I love my God. (Book 10, Ch. 6, para. 8, pp. 269–70)

Late have I loved Thee, O Beauty so ancient and so new, late have I loved Thee! And behold, Thou wert within and I was without. I was looking for Thee out there, and I threw myself, deformed as I was, upon those well-formed things which Thou hast made. Thou wert with me, yet I was not with Thee. These things held me far from Thee, things which would not have existed had they not been in Thee. Thou didst call and cry out and burst in upon my deafness; Thou didst shine forth and glow and drive away my blindness; Thou didst send forth Thy fragrance, and I drew in my breath, and now I pant for Thee; I have tasted, and now I hunger and thirst; Thou didst touch me, and I was inflamed with desire for Thy peace. (Book 10, Ch. 27, para. 38, p. 297)

And Thou sawest, O God, all the things that Thou hadst made, and, behold, 'they were very good'. We, too, see them, and, behold, they are all very good. For each kind of Thy works, when Thou hadst said that they were to be made, and they were made, Thou didst see that each in turn is good. I have counted seven times where it is written that Thou didst see that what Thou hast made is good; and this is the eighth, that Thou didst see all things that Thou hast made, and behold, they are not merely good, but even very good when taken all together. For, the individual things are merely good, but all together they are both good and very much so. All beautiful bodies express the same truth, for a body is far more beautiful, in the fact that it is constituted out of parts which are all beautiful, than are these parts taken individually; for, the whole is perfected by the most orderly gathering of these parts – even though they are also beautiful, when considered individually. (Book 13, Ch. 28, para. 43, pp. 447–8)

Source: *Saint Augustine, Confessions*, trans. Vernon J. Burke, Washington, The Catholic University of America Press, 1953.

1.11 Pseudo-Dionysius, from *The Divine Names*

Pseudo-Dionysius (working around 500) was a mystical theologian who sought to achieve a synthesis between Christian dogma and Neo-Platonist thought. He was the first theologian to present what might be called a theological aesthetics, dealing in particular with the idea of the beautiful. Here he stresses that everything in creation comes into existence through 'the One, the Good and the Beautiful'. The Good and the Beautiful are the cause, source, and goal of all being.

So then, the Good which is above all light is given the name 'light of the mind', 'beam and spring', 'overflowing radiance'. It crams with its light every mind which is above and beyond the world, or around it or within it. It renews all the powers of their minds. It steps beyond everything inasmuch as it is ordered beyond everything. It precedes everything inasmuch as it transcends everything. Quite simply, it gathers together and supremely anticipates in itself the authority of all illuminating power, being indeed the source of light and actually transcending light. And so it assembles into a union everything possessed of reason and of mind. For just as it is ignorance which scatters those in error, so it is the presence of the light of the mind which gathers and unites together those receiving illumination. It perfects them. It returns them toward the truly real. It returns them from their numerous false notions and, filling them with the one unifying light, it gathers their clashing fancies into a single, pure, coherent, and true knowledge.

The sacred writers lift up a hymn of praise to this Good. They call it beautiful, beauty, love, and beloved. They give it the names which convey that it is the source of loveliness and is the flowering of grace. But do not make a distinction between 'beautiful' and 'beauty' as applied to the Cause which gathers all into one. For we recognize the difference in intelligible beings between qualities that are shared and the objects which share them. We call 'beautiful' that which has a share in beauty, and we give the name of 'beauty' to that ingredient which is the cause of beauty in everything. But the 'beautiful' which is beyond individual being is called 'beauty' because of that beauty bestowed by it on all things, each in accordance with what it is. It is given this name because it is the cause of the harmony and splendour in everything, because like a light it flashes onto everything the beauty – causing impartations of its own well-spring ray. Beauty 'bids' all things to itself (whence it is called 'beauty') and gathers everything into itself. And they name it beautiful since it is the all-beautiful and the beautiful beyond all. It is forever so, unvaryingly, unchangeably so, beautiful but not as something coming to birth and death, to growth or decay, not lovely in one respect while ugly in some other way. It is not beautiful 'now' but otherwise 'then', beautiful in relation to one thing but not to another. It is not beautiful in one place and not so in another, as though it could be beautiful for some and not for others. Ah no! In itself and by itself it is the uniquely and the eternally beautiful. It is the superabundant source in itself of the beauty of every beautiful thing. In that simple but transcendent nature of all beautiful things, beauty and the beautiful uniquely preexisted in terms of their source. From this beauty comes the existence of everything, each being exhibiting its own way of beauty. For beauty is the cause of harmony, of sympathy, of community. Beauty unites all things and is the source of all things. It is the great creating cause which bestirs the world and holds all things in existence by the longing inside them to have beauty. And there it is ahead of all as Goal, as the Beloved, as the Cause toward which all things move, since it is the longing for beauty which actually brings them into being. It is a model to which they conform. The Beautiful is therefore the same as the Good, for everything looks to the Beautiful and the Good as the cause of being, and there is nothing in the world without a share of the Beautiful and the Good.

And I would even be so bold as to claim that nonbeing also shares in the Beautiful and the Good, because nonbeing, when applied transcendently to God in the sense of a denial of all things, is itself beautiful and good. This – the One, the Good, the Beautiful – is in its uniqueness the Cause of the multitudes of the good and the beautiful. From it derives the existence of everything as beings, what they have in common and what differentiates them, their identicalness and differences, their similarities and dissimilarities, their sharing of opposites, the way in which their ingredients maintain identity, the providence of the higher ranks of beings, the interrelationship of those of the same rank, the return upward by those of lower status, the protecting and unchanged remaining and foundations of all things amid themselves. Hence, the interrelationship of all things in accordance with capacity. Hence, the harmony and the love which are formed between them but which do not obliterate identity. Hence, the innate togetherness of everything. Hence, too, the intermingling of everything, the persistence of things, the unceasing emergence of things. Hence, all rest and hence, the stirrings of mind and spirit and body. There is rest for everything and movement for everything, and these come from that which, transcending rest and movement, establishes each being according to an appropriate principle and gives each the movement suitable to it.

The divine intelligences are said to move as follows. First they move in a circle while they are at one with those illuminations which, without beginning and without end, emerge from the Good and the Beautiful. Then they move in a straight line when, out of Providence, they come to offer unerring guidance to all those below them. Finally they move in a spiral, for even while they are providing for those beneath them they continue to remain what they are and they turn unceasingly around the Beautiful and the Good from which all identity comes.

The soul too has movement. First it moves in a circle, that is, it turns within itself and away from what is outside and there is an inner concentration of its intellectual powers. A sort of fixed revolution causes it to return from the multiplicity of externals, to gather in upon itself and then, in this undispersed condition, to join those who are themselves in a powerful union. From there the revolution brings the soul to the Beautiful and the Good, which is beyond all things, is one and the same, and has neither beginning nor end. But whenever the soul receives, in accordance with its capacities, the enlightenment of divine knowledge and does so not by way of the mind nor in some mode arising out of its identity, but rather through discursive reasoning, in mixed and changeable activities, then it moves in a spiral fashion. And its movement is in a straight line when, instead of circling in upon its own intelligent unity (for this is the circular), it proceeds to the things around it, and is uplifted from external things, as from certain variegated and pluralized symbols, to the simple and united contemplations.

The Good and the Beautiful is the cause of these three movements, as also of the movements in the realm of what is perceived, and of the prior remaining, standing, and foundation of each one. This is what preserves them. This is their goal, itself transcending all rest and all motion. It is the source, the origin, the preserver, the goal, and the objective of rest and of motion. The being and the life of the mind and of the soul derive from it. Also from it come the small, the equal, and the great in nature, the measure and the proportion of all things, the mixtures, the totalities, and the parts of things, the universal one and the many, the links between parts, the unity underlying everything, the perfection of wholes. From it come quality, quantity, magnitude and infinity, conglomeration and distinction, the limitless and the limited, boundaries, orders and super-achievements, elements and forms, all being, power, and activity, all states, perceptions, and expression, all conception, apprehension, understanding, all union. To put the matter briefly, all being drives from, exists in, and is returned toward the Beautiful and the Good. Whatever there is, whatever comes to be, *is* there and has being on account of the Beautiful and the Good. All things look to it. All things are moved by it. All things are preserved by it. Every source exists for the sake of it, because of it, and in it and this is so whether such source be exemplary, final, efficient, formal, or elemental. In short, every source, all preservation and ending, everything in fact, derives from the Beautiful and the Good. Even what is not still there exists transcendentally in the Beautiful and the Good. Here is the source of all which transcends every source, here is an ending which transcends completion. 'For from Him and through Him and in Him and to Him are all things' says holy scripture. And so it is that all things must desire, must yearn for, must love, the Beautiful and the Good. Because of it and for its sake, subordinate is returned to superior, equal keeps company with equal, superior turns providentially to subordinate, each bestirs itself and all are stirred to do and to will whatever it is they do and will because of the yearning for the Beautiful and the Good. And we may be so bold as to claim also that the Cause of all things loves all things in the superabundance of his goodness, that because of this goodness he makes all things, brings all things to perfection, holds all things together, returns all things. The divine longing is Good seeking good for the sake of the Good. That yearning which creates all the goodness of the world preexisted superabundantly within the Good and did not allow it to remain without issue. It stirred him to use the abundance of his powers in the production of the world. (para. 6–10, pp. 76–80)

This divine yearning brings ecstasy so that the lover belongs not to self but to the beloved. This is shown in the providence lavished by the superior on the subordinate. It is shown in the regard for one another demonstrated by those of equal status. And it is shown by the subordinates in their divine return toward what is higher. This is why the great Paul, swept along by his yearning for God and seized of its ecstatic power, had this inspired word to say: 'It is no longer I who live, but Christ who lives in me.' Paul was truly a lover and, as he says, he was beside himself for God, possessing not his own life but the life of the One for whom he yearned, as exceptionally beloved. And, in truth, it must be said too that the very cause of the universe in the beautiful, good superabundance of his benign yearning for all is also carried outside of himself in the loving care he has for everything. He is, as it were, beguiled by goodness, by love, and by yearning and is enticed away from his transcendent dwelling place and comes to abide within all things, and he does so by virtue of his supernatural and ecstatic capacity to remain, nevertheless, within himself. That is why those possessed of spiritual insight describe him as 'zealous' because his good yearning for all things is so great and because he stirs in men a deep yearning desire for zeal. In this way he proves himself to be zealous because zeal is always felt for what is desired and because he is zealous for the creatures for whom he provides. In short, both the yearning and the object of that yearning belong to the Beautiful and the Good. They preexist in it, and because of it they exist and come to be.

Why is it, however, that theologians sometimes refer to God as Yearning and Love and sometimes as the yearned-for and the Be-loved? On the one hand he causes, produces, and generates what is being referred to, and, on the other hand, he is the thing itself. He is stirred by it and he stirs it. He is moved to it and he moves it. So they call him the beloved and the yearned-for since he is beautiful and good, and, again, they call him yearning and love because he is the power moving and lifting all things up to himself, for in the end what is he if not Beauty and Goodness, the One who of himself reveals himself, the good procession of his own transcendent unity? He is yearning on the move, simple, self-moved, self-acting, preexistent in the Good, flowing out from the Good onto all that is and returning again to the Good. In this divine yearning shows especially its unbeginning and unending nature travelling in an endless circle through the Good, from the Good, in the Good and to the Good, unerringly turning, ever on the same centre, ever in the same direction, always proceeding, always remaining, always being restored to itself. (para. 13 and 14, pp. 82–3)

Source: *The Classics of Western Spirituality, Pseudo-Dionysius, The Complete Works*, trans. Colm Luibheid, ed. Paul Rorem, London, SPCK, 1987.

1.12 Maximus the Confessor, from *The Four Hundred Chapters on Love*

The Greek theologian, abbot and martyr Maximus (c.580–662) affirms that those who transcend everything are blessed as they rejoice in the beauty of God. Further, he distinguishes between image and likeness, and concludes that the 'good and wise' are not just made in the image but in the likeness of God. The New Testament emphasizes that Christ is the perfect likeness of God.

Blessed is the mind which has gone beyond all beings and takes unceasing delight in the divine beauty. (para. 19, p. 37)

In bringing into existence a rational and intelligent nature, God in his supreme goodness has communicated to it four of the divine attributes by which he maintains, guards, and preserves creatures: being, eternal being, goodness, and wisdom. The first two of these he grants to the essence, the second two to its faculty of will; that is, to the essence he gives being and eternal being, and to the volitive faculty he gives goodness and wisdom in order that what he is by essence the creature might become by participation. For this reason he is said to be made 'to the image and likeness of God': to the image of his being by our being, to the image of his eternal being by our eternal being (even though not without a beginning, it is yet without end); to the likeness of his goodness by our goodness, to the image of his wisdom by our wisdom. The first is by nature, the second by grace. Every rational nature indeed is made to the image of God; but only those who are good and wise are made to his likeness. (para. 25, p. 64)

Source: *Maximus Confessor, Selected Writings*, trans. and ed. George C. Berthold, Mahwah, NJ, Paulist Press, 1985.

2

The Divine Artist

2.1 Basil, from *Exegetical Works, On the Hexameron* *(Homily 1)*

In this homily Basil praises the lasting beauty and value of art, and he praises Moses for his emphasis on God as the creator of the world, which is 'a work of art'.

Yet, of the arts some are said to be creative, others practical, and others theoretical. The aim of the theoretical skills is the action of the mind; but that of the practical, the motion itself of the body, and, if that should cease, nothing would subsist or remain for those beholding it. In fact, there is no aim in dancing and flute playing; on the contrary, the very action ends with itself. However, in the case of the creative skills, even though the action ceases, the work remains, as that of architecture, carpentry, metal work, weaving, and of as many such arts as, even if the craftsman is not present, ably manifest in themselves the artistic processes of thoughts, and make possible for you to admire the architect from his work, as well as the metal worker and the weaver. That it might be shown, then, that the world is a work of art, set before all for contemplation, so that through it the wisdom of Him who created it should be known, the wise Moses used no other word concerning it, but he said: 'In the beginning he created'. He did not say: 'He produced', nor 'He fashioned', but 'he created'. Inasmuch as many of those who have imagined that the world from eternity coexisted with God did not concede that it was made by Him, but that, being, as it were, a shadow of His power, it existed of itself coordinately with Him, and inasmuch as they admit that God is the cause of it, but involuntarily a cause, as the body is the cause of the shadow and the flashing light the cause of the brilliance, therefore, the prophet in correcting such an error used exactness in his words, saying: 'In the beginning God created'. The thing itself did not provide the cause of its existence, but He created, as One good, something useful; as One wise, something beautiful; as One powerful, something mighty. Indeed, Moses showed you a Craftsman all but pervading the substance of the universe, harmonizing the individual parts with each other, and bringing to perfection a whole, consistent with itself, consonant, and harmonious. (para. 7, pp. 11–13)

Source: *The Fathers of the Church, Saint Basil, Exegetic Homilies*, trans. Agnes Clare Way, CDP, Washington, The Catholic University of America Press, 1963.

2.2 Gregory of Nyssa, from *On Perfection*

Gregory uses the analogy of a painter and of painting an imitation of a model in order to show how the followers of Christ must imitate the colours of virtues so as to be conformed to the Prototype, i.e. Christ.

Accordingly, this Person who is beyond knowledge and comprehension, the ineffable and the 'unspeakable' and the 'inexpressible', in order that He might again make Himself an 'image of God', because of His love for man, became Himself an 'image of the invisible God' so that he took on the form which He assumed among you, and again, through Himself, He fashioned a beauty in accord with the character of the Archetype. Therefore, if we also are to become an 'image of the invisible God', it is fitting that the form of our life be struck according to the 'example' of the life set before us. But what is that? It is living in the flesh, but not 'according to the flesh'. The Prototype, 'the image of the invisible God', living in His virginity, underwent all temptations because of the similarity of His nature to ours, but He did not share the experience of a single sin: 'Who did no sin, neither was deceit found in His mouth.' Therefore, just as when we are learning the art of painting, the teacher puts before us on a panel a beautifully executed model, and it is necessary for each student to imitate in every way the beauty of that model on his own panel, so that the panels of all will be adorned in accordance with the example of the beauty set before them; in the same way, since every person is the painter of his own life, and choice is the craftsman of the work, and the virtues are the paints for executing the image, there is no small danger that the imitation may change the Prototype into a hateful and ugly person instead of reproducing the master form if we sketch in the character of evil with muddy colours. But, since it is possible, one must prepare the pure colours of the virtues, mixing them with each other according to some artistic formula for the imitation of beauty, so that we become an image of the image, having achieved the beauty of the Prototype through activity as a kind of imitation, as did Paul, who became an 'imitator of Christ', through his life of virtue. If it is necessary to distinguish the individual colours through which the imitation comes about, one colour is meekness, for he says: 'Learn from me, for I am meek and humble of heart.' Another colour is patience which appears quantitatively in 'the image of the invisible God'. . . . Instead, He bore all these things in meekness and patience, legislating patience for your life through

Himself. Thus, it is possible to see all the features of the Prototype, the image of God. Looking towards that image and adorning our own form clearly in accordance with that One, each person becomes himself an 'image of the invisible God', having been portrayed through endurance. (pp. 110–11)

Source: *The Fathers of the Church, Gregory of Nyssa, Ascetical Works*, trans. Virginia Woods Callahan, Washington, The Catholic University of America Press, 1967.

2.3 Ambrose, from *Hexameron: Six Days of Creation: Six*

In this passage Ambrose affirms that God is the supreme artist, hence one should not interfere with God's superior work of art of truth, created through grace, by lesser 'deceitful' works, such as pictures made of wax or women's use of cosmetics. As with Tertullian, Ambrose's views on make-up are suspicious of the body, harsh and 'puritan'.

Man has been depicted by the Lord God, his artist. He is fortunate in having a craftsman and a painter of distinction. He should not erase that painting, one that is the product of truth, not of semblance, a picture, expressed not in mere wax, but in the grace of God. I speak, also, of women. They erase that painting by smearing on their complexion a colour of material whiteness or by applying an artificial rouge. The result is a work not of beauty, but of ugliness; not of simplicity, but of deceit. It is a temporal creation, a prey to perspiration or to rain. It is a snare and a deception which displeases the person you aim to please, for he realizes that all this is an alien thing and not your own. This is also displeasing to your Creator, who sees His own work obliterated. Tell me, if you were to invite an artist of inferior ability to work over a painting of another of superior talent, would not the latter be grieved to see his own work falsified? Do not displace the artistic creation of God by one of meretricious worth, for it is written: 'Shall I take the members of Christ and make them members of a harlot?' By no means! He commits a serious offence who adulterates the work of God. It is a serious charge to suppose that man is to be preferred to God as an artist! It is serious, indeed, when God has to say this about you: 'I do not recognize My colours or My image, not even the countenance which I have made. What is not Mine I reject. Take up your abode with him who has painted you. Seek your favours from him to whom you have given payment.' (para. 47, pp. 259–60)

Source: *The Fathers of the Church, Saint Ambrose, Hexameron, Paradise, and Cain and Abel*, trans. John J. Savage, New York, Fathers of the Church Inc., 1961.

2.4 Augustine, from *The City of God*

Clear echoes of Plato are apparent as Augustine defines beauty in terms of symmetry and proportion. Like Ambrose he refers to God as the supreme artist, whose power works invisibly, producing 'visible results'.

What, however, is true is that there is a hierarchy of created realities, from earthly to heavenly, from visible to invisible, some being better than others, and that the very reason of their inequality is to make possible an existence for them all. For, God is the kind of artist whose greatness in His masterpieces is not lessened in His minor works – which, of course, are not significant by reason of any sublimity in themselves, since they have none, but only by reason of the wisdom of their Designer. Take the case of the beauty of the human form. Shave off one eyebrow and the loss to the mere mass of the body is insignificant. But what a blow to beauty! For, beauty is not a matter of bulk but of the symmetry and proportion of the members. (Book 11, Ch. 22, p. 220)

When God made man according to His own image, He gave him a soul so endowed with reason and intelligence that it ranks man higher than all the other creatures of the earth, the sea, the air, because they lack intelligence. . . . We must not imagine the process in a material way, as though God worked, as ordinary artists do, with hands, shaping, as best they can, some earthly material into a form dictated by the rules of art. The 'hand' of God means the power of God which works in an invisible way to produce even visible results. (Book 12, Ch. 24, p. 290)

Source: *The Fathers of the Church, Saint Augustine, The City of God, Books 8–16*, trans. Gerald G. Walsh, SJ, and Grace Monahan, OSU, Washington, The Catholic University of America Press, 1952.

2.5 Paulinus of Nola, *Poem 27*

Paulinus (353/4–431), Bishop of Nola, ranks with Prudentius as one of the foremost Christian Latin poets of the early Christian epoch. Here he explores the imagery of God as musician and craftsman. In particular he considers the music of the Holy Spirit who intoxicates humans with various sounds and thereby 'brings sobriety'.

Think of a man playing a harp, plucking strings producing different sounds by striking them with the one quill. Or again the man who rubs his lips by blowing on woven reeds; he plays one tune from his one mouth, but there is more than one note, and he marshals the different sounds with controlling skill. He governs the shrill-echoing apertures with his breathing and his nimble fingers, closing and opening them, and thus a tuneful wind with haste of aery movement successively passes and returns along the hollow of the reed, so that the wind instrument becomes alive and issues forth a tune unbroken. This is how God works. He is the Musician who controls that universal-sounding harmony which He exercises through all the physical world. God is the Craftsman of all creation natural and contrived. In all this creation He is the Source and the End. He makes what is good and preserves it once made, abiding in Himself with that interchange of mutual love by which reigns the Father in the Word and the Son in the Father. Without Him nothing was made. Through Him all that comes to life abides in the same Being. He renews all things under the guidance of the Word, who mounting aloft from the gleaming cross with the purple of His precious blood reached the heights in swift ascent, flying on a cloud beyond the Cherubim! O He took His seat on the right hand of the Father, and from there poured forth on His followers the heavenly gift of the Holy Spirit.

The Holy Spirit proceeds from the only-begotten Son and the Father, and is Himself God coming forth from God! Though the Spirit is everywhere, His fiery presence was actually visible gliding speedily over the place where the harmonious gathering of young apostles was in session! Then, when a large number from Jerusalem had assembled at the unusual sound, the Spirit settled like a flame on all those present of every race, and with the same breath spoke differently but simultaneously to each of them. Like a musician strumming the strings of the lyre with fluent quill, the Spirit proclaimed the same message in different tongues, instilling into men's ears the varying sounds. Once such intoxication possessed these chosen souls, their hearts were drunk with God, and they belched forth from abstemious throats songs of sacred praise. Who will take pity on me and give me to drink from this stream which with its intoxication brings sobriety? (pp. 272–4)

Source: *Ancient Christian Writers, The Poems of Paulinus of Nola*, trans. and ed. P. G. Walsh, New York, Paramus, NJ, Newman Press, 1975.

3

Iconoclasm and Idolatry

— —

3.1 Justin Martyr, from *The First Apology*

In this passage Justin repudiates any form of idol worship and considers artisans who make such objects as morally objectionable. He encourages believers to live by virtue and to develop their faith through the faculty of the intellect.

We do not worship with many sacrifices and floral offerings the things men have made, set in temples, and called gods. We know that they are inanimate and lifeless and have not the form of God (for we do not think that God has that form; which some say they reproduce in order to give honour to Him) – but have the names and shapes of those evil demons who have appeared [to men]. Why should we tell you, who already know, into what different shapes the workmen fashion their material, by carving, cutting, molding, and hammering? From vessels destined for vile purposes, by merely changing their shape and by skillfully giving them a new form, they often make what they call gods. Thus, His name is applied to corruptible things that need constant care. This, we think, is not only stupid but also disrespectful to God, who is of ineffable glory and form. You are well aware of the fact that their skilled artisans are licentious men and, not to enter into details, are experienced in every known vice; they even defile the girls who work with them. What stupidity, that lustful men should carve and reshape gods for your veneration, and that such men should be appointed the guards of the temples wherein the gods are set up, not realizing that it is forbidden to declare or even think that men are the keepers of the gods.

But we have learned from tradition that God has no need, of the material gifts of men, since we see that He is the Giver of all things. We have been taught, are convinced, and do believe that He approves of only those who imitate His inherent virtues, namely, temperance, justice, love of man, and any other virtue proper to God who is called by no given name. We have also been instructed that God, in the beginning, created in His goodness everything out of shapeless matter for the sake of men. And if men by their actions prove themselves worthy of His plan, they shall, we are told, be found worthy to make their abode with

Him and to reign with Him, free from all corruption and pain. Just as in the beginning He created us when we were not, so also, we believe, He will consider all those who choose to please Him, because of their choice, to be worthy of eternal life in His presence. Our creation was not in our own power. But this – to engage in those things that please Him and which we choose by means of the intellectual faculties He has bestowed on us – this makes our conviction and leads us to faith. Indeed, we think it is for the good of all men that they are not prevented from learning these things, but are even urged to consider them. (Chs 9–10, pp. 41–3)

Source: *The Fathers of the Church, Saint Justin Martyr*, ed. Thomas B. Falls, Washington, The Catholic University of America Press in association with Consortium Books, 1948.

3.2 Lactantius, from *The Divine Institutes*

Lactantius (c.240–c.320) was a Christian apologist and teacher of rhetoric. Here he strongly argues against the making and worship of images since they are dead matter, while God is always present and alive. Instead of focusing on earthly things, made by human hands, the Christian ought to worship the heavenly Maker of all creation.

Now, I ask you, if anyone gazes often at the picture of a man who is away so that he may take comfort from it for sustaining the absence, he would not seem sane, would he, if, when the other has returned and is present, he should continue to gaze at the picture rather than wish to enjoy the sight of the man himself? Certainly, not at all sane. Still, the image of the man seems necessary when he is far away, but it will be superfluous when he is near at hand. The image of God, however, whose power and spirit, everywhere diffused, can never be absent, is certainly always superfluous. But they fear that their entire religion may be empty and vain if they see nothing before them to adore. So they set up like-nesses, which, because they are images of the dead, are very much like the dead: they lack all the senses. There ought to be a living sensible likeness of a god liv-ing to eternity. If this word takes its name from its quality of likeness, how can those images which neither feel nor are moved be considered like to God? Hence, the likeness of God is not that which is made by the hands of man from stone or bronze or any material whatever; it is man himself who feels, and is moved, and does many great actions. Men who are most foolish and absurd do not under-stand that, if likenesses could feel and be moved, they would willingly adore the man by whom they were fashioned, for they would be unfashioned and rough stone or unformed and raw material unless they had been put into shape by that man. Man, therefore, must be reckoned the parent, as it were, of those things which have come to be through his hands; it is through man that they have come to have form, shape, and beauty, and, therefore, he who made them is better than those things which were made. Yet no one looks up to and fears the very Maker; they are afraid of what He made, as though it were possible for the work to be of more avail than the workman. Rightly does Seneca in his moral books say that men venerate the likenesses of gods. 'They supplicate them with bended knee; they adore them; through the whole day they sit or stand near them; they throw offerings to them and slay victims for them; and while they look up to these so much they contemn the laborers who made them.' What is so self-contradictory as to despise a statue maker, to adore the statue, and not even to admit to social intercourse the man who makes your gods for you? What strength, then, what power can they have, when he who made them does not have any? But not even those powers which he possessed – sight, hearing, speech, movement – could he give to them. Is there anyone, therefore, so foolish that he thinks that there is something of a god in an image in which there is not even anything of man except a shadow? But no one considers these things. Men are infected with vain and stupid persuasion, and their minds have drunk in fully the juice of folly. So they who are themselves sensible adore insensible things; they who are wise adore irrational things; they who live adore lifeless things; with an origin from heaven they adore earthly things. . . .

Why then are you subjecting yourselves to inferior things? Why do you place earth upon your heads? When you submit yourselves to the earth and make yourselves lowlier, you sink beyond to the infernal regions and condemn yourselves to death because there is nothing inferior and more lowly than the earth except death and hell. If you wished to avoid these, you would despise the earth placed under your feet by preserving the normal stature of your body, an upright one, which you received for this reason – that you might be able to unite your eyes and your mind with Him who made them. Therefore, to despise and tread upon the earth is nothing else than not to adore images because they are made of earth; and, likewise, it is not to desire riches and to spurn the delights of the body, since wealth and the body itself, whose hospitality we make use of, is of the earth. Cherish the living, that you may live. It is necessary that he die who has assigned himself and his soul to the dead. (Book 1, Ch. 2, pp. 98–101)

Whoever, therefore, strives to regard the guaranty of man and to hold to the reason and plan of his nature, let him raise himself from the ground and with upright mind direct his eyes toward heaven. Let him not seek God under his feet nor take from his footsteps that which he may adore, for it must needs be that whatever lies beneath man is subject to man, but rather let him seek Him alone; let him seek in the heights, because nothing can be greater than man except what is above man. God is greater than man; therefore, He is above, not below, and He must not be sought in the lowest regions, but rather in the highest wherefore there is no doubt that there is no religion wherever there is a statue or image. For if religion consists of divine things, and if there is nothing divine except in things that are heavenly, images lack religion, since there can be nothing heavenly in that which is made of earth. (Book 2, Ch. 18, pp. 161–2)

Source: *The Fathers of the Church, Lactantius, The Divine Institutes*, trans. Mary F. McDonald, OP, Washington, The Catholic University of America Press, 1964.

3.3 Gregory the Great, from *Selected Epistles*

Pope Gregory I (the Great, c.540–604) was the last of the traditional Latin doctors of the Church. He was influential in the development of church music and liturgy. He also commented on pastoral issues for bishops and developed the doctrine of Purgatory. Further, he popularized the mystical writings of Pseudo-Dionysius. The letter below, to Serenus, Bishop of Massilia (Marseilles), deals with the question of iconoclasm, whereby Gregory takes a moderate stance. It is one of the most quoted texts in medieval and Reformation discussions on images.

But, while putting aside consideration of our wholesome admonitions, thou hadst come to be culpable, not only in thy deeds, but in thy questionings also. For indeed it had been reported to us that, inflamed with inconsiderate zeal, thou hadst broken images of saints, as though under the plea that they ought not to be adored. And indeed in that thou forbadest them to be adored, we altogether praise thee; but we blame thee for having broken them. Say, brother, what priest has ever been heard of as doing what thou hadst done? If nothing else, should not even this thought have restrained thee, so as not to despise other brethren, supposing thyself only to be holy and wise? For to adore a picture is one thing, but to learn through the story of a picture what is to be adored is another. For what writing presents to readers, this a picture presents to the unlearned who behold, since in it even the ignorant see what they ought to follow; in it the illiterate read. Hence, and chiefly to the nations, a picture is instead of reading. And this ought to have been attended to especially by thee who livest among the nations, lest, while inflamed inconsiderately by a right zeal, thou shouldest breed offence to savage minds. And, seeing that antiquity has not without reason admitted the histories of saints to be painted in venerable places, if thou hadst seasoned zeal with discretion, thou mightest undoubtedly have obtained what thou wert aiming at, and not scattered the collected flock, but rather gathered together a scattered one; that so the deserved renown of a shepherd might have distinguished thee, instead of the blame of being a scatterer lying upon thee. But from having acted inconsiderately on the impulse of thy feelings thou art said to have so offended thy children that the greatest part of them have suspended themselves from thy communion. When, then, wilt thou bring wandering sheep to the Lord's fold, not being able to retain those thou hast? Henceforth we exhort thee that thou study even now to be careful, and restrain thyself from this presumption, and make haste, with fatherly sweetness, with all endeavour, with all earnestness, to recall to thyself the minds of those whom thou findest to be disjoined from thee.

For the dispersed children of the Church must be called together, and it must be shewn then by testimonies of sacred Scripture that it is not lawful for anything made with hands to be adored, since it is written, *Thou shall adore the Lord thy God, and him only shalt serve* (Luke 4.8). And then, with regard to the pictorial representations which had been made for the edification of an unlearned people in order that, though ignorant of letters, they might by turning their eyes to the story itself learn what had been done, it must be added that, because thou hadst seen these come to be adored, thou hadst been so moved as to order them to be broken. And it must be said to them, If [sic] for this instruction for which images were anciently made you wish to have them in the church, I permit them by all means both to be made and to be had. And explain to them that it was not the sight itself of the story which the picture was hanging to attest that displeased thee, but the adoration which had been improperly paid to the pictures. And with such words appease thou their minds; recall them to agreement with thee. And if anyone should wish to make images, by no means prohibit him, but by all means forbid the adoration of images. But let thy Fraternity carefully admonish them that from the sight of the event portrayed they should catch the ardour of compunction, and bow themselves down in adoration of the One Almighty Holy Trinity.

Now we say all this in our love of Holy Church, and of thy Fraternity. Be not then shaken, in consequence of my rebuke, in the zeal of uprightness, but rather be helped in the earnestness of thy pious administration. (pp. 297–8)

Source: *A Select Library of the Nicene and Post-Nicene Fathers of the Christian Church, Second Series, vol. 13, Gregory the Great, Part 2, Selected Epistles*, Oxford, James Parker and Company/New York, The Christian Literature Company, 1898.

4

The Role of the Senses, Dress Codes, and Negative Views of Women

— —

4.1 Clement of Alexandria, from *Christ the Educator*

Clement of Alexandria (c.150–c.215), head of the School of Alexandria, concerned himself especially with christological questions. Here he discusses in depth the proper conduct of Christian life – one ought to live frugally, chaste and keep restraint in clothing, fragrances and cosmetics. He reflects on women, who should be a 'faithful reflection' of their husband, and should not present themselves in seductive fashion. These suspicious and ultimately oppressive views of women, influenced by Greek philosophy and certain biblical passages, were to shape much of future theological writing on the role of women in the Church.

For it is not right that garments and cosmetics that betray artificiality be allowed entry into a city of truth. Men of our way of life should be redolent, not of perfume, but of perfection, and women should be fragrant with the odour of Christ, the royal chrism, not that of powders and perfumes. Let her be ever anointed with the heavenly oil of chastity, taking her delight in holy myrrh, that is, the Spirit. Christ provides this oil of good odour for His followers, compounding His myrrh from sweet heavenly herbs. With this myrrh the Lord anoints Himself, as David says: 'Therefore, O God, thy God hath anointed thee with the oil of gladness above thy fellows. Myrrh and stacte and cassia from thy garments.'

Yet, let us not develop a fear of perfume, like vultures and scarabs who are said to die if anointed with the oil of roses. Let the women make use of a little of these perfumes, but not so much as to nauseate their husbands, for too much fragrance suggests a funeral, not married life. . . . Do you not realise that myrrh, a soft oil, is able to emasculate noble characters? Certainly it is. Just as we have already forbidden pampering the sense of taste, so, too, we proscribe indulgence of the sense of sight and of smell. Otherwise, we may reopen the doors of the soul without being aware of it, through the senses as through unfortified doors, to the very dissipation we had put to flight.

If anyone object that the great High Priest, the Lord, offers up to God incense of sweet odour, let this not be understood as the sacrifice and good odour of incense, but as the acceptable gift of love, a spiritual fragrance on the altar, that the Lord offers up. By its nature, oil is useful for softening the skin and for relaxing the muscles and removing the offensive odours of the body. For such purposes we may need oil, but the constant use of sweet odours bespeaks pampering, and pampering arouses lustful desires. The man without self-control is easily led about by anything: eating, sleeping, social gatherings, as well as by his eyes and ears and stomach, and particularly to the point, by his sense of smell. Just as cattle are led by rings through their noses and by ropes, so, too, the self-indulgent are led by odours and perfumes and sweet scents rising from their wreathes.

Since we make no allowance for pleasure not connected with a necessity of life, surely let us also make distinctions here and choose only what is useful. There are perfumes that are neither soporific nor erotic, suggestive neither of sexual relations nor of immodest harlotry, but wholesome and chaste and refreshing to the mind that is tired and invigorating to the appetite. We must not completely turn away from such things, but take advantage of myrrh as an aid and remedy to stimulate our failing powers, for catarrh and chills and indispositions (Book 2, para. 65–8, pp. 150–1)

Now, if Christ forbids solicitude once and for all about clothing and food and luxuries, as things that are unnecessary, do we need to ask Him about finery and dyed wools and multicolored robes, about exotic ornaments of jewels and artistic handiwork of gold, about wigs and artificial locks of hair and of curls, and about eye-shadowings and hair-plucking and rouges and powders and hair-dyes and all the other disreputable trades that practise these deceptions? (Book 2, para. 104, p. 180)

Both [men and women] have the same need of being protected; therefore, what they use as protection should be very similar, except, perhaps, that women ought to use a type of garment that will cover their eyes. If the female sex is rightly allowed more clothing out of deference to its weakness, then the practice of a degenerate way of life must be censured which accustoms men to unworthy customs that so often make them more womanish than the women. But we do not feel free to relax our strictness in any way. If we need to make any concessions, we might allow women to use softer garments, provided they give up fancy weaves, symptoms of vanity, and fabrics too elaborate in weave, or with gold thread, Indian silks and all products of the silk-worm. . . . These flimsy and luxurious things are proof of a shallow character, for, with the scanty protection they afford, they do nothing more than disgrace the body, inviting prostitution. An overly soft garment is no longer covering, since it cannot conceal the bare outline of the figure; the folds of such a garment clinging to the body and following its contours very flexibly take its shape and outline the woman's form so that even one not trying to stare can see plainly the woman's entire figure.

We disapprove also of dyed garments. They do not satisfy the demands either of necessity or of truth; besides, they give cause for defamation of character. They serve no useful purpose, for they do nothing to protect against the cold, nor do they add any advantage to that given by any other garment, save criticism alone. The enjoyment of these colours is injurious to the luxury-loving people who use them, to the point of provoking a strange eye-affliction. It is much more fitting that they who are pure and upright interiorly be clothed in pure white and plain garments. (Book 2, para. 107 and 108, pp. 182–3)

But we must moderate our severity for the sake of the women. We say, then, that their garment may be woven smooth and soft to the touch, but not adorned with gaudy colours, like a painting, just to dazzle the eye. . . .

The blessed John disdained sheep's wool because it savoured of luxury; he preferred camel's hair and clothed himself in it, giving us an example of simple, frugal living. Incidentally, he also ate only honey and locusts, food that is sweet and with a spiritual significance. So it was that he prepared the way of the Lord, and kept it humble and chaste. He fled from the false pretences of the city and led a peaceful life in the desert with God, away from all vanity and vainglory and servitude. How could he possibly have worn a purple mantle? Elias used a sheep-skin for his garment, and girded it tight with a belt made of hair. Isaias, another historic Prophet, went 'naked and without sandals', and often put on sack-cloth as a garment of humility. (Book 2, para. 111–12, pp. 185–6)

Therefore, we must avoid any irregularity in the type of garment we choose. We must also guard against all waywardness in our use of them. For instance, it is not right for a woman to wear her dress up over her knees, as the Laconian maidens are said to do, because a woman should not expose any part of her body. Of course, when someone tells her: 'Your arm is shapely', she can always cleverly make the witty reply: 'But it is not public property'; to 'Your legs are beautiful', this reply: 'But they belong to my husband'; or if he says: 'Your face is lovely', she can answer: 'But only for him to whom I am married'. (Book 2, para. 114, p. 187)

A woman should be adorned, assuredly, but interiorly; there she should be beautiful indeed. Beauty or ugliness is found only in the soul. Only he who is sincere is truly noble and virtuous, and only the noble can be considered good. 'Virtue alone is noteworthy even in a beautiful body,' and comes to full maturity afterwards in the flesh. The attractiveness of temperance is made manifest when the character glows with a brilliant appearance, as though with light. The beauty of anything, whether plant or animal, is admittedly in its perfection. But man's perfection is justice and temperance and courage and piety. Therefore, it is the just and temperate, or, in a word, the good man who is noble, and not the wealthy one. (Book 2, para. 121, pp. 193–4)

In fact, desire becomes everything, turns itself into a counterfeit of everything, and seeks to play the impostor to conceal man's true nature. But the man in whom reason dwells does not keep shifting, makes no false pretences, retains the form dictated by reason, is like God and possesses true beauty with no need of artificial beauty. Beauty is what is true, for it is in fact God. Such a man becomes God because God wills it. (Book 3, para. 1, p. 200)

But there is another sort of beauty for men: charity. 'Charity,' according to the Apostle, 'is patient, is kind, does not envy, is not pretentious, is not puffed up.' But artificial beauty is pretentiousness, because it presents the appearance of extravagance and superfluity. That is why he adds: 'It does not behave un-becomingly. . . . Truth calls what is proper to itself its own, while vanity seeks what is artificial, putting itself in opposition to God, to reason and to charity. The Spirit gives witness through Isaias that even the Lord became an unsightly spectacle.' And we saw Him, and there was no beauty or comeliness in Him, but the true beauty of body and soul: for the soul, the beauty of good deeds; for the body, that of immortality. (Book 3, para. 3, p. 201)

But now, debauched living and indulgence in illicit pleasures have gone to such a limit, and every sort of libertinism has become so rife in the cities, that they have become the norm. Women live in brothels, there offering their own bodies for sale to satisfy lustful pleasure, and boys are taught to renounce their own natures and play the role of women. Self-indulgence has turned everything upside down. Over-refinement in comfortable living has put humanity to shame. It seeks every-thing, it attempts everything, it forces everything, it violates even nature. Men have become the passive mate in sexual relations and women act as men; contrary to nature, women now are both wives and husbands. No opening is impenetrable to impurity. Sexual pleasure is made public property common to all the people, and self-indulgence their boon companion. What a pitiful spectacle! What unspeakable practices! They are the monuments to your wide-spread lack of self-control, and whores are the proof of your deeds. Alas, such disregard for law! (Book 3, para. 21, p. 217)

[W]e have received from our Educator those beautiful and holy mates, self-service and frugality. In fact, we must walk according to reason even if we have a wife and children in our home. A household is not a burden if it has but learned to follow in the lead of the wayfarer who knows self-control.

Invariably the wife who loves her husband will be his faithful reflection, both of them wayfarers carrying provisions best suited for a journey toward heaven: frugality, together with a united and determined practice of self-restraint. (Book 3, para. 38–9, p. 231)

Let me sketch a picture of the embellishment inspired by self-restraint. First of all, spiritual beauty is the most excellent; by it, the soul is made beautiful with the presence of the Holy Spirit and the adornments He confers: justice, prudence, fortitude, temperance, love of the good, and modesty. No colour has ever been seen as beautiful as these. Afterwards they may cultivate bodily beauty: 'symmetry of limbs and members, and a good complexion'. The adornment of good health also deserves mention in this category, for it is by health that an artificially produced image is transformed into reality according to the design planned by God. Self-control in drinking and moderation in eating are natural means of producing beauty, for they not only preserve the body's health, but also heighten beauty. A fiery substance generates a gleam and sparkle; moisture, brightness, and pleasantness; a dry substance begets courage and steadfastness; and a substance formed of air gives freshness and poise. It is with all these that the harmonious and beautiful image of the Word is adorned. Beauty is the noble flower of health. The one is caused within the body; the other, beauty, blossoming exteriorly, produces the good complexion that may be seen.

Courses of action that exercise the body are the most effective in maintaining beauty and health, and produce a beauty that is lasting and true because heat draws out all moisture and coldness of breath. (Book 3, para. 64–5, p. 249)

Source: *The Fathers of the Church, Clement of Alexandria, Christ the Educator*, trans. Simon Wood, CP, Washington, The Catholic University of America Press, 1954.

4.2.1 Tertullian, from *On the Soul*

Tertullian (c.160–c.225) wrote apologetic and ascetic works in defence of Christianity against heresies. In opposition to the Platonist philosophers, Tertullian stresses that the senses are the basis for our thinking, learning and our joy of life. If one denies the senses, one denies the humanity of Christ. He concludes that the intellect is not superior to, or separate from, sense perception, but dependent on it.

There also arises the question of the veracity of our five senses, of which we learn from earliest childhood, since the heretics seek to support their teaching on this score. They are the familiar five: sight, hearing, smell, taste, and touch.

The Platonists seriously attack their validity, and Heraclitus, Diocles, and Empedocles are said to agree with them. It is certain that Plato in the *Timaeus* declares sense knowledge to be irrational and capable of arriving at opinion, but not true knowledge. Our eyes deceive us, he says, in showing us oars under water as bent or broken in spite of our assurance that they are straight; thus, again, from a distance a square tower appears to be circular and on looking down a long corridor we seem to see the walls meeting at a point. Besides, we normally see on the horizon the meeting of the sea and the sky which is really high above it.

Likewise, our ears deceive us; we mistake thunder for the rumble of a cart or vice versa. The senses of smell and taste are also faulty in that we become so accustomed to perfumes and wines that we no longer advert to their specific bouquet. Touch also fails us in that the same pavement which scratches our hands is smooth to our feet; and at the first touch our bath water may seem to be scalding, yet shortly it seems quite comfortable.

Thus, they tell us, we are deceived by our senses and must continually revise our opinions. The Stoics are somewhat more moderate in that they do not always impugn the validity of all the senses. The Epicureans with complete consistency maintain that the senses always report the truth, but they explain the illusions in a way different from the Stoics. In their opinion, the senses report the truth, but our minds lead us astray. The function of the senses is to receive an impression, not to think; that is the function of the soul. They deny to the senses the power of thinking and to the soul all power of sensation.

But, what is the basis of thought, if not the senses? Whence does the mind get the idea the tower is really round, unless from the senses? Whence comes the act of sensation, if not from the soul? On the other hand, a soul without a body would experience no sensation. Therefore, sensation takes place in the soul and thought begins in the senses, but the soul is the root of it all. It is a fact that there is something which causes the senses to report things otherwise than they really are. If the senses can report things which do not correspond to reality, isn't it possible that such things are caused not by the senses at all, but by something that takes place between sensation and thought?

This fact ought surely be recognized. The water is the cause of making the oar appear bent or broken, because out of the water it is perfectly straight. Water is so delicate a medium that, when under the light of day it becomes a mirror, the slightest motion of the water will distort the image and appear to bend a straight line. (Ch. 17, para. 1–6, pp. 214–16)

So, you see, there is always a cause when our senses are mistaken. Now, if this cause deceives the senses and they in turn our opinions, then the error should not be imputed either to the senses which follow the cause or our opinions which are dependent on the data of our senses. (Ch. 17, para. 8, p. 216)

Further still, the blame for these errors is not to be imputed to these 'causes' either. For, although these things happen for specific reasons, reason should not be blamed for the mistake. The normal event should never be construed as a lie. Now, if we can absolve the 'causes' from blame, then surely we must acquit the senses which merely follow the 'causes'. The senses, then, can claim that they faithfully report the truth, since they never render any other account of their impressions save that which they receive from the oftenmentioned causes; this latter it is which produces the discrepancy between sensation and reality.

O Academics! What impudence you are showing! Don't you see that your assertions would destroy the normal conduct of human life and the very order of nature? Are you not claiming that Divine Providence was blind? The senses of man have been given the mastery over all God's creation that by them we might understand, inhabit, dispose of, and enjoy His goodness – and these you accuse of deliberate falsity! Is not all life dependent upon the senses? Are not our senses the second source of knowledge with which we are endowed? Whence, do you think, come the various arts, the ingenious developments in business, politics, commerce, medicine? Whence the technique of prudent advice and consolation, the resources that have made progress in all phases of human life and culture? Without his senses, man's life would be deprived of all joy and satisfaction, the only rational being in creation would thus be incapable of intelligence or learning, or even of founding an Academy! (Ch. 17, para. 10–11, p. 216–17)

We cannot, I insist, impugn the validity of the senses, for thus we will be denying that Christ really saw Satan cast down from heaven; that He ever heard His Father's voice testifying to Him; that He only *thought* He touched Peter's mother-in-law; that He never smelled the fragrance of the ointment given Him in preparation for His burial or of the wine He consecrated in memory of His Blood.

On this pernicious principle, Marcion denied that Christ had a real body and was but a phantom or a ghost. No, His Apostles really and truly perceived Him with their senses. They saw and heard Him at the Transfiguration; they tasted the wine changed from water at Cana in Galilee. Thomas believed when he touched the wound in His side. Finally, listen to the word of St. John: 'What we have seen, and heard, perceived with our eyes, what our hands have handled of the word of life.' The witness of St. John is false if we cannot believe the testimony of our eyes, our ears, and our hands. (Ch. 17, para. 13–14, p. 218)

We now come to the matter of the distinction between the sensitive and the intellectual powers, which is seen to be based on the nature of the objects perceived. While corporeal, visible, and tangible things belong to the province of sense, the spiritual, visible, and secret things are under the dominion of the mind. Yet, both classes come under the soul for the purpose of being at its service; thus, the soul perceives corporeal things with the help of the body and spiritual things by means of the mind, since the soul is really exercising sensation when it is thinking.

Isn't it true that to feel is to understand and to think is to have sensation? For, what else is sensation than the perception of the thing felt? Or what else is understanding than the perception of the thing known? Why, then, all torturing of simple truth into obscurity? Can you show me a sensation which does not understand what it feels or an intellect which does not perceive what it knows, so as to prove to me that one can get along without the other? If we must say that corporeal things are 'sensed' and spiritual things are 'understood', it is the nature *of those objects* which causes the distinction and not the abode of sensation and understanding, that is, the soul and the mind. By what faculty do we perceive corporeal things? If the mind does it, then the mind is a sensual as well as an intellectual faculty, because, when it understands, it feels, and, if it doesn't feel, it has no understanding. If, however, corporeal things are perceived by the soul, then the power of the soul is intellectual as well as sensual, because, when it feels something, it understands it; because, if there is no understanding, there is no sensation. Likewise, by which faculty are incorporeal things perceived? If by the mind, where does the soul fit in, and, if by the soul, the mind? Things that are distinct should be separate from each other in the exercise of their specific functions. (Ch. 18, para. 6–8, pp. 220–1)

On this matter we shall have to fight the heretics on their own ground. This work is concerned with the soul and we have to be careful lest the intellect should usurp the prerogative of superiority over the soul. Now, even though the object of the intellect, being spiritual, is superior to the object of sense – namely, material things – it is still merely a superiority in object – the exalted as against the humble – and not a superiority of intellect over sense. How can there be a real superiority of intellect over sense when the former depends on the latter for its guidance to the truth?

We know that truth is apprehended by means of visible images, that is, the invisible through the visible. For, St. Paul tells us: 'The invisible attributes of God from the creation of the world are understood from the things that are made.' Plato would tell the heretics: 'The things we see are merely the image of the hidden realities.' Hence, this world must be a representation of some other world, else why would the intellect use the senses as its guide, authority, and support, if without them it could attain to truth? How, then, can it be superior to that through which it exists, which it needs for its operation, and to which it owes all that it gains?

Two conclusions follow, therefore, from this discussion: (1) Intellect is not superior to sense on the argument that the instrument through which a thing exists is inferior to the thing itself. (2) Intellect must not be considered to be separate from the senses, since that by which a thing exists is united to that thing. (Ch. 18, para. 11–13, pp. 222–3)

Source: *The Fathers of the Church, Tertullian, Apologetical Works*, trans. R. Arbesmann, OSA, E. J. Daly, CSJ, and E. A. Quain, SJ, Washington, The Catholic University of America Press in association with Consortium Books, 1950.

4.2.2 Tertullian, from *On the Apparel of Women*

Tertullian's disparaging, misogynist view of women is in striking contrast with his more 'holistic' view of the relationship between intellect and sense perception. He viciously attacks women for having brought sin into the world and blames them even for Christ's death. Surprisingly, he admits to being envious of women, and reluctantly admits that men, too, are given to please through frivolous adornment.

Introduction. Modesty in apparel becoming to women, in memory of the introduction of sin into the world through a woman. . . . And do you not know that you are (each) an Eve? The sentence of God on this sex of yours lives in this age: the guilt must of necessity live too. *You* are the devil's gateway: *you* are the unsealer of that (forbidden) tree: *you* are the first deserter of the divine law: *you* are she who persuaded him whom the devil was not valiant enough to attack. *You* destroyed so easily God's image, man. On account of *your* desert, that is, death – even the Son of God had to die. And do you think about adorning yourself over and above your tunics of skins? Come, now; if from the beginning of the world the Milesians sheared sheep, and the Serians spun trees, and the Tyrians dyed, and the Phrygians embroidered with the needle, and the Babylonians with the loom, and pearls gleamed, and onyx-stones flashed; if gold itself also had already issued, with the cupidity (which accompanies it), from the ground; if the mirror, too, had licence to lie so largely, Eve, expelled from paradise, (Eve) already dead, would also have coveted *these* things, I imagine! No more then, ought she now to crave, or be acquainted with (if she desires to live again), what, when she *was* living, she had neither had nor known. Accordingly these things are all the baggage of woman in her condemned and dead state, instituted as if to swell the pomp of her funeral. (Book 1, Ch. 1, p. 14)

Men not excluded from these remarks on personal adornment. Of course, now, I, a man, as being envious of women, am banishing them quite from their own (domains). Are there, in our case too, some things which, in respect of the sobriety we are to maintain on account of the fear due to God, are disallowed? If it is true, (as it is,) that in men, for the sake of women (just as in women for the sake of men), there is implanted, by a defect of nature, the will to please; and if this sex of ours acknowledges to itself deceptive trickeries of form peculiarly its own . . . while yet, when (once) the knowledge of God has put an end to all wish to please by means of voluptuous attraction, all these things are rejected as frivolous, as hostile to modesty. For where God is, there modesty is; there is sobriety, her assistant and ally. How, then, shall we practise modesty without her instrumental mean that is, without sobriety? How, moreover, shall we bring sobriety to bear on the discharge of (the functions of) modesty, unless seriousness in appearance and in countenance, and in the general aspect of the entire man, mark our carriage? (Book 2, Ch. 8, p. 22)

Source: *The Ante-Nicene Fathers, The Writings of the Fathers down to* AD *325, vol. 4, Tertullian et al.*, eds James Donaldson and Alexander Roberts, Grand Rapids, MI, Eerdmans, 1965.

4.3 Ambrose, from *Paradise*

Ambrose here maintains what had been perceived as 'fact' since Plato, and was echoed in the early Christian era by Philo et al, i.e. the existence of woman as 'sense' (aisthesis) and emotion and as the one who instigates sin, and of man as 'mind' (nous). Mind is seen as a higher form of perception than sense.

Many people nevertheless are of the opinion that the Devil was not in Paradise, although we read that he stood with the angels in heaven. These persons interpret the statement of Scripture according to their own fancy. In this way they put aside any objection which they may have to the words of Scripture. We stand by the conviction held by one who preceded us that sin was committed by man because of the pleasure of sense. We maintain that the figure of the serpent stands for enjoyment and the figure of the woman for the emotions of the mind and heart. The latter is called by the Greeks *aisthesis*. When according to this theory, the senses are deceived, the mind, which the Greeks call *nous*, falls into error. Hence, not without reason the author to whom I refer accepts the Greek word *nous* as a figure of a man and *aisthesis* as that of a woman. Hence, some have interpreted Adam to mean an earthly *nous*. In the Gospel the Lord sets forth the parable of the virgins who awaited the coming of the bridegroom with either lighted or extinguished lamps. Thus He exemplifies either the pure emotions of the wise or the impure senses of the unwise. If Eve, that is, the emotions of the first woman, had kept her lamp lighted, she would not have enfolded us in the meshes of her sin. She would not have fallen from the height of immortality which is established as the reward of virtue.

   Paradise is, therefore, a land of fertility – that is to say, a soul which is fertile – planted in Eden, that is, in a certain delightful or well-tilled land in which the soul finds pleasure. Adam exists there as *nous* [mind] and Eve as sense. (para. 11 and 12, pp. 293–4)

Source: *The Fathers of the Church, Saint Ambrose, Hexameron, Paradise, and Cain and Abel*, trans. John J. Savage, New York, Fathers of the Church Inc., 1961.

Part 2

The Medieval Church

— —

Introduction

During the Middle Ages the themes pertaining to a theological aesthetics as they had emerged during the early Church continued to be further developed. These included the idea of beauty, the vision of God, the image of Christ, the iconodule–iconoclast conflict, and the strong presence of personally grounded and poetic doxologies.

The nature of beauty exercised the minds of several leading theologians, in particular, John Scotus Eriugena, Bonaventure, Thomas Aquinas and Nicholas of Cusa in their more abstract, theoretical arguments; and Bernard of Clairvaux and William of St Thierry in their allegorical commentaries and sermons on the Song of Songs. Yet, none of the medieval scholars ever developed a full theory of beauty as such. Edward Farley rightly raises the question that 'if to be is to be beautiful' – as the medievals insisted – why then was beauty so meagrely applied to interpretations of faith, morals and redemption in theological treatises on the whole? (cf. Farley, 2001, p. 22).

For Aquinas, the central voice of medieval theology who appropriated the Platonist and, especially, the Aristotelian heritage, beauty is made up of three criteria: *integritas* (perfection of form), *claritas* (the splendour of proportioned form) and *consonantia* (harmony of proportioned form). But, one might suggest, if everything that is, is beautiful precisely through its proportion and form, as Thomas and his contemporaries held, how can we think of God as being supreme beauty, if God is ultimately beyond any form and proportion? (Farley, 2001, p. 23). Schelling and Whitehead would tackle this problem much later.

Even though the medieval thinkers for the most part took on the Plato-Pseudo-Dionysius line of thought, a change occurred in their idea of the relationship between beauty and light. The early Christian theologians had said that beauty was *like* a light. Now the visible light itself was seen as an epiphany. Material things of light and colour, for example, the illuminated manuscripts and stained-glass windows, or even 'just' a stone or a piece of wood, as Eriugena exclaimed in somewhat panentheistic fashion, were regarded as light, as sources and epiphanies of divine beauty. Hugh of St Victor spoke of beauty as being 'the visible image of the invisible'. Thomas, too, with his Aristotelian background, had a more positive outlook on the created world. This appreciation of material beauty ultimately anticipated the focus on humanism and naturalism in the arts that would evolve during the Renaissance. The great Gothic cathedrals and the illuminated manuscripts are the most marvellous testimonies to these theological-aesthetic perceptions on light and beauty in this epoch. Yet, as with the early Christian theologians, the medievals would continuously assert that while beauty is found in 'every face' (Nicholas of Cusa), the transcendent God alone is absolute beauty – beauty itself.

Furthermore, the hugely oppressive views and treatment of women by males, in particular the clerical Church, continued unabated. The dualistic idea – fashioned by male thinkers – of woman as *aisthesis* and man as *nous* was not questioned in any way among those in power. Those who did present a challenge by their very lifestyle, their education and their intellectual interests, e.g. Hadewijch, the female mystical theologians in Helfta, as well as Mechthild of Magdeburg, remained on the margins and had to bear clerical suspicion. Aquinas, like Plato, held that a good thing is also beautiful, because it has form.

Something that is good, and thus beautiful, is also useful; it has a purpose. In this context it is important to remember that medieval artists and their predecessors were not actually considered artists in their own right – this only starts with the Renaissance – but essentially as artisans who remained largely anonymous creative makers of useful items. Yet Thomas significantly anticipated Kant's idea of aesthetic distance when he added that the good and the beautiful are not, in fact, synonymous. The good implies that which everyone desires and therefore involves purpose, whereas beauty 'has to do with knowledge'. It 'pleases the eye of the beholder'. Something may please and delight us, but we do not need to possess, touch or use it. In Kant's words we are faced with a 'purposiveness without purpose' (*Zweckmässigkeit ohne Zweck*) (cf. M. Hauskeller (ed.), *Was das Schöne sei*, München, dtv, 1994, p. 87).

Not surprisingly, the themes of the beauty of Christ and of Christ as *the* image of God also continue to feature in medieval thought. In our texts, this is especially manifested in the writings of John of Damascus and Theodore of Studios in their christologically grounded defence of images. Symeon the New Theologian writes his theology in the form of poetry; he lets Christ himself speak: 'It is only a ray of glory / and a streak of my light / that they contemplate and by which they are divinized. / For it is like a mirror / which receives the rays of the sun.' He employs the traditional metaphors of 'light' and 'glory' in his doxology, including the 'mirror', which already appears in the early writers, for example, in Ephrem and Gregory of Nyssa. It is through the mirror of Christ's Gospel that we come face to face with ourselves, with our own truth. Symeon, moreover, mentions what has been central to Eastern theology up to this day, namely the biblically inspired idea of divinization. This idea is centrally connected with the transfiguration of Christ. According to the Orthodox, this event was not only one whereby the disciples came to see Christ in glory but it anticipates our own future transfiguration or divinization. These themes of transfiguration, of Christ being the image of God, and of his beauty are reflected upon at length by Aquinas in his *Father, Son, and Holy Ghost (Summa Theologiae)* and by Gregory Palamas three centuries later. Bonaventure likewise passionately praised Christ for his 'extraordinary beauty'.

Relevant in relation to the beauty of Christ are also the mystical theologians and friends Bernard of Clairvaux and William of St Thierry. Both wrote commentaries on the Song of Songs, which they interpreted in the highly spiritualized allegorical mode of the Middle Ages as the relationship of the bridegroom Christ with his bride, the Church. Bernard writes: 'The Bridegroom's beauty is his love for the bride, all the greater in that it existed before hers.' Once again, love (goodness) and beauty go hand in hand, whereby the love of the beautiful Redeemer is eternal. Francis, in his poetic and wonderful yet more earthy imagery from the realm of nature, would also give praise to Christ.

One interesting metaphor for Christ, namely that of Mother, is applied by the mystic Julian of Norwich in her as one might put it strikingly 'gender-balanced' trinitarian theology: 'I saw and understood that the high might of the Trinity is our Father, and the deep wisdom of the Trinity is our Mother, and the great love of the Trinity is our Lord.' Christ is 'our Mother, brother and saviour'. This idea of God as Mother is already present in Beguine writings and in the German mystics Mechthild of Hackeborn and Gertrud of Helfta.

Poetry, rich imagery and metaphor abound in medieval times in theological language culminating in doxologies, especially in the contemplative, mystical and often highly imaginative writings of Symeon the New Theologian, Hildegard of Bingen, Bernard of Clairvaux, William of St Thierry and Julian of Norwich. But also Eriugena, with his more discursive style, speaks, like Augustine before him, of the universe as a marvellous harmony, which he likens to the 'art of music' which is made up of a 'variety of sounds . . . attuned to each other'. And again, in Anselm, as in Augustine, we find the analogy of God as the supreme artist and of the human artist who is always limited and confined. Nicholas of Cusa, likewise, marvels at the 'Artisan' who created the individual parts of the universe into a great harmony.

An analysis of the necessity of praising God is evident in both Aquinas and Nicholas of Cusa. Praise must come from the heart and is important, insists Thomas, and he goes into great detail concerning the proper conduct involved in singing hymns. His is a markedly spiritualized, ascetic, even 'puritan' approach. Singing, which merely gives pleasure, is to be avoided and so are musical instruments because they may arouse carnal delights. The purpose of singing must be spiritual devotion and he remarks that 'arousing men to devotion through preaching and teaching is a more excellent way than through singing'. Obviously the spoken word in discourse or preaching he considers more valuable than a form of art, i.e. music, in instilling faith. It is almost ironic to note that Thomas undermines precisely the revelatory power of the art of music, which through the ages has made people concretely feel *and know* the existence and presence of the beauty of the divine.

The rich variety of imagery in the medievals leads to the intrinsically related issue of the imagination in the human being and its place in, and implications for, theology. While descriptions of the imagination vary slightly, it is clear that the attitude to the imagination among these theologians was in general negative, fuelled by suspicion. In appropriating the tradition of Greek philosophy and biblical writing, medieval theologians with their onto-theological outlook mostly viewed the imagination as mimetic. Images were regarded as imitations, copies, representations, but not considered original in their own right. This idea of originality, especially in works of art, would only emerge with the Enlightenment and its turn to the human subject.

John of Damascus, who so forcefully defended icons, equates the imagination with fantasy; it is a faculty which belongs to the 'irrational part of the soul'. Richard of St Victor argues in a similar vein. He considers the imagination as an intermediary, a 'vestment' of the soul, communicating between the inner reason and the outer body. Reason needs the imagination and at the same time must transcend it because what really matters is the search for truth. This search for truth, for the highest being, God, and the 'proofs' of God's existence are to be undertaken as much as possible through reason and argument (cf. Kearney, 1994, pp. 122–3). For Bonaventure, too, the imagination has only an ancillary function on the ascent to God. The 'mirror' is the metaphor he employs; in our human imagining we, as *simulacra* of the divine, mirror God's primary imaging of creation. As Christians our task is to mirror the divine artist as faithfully as possible. Aquinas, like his fellow thinkers, equates imagination with fantasy. He affirms the mediating function of the imagination between mind and body and perceives it as 'a treasure-store of forms received through the senses' (*ST* I, 78, 4).

Despite the ambiguous, even suspicious, attitudes to the place, meaning and value of images and of the imagination, it is nevertheless remarkable that after more than a century of iconoclast controversies in the East (*c.*725–842), the icon-advocates under Empress Irene won their cause. Relevant extracts in this Reader include the great iconodule theologians John of Damascus and Theodore of Studios, as well as extracts from the Second Council of Nicaea (787) and the Fourth General Council of Constantinople (869–70). These are revelatory of the central issues and disputes, especially regarding the incarnation, that were to become the very basis for allowing images into places of worship. The latter Council states that the image of Christ 'must be venerated with the same honour as is given to the book of the holy Gospels'. At last, word and image were elevated to the same honoured rank.

Finally, all of the above touches in one way or another on one of the most fundamental concerns in terms of theological aesthetics, the search for the vision of God. This search, this hope for a glimpse of God in the here and now and for the beatific vision in the eschatological banquet, has continued through the ages. The medieval thinkers adopted this longing to see the divine into their theology directly or indirectly whenever their discussions and contemplative reflections, their poetry and hymns were concerned with beauty, with revelation, with the image of God in both Christ and humans, with the imagination and the defence of images, etc. In the writers present here this is particularly evident in Symeon the New Theologian, Anselm, Bonaventure, Meister Eckhart, Thomas, Hildegard, and Nicholas of Cusa, who was much influenced by Pseudo-Dionysius. It is also apparent in other thinkers and mystics, such as Mechthild of Magdeburg or Hadewijch. As was the case with their early Christian predecessors, the medieval writers contemplated God's light and glory. Anselm expresses an intense yearning to see the overwhelmingly bright light of God. Hugh of St Victor elaborates in detail the difference between seeing and believing. Nicholas of Cusa points out that 'seeing is tasting, seeking, having mercy, and working' and that the beauty of creation makes us glimpse the beauty of God. At the same time we find acknowledged in various writers the ultimate impossibility of seeing or knowing anything about God in this world, i.e. the apophatic dimension. As Meister Eckhart notes, to see the 'true light' of God 'one must be blind and must strip from God all that is "something". A master says whoever speaks of God in any likeness, speaks impurely of Him.' Thus, the final and total vision of God remains to be seen in the world to come, in the ultimate future, the light of the eschaton.

5

The Defence of Images

‒ ‒

5.1 From the *Second Council of Nicaea (787)*

In the eighth century emphatic iconoclastic outbursts occurred in the East. The outbursts began when in 730 Emperor Leo III ordered the destruction of icons which had been central to Byzantine worship. However, half a century later, at the Second Council of Nicaea, the iconodule theological position on the veneration of images, based on the incarnation of God in Christ, was officially affirmed.

To summarize, we declare that we defend free from any innovations all the written and unwritten ecclesiastical traditions that have been entrusted to us. One of these is the production of representational art; this is quite in harmony with the history of the spread of the gospel, as it provides confirmation that the becoming man of the Word of God was real and not just imaginary, and as it brings us a similar benefit. For, things that mutually illustrate one another undoubtedly possess one another's message. Given this state of affairs and stepping out as though on the royal highway, following as we are the God-spoken teaching of our holy fathers and the tradition of the catholic church – for we recognize that this tradition comes from the holy Spirit who dwells in her – we decree with full precision and care that, like the figure of the honoured and life-giving cross, the revered and holy images, whether painted or made of mosaic or of other suitable material, are to be exposed in the holy churches of God, on sacred instruments and vestments, on walls and panels, in houses and by public ways; these are the images of our Lord, God and saviour, Jesus Christ, and of our Lady without blemish, the holy God-bearer, and of the revered angels and of any of the saintly holy men. The more frequently they are seen in representational art, the more are those who see them drawn to remember and long for those who serve as models, and to pay these images the tribute of salutation and respectful veneration. Certainly this is not the full adoration in accordance with our faith, which is properly paid only to the divine nature, but it resembles that given to the figure of the honoured and life-giving cross, and also to the holy books of the gospels and to other sacred cult objects. Further, people are drawn to honour these images with the offering of incense and lights, as was piously established by ancient custom. Indeed, the honour paid to an image traverses it, reaching the model; and he who venerates the image, venerates the person represented in that image. So it is that the teaching of our holy fathers is strengthened, namely, the tradition of the catholic church which has received the gospel from one end of the earth to the other. So it is that we really follow Paul, who spoke in Christ, and the entire divine apostolic group and the holiness of the fathers, clinging fast to the traditions which we have received. . . . Therefore all those who dare to think or teach anything different, or who follow the accursed heretics in rejecting ecclesiastical traditions, or who devise innovations, or who spurn anything entrusted to the church (whether it be the gospel or the figure of the cross or any example of representational art or any martyr's holy relic), or who fabricate perverted and evil prejudices against cherishing any of the lawful traditions of the catholic church, or who secularize the sacred objects and saintly monasteries, we order that they be suspended if they are bishops or clerics, and excommunicated if they are monks or lay people.

Anathemas concerning holy images. 1. If anyone does not confess that Christ our God can be represented in his humanity, let him be anathema. 2. If anyone does not accept representation in art of evangelical scenes, let him be anathema. 3. If anyone does not salute such representations as standing for the Lord and his saints, let him be anathema. (pp. 135–7)

Source: Norman P. Tanner, SJ, *Decrees of the Ecumenical Councils, vol. 1*, London, Sheed & Ward, Georgetown University Press, 1990.

5.2 From the *Fourth General Council of Constantinople (869–70)*

Despite the solemn declaration on the veneration of images at the Second Council of Nicaea (787), iconoclastic outbursts revived two decades later. Three iconoclastic emperors from Asia ordered persecutions of iconodule monks and patriarchs. Finally, however, persecutions were brought to an end. At the Fourth General Council of Constantinople, the crisis was settled. The veneration of the image and of the written word were placed on the same level, and images were cherished as an expression of language accessible to the illiterate.

On the veneration of sacred images [1253] *Canon* 3: We decree that the sacred image of our Lord Jesus Christ, the liberator and Saviour of all people, must be venerated with the same honour as is given to the book of the holy Gospels. For, as through the language of the words contained in this book all can reach salvation, so, due to the action which these images exercise by their colours, all, wise and simple alike, can derive profit from them. For, what speech conveys in words, pictures announce and bring out in colours. It is fitting, in accordance with sane reason and with the most ancient tradition, since the honour is referred to the principal subject, that the images derived from it be honoured and venerated, as is done for the sacred book of the holy Gospels and for the image of the precious cross. (p. 360)

Source: J. Neuner, SJ, and J. Dupuis, SJ (eds), *The Christian Faith in the Doctrinal Documents of the Catholic Church*, 7th enlarged edition, New York, Alba House, Society of St Paul, 2001.

5.3 John of Damascus, from *Orthodox Faith*

John of Damascus (c.675–c.749), priest and theologian, is remembered especially for his defence of icons in the Byzantine iconoclastic controversies of the eighth and ninth centuries. In this passage he presents a view of the imagination, which seems rather limited, even negative, as he locates it in the realm of the irrational. Yet he puts forward a detailed explanation of sense, sensible things, and the function of the five senses.

The *imagination* is the faculty belonging to the irrational part of the soul. It acts through the sense organs and is called a sensation. Moreover, that which comes within the province of the imagination and the senses is the imaginative and the sensible, just as the visible – say, a stone or something of the sort – comes within the province of sight, which is the power of vision. An *imagination*, or fantasy, is an affection of the irrational part of the soul arising from some imaginable object. But an *imagining*, or phantasm, is an empty affection arising in the irrational parts of the soul from no imaginable object at all. The organ of the imagination is the anterior ventricle of the brain.

Sense is a faculty of the soul by which material things are perceived, or distinguished. The sense organs are the organs or members by means of which we perceive. *Sensible* things are those which come within the province of the senses. The animal endowed with sense is *sensitive*. There are five senses and, likewise, five sense organs. The first sense is that of *sight*. The sense organs or media of sight are the nerves leading from the brain and the eyes. Fundamentally, it is the visual impression of colour that is received, but along with the colour the sight distinguishes the coloured body, also its size and shape, the place where it is and the intervening distance, its number, its motion or motionlessness, its roughness or smoothness, its evenness or unevenness, sharpness or bluntness, and whether it has the consistency of water or that of earth; in other words, whether it is liquid or solid. The second sense is that of *hearing*. This is capable of discerning

voices and sounds, of which it distinguishes the high or low pitch, the degree of smoothness, and the volume. Its organs are the soft nerves leading from the brain and the apparatus of the ears. Moreover, only man and the monkey do not move their ears. The third sense is that of *smell* which originates with the nose sending the odours up to the brain and is terminated at the extremities of the anterior ventricles of the brain. The sense of smell is capable of discerning and perceiving odours. The most general division of odours is into sweet-smelling and foul-smelling and that which stands midway between these and is neither the one nor the other. Thus, a sweet smell arises when the juices in bodies have been cooked to a nicety. When they have been cooked middling well, the result is middling. But when they have been very poorly or incompletely cooked, then there is a foul smell. The fourth sense is that of *taste*. This sense is capable of perceiving or discerning flavours. Its organs are the tongue – especially its tip – and the palate, which some call the roof [of the mouth]. The nerves leading from the brain have been broadened out in these and report back to the authoritative part of the soul the impression or sensation received. The so-called taste qualities or flavours are as follows: sweetness, bitterness, acidity, sourness, tartness, pungency, saltiness, greasiness, and stickiness. For it is these that the sense of taste can distinguish. Water, however, in so far as these qualities are concerned, is tasteless, because it has none of them. Sourness is an intense and excessive tartness. The fifth sense is that of *touch*, which is common to all animals. It comes from the nerves leading out from the brain into the entire body, for which reason both the entire body and the other sense organs, too, possess the sense of touch. Subject to touch are heat and cold, softness and hardness, stickiness and friability, and heaviness and lightness, because these things are recognized only by the sense of touch. Common to both the sense of touch and that of sight are: roughness and smoothness; dryness and wetness; thickness and thinness; up and down; place; size, whenever it is such as can be determined with one application of the sense of touch; compactness and looseness, or density; roundness, if on a small scale, and various other shapes. Similarly, with the aid of the memory and the understanding, it can also perceive the approach of a body, as well as number, too, up to two or three, provided the objects be small and easily grasped. Sight, however, is more perceptive of these than is touch. One should note that the Creator constructed each one of the sense organs in pairs, so that, should one be harmed, the other might fulfill the function. Thus, there are two eyes, two ears, two nostrils, and two tongues. These last, however, while they are separate in some animals, such as snakes, in others, such as man, are joined together. On the other hand, the sense of touch is in the entire body, with the exception of the bones, nerves, nails and horns, hair, sinews, and certain other parts of the same sort. One should note that sight sees along straight lines, but that smell and hearing get their impressions not only along straight lines, but from all directions. Touch and taste, however, get their impressions neither along straight lines nor along any line, but only when their proper organs are in contact with their objects.
(Book 2, Chs 17–18, pp. 241–4)

Since there are certain people who find great fault with us for adoring and honouring both the image of the Saviour and that of our Lady, as well as those of the rest of the saints and servants of Christ, let them hear how from the beginning God made man to His own image. For what reason, then, do we adore one another, except because we have been made to the image of God? As the inspired Basil, who is deeply learned in theology, says: 'the honour paid to the image redounds to the original', and the original is the thing imaged from which the copy is made. For what reason did the people of Moses adore from round about the tabernacle which bore an image and pattern of heavenly things, or rather, of all creation? Indeed, God had said to Moses: 'See that thou make all things according to the pattern which was shewn thee on the mount.' And the Cherubim, too, that overshadowed the propitiatory, were they not the handiwork of men? And what was the celebrated temple in Jerusalem? Was it not built and furnished by human hands and skill? Now, sacred Scripture condemns those who adore graven things, and also those who sacrifice to the demons. The Greeks used to sacrifice and the Jews also used to sacrifice; but the Greeks sacrifice to the demons, whereas the Jews sacrificed to God. And the sacrifice of the Greeks was rejected and condemned, while the sacrifice of the just was acceptable to God. Thus, Noe sacrificed 'and the Lord smelled a sweet savour' of the good intention and accepted the fragrance of the gift offered to Him. And thus the statues of the Greeks happen to be rejected and condemned, because they were representations of demons. But, furthermore, who can make a copy of the invisible, incorporeal, uncircumscribed, and unportrayable God? It is, then, highly insane and impious to give a form to the Godhead. For this reason it was not the practice in the Old Testament to use images. However, through the bowels of His mercy God for our salvation was made man in truth, not in the appearance of man, as He was seen by Abraham or the Prophets, but really made man in substance. Then He abode on earth, conversed with men, worked miracles, suffered, was crucified, rose again, and was taken up; and all these things really happened and were seen by men and, indeed, written down to remind and instruct us, who were not present then, so that, although we have not seen, yet hearing and believing we may attain to the blessedness of the Lord. Since, however, not all know letters nor do all have leisure to read, the Fathers deemed it fit that these events should be depicted as a sort of memorial and terse reminder. It certainly happens frequently that at times when we do not have the Lord's Passion in mind we may see the image of His crucifixion and, being thus reminded of His saving Passion, fall down and adore. But it is not the material which we adore, but that which is represented; just as we do not adore the material of the Gospel or that of the cross, but that which they typify. (Book 4, Ch. 16, pp. 370–2)

Source: *The Fathers of the Church, Saint John of Damascus, Writings*, trans. Frederic H. Chase, Jr, Washington, The Catholic University of America Press, 1958.

5.4 Theodore of Studios, from *On the Holy Icons*

Like John of Damascus, the monastic reformer Theodore of Studios (759–
826) was a theologian in the East who defended the use of images. Images of
the divine should be allowed on the basis of the incarnation. He emphasizes
that it is not the material thing but the prototype that is venerated.

First Refutation of the Iconoclasts

The heretics say, 'Surely there is not just one veneration, if our piety is shown to
have many objects of veneration by the erection of icons, a practice which by
some wile of the devil has been transferred from pagan tradition, bringing the
veneration of idols into the catholic church. For every theologian agrees that the
Godhead is entirely incomprehensible and uncircumscribable.' It is obvious to
everyone that the Godhead is incomprehensible and uncircumscribable, and I
may add boundless, limitless, formless, and whatever adjectives signify the
privation of what the Godhead is not. But 'What fellowship does light have with
darkness?' here also it is appropriate to say, or 'What agreement does Christ
have with Belial?' What do the holy icons have in common with the idols
of pagan gods? If we were worshipping idols, we would have to worship and
venerate the causes before the effects, namely Astarte and Chamos the abomination of the Sidonians, as it is written, and Apollo, Zeus, Kronos, and all the other
diverse gods of the pagans, who because they were led astray by the devil transferred their worship unwittingly from God the maker to the products of His
workmanship, and, as it is said, 'worshipped the creation instead of the Creator',
slipping into a single abyss of polytheism.

We, however, have only one God whom we venerate as Trinity. And in regard
to the doctrine of theology, so far from inventing some kind of circumscription
or comprehension (perish the idea! for this was an invention of pagan thought),
we do not even know that the Godhead exists at all, or what sort of thing it is, as
it alone understands about itself. But because of His great goodness one of the
Trinity has entered human nature and become like us. There is a mixture of the
immiscible, a compound of the uncombinable: that is, of the uncircumscribable
with the circumscribed, of the boundless with the bounded, of the limitless with
the limited, of the formless with the well-formed (which is indeed paradoxical).
For this reason Christ is depicted in images, and the invisible is seen. He who in
His own divinity is uncircumscribable accepts the circumscription natural to His
body. Both natures are revealed by the facts for what they are: otherwise one or
the other nature would falsify what it is, as your opinions imply.

'But,' the heretics say, 'the Godhead does not remain uncircumscribed when
Christ is circumscribed bodily. If the divinity is united to the flesh by a hypostatic
union, the uncircumscribable divinity must be co-circumscribed in the circumscription of the flesh. Neither can be separated from the other, or else some
abominable kind of division would be introduced.' According to the word-play

which you call an argument, neither could the Godhead remain incomprehensible in being comprehended – but it was wrapped in swaddling clothes! Nor could it remain invisible in being seen – but it was seen! Nor could it remain intangible in being touched – but it was touched! Nor could it remain impassible in suffering – but it was crucified! Nor could it remain immortal in dying – but it was put to death! In the same way you should understand that the Godhead has also remained uncircumscribable in being circumscribed. For these are properties just as those others are; but the properties of the uncircumscribable nature are those in which Christ is recognized to be God, while the properties of the circumscribed nature are those in which He is confessed to be man. Neither one makes the other into something new, nor departs from what it was itself; nor is one changed into the other (for such a change would produce the confusion which we have refused to admit); but He is one and the same in His hypostasis, with His two natures unconfused in their proper spheres. Therefore you must either accept the 'circumscribed', or if not, then take away the 'visible' and 'tangible' and 'graspable' and whatever adjectives are in the same category. Then it would become obvious that you utterly deny that the Word became flesh – which is the height of impiety. (pp. 20–2)

Third Refutation of the Iconoclasts

If Christ is uncircumscribable, as you say, not only in respect to His divinity, but also in respect to His humanity, then His humanity is also divinity. For things which have the same properties also have one nature. But if He is of two natures, He is therefore also of two properties: otherwise, by the removal of circumscription, the nature of humanity would also be removed.

If every image is an image of form, shape, or appearance and of colour, and if Christ has all these, since the Scriptures say, 'He took the form of a servant . . . and was found in human shape,' and had an 'ignoble and inferior' appearance, which signifies the body: then He is portrayed in just such a circumscription in His likeness. (p. 81)

Every image has a relation to its archetype; the natural image has a natural relation, while the artificial image has an artificial relation. The natural image is identical both in essence and in likeness with that of which it bears the imprint: thus Christ is identical with His Father in respect to divinity, but identical with His mother in respect to humanity. The artificial image is the same as its archetype in likeness, but different in essence, like Christ and His icon. Therefore there is an artificial image of Christ, to whom the image has its relation. . . .

The fact that man is made in the image and likeness of God shows that the work of iconography is a divine action. But since an image can be copied from an image, inasmuch as Christ is man, though also God, He can be portrayed in an image, not in spirit but in body. But if He is portrayed in one of the two, then obviously He has an image exactly resembling Him which reveals the shared likeness.

If Adam the first man is circumscribed by His form, then also Christ the second Adam, as He is both God and man, can equally be portrayed in His bodily form. If, moreover, 'As was the man of dust, so are those who are of the dust; and as is the man of heaven, so are those who are of heaven,' and if we who are of heaven can be portrayed, then Christ, as He is the originator of the salvation of all, is also the original of His own image. . . .

An objection as from the iconoclasts: 'If everything which is made in the likeness of something else inevitably falls short of equality with its prototype, then obviously Christ is not the same as His portrait in regard to veneration. And if these differ, the veneration which you introduce differs also. Therefore it produces an idolatrous worship.'

Answer: The prototype is not essentially in the image. If it were, the image would be called prototype, as conversely the prototype would be called image. This is not admissable, because the nature of each has its own definition. Rather, the prototype is in the image by the similarity of hypostasis, which does not have a different principle of definition for the prototype and for the image. Therefore we do not understand that the image lacks equality with the prototype and has an inferior glory in respect to similarity, but in respect to its different essence. The essence of the image is not of a nature to be venerated, although the one who is portrayed appears in it for veneration. Therefore there is no introduction of a different kind of veneration, but the image has one and the same veneration with the prototype, in accordance with the identity of likeness.

It is not the essence of the image which we venerate, but the form of the prototype which is stamped upon it, since the essence of the image is not venerable. Neither is it the material which is venerated, but the prototype is venerated together with the form and not the essence of the image. But if the image is venerated, it has one veneration with the prototype, just as they have the same likeness. Therefore, when we venerate the image, we do not introduce another kind of veneration different from the veneration of the prototype. (pp. 100–3)

Source: *St Theodore the Studite, On Holy Icons*, trans. Catherine P. Roth, Crestwood, NY, St Vladimir's Seminary Press, 1981.

6

Seeing God; Beauty and Goodness

— —

6.1 John Scotus Eriugena, from *Periphyseon*

Eriugena (c.810–c.877) was Irish, a Neo-Platonist, and one of the foremost philosopher-theologians in the Middle Ages. He was involved in controversies on predestination and the Eucharist. In this passage he points out that the beauty of all creation is established by the divine will who brings contrasts and opposites into harmony and unity, quite like in a symphony of music.

Furthermore, the beauty of the whole established universe consists of a marvellous harmony of like and unlike in which the diverse genera and various species and the different orders of substances and accidents are composed into an ineffable unity. For as instrumental melody is made up of a variety of qualities and quantities of sounds which when they are heard individually and separately are distinguished from one another by widely differing proportions of tension or relaxation, but when they are attuned to each other in accordance with the fixed and rational rules of the art of music give forth through each piece of music a natural sweetness, so the harmony of the universe is established in accordance with the uniform will of its Creator out of the diverse subdivisions of its one nature which when regarded individually clash with one another. (Book III, pp. 255–6)

Thus it seems to me that He who created and ordained the universal creation allowed the perverse impulses of the human and angelic will to be punished within their nature (although the nature itself ever remains unimpaired and totally free from the conflict of the passions) for this reason: that 'by comparison with the perverse will of the wicked,' as St Augustine says, 'the rational will of the righteous might be raised to the greater glory. For,' says he, 'the artist introduces black into the colours of his picture so that by comparison with its obscurity, the other colours may shine forth more brightly.' For that which in some part of nature appears to be deformed in itself, considered in nature as a whole is not only beautiful and beautifully ordered, but is the efficient cause of the beauty of the whole: Wisdom is manifested by comparison with foolishness, and knowledge by comparison with ignorance, which is the absence and deprivation of it; life is revealed by comparison with death which is the absence of life, and light is glorified by contrast with darkness which is the deprivation of light: and, in a word, not only is it by contrast with their opposing vices that all virtues are glorified, but without that comparison they would be without glory. . . . For whatsoever is ordained by the dispositions of the Divine Providence is good and beautiful and just. For what is more desirable than that the immeasurable glory both of the Universe and its Creator should be manifested by the contrast of opposites? What is more just than that those who have deserved well should occupy the highest place in nature, and those who have deserved will occupy the lowest? What is more honourable than that the Universe of all things should be adorned by the properties of the individuals it contains? Therefore no true philosopher believes that there can be any wickedness or wicked man, any impiety or impious man, any misery or miserable man, any punishment or punished man, any torment or anyone liable to torment, any baseness or base man, any dishonour or dishonourable man, in the noble harmony of the whole Universe than which nothing is more excellent, nothing more holy, nothing more blessed and free from punishment, nothing more beautiful, nothing happier and nothing more honourable: for it is created and ordained by Him who is the highest honour, the highest beauty, the highest happiness, the highest peace, the highest bliss, the highest holiness, the highest good. For what we contemplate in the parts of the Universe appears differently when we consider it in relation to the whole. Thus, what in the part seems discordant, in the whole is found to be not only not discordant, but an addition to its beauty. Hell, which the Greeks call 'hades' that is, sorrow, or the deprivation of joy is known by the evil to be evil when it is considered by itself: but when it is considered as forming a part of the perfect beauty of the Universe it is made for the good a good, for not only does it show forth the severity of the most just of all judges and the irrevocability of His judgments but it also adds to the glory and embellishes the beauty of the blessed state of the angels and the Saints. (Book 5, pp. 633–4)

Source: *John Scotus Eriugena, Periphyseon*, trans. I. P. Sheldon-Williams, Revd John O'Meara, Montreal, Washington, Bellarmin, 1987.

6.2 Anselm of Canterbury, from *Proslogium*

Anselm (c.1033–1109), Archbishop of Canterbury, was one of the foremost thinkers of the early Scholastic period who desired to defend the Christian faith through intellectual reasoning rather than through biblically based arguments. However, in this rather personal passage, Anselm expresses his deep longing to see and feel God. He knows that God, whose attributes are of sensuous beauty, is always present to him, yet always remains hidden from his vision.

This is the unapproachable light wherein he dwells

TRULY, O Lord, this is the unapproachable light in which thou dwellest for truly there is nothing else which can penetrate this light, that it may see thee there. Truly, I see it not, because it is too bright for me. And yet, whatsoever I see, I see through it, as the weak eye sees what it sees through the light of the sun, which in the sun itself it cannot look upon. My understanding cannot reach that light, for it shines too bright. It does not comprehend it, nor does the eye of my soul endure to gaze upon it long. It is dazzled by the brightness, it is overcome by the greatness, it is overwhelmed by the infinity, it is dazed by the largeness, of the light. O supreme and unapproachable light! O whole and blessed truth, how far art thou from me, who am so near to thee! How far removed art thou from my vision, though I am so near to thine! Everywhere thou art wholly present, and I see thee not. In thee I move, and in thee I have my being; and I cannot come to thee. Thou art within me, and about me, and I feel thee not. (Ch. 16, pp. 22–3)

In God is harmony, fragrance, sweetness, pleasantness to the touch, beauty, after his ineffable manner

STILL thou art hidden, O Lord, from my soul in thy light and thy blessedness; and therefore my soul still walks in its darkness and wretchedness. For it looks, and does not see thy beauty. It hearkens, and does not hear thy harmony. It smells, and does not perceive thy fragrance. It tastes, and does not recognise thy sweetness. It touches, and does not feel thy pleasantness. For thou hast these attributes in thyself, Lord God, after thine ineffable manner, who hast given them to objects created by thee, after their sensible manner; but the sinful senses of my soul have grown rigid and dull, and have been obstructed by their long list-lessness. (Ch. 17, p. 23)

Source: *St Anselm, Basic Writings, Proslogium, Monologium, Cur Deus Homo, Gaunilo's In Behalf of the Fool*, trans. Sidney Norton Deane, Chicago, The Open Court Publishing Company, 1903.

6.3 Hugh of St Victor, from *On the Sacraments of the Christian Faith*

Hugh of St Victor (d. 1142), mystical theologian and philosopher, points out how the human being through the soul, which is the 'better part' of the human, is made in the image and likeness of the divine. Further he examines how seeing and believing differ. In seeing we witness the things that we have seen ourselves, in believing we trust in, and rely on, the testimony of others.

How man was made to the image and likeness of God

Man was made to the image and likeness of God, because in the soul, which is the better part of man, or rather was man himself, was the image and likeness of God: image according to reason, likeness according to love; image according to understanding of truth, likeness according to love of virtue; or image according to knowledge, likeness according to substance; image, because all things in it are according to wisdom; likeness, because it is itself one and simple according to essence; image because rational, likeness because spiritual; image pertains to figure, likeness to nature. Now these things were made in the soul alone, because corporeal nature could not have received likeness of the Godhead, which was far from its excellence and likeness in this very fact, that it was corporeal. (Book 1, Part 6, para. 2, p. 95)

What is the difference between seeing and believing

We say that there is this difference between seeing and believing, that things present are seen, things absent are believed. Indeed it is perhaps enough if by those things present we understand in this place the words which are at hand for the senses either of soul or of body. Therefore too, when words are uttered they are called present. For just as I clearly see this light by a sense of the body, so too I see my will because it is at hand to the senses of my spirit and is present within me. If anyone indeed indicates his will to me, whose face and voice are present to me, yet since the will which he indicates to me escapes the sense of the body and of my spirit, I believe, I do not see. Or if I think that he lies, I do not believe, even if by chance it might be as he says. Therefore, those things which are absent from our senses are believed, if what is offered as proof for them seems sufficient. And not because I have said that those things are believed which are absent from our senses could they so be accepted as to be placed among those things which we have seen and are certain of, because they are not present then when they are recalled by us. For they are not classed among the things believed but among those seen and so they are known, not because we had faith in other witnesses but because we recall without doubt and know that we have seen them. Therefore, our knowledge is established from things seen and believed, but in those things which we see or have seen we ourselves are the witnesses. But in those things which we believe, we are moved to faith by other witnesses, when of those things which we neither recall having seen nor see, signs are given either in words or in letters or in any documents whatever, on seeing which the unseen things are believed. Now not unfittingly do we say that we know not only those things which we have seen and see but also those which we believe by proper testimonies and witnesses. . . . The Scriptures have to do with impressions on the body: on the eyes, if one reads them; or on the ears, if one has heard them. This, therefore, I do not show in such a way that it be held seen or perceived by a sense of the body or the soul, and yet I do say something which must indeed be either true or false but is seen by neither of these two; it remains only that it either be believed or not believed. But if it is confirmed by the clear authority of these Scriptures, specifically which in the Church are called canonical, it must be believed without any doubt. Indeed in other witnesses or testimonies in which we are persuaded to have some credence, you may either believe or not believe according as you consider that I either do or do not possess what causes trust in him who advises of these things. . . .

You have learned sufficiently, in my opinion, from this preamble of mine what it is to see either by mind or by body and how believing differs from this, which indeed is done by the mind and is seen by the mind, since our faith is clear to our mind. But yet what is believed by the same faith is absent both from the sight of our body, as the body is absent in which Christ arose, and from the sight of another's mind, as is your faith from the sight of our mind; although I believe that it is in you, when I do not see with the body what you cannot nor with the mind what you can, just as I can see my faith which you cannot. (Book 2, Part 18, para. 17, pp. 472–3)

Source: *Hugh of Saint Victor, On the Sacraments of the Christian Faith (De Sacramentis)*, trans. Roy J. Deferrari, Cambridge, MA, The Medieval Academy of America, 1951.

6.4 Richard of St Victor, from *The Mystical Ark*

Richard of St Victor (d. 1172) was a Scholastic theologian and mystic. He contributed especially to the development of trinitarian thought. His stress on argument and demonstration in theology is evidenced in this passage, in which he distinguishes and analyses six modes of contemplation. Thereby he relates that the imagination and reason focus on the perception of created things, while the fifth and sixth contemplation – above and even contradictory to reason – perceive the transcendent divine things.

How many and what the kinds of contemplation are

There are six kinds of contemplations in themselves, and within each there are many divisions. The first is in imagination and according to imagination only.

The second is in imagination and according to reason. The third is in reason and according to imagination. The fourth is in reason and according to reason. The fifth is above but not beyond reason. The sixth is above reason and seems to be beyond reason. And so, there are two in imagination, two in reason and two in understanding. Without doubt, our contemplation is engaged in imagination when the form and image of those visible things are brought into consideration and we, being amazed, give attention, and in giving attention are amazed how many, how great, how diverse, how beautiful and joyful are these corporeal things that we imbibe by means of corporeal sense. Marvelling we venerate and venerating we marvel at the power, wisdom and generosity of that superessential creatrix. However our contemplation is engaged in imagination and is formed according to imagination only when we seek nothing by means of argumentation and investigate nothing by means of reasoning, but rather our mind runs freely here and there, wherever wonder carries it away in this kind of manifestation. The second kind of contemplation is that which is in imagination, but yet is formed by and proceeds according to reason, since it comes about when we seek and find a rational principle for those things which we engage in imagination and which belong, as we have already said, to the first kind of contemplation. Indeed, with wonder we bring discovery and knowledge into consideration. In the first kind of contemplation we look at, examine and marvel at things themselves; in the second kind we do the same with the reason, order and disposition of these things, and the cause, mode and benefit of any one thing. And so this contemplation is in imagination but according to reason, because it proceeds by means of reasoning about those things which are engaged in the imagination. And although this contemplation in which the rational principle of visible things is sought seems to be in reason according to something, nevertheless it is rightly said to be in the imagination because whatever we seek or find in it by means of reasoning, we undoubtedly accommodate to those things which we engage in imagination when we apply ourselves to those things by reasoning about them. We have said that the third kind of contemplation is that which is formed in reason according to imagination. We truly use this kind of contemplation when by means of the similitude of visible things we are raised up to speculation of invisible things. This speculation is in reason, because it applies only to those things which go beyond imagination by means of attention and investigation, since it directs attention toward invisible things only, toward those only which it grasps by reason. But it is said to be formed according to imagination because in this speculation a similitude is drawn from an image of visible things, and the soul is assisted by this similitude in the investigation of invisible things. And indeed, although it is advanced by reasoning, this contemplation is rightly said to be in reason but according to imagination, because all its reasoning and argumentation begin with a foundation and acquire support in imagination, and it draws the reason for its investigation and assertion from the particular nature of things that are imaginable. The fourth kind of contemplation is that which is formed in reason and according to reason: because it is when, far removed from every function of imagination, the rational soul directs its attention toward only those things which the imagination does not know but which the mind gathers from reasoning or understands by means of reason. We apply ourselves to speculation of this kind when we bring into consideration the invisible things of ourselves which we know through experience and acquire from understanding; and we rise up from consideration of these things to contemplation of celestial souls and highest goods. However, this contemplation is in reason because it gives its attention only to things of the understanding that are far removed from things of sense. And indeed, this contemplation seems to take a beginning and to acquire a foundation especially from those invisible things of ourselves which it is agreed that the human soul knows by experience and understands by means of common understanding. But in this case alone, this contemplation is also rightly said to be in reason, because these invisible things of ourselves are understood by reason, and in this, the mode of reasoning is not surpassed in the least. This contemplation, therefore, advances according to reason alone because it gathers some things from invisible things that are known by experience, and other things that it does not know from experience it gathers by reasoning. In this contemplation the human soul makes use for the first time of pure understanding, and since it is far removed from every function of imagination, our understanding itself seems in this activity to understand itself by means of itself for the first time. Although the understanding seems not to be absent in those previous kinds of contemplation, yet it is almost nowhere present, except where reason or even imagination meditates. In the previous kinds of contemplation reason uses, as it were, an instrument and gazes, for example, into a mirror. In the present kind of contemplation it operates by means of itself and gazes, as it were, by means of sight. Accordingly, here it inclines itself to the lowest part, as it were, since it does not have anything by which it might descend lower by itself. We have said that the fifth kind of contemplation is that which is above reason yet not beyond reason. However, we rise up into this watchtower of contemplation by the raising up of the mind, when by means of a divine showing we know things that we are not capable of sufficiently grasping fully by any human reason or investigating fully by any of our reasoning. Such things are those which we believe and prove by the authority of divine Scripture concerning the nature of Divinity and that simple essence. Thus our contemplation truly rises above reason when, by means of the raising up of the mind, the rational soul perceives that which transcends the limits of human capacity. It ought to be held to be above reason yet not beyond reason, when human reason is not able to oppose that which is perceived by the fine point of the understanding, but rather, it more easily gives assent and alludes to the attestation of such. The sixth kind of contemplation is that which is engaged with those things which are above reason and seem to be beyond or even against reason. In this highest and most worthy watchtower of all contemplations, the rational soul especially rejoices and dances when from the irradiation of divine light it learns and considers those things against which all human reason cries out. Such things are almost all the things that we are told to believe concerning the Trinity of persons. When human reason is consulted concerning these, it seems to do nothing other than to oppose them. (Ch. 6, pp. 161–4)

What things are common to them

And so two of these are in the imagination, because they direct attention toward sensible things only. Two are in reason, because they apply themselves to intelligible things only. Two subsist in understanding, because they direct attention toward intellectible things only. I call 'sensible' whatever is visible and perceptible by corporeal sense. However, I call 'intelligible' those invisible things which can nevertheless be understood by reason. In this place, I call 'intellectible' those invisible things which cannot be understood by human reason. Thus, among these six kinds of contemplation, the lower four are engaged especially with created things while the two highest are engaged with uncreated and divine things. Again: Among the first four, the two higher are engaged concerning invisible things; the two lower, concerning visible and corporeal things. Without doubt the lowest two are engaged with visible and created things. However, the highest two are especially engaged with invisible and uncreated things. The middle two are engaged especially with invisible and created things. I have said 'especially' for the reason that there are some things concerning invisible and created things that cannot be grasped in any way by human reason. According to this they go with the number of intellectible things and show themselves to pertain more to the two highest kinds of contemplations. Similarly, concerning the highest and uncreated things, it seems that some are accessible to human reason, and according to this ought to be counted among intelligible things and to be adapted especially to those two middle kinds of contemplations. And so it seems that the first two have this in common, that both are engaged about visible things. Yet they seem to differ especially in this, that the first, being impelled by wonder, is accustomed to run here and there without any function of reason. However, in the second, a rational principle is sought and assigned to those things which are engaged in the mind by imagination, and that which is already known to us in a familiar way is led into wonder. The second and third have this in common but uniquely so in comparison with the others: that equally in both, imagination seems to be mixed with reason and reason with imagination. However, they differ in this: that in the second a rational principle is sought for and adapted to visible things, as has been said; while in the third, a rational principle is drawn from visible things for the investigation of invisible things, and in the latter we are often instructed concerning invisible things by visible things and we are clearly shown some things by other things. In this we advance from the examination of visible things to knowledge of invisible things. The third and fourth have in common that they direct attention, as is agreed, toward invisible and intelligible things, but they especially differ in this, that in the third, reason is mixed with imagination, while in the fourth pure understanding is mixed with reason. In the fourth and fifth, reason and understanding come together in unity, and in this they especially agree in harmony. But in the fourth, understanding advances by means of reason. But in the fifth, reason does not go before understanding at all, but it follows or at the most accompanies it. For what is first recognized by means of divine inspiration is afterward affirmed by the testimony of reason. It happens jointly in the fifth and sixth that both of them pursue intellectible things. In the fifth, human reason seems sufficiently to concur. But in the sixth, all human reason seems to be contrary, unless it is supported by a mixture of faith. (Ch. 7, pp. 164–5)

Source: *The Classics of Western Spirituality, Richard of St Victor, The Twelve Patriarchs, The Mystical Ark, Book Three of the Trinity*, trans. and ed. Grover A. Zinn, New York, Mahwah, NJ, Paulist Press, 1979.

6.5 Hildegard of Bingen, from *Scivias*

Hildegard (1098–1179), mystic, musician, author and Benedictine abbess, had a wide influence through her diverse writings on theology, spirituality and healing. Her main work, Scivias, *is a recording of, and commentary on, 26 prophetic visions and auditions. The doctrine of the Trinity shapes this work, which has at its centre the way of salvation which God makes known to us in Christ, by whom we are led back to God. Hildegard employs a wide breadth of images. In this passage she describes the figurative 'appearance' of central Christian virtues and finally the appearance of divine grace.*

Humility and her appearance

So *the first figure* designates Humility, who first manifested the Son of God when God, Who holds heaven and earth in His power, did not disdain to send His Son into the world. Thus she *wears a gold crown on her head, with three higher prongs*, because she surpasses and sweetly precedes the other virtues, and so is crowned with the gold crown of the precious and resplendent Incarnation of the Saviour. For He adorned her head with this mystery when He became incarnate. The crown is triangular, for the Trinity is in the Unity and the Unity in the Trinity; the Son with the Father and the Holy Spirit is One True God, excelling all things in the height of Divinity. *It is radiantly adorned with green and red precious stones and white pearls.* For the Humanity of the Saviour manifests the high and profound goodness of His works; the Son of God wrought them in the greenness of the blossoming of the virtues in His teachings, and in the redness of His blood when He suffered death on the cross to save humanity, and in the whiteness of His resurrection and ascension. And with all of these the Church is lighted and adorned, like an object set with precious stones. *And on her breast she has a shining mirror, in which appears with wondrous brightness the image of the incarnate Son of God.* This is to say that in Humility, who stands in the heart of the sacred temple in blessed and shining knowledge, gratefully and humbly but splendidly and permanently, there shines forth the Only-Begotten of God, in all the works He performed in the body in which He showed Himself to the world. And so the noblest impulses of the hearts of the faithful elect are sealed by this figure, who sets up her tribunal in them and rules and directs all their actions. For she is the solid foundation of all human good deeds, as she shows in the maternal admonition already quoted. (Book 3, Vision 8, para. 18, p. 442)

Fear of the Lord and her appearance

And *the third figure* signifies Fear of the Lord, who arose in the minds of the faithful after the Charity God showed humanity when He willed His Son to undergo death for its sake. And this Fear arose that people might understand the heavenly commands more fully and perfectly than they previously had when doing them. Now *you see her in the same form as you did in your previous vision;* for the immutable God, as was declared to you before, must be held in equal and similar honour and reverence in every thing and creature of His. And *she is greater and taller of stature than the other virtues, and non-human in form;* for she above all the others brings people anguish and trembling. They look with sharp vision upon the greatness of the Supreme Majesty and the loftiness of His Divinity, and they grow afraid; for God is to be dreaded and venerated by all people, since they were created by Him and not another. For which reason this virtue does not resemble a human being; for, as was mentioned, she rejects the perverseness that opposes God with evil deeds, and fixes her inner eye on God alone and walks the righteous paths of His will. Thus *she is covered with eyes all over her body, for she lives wholly in wisdom.* For, with the eyes of good understanding, she looks all around her and contemplates God in all His wonders, so as to pick out the right path of good works and bypass the Devil's morass of evil works by that knowledge of God. She shines with wisdom, for she despises the deadly things that harm the spirit; she flees death and abandons iniquity, and wisely builds herself a house in life.

She wears a shadowy garment through which the eyes can look out. For she is surrounded by the severe abstinence that destroys carnal desire in humans; and in that abstinence she looks toward the light of life, in which Man is wondrously brilliant in beatitude. (Book 3, Vision 8, para. 20, p. 444)

Chastity and her appearance

And *the seventh* designates Chastity. For after people have placed their hope fully in God, the perfect work increases in them, and then by Chastity they start wanting to restrain themselves from the desires of the flesh. For abstinence in the flower of the flesh feels strongly, as a young girl who does not want to look on a man nonetheless feels the fire of desire. But Chastity renounces all filth and longs with beautiful desire for her sweet Lover, the sweetest and loveliest odour of all good things, for Whom those who love Him wait in timid beauty of soul. Thus she *is dressed in a tunic more brilliant and pure than crystal, which shines resplendent like water when the sun reflects from it.* It is brilliant because of her simple intent, and pure because not covered with the dust of burning desire; miraculously strengthened by the Holy Spirit, she is enwrapped in the garment of innocence, which shines in the bright light of the Fountain of living water, the splendid Sun of eternal glory. *And a dove is poised over her head, facing her with its wings spread as if to fly.* This is to say that Chastity at her beginning, at her head, as it were, is protected by the extended and overshadowing wings of the Holy Spirit; and so she can fly through the Devil's snares, one after another. For the Spirit comes with the ardent love of holy inspiration to wherever Chastity shows her sweet face. Therefore too, *in her womb as if in a pure mirror appears a pure infant, on whose forehead is written 'Innocence'.* For in the heart of this purest and brightest of virtues there lives inviolable, beautiful and sure integrity. Its form is immature because it is simple infancy that has integrity; and its forehead, which is to say its knowledge, shows no arrogance and pride but only simple innocence. And *in her right hand she holds a royal sceptre, but she has laid her left hand on her breast.* This is to say that on the right, the side of salvation, life is shown in Chastity through the Son of God who is the King of all people. And through Him as defender, Chastity confounds the left, the side of lust, and reduces it to nought in the hearts of those who love her.

The Grace of God and its appearance

But *at the summit of the shadowed pillar you see another beautiful figure.* This is to say that, by the supreme and surpassing loving kindness of the Almighty in the Incarnation of the Saviour, another resplendent virtue was manifested, namely the Grace of God. And it is powerful and full of God, admonishing people to repent, so that all their villainies may be forgiven through it. *It stands bareheaded*; for its dignity and glory are revealed to all who seek it. *It has curly black hair*; for the Only-Begotten of God clothed Himself in virginal flesh without a stain of sin in the time of the Jewish people, who were tangled and knotted up in their black unfaithfulness. And *it has a manly face so ardently bright that you cannot look on it clearly like a human one.* For God's Grace, in the powerful might of Divinity, appeared to give life in life, and it burns so ardently in that glorious Divinity that no human being can see it with inner or outer sight while he is still weighed down by the heaviness of the body. So it does not stand with its secrets revealed to human judgment, but is mysterious; for the judgments of divine grace are hidden. *It is clad* in a *tunic of purple and black*, which is to say that the work of Grace, which burns in charity, leans down over the blackness of sins as if it were clothing people. How? It warns people toward salvation, and lifts them from the mire of sin toward the vision of the light by means of penitence. For, as day puts the darkness to flight, it builds up sinners toward life by taking away their misdeeds through repentance. *This tunic has a stripe of red over one shoulder and a stripe of yellow over the other, which fall to its feet* in *front and back.* For the Grace of God, in its strength and piety, bends down to the faithful and lifts them on high to heavenly places. How? By the two ways of the stripes. It grasps the anguish of the frail flesh, worn out by bloody battle, and the strength of the soul, grown tepid in the body, and draws them up to love of heavenly things by the red and yellow splendour of the Humanity and the Divinity of the Son of God, the most serene Sun. And so the faithful person who is touched by the integrity of Grace can resist his own sinful desires; he can put virtue in front of him and mortify vice behind him, and thus courageously consummate his works and be clothed in them as in lovely and delightful clothes. And *around its neck it has a bishop's stole, wonderfully adorned with gold and precious gems.* This is to say that Christ, the Son of God, Who is the High Priest of the Father, has the high power of the priestly office everywhere in the world; and so that office should be adorned by the Grace of God with the gold of wisdom and the gems of virtues by the faithful who are His imitators and members. But *a pure radiance so surrounds it that you cannot look at it, except from head to foot in front;* for the Grace of the Omnipotent is surrounded by the serene whiteness of His mercy. In the times before the Humanity of the Saviour, Grace was hidden, invisible and unknown, in the mystery of the Divinity; only from the time of His Incarnation down to the last of His members, who will live at the end of the world, does Grace show forth as far as possible to human understanding, openly manifested in its works. But *its arms and hands and feet are concealed from your sight;* for the true power and deeds and goal of the Grace of God working in humans can be fully known to no one who is weighed down by a body. And *that radiance around it is full of eyes on all sides, and is all alive.* This is to say that the divine pity, which dwells in the Grace of God, manifests His many mercies and His abundant compassion in the form of many eyes, which look upon the sorrows of the people who try to follow God. And that radiance is all alive to console and save their souls, and does not prepare perdition for them, but life. *And that radiance changes its form like a cloud;* for Grace goes before the just, that they may watch themselves and not fall, but follows sinners, that they may repent and rise again. (Book 3, Vision 8, para. 24–5, pp. 445–8)

Source: *The Classics of Western Spirituality, Hildegard of Bingen, Scivias,* trans. Mother Columba Hart, OSB, New York, Mahwah, Paulist Press, 1990.

6.6.1 Bonaventure, from *The Soul's Journey into God*

The Franciscan theologian Bonaventure (1217–74) stressed the futility of human reason in the light of God's mystical illumination of the Christian believer. He was influenced by Richard of St Victor's treatment of the soul's contemplative ascent to God. For Bonaventure, as for his contemporaries, the imagination is mimetic; thus he employs the mirror as a central metaphor. In this extract he analyses how the macrocosm of the world enters the microcosm of the soul through the senses. The objects are perceived through apprehension out of which we derive pleasure. Through judgement, which is the property of the rational soul, humans decide why something is pleasurable or beautiful.

On contemplating God in his vestiges in the sense world

> Concerning the mirror of things
> perceived through sensation,
> we can see God
> not only through them as through his vestiges [i.e. traces],
> but also in them
> as he is in them
> by his essence, power and presence.
>
> (Ch. 2, para. 1, p. 69)

The entire sense world, therefore, in its three classes of objects, enters the human soul through apprehension. The exterior sense objects are the first which enter into the soul through the gates of the five senses. They enter, I say, not through their substance, but through their likenesses, which are first produced in the medium; and from the medium they enter into the organ and from the exterior organ into the interior organ and from this into the apprehensive faculty. And thus the production of the image in the medium and from the medium in the organ and the turning of the apprehensive faculty upon it bring about the apprehension of all objects that the soul grasps from outside.

From this apprehension, if it is of a suitable object, there follows pleasure. The senses take delight in an object perceived through an abstracted likeness either because of its beauty, as in sight, or because of its sweetness, as in smell and hearing, or because of its wholesomeness, as in taste or touch, if we speak by way of appropriation. Now, all enjoyment is based on proportion. But the species has the notion of form, power or operation according to whether it is viewed in relation to the principle from which it flows; or to the medium through which it passes; or to the term on which it acts. Therefore proportion can be viewed in the likeness, insofar as it involves species or form, and then it is called beauty since 'beauty is nothing other than harmonious symmetry' or 'a certain arrangement of parts with pleasing colour'. Or proportion can be viewed as involving potency or power, and then it is called agreeableness since the acting power does not disproportionally exceed the recipient; for the senses are pained by extremes and delighted in the mean. Or proportion can be viewed as productive and impressive; it is proportioned when the agent by its impression fills a need of the recipient, that is, strengthening and nourishing the recipient, which is most apparent in taste and touch. And thus through pleasure, exterior agreeable objects enter into the soul by their likenesses according to a threefold form of delight.

After this apprehension and pleasure comes judgment, by which we determine not only whether something is white or black, because this pertains to a particular sense, not only whether it is wholesome or harmful, because this pertains to an interior sense, but we judge also and give a reason why it is pleasurable. In this judgment we inquire into the reason of the pleasure which is experienced in the senses from the object. Now this occurs when we ask the reason why a thing is beautiful or pleasant or wholesome, and we find that the reason lies in the proportion of harmony. The basis of harmony is the same in large and small objects; neither is it increased by size nor does it change or pass away as things pass away, nor is it altered by motion. It abstracts, therefore, from place, time and motion, and consequently is unchangeable, unlimited, endless and is completely spiritual. Judgment, therefore, is an action which causes the sensible species, received in a sensible way through the senses, to enter the intellective faculty by a process of purification and abstraction. And thus the whole world can enter into the human soul through the doors of the senses by the three operations mentioned above.

All these are vestiges in which we can see our God. For the species which is apprehended is a likeness generated in a medium and then impressed on the organ itself. Through this impression, it leads to its source, namely the object to be known. This clearly suggests that the Eternal Light generates from itself a coequal Likeness or Splendour, which is consubstantial and coeternal. It further suggests that he who is *the image of the invisible God* (Col. 1.15) and *the brightness of his glory and the image of his substance* (Heb. 1.3), who is everywhere through his initial generation, as the object generates its likeness in the entire medium, is united by the grace of union to an individual of rational nature, as the species is united to the bodily organ. Through this union he leads us back to the Father as to the fountain-source and object. If, therefore, all things that can be known generate a likeness of themselves, they manifestly proclaim that in them as in mirrors we can see the eternal generation of the Word, the Image and Son, eternally emanating from God the Father.

In this way the species which delights as beautiful, pleasant and wholesome suggests that there is primordial beauty, pleasure and wholesomeness in that first Species, in which there is supreme proportion and equality with the generating Source, in which there is power flowing not from images of the imagination but from the truth of apprehension, in which there is an impression which preserves and satisfies and dispels all need in the one who apprehends. If, therefore,

'pleasure is the union of the harmonious with the harmonious', and if the
Likeness of God alone contains in the highest degree the notion of beauty, delight
and wholesomeness and if it is united in truth and intimacy and in a fulness that
fulfills every capacity, it is obvious that in God alone there is primordial and true
delight and that in all of our delights we are led to seek this delight. (Ch. 2, para.
4–8, pp. 71–3)

From the first two stages
in which we are led to behold God
in vestiges,
like the two wings covering the Seraph's feet,
we can gather that all the creatures of the sense world
lead the mind
of the contemplative and wise man
to the eternal God.
For these creatures are
shadows, echoes and pictures
of that first, most powerful, most wise and most perfect
Principle,
of that eternal Source, Light and Fulness,
of that efficient, exemplary and ordering Art.
They are
vestiges, representations, spectacles
proposed to us
and signs divinely given
so that we can see God.
These creatures, I say, are
exemplars
or rather exemplifications
presented to souls still untrained
and immersed in sensible things
so that through sensible things
which they see
they will be carried over to intelligible things
which they do not see
as through signs to what is signified.

(Ch. 2, para. 11, pp. 75–6)

From all this, one can gather that
from the creation of the world
the invisible attributes of God are clearly seen,
being understood
through the things that are made.

And so those who do not wish to heed these things,
and to know, bless and love
God
in all of them
are without excuse;
for they are unwilling to be transported
out of darkness
into the marvellous light of God.
But thanks be to God
through our Lord Jesus Christ,
who *has transported* us
out of darkness
into his marvellous light
when through these lights exteriorly given
we are disposed to reenter
the mirror of our mind
in which divine realities shine forth.

(Ch. 2, para. 13, pp. 77–8)

Source: *The Classics of Western Spirituality, Bonaventure, The Soul's Journey into God, The Tree of Life, The Life of St Francis*, trans. and ed. Ewert Cousins, New York, Paulist Press, 1978.

6.6.2 Bonaventure, from *The Tree of Life*

In this brief passage Bonaventure praises the beauty of Christ and exclaims that happiness is found in the vision of God.

Jesus, Extraordinary Beauty This most beautiful *flower of the root of Jesse* (Isa 11.1), which had blossomed in the incarnation and withered in the passion, thus blossomed again in the resurrection so as to become the beauty of all. For that most glorious body – subtle, agile and immortal – was clothed in glory so as to be truly more radiant than the sun, showing an example of the beauty destined for the risen human bodies. Concerning this the Saviour himself said: *'Then the just will shine forth like the sun into the kingdom of their Father'* (Matt 13.43), that is, in eternal beatitude. And if the just will shine forth like the sun, how great do you think is the radiance of the very Sun of justice himself? So great is it, I say, that it is *more beautiful than the sun and surpasses every constellation of the stars* (Wisd 7.29); compared to light, his beauty is deservedly judged to be pre-eminent.

Happy the eyes that have seen!
But you will be truly *happy*
if there will be remnants of your seed
to see
both interiorly and exteriorly
that most desired *splendour.*

(para. 35, pp. 160–1)

Source: *The Classics of Western Spirituality, Bonaventure, The Soul's Journey into God, The Tree of Life, The Life of St Francis*, trans. and ed. Ewert Cousins, New York, Paulist Press, 1978.

6.7.1 Thomas Aquinas, from *Summa Theologiae, Existence and Nature of God (Ia. 2–11)*

In this brief but important section, the foremost medieval philosopher-theologian, Thomas Aquinas (1225–74), relates how and why something that is good is also beautiful. His argument here, as in all his writing, is largely based on the Platonist and especially on the Aristotelian tradition. Interestingly, he also speaks of beauty in subjective terms as being in the eye of the beholder and of the cognitive element in the perception of beauty. These views anticipate Kant's aesthetics by several centuries.

ST, Ia. q. 5 *The General Question of Good*, a. 4 *what kind of causality is implicit in the notion of goodness* . . . Hence: I. A good thing is also in fact a beautiful thing, for both epithets have the same basis in reality, namely, the possession of form; and this is why *the good is esteemed beautiful.* Good and beautiful are not however synonymous. For good (being *what all things desire*) has to do properly with desire and so involves the idea of end (since desire is a kind of movement towards something). Beauty, on the other hand, has to do with knowledge, and we call a thing beautiful when it pleases the eye of the beholder. This is why beauty is a matter of right proportion, for the senses delight in rightly proportioned things as similar to themselves, the sense-faculty being a sort of proportion itself like all other knowing faculties. Now since knowing proceeds by imaging, and images have to do with form, beauty properly involves the notion of form. (pp. 71, 73)

Source: *Summa Theologiae, vol. 2, Existence and Nature of God (Ia. 2–11)*, trans. and ed. Timothy McDermott, OP, London, Blackfriars, 1964.

6.7.2 Thomas Aquinas, from *Summa Theologiae, The Emotions (Ia2æ. 22–30)*

In his discussion of what causes love, Aquinas refers to Pseudo-Dionysius'
claim that humans do not simply love what is good but also what is beauti-
ful. He argues similarly as in Ia. q. 5 in Existence and Nature of God.

ST, Ia.2æ. q. 27 *the causes of love* . . . a I. *is love caused only by what is good?*
. . . Hence: . . . 3. 'Good' and 'beautiful' have the same reference but differ in
meaning. For the good, being 'what all things want', is that in which the orexis
[*i.e. desire] comes to rest; whereas the beautiful is that in which the orexis
comes to rest through contemplation or knowledge. Those senses are therefore
chiefly associated with beauty which contribute most to our knowledge, viz.
sight and hearing when ministering to reason; thus we speak of beautiful sights
and beautiful sounds, but not of beautiful tastes and smells: we do not speak of
beauty in reference to the other three senses. 'Beautiful' therefore adds to 'good'
a reference to the cognitive powers; 'good' refers simply to that in which the
orexis takes pleasure: 'beautiful' refers to that which gives pleasure when it is
perceived or contemplated. (pp. 75, 77)

Source: *Summa Theologiae, vol. 19, The Emotions (Ia2æ. 22–30)*, ed. Eric D'Arcy, London,
Blackfriars, 1967.

6.7.3 Thomas Aquinas, from *Summa Theologiae, Temperance (2a2æ. 141–154)*

In this extract Aquinas examines the relationship between the honourable
and the beautiful. He distinguishes between physical and spiritual beauty
and concludes that it is the beauty of spirit, which 'is of the essence of the
honourable'.

ST, 2a2æ. q. 145 *the sense of honour* . . . a. 2. *is the honourable the same as the*
beautiful? THE SECOND POINT: I. Apparently not. The honourable is lovable
for its own sake, says Cicero; it is a quality of being desirable, and therefore
relates to appetite, whereas the quality of being beautiful relates to vision, which
delights in it. Therefore the two are not the same. 2. Moreover, beauty requires a
certain splendour, a quality of glory. But glory and honour are rather different, as
we have noted. So, therefore, are the beautiful and the honourable. 3. Further, the
honourable has been identified with the virtuous. Yet beauty can be contrary to
virtue; thus *Ezekiel, Trusting in thy beauty thou playest the harlot because of thy*
renown. Therefore the honourable is not identical with the beautiful. ON THE
OTHER HAND there is St Paul, *Those that are our not-presentable parts have*
more abundant comeliness, but our comely parts have no need. He is referring to

our lower and higher faculties. And in effect identifying the virtuous with the beautiful. REPLY: As may be gathered from Dionysius, beauty or handsomeness arises when fine proportions and brightness run together; he says that God is named Beautiful because he is *the cause of the consonance and clarity of the universe.* So beauty of body consists in shapely limbs and features having a certain proper glow of colour. So also beauty of spirit consists in conversation and actions that are well-formed and suffused with intelligence. Since this is of the essence of the honourable, which we have identified with the virtuous or the tempering of human affairs by intelligence, it follows that the honourable is the spiritually beautiful. Accordingly Augustine remarks, *By the honourable I mean what is beautiful to the mind, and this we properly designate* as *spiritual.* And, he goes on, *There are many things lovely to the eye which it would be hardly proper to call honourable.* Hence: 1. The object rousing the appetite is a good that is apprehended. When in the very apprehending it is seen as a beauty it is received as desirable and just right, by the mind. And so Dionysius says, *The beautiful and good is beloved by all.* Thus the honourable by its spiritual beauty becomes desirable. And so Cicero reflects, *Thou perceivest the very figure and the features so to speak of honourable worth; were it to be seen with the eyes, what wondrous loves, as Plato declares, it would arouse for wisdom.* 2. We have discussed how glory is an effect of honour; through being praised and honoured a person gains renown in the sight of others. And so because the same deed causes honour and glory, so also is it honourable and beautiful. 3. The objection applies to bodily beauty. Though you might also care to answer that there is a spiritual fornication when a person prides himself on how honourable he is, according to *Ezekiel, Thy heart was lifted up with thy beauty, thou hast lost thy wisdom in thy beauty.* (pp. 73, 75, 77)

Source: *Summa Theologiae, vol. 43, Temperance (2a2æ. 141–54),* ed. Thomas Gilbey, OP, London, Blackfriars, 1968.

6.7.4 Thomas Aquinas, from *Summa Theologiae, The Life of Christ (3a. 38–45)*

The transfiguration of Christ is discussed by Aquinas at length, whereby, referring to Augustine and John of Damascus, he points out that Christ's splendour in the transfiguration was a manifestation which belonged to his essence as it derived from his divinity and the splendour of his soul. The emphasis in the Eastern Church on divinization appears to be reflected in his reference to Christ's resplendent clothes – a metaphor for the saints in their future splendour in eschatological union with Christ.

ST, 3a. q. 45. *Christ's transfiguration . . . a. I. whether it was fitting for Christ to be transfigured . . .* REPLY: *. . .* And so it was fitting for him to manifest his glorious splendour (which is to be transfigured), according to which he will configure those who belong to him; as it is written, *He will configure these wretched bodies of ours into copies of his glorious body*. For this reason Bede says, *By his loving foresight he prepared them to endure adversity bravely by allowing them to taste for a short time the contemplation of everlasting joy*. Hence: 1. As Jerome says, *Let no one think that Christ*, because it is said he was transfigured, thereby *lost his original form and countenance, or laid aside his real body and took up a spiritual or ethereal body. Now the Evangelist describes how he was transformed, when he says, His face shone like the sun and his clothes became as white as snow. The brightness of countenance which is manifested, and the whiteness of clothes which is described, indicates not that his substance is taken away, but rather that his glory undergoes a change*. 2. Figure has to do with the outline of a body, for a figure is *that which is encompassed by a boundary or boundaries*. Therefore whatever has to do with the outline of a body seems to pertain somehow to the figure. Now the splendour, just as the colour, of a non-transparent body is perceived on its surface, and so the assumption of splendour is called transfiguration. 3. Among the aforementioned endowments, only splendour is a quality of the very person in himself; the other three qualities, however, cannot be perceived except in some action or movement, or in some passion. Christ, then, showed in himself certain signs of possessing these three qualities of agility, for example, when he walked on the waves of the sea; of subtlety, when he came forth from the closed womb of the Virgin; of impassibility, when he escaped unhurt from the hands of the Jews who wished to hurl him down or to stone him. Nevertheless, it is not said, on account of these, that he was transfigured, but only on account of his splendour, which pertains to his personal appearance.

a. 2. *whether his splendour was the splendour of glory* . . . REPLY: The splendour which Christ assumed in the transfiguration was the splendour of glory as to essence, but not as to mode of being. For the splendour of the glorious body is derived from the splendour of the soul, as Augustine says. And similarly, the splendour of Christ's body in the transfiguration was derived from his divinity, as Damascene says, and from the glory of his soul. That the glory of his soul did not overflow into his body from the first moment of Christ's conception was a divine dispensation, that, as stated above, he might fulfil the mysteries of our redemption in a passible body. This did not, however, deprive Christ of the power to let the glory of his soul flow into his body. And as regards splendour, this is what he did in the transfiguration, but other than in a glorious body. For splendour flows from the soul into the glorified body, by way of a permanent quality affecting the body. And so bodily refulgence is not miraculous in a glorified body. But in Christ's transfiguration, splendour flowed from his divinity and from his soul into his body, not by way of an inherent quality of his body, but rather by way of a transient passion, as when the air is lit up by the sun. And so the refulgence, which appeared in Christ's body, was miraculous; just as the fact that he walked upon the waves of the sea. For this reason Dionysius says, *Christ excelled man in doing what is natural to man: this is shown both by the Virgin conceiving him supernaturally, and by the unstable water sustaining the weight of material and earthly feet.* For this reason it should not be maintained, as Hugh of St Victor said, that Christ was endowed with the gift of splendour at his transfiguration, of agility when he walked upon the sea, of subtlety when he came forth from the Virgin's closed womb, and impassibility at the Supper when, without its being divided, he gave of his body to be eaten: because these gifts are inherent qualities of a glorified body. Rather, he was endowed miraculously with what pertained to these gifts. And so the explanation, as regards his soul, is similar to what is stated in the Second Part concerning the vision in which Paul saw God in a rapture. Hence: 1. These words do not prove that the splendour of Christ was not the splendour of glory, but that it was not the splendour of a glorious body, because Christ's body was not as yet immortal. For just as it was by dispensation that in Christ the glory of the soul did not overflow into the body, so likewise it was possible that by dispensation the glory might overflow as the gift of splendour but not as the gift of impassibility. 2. This splendour is said to have been imaginary, not as though it were not really the splendour of glory, but because it was a kind of image representing that perfection of glory according to which the body will be glorious. 3. Just as the splendour of Christ's body represented the future splendour of his body, so the splendour of his clothes signified the future splendour of the saints, which will be surpassed by the splendour of Christ, just as the brightness of the snow is surpassed by the brightness of the sun. For this reason Gregory says that Christ's clothes became resplendent, *because in the heights of heavenly splendour all the saints will cling to him as they shine brightly with the light of righteousness. For his clothes signify the righteous, whom he will unite to himself;* according to *Isaiah, You will be clothed with all these as with jewels.* The bright cloud, however, signifies the glory of the Holy Spirit or *the power of the Father,* as Origen says, by which the saints will be covered in their future state of glory. Although it could also fittingly signify the splendour of the world made new, which splendour will cover the saints as a tent. And so, when Peter suggested that they make tents, *a bright cloud overshadowed* the disciples. (pp. 149, 151, 153, 155)

Source: *Summa Theologiae, vol. 53, The Life of Christ (3a. 38–45),* eds Samuel Parsons, OP and Albert Pinheiro, OP, London, Blackfriars, 1971.

6.8 Meister Eckhart, *Sermon 19, Surrexit autem Saulus de terra apertisque oculis nihil videbat (Acts 9.8)*

The German Dominican preacher and mystic Meister Eckhart (c.1260– 1327) here takes Paul's conversion experience for inspiration and discusses how by seeing nothing one sees God, the 'divine Nothing'. In this passage thus we find a significant example of apophatic mystical theology.

This text which I have quoted in Latin is written by St Luke in *Acts* about St Paul. It means: 'Paul rose from the ground and with open eyes saw nothing.' I think this text has a fourfold sense. One is that when he rose up from the ground with open eyes he saw Nothing, and the Nothing was God; for when he saw God he calls that Nothing. The second: when he got up he saw nothing but God. The third: in all things he saw nothing but God. The fourth: when he saw God, he saw all things as nothing. He previously told how a light came suddenly from heaven and felled him to the ground. Note, he says that a light came from heaven (Acts 9.3). Our best masters say that heaven has light within itself, and yet does not shine. The sun also has light within itself, and does shine. The stars too have light, though it is conveyed to them. Our masters say fire in its simple, natural purity gives no light at its highest place. Its nature (there) is so pure that no eye can see it in any way. It is so subtle and so alien to the eyes, that if it were down here before the eyes, they could not touch it by the power of sight. But in an alien object one can easily see it, where it has been caught by a piece of wood or a lump of coal. By the light of heaven we mean the light that is God, to which no man's senses can attain. Hence St Paul says, 'God dwells in a light that no man can approach' (1 Tim. 6.16). He says God is a light to which there is no approach. There is no way in to God. No man still on the way up, still on the increase in grace and light, ever yet got into God. God is not a growing light, yet one must have got to Him by growing. During the growing we do not see God. If God is to be seen, it must be in the light that is God Himself. A master says, 'In God there is no less or more, no this or that.' As long as we are on the approaches, we cannot get in. Now he says: 'A light from heaven shone about him.' That means that everything pertaining to his soul was enveloped. A master says that in this light all the soul's powers are lifted up and exalted: the outer senses we see and hear with, and the inner senses we call thoughts. The reach of these and their profundity is amazing. I can think as easily of a thing overseas as of something close at hand. Above thoughts is the intellect which still seeks. It goes about looking, spies out here and there, picks up and drops. But above the intellect that seeks there is another intellect which does not seek, but stays in its pure, simple being, which is embraced in that light. And I say that it is in this light that all the powers of the soul are exalted. The senses rise up into the thoughts. How high and how fathomless these are, none knows but God and the soul. Our masters say – and it is a knotty question – that even the angels know nothing

about thoughts unless they break out and rise into the questing intellect, and this seeking intellect springs up into the intellect that does not seek, which is pure light in itself. This light embraces in itself all the powers of the soul. Therefore he says: 'The light of heaven shone about him.' A master says that all things that have an emanation receive nothing from things below them. God flows into all creatures, and yet remains untouched by them all. He has no need of them. God gives nature the power to work, and her first work is the heart. And so some masters held that the soul is entirely in the heart and flows out thence, giving life to the other members. That is not so. The soul is entire in every single member. It is true that her first work is in the heart. The heart lies in the middle, and needs protecting on all sides, just as heaven suffers no alien influence and receives nothing from anywhere, for it possesses all things. It touches all things and remains untouched. Even fire, exalted as it is in its highest part, cannot touch heaven. In the encircling light he fell to earth and his eyes were opened, so that with open eyes he saw all things as naught. And when he saw all things as naught, he saw God. . . . There is no night that is without light, but it is veiled. The sun shines in the night, but is hidden from view. By day it shines, and eclipses all other lights. So does the light of God, it eclipses all other lights. Whatever we seek in creatures, all that is night. I mean this: whatever we seek in any creature, is but a shadow and is night. Even the highest angel's light, exalted though it be, does not illumine the soul. Whatever is not the first light is all darkness and night. [. . .]
'Paul rose from the ground and with open eyes saw nothing.' I cannot see what is one. He saw nothing, that is: God. God is a nothing and God is a something. What is something is also nothing. What God is, that He is entirely. Concerning this the illumined Dionysius, in writing about God, says: 'He is above being, above life, above light.' He attributes to Him neither this nor that, but makes Him out to be I know not what that far transcends these. Anything you see, or anything that comes within your ken, that is not God, just because God is neither this nor that. Whoever says God is here or there, do not believe him. The light that God is shines in the darkness. God is the true light: to see it, one must be blind and must strip from God all that is 'something'. A master says whoever speaks of God in any likeness, speaks impurely of Him. But to speak of God with nothing is to speak of Him correctly. When the soul is unified and there enters into total self-abnegation, then she finds God as in Nothing. It appeared to a man as in a dream – it was a waking dream – that he became pregnant with Nothing like a woman with child, and in that Nothing God was born, He was the fruit of nothing. God was born in the Nothing. Therefore he says: 'He arose from the ground with open eyes, seeing nothing.' He saw God, where all creatures are nothing. He saw all creatures as nothing, for He has the essence of all creatures within Him. He is an essence that contains all essence. A second thing he means by saying 'He saw nothing'. Our masters say that whoever perceives external things, something must enter into him, at least an impression. If I want to get an image of anything, such as a stone, I draw the coarsest part of it into myself,

stripping it off externally. But as it is in the ground of my soul, there it is at its highest and noblest, *there* it is nothing but an image. Whatever my soul perceives from without, an alien element enters in. But when I perceive creatures in God, nothing enters but God alone, for in God there is nothing but God. When I see all creatures in God, I see nothing. He saw God, in Whom all creatures are nothing. The third reason why he saw nothing: the nothing was God. A master says, all creatures are in God as naught, for He has in Him the essence of all creatures. He is the essence that contains all essence. A master says there is nothing under God, however near it may be to Him, but has some alien taint. A master says an angel knows himself and God without *means*. But into all else he knows, there comes an outside element – there is an impression, however slight. If we are to know God it must be without means, and then nothing alien can enter in. If we do see God in this light, it must be quite private and indrawn, without the intrusion of anything created. *Then* we have an immediate knowledge of eternal life. 'Seeing nothing, he saw God.' The light that is God flows out and darkens every light. The light in which Paul saw revealed God to him and nothing else. Therefore Job says: 'He commands the sun not to shine and has sealed up the stars beneath Him as with a seal' (Job 9.7). Being enveloped in this light, he could see nothing else, for all pertaining to his soul was troubled and preoccupied with the light that is God, so that he could take in nothing else. And that is a good lesson for us, for when we concern ourselves with God we are little concerned with things from without. Fourthly, why he saw nothing: the light that is God is unmingled, no admixture comes in. This was a sign that it was the true light he saw, which is Nothing. By the light he meant quite simply that with his eyes open he saw nothing. In seeing nothing, he saw the divine Nothing. St Augustine says: 'When he saw nothing, he saw God'. He who sees nothing else and is blind, sees God. . . . Whatever is without colour, with that we can see all colours, even if it were down in our feet. God is an essence that embraces all essence. For God to be perceived by the soul, she must be blind. Therefore he says, 'He saw the Nothing', from whose light all lights come, from whose essence all essence comes. . . . I could not properly see the light that shines on the wall unless I turned my gaze to where it comes from. And even then, if I take it where it wells forth, I must be free of this welling forth: I must take it where it rests in itself. And yet I say even that is wrong. I must take it neither where it touches nor where it wells forth nor where it rests in itself, for these are still all modes. We must take God as mode without mode, and essence without essence, for He has no modes. Therefore St Bernard says, 'He who would know thee, God, must measure thee without measure.' Let us pray to our Lord that we may come to that understanding that is wholly without mode and without measure. May God help us to this. Amen. (pp. 153–61)

Source: *Meister Eckhart, Sermons and Treatises, vol. 1*, trans. and ed. M. O'Connell Walshe, Shaftesbury, Dorset, Element Books, 1987.

6.9 Gregory Palamas, from *The Triads*

The Triads *is a defence of the Hesychasts, who emphasized inner mystical prayer through union of mind and heart, as well as the human vision of God. In this passage, the Greek theologian and monk on Mount Athos, Palamas (c.1296–1359), reflects, with reference especially to John of Damascus, on the vision of Christ's glory, on divine illumination, and on the transfiguration and our divinization. These themes have played a central role in Orthodox theology through history.*

The Deification of Christ

It is our purpose to communicate the teaching on the light of grace of those long-revered saints whose wisdom comes from experience, proclaiming that 'such is the teaching of Scripture'. Thus we set forth as a summary the words of Isaac, the faithful interpreter of these things: 'Our soul', he affirms, 'possesses two eyes, as all the Fathers tell us. . . . [sic] Yet the sight which is proper to each "eye" is not for the same use: with one eye, we behold the secrets of nature, that is to say, the power of God, His wisdom and providence towards us, things comprehensible by virtue of the greatness of His governance. With the other eye, we contemplate the glory of His holy nature, since it pleases God to introduce us to the spiritual mysteries.' Since then these are eyes, what they see is a light; but since each possesses a power of vision designed for a particular use, a certain duality appears in the contemplation of this light, since each eye sees a different light, invisible to the other eye. As the divine Isaac has explained, the one is the apprehension of the power, wisdom and providence of God, and in general, knowledge of the Creator through the creatures; the other is contemplation, not of the divine nature . . . [sic] but of the *glory* of His nature, which the Saviour has bestowed on His disciples, and through them, on all who believe in Him and have manifested their faith through their works. This glory He clearly desired them to see, for He says to the Father, 'I will that they contemplate the glory You have given Me, for You have loved Me since the foundation of the world.' And again, 'Glorify Me, Father, with that glory I have had from You since before the world began.' Thus to our human nature He has given the glory of the Godhead, but not the divine nature; for the nature of God is one thing, His glory another, even though they be inseparable one from another. However, even though this glory is different from the divine nature, it cannot be classified amongst the things subject to time, for in its transcendence 'it is not', because it belongs to the divine nature in an ineffable manner. Yet it is not only to that human composite which is united to His hypostasis that He has given this glory which transcends all things, but also to His disciples. 'Father,' He says, 'I have given them the glory which You gave Me, so that they may be perfectly one.' But He wishes also that they should see this glory, which we possess in our inmost selves and through which properly speaking we see God.

How then do we possess and see this glory of the divine nature? Is it in examining the causes of things and seeking through them the knowledge of the power, wisdom and providence of God? But, as we have said, it is another eye of the soul which sees all this, which does not see the divine light, 'the glory of his nature' (in St Isaac's words). This light is thus different from the light synonymous with knowledge. Therefore, not every man who possesses the knowledge of created things, or who sees through the mediation of such knowledge has God dwelling in him; but he merely possesses knowledge of creatures, and from this by means of analogy he infers the existence of God. As to him who mysteriously possesses and sees this light, he knows and possesses God in himself, no longer by analogy, but by a true contemplation, transcendent to all creatures, for he is never separated from the eternal glory. Let us not, then, turn aside incredulous before the superabundance of these blessings; but let us have faith in Him who has participated in our nature and granted it in return the glory of His own nature, and let us seek how to acquire this glory and see it. How? By keeping the divine commandments. For the Lord has promised to manifest Himself to the man who keeps them, a manifestation He calls His own indwelling and that of the Father, saying, 'If anyone loves Me, he will keep My word, and My Father will love him, and We will come to him and will make our abode with him' and 'I will manifest Myself to him.' And it is clear that in mentioning His 'word', He means His commandments, since earlier He speaks of 'commandments' in place of 'word': 'He who possesses and keeps My commandments, that is the man who loves Me.' (Ch. D, para. 15–16, pp. 59–61)

The Uncreated Glory

However, the disciples would not even have seen the symbol, had they not first received eyes they did not possess before. As John of Damascus puts it, 'From being blind men, they began to see', and to contemplate this uncreated light. The light, then, became accessible to their eyes, but to eyes which saw in a way superior to that of natural sight, and had acquired the spiritual power of the spiritual light. This mysterious light, inaccessible, immaterial, uncreated, deifying, eternal, this radiance of the Divine Nature, this glory of the divinity, this beauty of the heavenly kingdom, is at once accessible to sense perception and yet transcends it. Does such a reality really seem to you to be a symbol alien to divinity, sensible, created and 'visible through the medium of air'? Listen again to Damascene's assertion that the light is not alien but natural to the divinity. 'The splendour of divine grace is not something external, as in the case of the splendour possessed by Moses, but belongs to the very nature of the divine glory and splendour.' And again: 'In the age to come, we will be always with the Lord, and contemplate Christ resplendent in the light of the Godhead, a light victorious over every nature.' And again: 'He takes with Him the leaders of the apostles as witnesses of His own glory and divinity, and reveals to them His own divinity', which transcends all things, unique, utterly perfect and anticipating the End. That this light is not visible through the mediation of air is shown by the great Denys, and those who with him call it the 'light of the age to come', an age in which we will no longer need air. Basil the Great similarly states that it is visible to the eyes of the heart. The fact that it is not visible through the medium of air shows us it is not a sensible light. Indeed, when it was shining on Thabor more brilliantly than the sun, the people of the area did not even see it! (Ch. E, para. 22, p. 80)

Essence and Energies in God

We do not see distant objects as if they were in front of our eyes, nor the future as if it were the present; we do not know the will of God concerning us before it comes to be. Yet the prophets knew the designs of God which eternally pre-existed in God, even before they were accomplished. Similarly, the chosen disciples saw the essential and eternal beauty of God on Thabor (as the Church sings) . . . not the glory of God which derives from creatures, as you think, but the superluminous splendour of the beauty of the Archetype; the very formless form of the divine loveliness, which deifies man and makes him worthy of personal converse with God; the very Kingdom of God, eternal and endless, the very light beyond intellection and unapproachable, the heavenly and infinite light, out of time and eternal, the light that makes immortality shine forth, the light which deifies those who contemplate it. They indeed saw the same grace of the Spirit which would later dwell in them; for there is only one grace, of the Father, Son and Spirit, and they saw it with their corporeal eyes, but with eyes that had been opened so that, instead of being blind, they could see – as St John of Damascus puts it, they contemplated that uncreated light which, even in the age to come, will be ceaselessly visible only to the saints, as Sts. Denys and Maximus teach. (Ch. F, para. 9, p. 106)

Source: *The Classics of Western Spirituality, Gregory Palamas, The Triads*, ed. John Meyendorff, trans. Nicholas Gendle, New York, Paulist Press, London, SPCK, 1983.

6.10 Nicholas of Cusa, from *On the Vision of God*

German philosopher-theologian and Cardinal Nicholas of Cusa (1401–64) worked for church reforms and wrote on the apophatic dimension in God. In this work the author addresses God directly and praises God's supremely beautiful face, the face of faces, who enables our vision of God. Moreover, he discusses Jesus' vision and how, as the most perfect human being, he has the divine light of truth that illumines every intellect.

That Seeing Is Tasting, Seeking, Having Mercy, and Working

How great is the multitude of your sweetness, which you have hidden away for those who fear you! It is an inexhaustible treasure of the most joyous of gladness.

For to taste your sweetness is to know through the touch of experience the sweetness of every delight at its source. It is to attain in your wisdom to the reason of every desirable thing. Therefore, to see Absolute Reason, the Reason of all things, is nothing other than mentally to taste you, O God, because you are the sweetness itself of being, of life, and of intellect. What other, O Lord, is your seeing, when you look upon me with the eye of mercy, than your being seen by me? In seeing me you, who are the hidden God, I give yourself to be seen by me. No one can see you except in the measure you grant to be seen. Nor is your being seen other than your seeing one who sees you. (Ch. 5, para. 13, p. 241)

On Facial Vision

The longer I behold your face, O Lord, my God, the more keenly you seem to fix your glance on me. And your gaze prompts me to consider how this image of your face is thus portrayed in a sensible fashion since a face could not have been painted without colour and colour does not exist without quantity. But I see the invisible truth of your face, represented in this contracted shadow here, not with the eyes of flesh, which examine this icon of you, but with the eyes of the mind and the intellect. Your true face is absolute from every contraction. It has neither quality nor quantity, nor is it of time or place, for it is the absolute form, which is the face of faces.

When, therefore, I consider how this face is the truth and the most adequate measure of all faces, I am numbed with astonishment. For this face, which is the truth of all faces, is not a face of quantity. It is, therefore, neither greater nor smaller nor equal to any, since it is not of quantity but is absolute and super-exalted. Therefore, it is the truth, which is equality, absolute from all quantity. Thus, O Lord, I comprehend that your face precedes every formable face, that it is the exemplar and truth of all faces and that all are images of your face, which is not subject to contraction and participation. Every face, therefore, which can behold your face sees nothing that is other or different from itself, because it sees there its own truth. Moreover, the truth of the exemplar cannot be other or different, but otherness and diversity happen to the image because the image is not itself the exemplar.

Therefore, while I look at this painted face from the east, it likewise appears that it looks at me in the east, and when I look at it from the west or from the south it also appears to look at me in the west or south. In whatever direction I turn my face, its face seems turned toward me. Thus, too, your face is turned to all faces which look on you. Your vision, Lord, is your face. Consequently, whoever looks on you with a loving face will find only your face looking on oneself with love. And the more one strives to look on you with greater love, the more loving will one find your face. Whoever looks on you with anger will likewise find your face angry. Whoever looks on you with joy will also find your face joyous, just as is the face of the one who looks on you. So indeed the eye of flesh, while peering through a red glass, judges that everything it sees is red or if through a green glass, that everything is green. In the same way, the eye of the mind, wrapped up in contraction and passivity, judges you, who are the object of the mind, according to the nature of the contraction and passivity. A human being cannot judge except in a human way. When a person attributes a face to you, one does not seek it outside the human species since one's judgment is contracted within human nature and in judging does not depart the passivity of this contraction. In the same manner, if a lion were to attribute a face to you, it would judge it only as a lion's face; if an ox, as an ox's; if an eagle, as an eagle's. O Lord, how wonderful is your face, which a young man, if he wished to conceive it, would fashion as youthful; a grown man as manly; and an older man as elderly!

Who could conceive of this sole, truest, and most adequate exemplar of all faces, in such a way that it is the exemplar of all and of each individually and is so most perfectly the exemplar of each as if it were the exemplar of no other? One must leap beyond the forms of all formable faces and beyond all figures. And how would one conceive a face when one would transcend all faces, and all likenesses and figures of all faces, and all concepts that can be formed of a face, and all colour, decoration, and beauty of all faces? Whoever, therefore, undertakes to see your face, so long as one conceives anything, is far removed from your face. For every concept of a face is less than your face, O Lord. And every beauty that can be conceived is less than the beauty of your face. Every face has beauty, but none is beauty itself. Your face, Lord, has beauty, and this having is being. It is thus absolute beauty itself, which is the form that gives being to every form of beauty. O immeasurably lovely Face, your beauty is such that all things to which are granted to behold it are not sufficient to admire it.

In all faces the face of faces is seen veiled and in enigma. It is not seen unveiled so long as one does not enter into a certain secret and hidden silence beyond all faces where there is no knowledge or concept of a face. This cloud, mist, darkness, or ignorance into which whoever seeks your face enters when one leaps beyond every knowledge and concept is such that below it your face cannot be found except veiled. But this very cloud reveals your face to be there beyond all veils, just as when our eye seeks to view the light of the sun, which is the sun's face, it first sees it veiled in the stars and in the colours and in all the things which participate its light. But when the eye strives to gaze at the light unveiled, it looks beyond all visible light, because all such light is less than what it seeks. But since the eye seeks to see the light which it cannot see, it knows that so long as it sees anything, what it sees is not what it is seeking. Therefore, it must leap beyond every visible light. Whoever, therefore, has to leap beyond every light must enter into that which lacks visible light and thus is darkness to the eye. And while one is in that darkness, which is a cloud, if one then knows one is in a cloud, one knows one has come near the face of the sun. For that cloud in one's eye originates from the exceeding brightness of the light of the sun. The denser, therefore, one knows the cloud to be the more one truly attains the invisible light in the cloud. I see, O Lord, that it is only in this way that the inaccessible light, the beauty, and the splendour of your face can be approached without veil. (Ch. 6, para. 17–21, pp. 242–4)

How God's Vision Is the Loving, Causing, Reading, and Holding in Itself of All Things

You, Lord, see and have eyes. You are, therefore, an eye, because your having is being. You thus observe all things in yourself. For if in me my sight were an eye as in you, my God, then in myself I would see all things. For the eye is like a mirror, and a mirror, however small, figuratively takes into itself a vast mountain and all that exists on the mountain's surface. And in this way the species of all things are observed in the eye. Nevertheless, our sight, through the mirror of the eye, sees only, and in a particular manner, the object toward which it turns its attention, because its power can be determined only in a particular manner by the object. Therefore, it does not see all the things that are captured in the mirror of the eye. But since your sight is an eye or living mirror, it sees all things in itself. Even more, since it is the cause of all that can be seen, it embraces and sees all things in the cause and reason of all, that is, in itself. Your eye, O Lord, reaches toward all things without turning. Our eye must turn itself toward an object because of the quantum angle of our vision. But the angle of your vision, O God, is not quantum but infinite. It is also a circle, or rather, an infinite sphere because your sight is an eye of sphericity, and of infinite perfection. For your sight sees all things simultaneously around and above and below. (Ch. 8, para. 30, p. 249)

How God Is Seen Beyond the Coincidence of Contradictories, and How Seeing is Being

. . . For you are there where speaking, seeing, hearing, tasting, touching, reasoning, knowing, and understanding are the same and where seeing coincides with being seen, hearing with being heard, tasting with being tasted, touching with being touched, speaking with hearing, and creating with speaking. If I were to see just as I am visible, I would not be a creature, and if you, O God, did not see just as you are visible, you would not be God, the Almighty. You are visible by all creatures and you see all. In that you see all you are seen by all. For otherwise creatures cannot exist since they exist by your vision. If they did not see you who see, they would not receive being from you. The being of a creature is equally our seeing and your being seen. By your word, you speak to all that are and call into existence all that are not. You call them to hear you, and when they hear you, then they are. When, therefore, you speak, you speak to all and all to which you speak hear you. You speak to the earth, and you call it into human nature. The earth hears you, and its hearing this is its becoming human being. You speak to nothing as if it were something, and you call nothing into something, and nothing hears you since what was nothing becomes something.

O infinite Power, your conceiving is your speaking. You conceive sky, and it exists as you conceive it. You conceive earth, and it exists as you conceive it. While conceiving, you see and you speak and you work and you do all else that one is able to name. (Ch. 10, para. 40–1, p. 253)

That Where the Invisible Is Seen, the Uncreated Is Created

Formerly you appeared to me, O Lord, as invisible by every creature because you are a hidden, infinite God. Infinity, however, is incomprehensible by every means of comprehending. Later you appeared to me as visible by all, for a thing exists only as you see it, and it would not actually exist unless it saw you. For your vision confers being, since your vision is your essence. Thus, my God, you are equally invisible and visible. As you are, you are invisible; as the creature is, which exists only insofar as the creature sees you, you are visible. You, therefore, my invisible God, are seen by all, and in all sight you are seen by everyone who sees. You who are invisible, who are both absolute from everything visible and infinitely superexalted, are seen in every visible thing and in every act of vision. Therefore, I must leap across this wall of invisible vision to where you are to be found. But this wall is both everything and nothing. For you, who confront as if you were both all things and nothing at all, dwell inside that high wall which no natural ability can scale by its own power.

At times you confront me so that I think you see all things in yourself as a living mirror in which all things are reflected. But because your seeing is knowing, then it occurs to me that you do not see all things in yourself as a living mirror would, for in this case your knowledge would arise from things. Then you seem to me to see all things in yourself as a power looking on itself. If, for example, the power of the seed of a tree looked on itself, it would see in itself the virtual tree, since the power of the seed is virtually the tree. But, afterward, it occurs to me that you do not see yourself and all things in yourself as a power. For to see a tree in the potency of its power is different from the sight by which a tree is seen in actuality. And then I discover how your infinite power surpasses the power of a mirror or a seed and exceeds the coincidence of radiating and reflecting and of both cause and effect. I learn how your absolute power is absolute vision, which is perfection itself and above all the modes of seeing; for your vision, which is your essence, my God, is, without mode, all the modes, which make manifest the perfection of vision. (Ch. 12, para. 47–8, p. 256)

How Jesus Sees and Has Worked

The eye of the mind cannot be satiated in seeing you, O Jesus, because you are the completion of all mental beauty, and at this icon I conjecture about your exceedingly wonderful and astonishing gaze, O Jesus, who are blessed above all. For while you walked in this world of sense, you, Jesus, used eyes of flesh similar to ours. With them you saw objects one after another, no differently than we human beings, for there was in your eyes a certain spirit that was the form of the organ, like the sensible soul in an animal's body. In this spirit was a noble and discriminative power by which you, Lord, saw distinctly and discretely this object as coloured in one way and that object as coloured in another. And even more, according to the forms of the face and of the eyes of the people whom you saw, you were the true judge of the soul's passions, of its anger, joy, and sorrow. And more subtly still, from a few signs you comprehended what lay hidden in the mind of a human being. For nothing is conceived in the mind that is not in some way signalled in the face, most greatly in the eyes, because the face is the heart's messenger. (Ch. 22, para. 94, p. 278)

Thus, in you who are one, O Jesus, I see that the human intellectual nature was united in a similar way to the divine nature and that as human being you did many works and at the same time as God many wonderful and superhuman works. I see, most merciful Jesus, that the intellectual nature is absolute in regard to the sensible and not at all, as is the sensible, limited and bound to an organ, as, for example, the visual faculty of the senses is bound to the eye; but the divine power is incomparably more absolute and above the intellectual. For the human intellect, to be brought into act, needs phantasms, and phantasms cannot be acquired without the senses, and the senses do not subsist without the body. Consequently, dependent on these, the power of the human intellect is contracted and slight. But the divine intellect is necessity itself, independent and requiring nothing; yet all. Things require it, and without it they cannot exist. (Ch. 22, para. 98, p. 280)

Therefore, in you, my Jesus, I see all perfection. For since you are the most perfect human, I see that in you the intellect is united to the rational or discursive power, which is the summit of sensible power. And thus I see that the intellect is in reason as in its own place, like a candle placed in a room, which illuminates the room and all the walls and the whole building, according, however, to the greater or less degree of distance they are from it. Then I see that the divine Word is united to the intellect in its highest and the intellect itself is the place where the Word is received, just, as in regard to ourselves, we discover that the intellect is the place where the word of a teacher is received, as if the light of the sun were joined to the candle just mentioned. For the Word of God illumines the intellect just as the light of the sun illumines this world. Therefore, in you, my Jesus, I see the sensible life as illumined by the intellectual light, the intellectual life as a light that illumines and is illumined, and the divine life as a light that illumines only. For in your intellectual light I see the Fountain of light, that is, the Word of God, which is the Truth enlightening every intellect. You alone, therefore, are the highest of all creatures, because you are creature in such a way that you are the blessed Creator. (Ch. 22, para. 100, p. 281)

Source: *The Classics of Western Spirituality, Nicholas of Cusa, Selected Spiritual Writings*, trans. and ed. H. Lawrence Bond, New York, Mahwah, Paulist Press, 1997.

7

Images of God

— —

7.1 Anselm of Canterbury, from *Monologium*

Here Anselm examines the analogy of Creator and artisan. He points out that while God's creative power is unlimited, the artist always works within the confines of his or her human limitations.

The analogy, however, between the expression of the Creator and the expression of the artisan is very incomplete. But, though it is most certain that the supreme Substance expressed, as it were, within itself the whole created world, which it established according to, and through, this same most profound expression, just as an artisan first conceives in his mind what he afterwards actually executes in accordance with his mental concept, yet I see that this analogy is very incomplete. For the supreme Substance took absolutely nothing from any other source, whence it might either frame a model in itself, or make its creatures what they are; while the artisan is wholly unable to conceive in his imagination any bodily thing, except what he has in some way learned from external objects, whether all at once, or part by part; nor can he perform the work mentally conceived, if there is a lack of material, or of anything without which a work premeditated cannot be performed. For, though a man can, by meditation or representation, frame the idea of some sort of animal, such as has no existence; yet, by no means has he the power to do this, except by uniting in this idea the parts that he has gathered in his memory from objects known externally. Hence, in this respect, these inner expressions of the works they are to create differ in the creative substance and in the artisan: that the former expression, without being taken or aided from any external source, but as first and sole cause, could suffice the Artificer for the performance of his work, while the latter is neither first, nor sole, nor sufficient, cause for the inception of the artisan's work. Therefore, whatever has been created through the former expression is only what it is through that expression, while whatever has been created through the latter would not exist at all, unless it were something that it is not through this expression itself. (Ch. 11, pp. 58–9)

Source: *St Anselm, Basic Writings, Proslogium, Monologium, Cur Deus Homo, Gaunilo's In Behalf of the Fool*, trans. Sidney Norton Deane, Chicago, The Open Court Publishing Company, 1903.

7.2 Thomas Aquinas, from *Summa Theologiae, Father, Son and Holy Ghost (Ia. 33–43)*

Aquinas discusses how 'image' ought to be understood in itself, and in relation to the Trinity, especially, to the Son, and how it can be used for humans in relation to God. Further he asserts Augustine's application of the attribute of beauty to the second person in the Trinity.

ST, Ia q. 35 *the name 'Image'* . . . a I. *whether in the godhead 'Image' is a personal name* . . . For something to be an image in the full sense, then, it must proceed from another as like the other in species or at least in a mark of the species. Now in God whatever implies procession, i.e. origin, is personal. Hence this name 'Image' is personal. Hence: 1. That is called an image in a literal sense which originates as the likeness of another; that in whose likeness something originates is strictly speaking an exemplar and an image only in an imprecise sense. Yet it is in this sense that Augustine uses the term in stating that the divinity of the Holy Trinity is the Image after which man is fashioned. 2. The term 'species' as Hilary put it into the definition of image connotes a form derived in one thing from another. In such a usage an image means the species of something in the way that anything made like another is said to be in the form of the other, namely by having a like form. 3. Among the divine persons imitation indicates not subordination but simply likeness.

2. *whether 'Image' is a name proper to the Son* . . . The teaching of the Greek doctors generally is that the Holy Spirit is the Image of Father and Son. Latins, however, ascribe the name 'Image' to the Son alone, since in the canonical Scriptures we find it used only of the Son; *thus Colossians, Who is image of the invisible God the firstborn of creatures; Hebrews, Who, being the brightness of his glory and the figure of his substance.* . . . Hence: 1. The Damascene, and the Greek theologians generally, employ the term 'image' to convey the absolute likeness of the Holy Spirit. 2. For the reason already given, even though the Holy Spirit is like the Father and the Son, it does not follow that he is an image. 3. The image of one thing is present in another in one of two ways. The first, as in a being of the same specific nature, e.g. the king's image in his son; the second, as in a being of a different nature, e.g. the king's image on a coin. The Son is the Image of the Father in the first manner; man is the image of God in the second. In order, therefore, to bring out that there is less of an image in man, Scripture does not just say that man is made the image, but made to the image of God, thereby implying a kind of process tending towards completion. Because the Son is the absolute Image, on the other hand, he cannot be said to be 'to the Father's image'.

ST, Ia q. 39 *Persons and Essence* . . . a. 8 *whether the holy doctors have correctly assigned essential attributes to the persons* . . . Comeliness or beauty bears a resemblance to the properties of the Son. Beauty must include three qualities: integrity or completeness – since things that lack something are thereby ugly; right proportion or harmony; and brightness – we call things bright in colour beautiful. Integrity is like the Son's property, because he is a Son who in himself has the Father's nature truly and fully. To suggest this Augustine, commenting on Hilary, says, *In whom*, namely the Son, *there is life, primal and supreme*, etc. Right proportion is consonant with what is proper to the Son inasmuch as he is the express Image of the Father; thus we notice that any image is called beautiful if it represents a thing, even an ugly thing, faithfully. Augustine touches on our point, saying, *In whom there is so complete a reflection and such absolute equality*, etc. Brightness coincides with what is proper to the Son as he is the Word, *the light and splendour of the mind*, in Damascene's description. Augustine alludes to this in the same text, as *complete Word, from whom nothing is wanting, and the Art, as it were, of the Almighty*, etc. (pp. 43, 45, 47, 49, 129, 133, 135)

Source: *Summa Theologiae, vol. 7, Father Son and Holy Spirit (Ia. 33–43)*, ed. T. C. O'Brien, London, Blackfriars, 1976.

7.3 Julian of Norwich, from *Showings*

The female English mystic (c.1342–after 1413) reflects on the Trinity and the triune God's relationship with us. In rather unusual fashion in the history of trinitarian theology she speaks of God as Mother and Father, and about God being present in our sensuality, and of the union of body and soul. Julian thus sketches a holistic view of God and of the human being, which seems remarkably 'modern' and is therefore of interest to contemporary (feminist) theology.

Our faith comes from the natural love of our soul, and from the clear light of our reason, and from the steadfast memory which we have from God in our first creation. And when our soul is breathed into our body, at which time we are made sensual, at once mercy and grace begin to work, having care of us and protecting us with pity and love, in which operation the Holy Spirit forms in our faith the hope that we shall return up above to our substance, into the power of Christ, increased and fulfilled through the Holy Spirit. So I understood that our sensuality is founded in nature, in mercy and in grace, and this foundation enables us to receive gifts which lead us to endless life. For I saw very surely that our substance is in God, and I also saw that God is in our sensuality, for in the same instant and place in which our soul is made sensual, in that same instant and place exists the city of God, ordained for him from without beginning. He comes into this city and will never depart from it, for God is never out of the soul, in which he will dwell blessedly without end. And this was said in the sixteenth revelation, where it says: The place that Jesus takes in our soul he will never depart from. And all the gifts which God can give to the creature he has given to his Son Jesus for us, which gifts he, dwelling in us, has enclosed in him until the time that we are fully grown, our soul together with our body and our body together with our soul. Let either of them take help from the other, until we have grown to full stature as creative nature brings about; and then in the foundation of creative nature with the operation of mercy, the Holy Spirit by grace breathes into us gifts leading to endless life. And so my understanding was led by God to see in him and to know, to understand and to recognize that our soul is a created trinity, like the uncreated blessed Trinity, known and loved from without beginning, and in the creation united to the Creator, as is said before. This sight was sweet and wonderful to contemplate, peaceful and restful, secure and delectable. And because of the glorious union which was thus made by God between the soul and the body, mankind had necessarily to be restored from a double death, which restoration could never be until the time when the second person in the Trinity had taken the lower part of human nature, whose highest part was united to him in its first creation. And these two parts were in Christ, the higher and the lower, which are only one soul. The higher part was always at peace with God in full joy and bliss. The lower part, which is sensuality, suffered for the salvation of mankind. And these two parts were seen and felt in the eighth revelation, in which my body was filled full of feeling and memory of Christ's Passion and his dying. And furthermore, together with this there was a perception and a secret inward vision of the higher part, and that was shown at the same time, when I could not, in response to the intermediary's suggestion, look up to heaven. And that was because of that same mighty contemplative vision of the inward life, which inward life is that high substance, that precious soul which is endlessly rejoicing in the divinity. (Ch. 55, pp. 286–8)

And therefore if we want to have knowledge of our soul, and communion and discourse with it, we must seek in our Lord God in whom it is enclosed. And of this enclosing I saw and understood more in the sixteenth revelation, as I shall say, and as regards our substance, it can rightly be called our soul, and as regards our sensuality, it can rightly be called our soul, and that is by the union which it has in God. That honourable city in which our Lord Jesus sits is our sensuality, in which he is enclosed; and our natural substance is enclosed in Jesus, with the blessed soul of Christ sitting in rest in the divinity. And I saw very certainly that we must necessarily be in longing and in penance until the time when we are led so deeply into God that we verily and truly know our own soul; and I saw certainly that our good Lord himself leads us into this high depth, in the same love with which he created us and in the same love with which he redeemed us, by mercy and grace, through the power of his blessed Passion. And all this notwithstanding, we can never come to the full knowledge of God until we first clearly know our own soul. For until the time that it is in its full powers, we cannot be all holy; and that is when our sensuality by the power of Christ's

Passion can be brought up into the substance, with all the profits of our tribulation which our Lord will make us obtain through mercy and grace. (Ch. 56, p. 289)

And so in our making, God almighty is our loving Father, and God all wisdom is our loving Mother, with the love and the goodness of the Holy Spirit, which is all one God, one Lord. And in the joining and the union he is our very true spouse and we his beloved wife and his fair maiden, with which wife he was never displeased; for he says: I love you and you love me, and our love will never divide in two. I contemplated the work of all the blessed Trinity, in which contemplation I saw and understood these three properties: the property of the fatherhood, and the property of the motherhood, and the property of the lordship in one God. In our almighty Father we have our protection and our bliss, as regards our natural substance, which is ours by our creation from without beginning; and in the second person, in knowledge and wisdom we have our perfection, as regards our sensuality, our restoration and our salvation, for he is our Mother, brother and saviour; and in our good Lord the Holy Spirit we have our reward and our gift for our living and our labour, endlessly surpassing all that we desire in his marvellous Courtesy, out of his great plentiful grace. For all our life consists of three: In the first we have our being, and in the second we have our increasing, and in the third we have our fulfillment. The first is nature, the second is mercy, the third is grace. As to the first, I saw and understood that the high might of the Trinity is our Father, and the deep wisdom of the Trinity is our Mother, and the great love of the Trinity is our Lord; and all these we have in nature and in our substantial creation. And furthermore I saw that the second person, who is our Mother, substantially the same beloved person, has now become our mother sensually, because we are double by God's creating, that is to say substantial and sensual. Our substance is the higher part, which we have in our Father, God almighty; and the second person of the Trinity is our Mother in nature in our substantial creation, in whom we are founded and rooted, and he is our Mother of mercy in taking our sensuality. And so our Mother is working on us in various ways, in whom our parts are kept undivided; for in our Mother Christ we profit and increase, and in mercy he reforms and restores us, and by the power of his Passion, his death and his Resurrection he unites us to our substance. So our Mother works in mercy on all his beloved children who are docile and obedient to him, and grace works with mercy, and especially in two properties, as it was shown, which working belongs to the third person, the Holy Spirit. He works, rewarding and giving. Rewarding is a gift for our confidence which the Lord makes to those who have laboured; and giving is a courteous act which he does freely, by grace, fulfilling and surpassing all that creatures deserve. Thus in our Father, God almighty, we have our being, and in our Mother of mercy we have our reforming and our restoring, in whom our parts are united and all made perfect man, and through the rewards and the gifts of grace of the Holy Spirit we are fulfilled. And our substance is in our Father, God almighty, and our substance is in our Mother, God all wisdom, and our substance is in our Lord God, the Holy Spirit, all goodness, for our substance is whole in each person of the Trinity, who is one God. And our sensuality is only in the second person, Christ Jesus, in whom is the Father and the Holy Spirit; and in him and by him we are powerfully taken out of hell and out of the wretchedness on earth, and gloriously brought up into heaven, and blessedly united to our substance, increased in riches and nobility by all the power of Christ and by the grace and operation of the Holy Spirit. (Ch. 58, pp. 293–5)

Source: *The Classics of Western Spirituality, Julian of Norwich, Showings*, trans. and ed. Edmund Colledge, OSA and James Walsh, SJ, London, SPCK, 1978.

7.4 Nicholas of Cusa, from *On Learned Ignorance*

In this passage of Cusa's most well-known work, he – like Ambrose, Augustine and Anselm before him – describes God as artisan and affirms that it is through seeing the visible beauty of creation that we come to see the invisible beauty of God. Furthermore, he explores the metaphors of fire and light for God.

On the Wonderful Divine Art in the Creation of the World and Its Elements

Since it is the unanimous opinion of the wise that through these visible things and their magnitude, beauty, and order we are led to marvel at the divine art and excellence and since we touched upon several of the handiworks of God's marvellous knowledge, let us briefly and in wonder add, regarding the creation of the universe, a few more words about the placement and order of its elements. In the creation of the world God made use of arithmetic, geometry, music, and astronomy, which we also use when we investigate the proportions of things, including elements and motions. For through arithmetic God joined things together; through geometry God fashioned them in such a way that they receive steadfastness, stability, and mobility, according to their conditions; with music God gave them such proportion that there is not more earth in earth than water in water, air in air, and fire in fire, so that no element is wholly resoluble into another. Therefore, the machine of the world cannot perish. (Book 2, Ch. 13, para. 175, p. 166)

And, as it were, the earth is to fire as the World is to God. For in relation to the earth, fire has many likenesses to God. There is no limit to its power; it works, penetrates, and illumines all the things on earth and distinguishes and forms all by means of air and water. Hence, it is as if in all things that are brought forth from earth there is nothing except one or another activity of fire, so that the forms of things are different because of the diversity in fire's brightness. Fire, however, is immersed in things, and without them it does not exist, nor do earthly things exist without it. But God alone is absolute. Hence, God, who is light and in whom there is no darkness, is called by the ancients 'Absolute Consuming Fire', and 'Absolute Brightness'. It is God's fiery splendour and brightness, as it were, that all things strive, as far as they can, to participate, as we observe in all the stars, where such brightness is found materially contracted. And this discerning and penetrating brightness is, as it were, immaterially contracted in the life of those who are living by an intellective life.

Who would not marvel at this Artisan, who in the spheres and stars and the astral regions also employed such skill that, although without complete precision, there is a harmony of all things as well as a diversity? This Artisan weighed in advance the vastness of the stars and their position and movement in the one world and so ordained the distances between them that unless each region were just as it is, it could neither exist nor exist in such position and order, nor could the universe itself exist. This Artisan gave to all the stars a differing brightness, influence, shape, and colour, as well as heat, which causally accompanies the brightness. And this Artisan so proportionately established the proportion of parts to one another that in each thing the movement of the parts is in relation to the whole, with heavy things having downward motion toward the centre and with light things having upward motion from the centre and around the centre, as, for example, we perceive the movement of the stars to be circular. (Book 2, Ch. 13, para. 177–8, pp. 167–8)

Source: *The Classics of Western Spirituality, Nicholas of Cusa, Selected Spiritual Writings,* trans. and ed. H. Lawrence Bond, New York, Mahwah, NJ, Paulist Press, 1997.

8

Praising God: Architecture, Poetry and Music

— —

8.1 Symeon the New Theologian, from *Hymns of Divine Love*

The numerous hymns of the spiritual writer and Byzantine mystic Symeon (949–1022) present a poetic example of doxology. The vision of the light of God is central to his thought. In Hymn 35 *he contemplates the vision of God's glory by letting Christ himself speak.*

Hymn 35 That all the Saints, having been illumined, are seen bathed in the light and contemplate the glory of God as far as it is possible to human nature to see God.

Look down from above, my God
and be pleased to appear
and converse with a poor person.
Reveal Your light,
opening up Heaven to me,
or rather, open my mind
and enter now deeply within me!
Speak as earlier
through means of my stained tongue,
concerning the things certain persons say
that today there is no one
who has seen God consciously
and that there never was anyone
in prior times, except the Apostles.
But not even those themselves, they say,
saw your God and Father distinctly,
but He is unknowable to all as well as invisible.

They declare solemnly
that this is so, citing the word
of Your very beloved
disciple, John,
who said, 'Nobody among men has ever seen God.'
Yes, my Christ, speak quickly
so that before those foolish ones
I may not appear to be talking nonsense!
'Write,' He said, 'what I tell you.
Write and do not fear!
I, God, was before all days,
all hours and times
but also before all ages
and before all creation,
visible and spiritual.
I exceeded every mind and reason,
beyond every thought,
Unique Intimacy of the Unique with the Unique.
Nothing of the visible creatures
and nothing even of the invisible creatures
existed before actually coming into existence.
I alone am uncreated
with My Father and My Spirit.
I am the only One without a beginning,
coming from My Father who is without a beginning.
No one among the angels,
not even among the archangels
nor among the other angelic orders,
has ever seen My nature
nor Myself, the Creator,
in My total being such as I am.
It is only a ray of glory
and a streak of My light
that they contemplate and by which they are divinized.
For it is like a mirror
which receives the rays of the sun
or a crystal stone
which radiates brilliantly in mid-day.
In like manner, they all receive the rays of My divinity.
But to contemplate Me totally,
this never has anyone been considered worthy to do
not among the angels
nor men nor the holy Powers.
For I am beyond all creatures

and invisible to all.
It is not because I bear at all bad will towards them
that they do not contemplate me,
nor because I am lacking in beauty
that I hide Myself so as not to manifest Myself to them.
But it is because none of them
is found worthy of My divinity.
There is no creature
who is equal in power to the Creator.
For such a thought is unfitting.
But, having seen a small ray of light,
they receive a revelation that I really exist
and they know that I am God
and that I brought them into existence.
And in wonderment and fear, they celebrate Me in song.'
For it is impossible that there be created another
who is God by nature,
equal in power with the Creator,
having the same nature as He.
It is indeed completely impossible
that any creature be
of the same essence as the Creator.
For how could the created
ever become equal to the Uncreated?
Created beings are inferior
to Him who is always equally
both eternal and uncreated.
And indeed you bear witness
that this is so
and that there is as much difference
as between a plow or a scythe
and the one who made them.
How therefore can the plow completely understand the one
who made it?
And how can the scythe know the one, tell me, who uses it?
At least if he does not give to them such a knowledge;
at least if he does not give them sight, he who has built them?
Is this not then impossible for all creatures?
Indeed no man, not even an angel has received completely the power
to bestow the Spirit upon others
or to give them life,
but only the Lord of all who has the power,
who has the might, as being the source of life.
He brings forth living beings endowed with souls,

such exactly as He wishes, and He graces each one,
as an artisan, as a master,
with all that He desires and wishes. To Him be glory and power,
now, always and forever and ever. Amen.

(pp. 191–3)

Source: *Symeon the New Theologian, Hymns of Divine Love*, Introduction and trans. George A. Moloney, SJ, Denville, NJ, Dimension Books, date not given.

8.2 Abbot Suger, from *On the Abbey Church of St. Denis and Its Art Treasures*

Suger was abbot of St Denis near Paris from 1122. The new church at St Denis, for which he was responsible, was to be influential for the whole development of Gothic church art and architecture. Suger wrote an account of the building process. In these selected sections he comments on the doors and the main altar, whereby he emphasizes the importance of craftsmanship. The central role of the Eucharist is raised in his advocacy of using the most splendid vessels for the celebration of the sacrament.

Of the Cast and Gilded Doors Bronze casters having been summoned and sculptors chosen, we set up the main doors on which are represented the Passion of the Saviour and His Resurrection, or rather Ascension, with great cost and much expenditure for their gilding as was fitting for the noble porch. Also [we set up] others, new ones on the right side and the old ones on the left beneath the mosaic which, though contrary to modern custom, we ordered to be executed there and to be affixed to the tympanum of the portal. We also committed ourselves richly to elaborate the tower[s] and the upper crenelations of the front, both for the beauty of the church and, should circumstances require it, for practical purposes. Further we ordered the year of the consecration, lest it be forgotten, to be inscribed in copper-gilt letters in the following manner:

'For the splendour of the church that has fostered and exalted him,
Suger has laboured for the splendour of the church.
Giving thee a share of what is thine, O Martyr Denis,
He prays to thee to pray that he may obtain a share of Paradise.
The year was the One Thousand, One Hundred, and Fortieth
Year of the Word when [this structure] was consecrated.'

The verses on the door, further, are these:

'Whoever thou art, if thou seekest to extol the glory of
    these doors,
Marvel not at the gold and the expense but at the
    craftsmanship of the work.
Bright is the noble work; but, being nobly bright, the work
Should brighten the minds, so that they may travel,
    through the true lights,
To the True Light where Christ is the true door.
In what manner it be inherent in this world the golden
    door defines:
The dull mind rises to truth through that which is
    material
And, in seeing this light, is resurrected from its
    former submersion.'

And on the lintel:

'Receive, O stern Judge, the prayers of Thy Suger;
Grant that I be mercifully numbered among Thy own sheep.'

(Ch. XXVII, p. 47, 49)

We hastened to adorn the Main Altar of the blessed Denis where there was only
one beautiful and precious frontal panel from Charles the Bald, the third
Emperor; for at this [altar] we had been offered to the monastic life. We had it all
encased, putting up golden panels on either side and adding a fourth, even more
precious one; so that the whole altar would appear golden all the way round. On
either side, we installed there the two candlesticks of King Louis, son of Philip,
of twenty marks of gold, lest they might be stolen on some occasion; we added
hyacinths, emeralds, and sundry precious gems; and we gave orders carefully to
look out for others to be added further. The verses on these [panels] are these.
    On the right side:

'Abbot Suger has set up these altar panels
In addition to that which King Charles has given before.
Make worthy the unworthy through thy indulgence, O Virgin Mary.
May the fountain of mercy cleanse the sins both of the King and
the Abbot.'

On the left side:

'If any impious person should despoil this excellent altar
May he perish, deservedly damned, associated with Judas.'

But the rear panel, of marvellous workmanship and lavish sumptuousness (for the barbarian artists were even more lavish than ours), we ennobled with chased relief work equally admirable for its form as for its material, so that certain people might be able to say: *The workmanship surpassed the material.* Much of what had been acquired and more of such ornaments of the church as we were afraid of losing – for instance, a golden chalice that was curtailed of its foot and several other things – we ordered to be fastened there. And because the diversity of the materials [such as] gold, gems and pearls is not easily understood by the mute perception of sight without a description, we have seen to it that this work, which is intelligible only to the literate, which shines with the radiance of delightful allegories, be set down in writing. Also we have affixed verses expounding the matter so that the [allegories] might be more clearly understood:

> 'Crying out with a loud voice, the mob acclaims Christ:
> "Osanna".
> The true Victim offered at the Lord's Supper has carried
> all men.
> He Who saves all men on the Cross hastens to carry the
> cross.
> The promise which Abraham obtains for his seed is sealed by
> the flesh of Christ.
> Melchizedek offers a libation because Abraham triumphs over
> the enemy.
> They who seek Christ with the Cross bear the cluster of
> grapes upon a staff.'

Often we contemplate, out of sheer affection for the church our mother, these different ornaments both new and old; and when we behold how that wonderful cross of St Eloy – together with the smaller ones – and that incomparable ornament commonly called 'the Crest' are placed upon the golden altar, then I say, sighing deeply in my heart: *Every precious stone was thy covering, the sardius, the topaz, and the jasper, the chrysolite, and the onyx, and the beryl, the sapphire, and the carbuncle, and the emerald.* To those who know the properties of precious stones it becomes evident, to their utter astonishment, that none is absent from the number of these (with the only exception of the carbuncle), but that they abound most copiously. Thus, when – out of my delight in the beauty of the house of God – the loveliness of the many-coloured gems has called me away from external cares, and worthy meditation has induced me to reflect, transferring that which is material to that which is immaterial, on the diversity of the sacred virtues: then it seems to me that I see myself dwelling, as it were, in some strange region of the universe which neither exists entirely in the slime of the earth nor entirely in the purity of Heaven; and that, by the grace of God, I can be transported from this inferior to that higher world in an anagogical manner. I used to converse with travellers from Jerusalem and, to my great delight, to learn from those to whom the treasures of Constantinople and the ornaments of Hagia Sophia had been accessible, whether the things here could claim some value in comparison with those there. When they acknowledged that these here were the more important ones, it occurred to us that those marvels of which we had heard before might have been put away, as a matter of precaution, for fear of the Franks, lest through the rash rapacity of a stupid few the partisans of the Greeks and Latins, called upon the scene, might suddenly be moved to sedition and warlike hostilities; for wariness is preeminently characteristic of the Greeks. Thus it could happen that the treasures which are visible here, deposited in safety, amount to more than those which had been visible there, left [on view] under conditions unsafe on account of disorders. From very many truthful men, even from Bishop Hugues of Laon, we had heard wonderful and almost incredible reports about the superiority of Hagia Sophia's and other churches' ornaments for the celebration of Mass. If this is so – or rather because we believe it to be so, by their testimony – then such inestimable and incomparable treasures should be exposed to the judgment of the many. *Let every man abound in his own sense.* To me, I confess, one thing has always seemed preeminently fitting: that every costlier or costliest thing should serve, first and foremost, for the administration of the Holy Eucharist. *If* golden pouring vessels, golden vials, golden little mortars used to serve, by the word of God or the command of the Prophet, to collect the *blood of goats or calves or the red heifer: how much more* must golden vessels, precious stones, and whatever is most valued among all created things, be laid out, with continual reverence and full devotion, for the reception of the *blood of Christ! Surely* neither we nor our possessions suffice for this service. If, by a new creation, our substance were re-formed from that of the holy Cherubim and Seraphim, it would still offer an insufficient and unworthy service for so great and so ineffable a victim; and yet we have so great a propitiation for our sins. The detractors also object that a saintly mind, a pure heart, a faithful intention ought to suffice for this sacred function; and we, too, explicitly and especially affirm that it is these that principally matter. [But] we profess that we must do homage also through the outward ornaments of sacred vessels, and to nothing in the world in an equal degree as to the service of the Holy Sacrifice, with all inner purity and with all outward splendour: For it behooves us most becomingly to serve Our Saviour in all things in a universal way – Him Who has not refused to provide for us in all things in a universal way and without any exception; Who has fused our nature with His into one admirable individuality; Who, *setting us on His right hand*, has promised us in truth *to possess His kingdom*; our Lord Who *liveth and reigneth for ever and ever.* (Ch. XXXIII, pp. 61, 63, 65, 67)

Source: *Abbot Suger, On the Abbey Church of St. Denis and Its Art Treasures*, ed. and trans. Erwin Panofsky, 2nd edn, ed. Gerda Panofsky-Soergel, Princeton, NJ, Princeton University Press, 1979.

8.3 Bernard of Clairvaux, from *On the Song of Songs II*

*St Bernard (1090–1153) was a Cistercian, Abbot of Clairvaux and an emi-
nent mystical theologian. In his sermons he developed the most famous of
the medieval allegorical interpretations of the* Song of Songs, *of Christ's
loving relationship with his Church and with the believing soul. The following provides a taste of his highly spiritualized interpretation, which, like his
friend William of St Thierry's, is, in fact, passionate doxology. In particular,
Bernard speaks of the soul's and of Christ's beauty.*

Sermon 45

'Behold how beautiful you are, my dearest, O how beautiful, your eyes are like
doves!' How beautifully said, how excellent. The bride's presumption springs
from her love, the Bridegroom's anger from his love. The circumstances prove
this. For correction followed the presumption, amendment the correction, and
reward the amendment. The master is gone, the king has disappeared, dignity is
put off, reverence is laid aside, only the Beloved is present. As love grows strong,
pride melts away. And just as Moses once spoke to God as a friend to a friend
and God answered him, so now the Word and the soul converse with mutual
enjoyment, like two friends. And no wonder. The two streams of their love have
but a single source from which they are equally sustained. Winged words honey-
sweet fly to and fro between them, and their eyes like heralds of holy love, betray
to each other their fullness of delight. He calls her his dearest one, proclaims her
beauty, repeats that proclamation, only to win a like response from her. It is no
idle repetition that gives firm assurance of love, and hints at something that
demands investigation.

   Let us see what is meant by the soul's twofold beauty, for that is what seems
to be intimated here. Humility is the soul's loveliness. This is not my opinion
merely, the Prophet has already said: 'Sprinkle me with hyssop and I shall be
cleansed,' symbolizing in this lowly herb the humility that purifies the heart. He
who was once both king and prophet trusts that this will wash him clean from
his grave offence, and give him back the snowy brightness of his innocence. But
though we are attracted by the humility of one who has gravely sinned, we may
not admire it. If, however, a man retains an innocence now graced with humility,
do you not think that his soul is endowed with loveliness? Mary never lost her
holiness, yet she did not lack humility; and so the king desired her loveliness,
because she joined humility to innocence. As she said: 'He looked graciously
upon the lowliness of his handmaid.' Happy then are those who keep their
garments clean, who guard their simplicity and innocence, but on condition that
they strive for the loveliness of humility. One so endowed will hear words like
these: 'Behold, how beautiful you are my dearest, O how beautiful.' Lord Jesus,
if only you would once say to my soul: 'How beautiful you are.' Safeguard
my humility! For I have poorly kept my robe of innocence. I am your servant. I

cannot presume to profess myself your friend, for I fail to hear your voice repeat its witness to my beauty. It would be enough for me to hear it even once. But what if this too should be questionable: I know what I will do: servant though I am I shall have recourse to her who is the friend. In my dwarfish ugliness I shall be filled with wonder by her multiform loveliness; I shall rejoice at the voice of the Bridegroom as he too marvels at a beauty so great. Who knows but I may so find favour in the eyes of the bride, and with her support be numbered among the friends. Then as the Bridegroom's friend I shall stand and experience the greatest joy at hearing the Bridegroom's voice, the voice that is meant for the ear of his beloved. Let us listen and be glad. They are present to each other, they speak together. Let us also attend; no worldly cares, no carnal pleasures must distract us from this conversation.

'Behold, how beautiful you are, my dearest,' he said, 'how beautiful.' 'Behold', is an expression of his admiration; the rest, his praise. And how worthy of admiration she is, in whom not the loss but the preservation of holiness fostered humility. Rightly too is this beauty praised twice over, since she lacked neither of the two sources of beauty. This is a rare bird on earth, where neither innocence is lost nor humility excluded by innocence. Consequently she who retained both is truly blessed. The proof is that though conscious of no fault she did not reject the connection. We, when we sin gravely, can scarcely tolerate reproof; she on the contrary listens with equanimity to bitter reprimands, and does not sin. . . . What he actually says is: 'Behold, how beautiful you are.' And he repeats this encomium to show that the grace of humility is joined to the glory of holiness: 'Behold, how beautiful you are, my dearest, how beautiful.' Now I know that you are beautiful, not merely because of my love for you but also because of your humility. I am not now praising your beauty among women nor the beauty of your cheeks and neck as I have previously done. I make no comparison of your beauty, nor qualification nor any other distinction. I speak of your beauty as such. (para. 1–3, pp. 232–4)

The bride speaks in her turn: 'Behold, how beautiful you are, my love, how beautiful.' See how she takes her stand on the heights, see how her loftiest aspirations reach into the heavens, how with a personal right she claims as her beloved him who is Lord of the universe. Take note that she does not simply say 'love', but 'my love', as if insisting on a special prerogative. A tremendous vision indeed that endows her with such confidence and prestige that she greets this Lord of all things not as her lord but as her beloved. For I believe that in this vision images of his flesh, or of the cross, or in any way suggestive of physical frailty, were not imprinted on her imagination, since the Prophet tells us that under these forms he possessed neither beauty nor majesty. But as she now contemplates him, she declares him both beautiful and majestic, making it clear that her present vision transcended all others. He speaks to her face to face as once he spoke to Moses, and she for her part sees God plainly, not through riddles and symbols. Her words declare what her mind perceives in that sublime vision so full of delight. Her eyes beheld the king in his beauty, though to her he was not king but her beloved. One man has seen him sitting on a lofty and exalted throne, another testifies that he appeared to him face to face; but for me this vision of the bride surpasses them, for there we read that he was seen as Lord, here as the beloved. One text runs: 'I saw the Lord seated on a high and lofty throne'; another: 'I have seen God face to face and yet my life is preserved.' But he says: 'If I am a master, where is my fear?' If the revelation accorded to them was accompanied by fear, since where the Lord is there too is fear of him, I for my part, given the choice should embrace with greater willingness and love the vision seen by the bride, because it comes about through a more wonderful passion, that of love. For to fear is to expect punishment, but perfect love casts out fear. There is a vast difference between him who appears so terrible in his deeds among men, and him who surpasses men in beauty of form. 'Behold, you are beautiful, my beloved, truly lovely.' These words are vibrating with love, not fear.

But perhaps you are thinking and asking yourselves with increasing doubt: 'How can the words of the Word be spoken to the soul and those of the soul to the Word, so that she hears his voice telling her that she is beautiful, and she in return offers a similar compliment to him? How can this happen? It is not the word that speaks, it is we who speak the word. So too, the soul has no means of uttering speech unless the body's mouth forms and speaks the words.' It is a good question; but take note that it is the Spirit who speaks, and whatever is said must be spiritually understood. So whenever you hear or read that the Word and the soul converse together, and contemplate each other, do not imagine them speaking with human voices nor appearing in bodily form. Listen, this is rather what you must think about it: The Word is a spirit, the soul is a spirit; and they possess their own mode of speech and mode of presence in accord with their nature. The speech of the Word is loving kindness, that of the soul, the fervour of devotion. The soul without devotion is a speechless infant that can never enjoy such intercourse with the Word. But when the Word addresses such a soul, desiring to speak to it, that soul cannot but hear, for 'the word of God is living and active, sharper than any two-edged sword, piercing to the division of soul and spirit'. And again when the soul decides to speak, much less can the Word hide from it, not merely because he is present everywhere, but rather because without his inspiration the soul will lack the devotion that urges speech.

When the Word therefore tells the soul, 'You are beautiful', and calls it friend, he infuses into it the power to love, and to know it is loved in return. And when the soul addresses him as beloved and praises his beauty, she is filled with admiration for his goodness and attributes to him without subterfuge or deceit the grace by which she loves and is loved. The Bridegroom's beauty is his love of the bride, all the greater in that it existed before hers. Realizing then that he was her lover before he was her beloved, she cries out with strength and ardour that she must love him with her whole heart and with words expressing deepest affection. The speech of the Word is an infusion of grace, the soul's response is wonder and thanksgiving. The more she feels surpassed in her loving the more she gives in love; and her wonder grows when he still exceeds her. Hence, not satisfied to tell him once that he is beautiful, she repeats the word, to signify by that repetition the pre-eminence of his beauty.

Again, this repetition may have expressed her admiration at the beauty in each of Christ's natures, the beauty of nature and the beauty of grace. How beautiful you appear to the angels, Lord Jesus, in the form of God, eternal, begotten before the daystar amid the splendours of heaven, 'the radiant light of God's glory and the perfect copy of his nature', the unchanging and untarnished brightness of eternal life? How beautiful you are to me, my Lord, even in the very discarding of your beauty! When you divested yourself of the native radiance of the unfailing light, then your kindness was thrown into relief, your love shone out more brightly, your grace was wider in its sweep. Star out of Jacob, how brilliant your rising above me! How fair the flower, as you spring from the root of Jesse! How pleasant your light as you come to me in darkness, rising from on high! How stupendous, how admirable in the sight of the angelic hosts, is your conception from the Holy Spirit, your birth from the Virgin, your sinless life, your wealth of doctrine, your glorious miracles, your revelation of mysteries. And how you rose from the heart of the earth, gleaming after your setting, Sun of Righteousness! And finally, with robes of splendour, how you ascended to the heights of heaven, the King of Glory! Because of all these marvels shall not all my bones cry out: Lord who is like you? (para. 6–9, pp. 236–9)

Source: *Cistercian Fathers Series, no. 7, The Works of Bernard of Clairvaux, vol. 3, On the Song of Songs II*, trans. Kilian Walsh, OCSO, Kalamazoo, Michigan, Cistercian Publications, London/Oxford, Mowbray, 1976.

8.4 Francis of Assisi, *The Praises of God* and *The Canticle of the Creatures*

One of the most cherished saints in the history of the Church due to his simple, exemplary life, Francis (1181/2–1226), founder of the Franciscan order, here gives praise to God in poetic form. He uses imagery from the realm of creation and includes both female and male metaphors.

The Praises of God

Thou are the holy Lord God Who does wonderful things.
You are strong. You are great. You are the most high.
You are the almighty king. You holy Father,
King of heaven and earth.

You are three and one, the Lord God of gods;
You are the good, all good, the highest good,
Lord God living and true.

You are love, charity; You are wisdom, You are humility,
You are patience, You are beauty, You are meekness,
You are security, You are rest,
You are gladness and joy, You are our hope, You are justice,
You are moderation, You are all our riches to sufficiency.

You are beauty, You are meekness,
You are the protector, You are our custodian and defender,
You are strength, You are refreshment. You are our hope,
You are our faith, You are our charity,
You are all our sweetness, You are our eternal life:
Great and wonderful Lord, Almighty God, Merciful Saviour.

(p. 109)

The Canticle of the Creatures

Most High, all-powerful, good Lord,
    Yours are the praises, the glory, and the honour, and all blessing,
To You alone, Most High, do they belong,
    and no human is worthy to mention Your name.
Praised be You, my Lord, with all Your creatures,
    especially Sir Brother Sun,
    Who is the day and through whom You give us light.
And he is beautiful and radiant with great splendour;
    and bears a likeness of You, Most High One.
Praised be You, my Lord, through Sister Moon and the stars,
    in heaven You formed them clear and precious and beautiful.
Praised be You, my Lord, through Brother Wind,
    and through the air, cloudy and serene, and every kind of weather,
    through whom You give sustenance to Your creatures.
Praised be You, my Lord, through Sister Water,
    who is very useful and humble and precious and chaste.
Praised be You, my Lord, through Brother Fire,
    through whom You light the night,
    and he is beautiful and playful and robust and strong.
Praised be You, my Lord, through our Sister Mother Earth,
    who sustains and governs us,
    and who produces various fruit with coloured flowers and herbs.
Praised be You, my Lord through those who give pardon for Your love,
    and bear infirmity and tribulation.

Blessed are those who endure peace
  for by You, Most High, shall they be crowned.
Praised be You, my Lord, through our Sister Bodily Death,
  From whom no one living can escape.
  Woe to those who die in mortal sin.
  Blessed are those whom death will find in Your most holy will,
  For the second death shall do them no harm.
Praise and bless my Lord and give Him thanks
  And serve Him with great humility.

(pp. 113–14)

Source: *Francis of Assisi, Early Documents, vol. 1*, ed. Regis J. Armstrong, J. A. Wayne Hellmann and William J. Short, New York, New City Press, 1999.

8.5 Thomas Aquinas, from *Summa Theologiae, Religion and Worship (2a2æ. 80–91)*

Aquinas asserts that we need to praise God vocally in song. Yet, he is quick to point out that one might merely take pleasure in the music itself. Rather music ought to lead to devotion. Moreover, he places teaching and preaching above singing in encouraging devotion and he advises that those involved in teaching and preaching should refrain from singing.

ST, 2a2æ. q. 91. *use of God's name in prayer or praise* . . . a I. *should God be praised vocally?* . . . Hence: 1. We may speak of God in two ways. First, in regard to his essence, and as such he is incomprehensible, ineffable, and above all praise. In this respect we owe him the reverence and honour of religious worship, as Jerome's translation of Psalm 64 indicates. Secondly, we may speak of God in so far as he effects our good, and in this respect we owe him praise, as it is written, *The favours of the Lord I will recall, I will praise the Lord for all things he has done for us.* Moreover, Dionysius says, *You will find that all sacred hymns, that is, divine praise, are directed to the processions within the Godhead and to show-ing forth and praising the names of God.* 2. Vocal praise is useless if it does not come from the heart, for one should praise God while meditating with affection upon his glorious works. Vocal praise, however, arouses the interior affection of the one praising and prompts others to praise God, as explained above. 3. We praise God, not for his benefit, but for ours, as stated above.

a. 2 *should songs be used in praising God?* . . . Hence: 1. The name spiritual canticle may be applied not only to those sung in the spirit, but also to those that are vocal in so far as they arouse spiritual devotion. 2. Jerome does not condemn singing absolutely, but he corrects those who sing theatrically, or who sing not in order to arouse devotion but to show off or to provoke pleasure. Hence Augustine says, *When it happens that I am more moved by the voice than the words sung, I confess to have sinned, and then I would rather not hear the singer.* 3. Arousing men to devotion through preaching and teaching is a more excellent way than through singing. Deacons and prelates, therefore, who lead souls to God through preaching and teaching should not be involved in singing lest they neglect greater things. Hence Gregory says, *It is a most discreditable custom for those who have been raised to the diaconate to serve as choristers, for it behoves them to give their whole time to the duty of preaching and to taking charge of alms.* 4. As Aristotle says, *Teaching should not be accompanied by the flute or any artificial instrument such as the harp, or anything of this kind, but only with such things as foster attentive listeners.* Musical instruments usually move the soul to pleasure rather than create a good disposition in it. In the Old Testament instruments of this kind were used both because the people were more coarse and carnal, so that they needed to be aroused by such instruments as well as with promises of temporal wealth, and because these instruments presaged the future. 5. The soul is distracted from the meaning of a song when it is sung merely to arouse pleasure. But if one sings out of devotion, he pays more attention to the content and meaning, both because he lingers more on the words, and because, as Augustine says, *each affection of our spirit, according to its variety, has its own appropriate measure in the voice and singing, by some hidden correspondence wherewith it is stirred.* The same is true of the hearers, for even if they do not understand what is sung, they understand why it is sung, namely, for God's honour, and this is enough to arouse their devotion. (pp. 245, 247, 249, 251)

Source: *Summa Theologiae, vol. 39, Religion and Worship (2a2æ. 80–91)*, ed. Kevin D. O'Rourke, OP, London, Blackfriars, 1964.

Part 3

The Reformation

— —

Introduction

Unlike the two previous sections, each of which span several centuries, this section focuses on the sixteenth century only, the period of the Reformation.

The fundamental changes that affected the Church and theology during this time are also reflected in the area of theological aesthetics. The central issue in this context is the theology of the image, in particular, idolatry and iconoclasm. Although each of the major Reformers commented on this subject, the responses were far from univocal. While one might assume that the Reformers shared the same opinions on the matter, this is not the true picture. In fact, a glance around older and more modern church buildings of different denominations will provide us with a general idea of the various views adopted and developed by Luther, Zwingli and Calvin.

In most Lutheran church buildings, works of art are quite liberally displayed: candles on the altar, often an imposing crucifix or at least a cross in the sanctuary over or behind the altar. The church may have stained glass as well as ornate architecture and interior design. One might also find statues and sculptures of predominantly biblical figures. One might even come across exhibitions of contemporary art. Compared to a Roman Catholic church interior, the only definite differences are the tabernacle, sanctuary lamp, and Stations of the Cross. There is also a greater emphasis on Marian veneration in Catholic places of worship. A somewhat similar scenario is evident in Anglican churches, even if there are significant differences between 'high church' interiors (more like Lutheran churches) and 'low church' buildings (more like Reformed churches). However, in Anglican churches statues and images are far less prevalent than in Lutheran or Roman Catholic places of worship. Reformed churches in the Calvinist tradition and Methodist churches are generally markedly different. These often strike the worshipper – at least those who do not belong to the Reformed tradition – as lacking in aesthetic appeal. Pictures and statues are absent, candles are few, crucifixes or crosses are largely absent, too. While the buildings, especially older ones, might convey an atmosphere of austere grandeur, the stark, 'puritan' interiors are of lesser appeal to the aesthetic eye. What truly matters here is the word of God, the word preached and heard by the congregation.

This is, of course, a very brief and general account within the scope of our introduction. That there are notable exceptions, whether in Lutheran, Anglican, Roman Catholic, or Reformed churches, shall not be disputed or denied. The intention is merely to create something of an impression of the various kinds of liturgical places and their interiors. To this day the spaces of worship reflect more or less directly the theological aesthetics of each Reformer and of the Council of Trent. It must be said, however, that in the latter half of the twentieth century with Vatican II and the ecumenical movement, and with the rapid development in recent years of the dialogue between theology and the arts, the churches now hold more ideas in common with regard to furnishings, aesthetics, etc. (see also Part 5).

The Reformation concerns included the place of images and relics and the role of the saints in the Church. Given that the veneration of these was very much part of church life – sometimes in an exaggerated fashion – in the late Middle Ages, Luther *et al* saw the need to tackle this issue. If one reads and compares the Reformers in this context, one is struck by the reasonable and tolerant approach Luther adopted. For Luther images are basically a 'small matter'. Justification through grace by faith was his primary concern. And yet, these topics are interrelated. He points out that the worst misuse is not the veneration of images but believers placing 'images in churches because they think they are thereby doing a good work and a service to God'. It is not the presence of images that Luther attacks, but the spirit and reason by which they are installed. This, of course, connects with his overall concern that the Christian is saved through grace alone. For Luther visual images 'are neither good nor bad'. They are 'unnecessary and we are free to have them or not, although it would be much better if we did not have them at all'. He even asserts that they may be of considerable benefit in preaching and teaching the good news, i.e. as educational tools. He attacks the 'papists' but also at least as strongly, his fellow Wittenberg Reformer Karlstadt and the 'heavenly prophets' who had started to destroy images in churches in Wittenberg during his absence: 'To have images is not wrong . . . we cannot prove it right to mutilate and burn them . . .' Therefore images of the saints and of Christ and crucifixes should be allowed as long as they are not worshipped but used 'for memorial and witness'. Works of art, he notes, can also be used for pleasure and decoration. Karlstadt, on the other hand, wanted to have statues and works of art in churches destroyed. Luther countered that Karlstadt failed to get rid of the *true* idols, the idols *of the heart*. These *inner* idols we create and desire for ourselves – mammon, power, good works as means of securing a place in heaven – these are the really dangerous idols we need to destroy. The outward material images are not the real issue, but the false images and idols in the heart. This, one would argue, is Luther's most important observation on this issue and still valid. We may have images, but, as Luther notes, one's trust must not be in them but in God alone. He concludes: 'If it is not a sin but good to have the image of Christ in my heart, why should it be a sin to have it in my eyes?'

In this context it is worth remembering that Luther's and Melanchton's Reformation aims were significantly supported by the painter Lucas Cranach and his workshop. The famous Reformation altarpiece by Cranach in the town church in Wittenberg bears testimony to the Reformers' ideas of what it means to be the true Church: the preaching of, and faith in, the crucified Christ, and the proper administration of the sacraments.

Huldrych Zwingli did not only fall out with Luther over different understandings of the Eucharist; his ideas on images were also far more extreme than Luther's. Zwingli's arguments are strongly biblically based, in particular on the Hebrew Testament. He asserts that 'images are forbidden by God' and that everyone ought to learn that they should be abolished: 'If one has them in a church then one has already given them honour.' He rejects them as teaching aids and insists that we 'should be taught solely by the word of God'. Like Luther, he rightly notes that the 'idle priests' failed to do their duty in teaching the 'poor simple people'. Thus the faithful had been led to trust in images instead. While his views were appropriate he, nevertheless, remained one-sided as he gave no credit to the positive role images can play. Zwingli ordered the systematic destruction of images and statues in the Minster in Zürich in 1524.

Jean Calvin, less than a generation after Luther, formulates his views on images and art in a detailed discourse in *The Institutes of the Christian Religion* (1539). While Luther wrote in response to the issues of his day, Calvin's method and treatment are far more systematic. However, despite his more 'academic' approach, one is almost taken aback by his, at times, intensely emotional, polemical, aggressive, and even condescending tone. He, like Zwingli and Luther, argues from a biblical perspective and also comments on the views of the early doctors of the church. Like Zwingli, Calvin rejects any presence of images in churches 'for God himself is the sole and proper witness of himself'. He considers it 'brute stupidity' to 'pant after visible figures of God'. Images are 'contrary to Scripture' and he, like Zwingli, laments that had the Church fulfilled its duty to educate the faithful properly, they would not have been fed this 'trash'. The use of images leads to superstition and idolatry, and he adds that it was 'the vulgar sort' who defended images as mediating the invisible presence of a saint or of Christ through a visible object. He thus refutes the whole iconodule tradition since the days of John of Damascus and Theodore of Studios. Calvin denigrates the arguments of the Council of Nicaea (787) as 'childish' and comments that John of Damascus and the Eastern theologians did not really make the distinction between *latria* (worship) and *dulia* (veneration), as they had claimed. In a passage on the 'functions and limits of art', he makes one concession. Paintings and sculptures as 'gifts of God' are permissible, but only when those things 'which the eyes are capable of seeing' are painted and sculpted. Hence depictions of historical events, landscape or of the human body are allowed either for teaching purposes or for pleasure. It is interesting to note that this is precisely what happened with the Reformation in the Low Countries. Religious images were abandoned for genre subjects, still life and historical painting. Yet, in many of these non-religious works, distinctly moral messages, such as the symbolical inclusion of the seven deadly sins, were retained and developed.

The Council of Trent, in its response to the Reformers, reiterated mainly what the Second Council of Nicaea had affirmed about 800 years earlier. Those responsible for teaching the Catholic faith were to 'instruct the faithful diligently' regarding the saints, relics and images. Unlike the Reformers, the Council encouraged the invocation of saints and a proper honouring of relics. Those who deny the honour due to relics of the saints should be 'condemned absolutely'. Further, the veneration of images of holy persons was to be 'preserved'. The Council clearly points out that the honour is paid to the 'original subjects', not to the material image.

Aside from the pervading issue of images, there are a few other noteworthy aspects pertaining to theological aesthetics in the Reformation period. Pannenberg, among others, has remarked that all theology is ultimately doxology. This is true, yet at times the element of praising the divine is more pronounced than at others. Luther's contribution to, and espousal of, music as a means of doxology was to be significant for the whole development of liturgical life and the musical tradition in Protestant churches. Not only did Luther play the lute and compose hymns, but he wrote about music on several occasions, noting that 'next to the Word of God, music deserves the highest praise'. The human being ought to praise God through 'word and music'. He describes music in the highest terms 'as the excellent gift of God', and in the face of its 'diversity and magnitude of its virtue' he finds himself unable to conceive of sufficient words of praise.

The theme of doxology leads us to two other writers in the rather different location and situation of Spain, the famous mystics and Carmelites, Teresa of Avila and John of the Cross. Teresa of Avila wrote of her vision of Christ's face and hands and marvelled at their overwhelming, glorious beauty. She emphasizes the great fear and confusion it caused her and also that it is impossible to truly describe that vision without destroying it. At the same time, she finds – as a woman who was led to deeply doubt her own intellectual powers – that she needs to defend herself against her male confessors asserting that this is a *genuine* vision. It is clear from the text included here that her confessors told her that purely 'intellectual', 'imageless' visions were superior to hers. However, Teresa's vision of the beauty of Christ serves as one more example of the rich intellect, imagination and visionary life of important mystics and theologians of the Middle Ages and beyond, ranging from Hadewijch and Hildegard of Bingen, to Julian of Norwich and Meister Eckhart.

John of the Cross, who excelled as a mystical poet, maintained that the believer's finding of God's Spirit begins with God leading her or him through 'visions, forms, images and other sensitive and spiritual knowledge' to Godself. Spiritual 'goods' thus can be conveyed through the senses. Yet, John emphasizes that these are only initial steps; the more the soul approaches God, the more detached the individual will become from the realm of the senses. He concludes that 'the perfect spirit pays no attention to the senses; it neither receives anything through them, nor uses them principally, nor judges them to be requisite in its relationship with God, as it did before its spiritual growth'. He repeatedly insists that the mature believer must ultimately renounce the senses so as to concentrate wholly on the supernatural and the spiritual. Despite his wonderful poetry – abundant with images, enthusiasm and passion – and his in part positive evaluation of the senses, images and the imagination, this mystic's view therefore remained essentially attached to the traditional dualistic view of mind and body.

Theologically, the sixteenth century was one of the most important and tension-filled in Christian history. This brief introduction and the following selection of texts, it is hoped, will bring out the diversity of thought among theologians of the time, especially on the most central issue in relation to theological aesthetics, iconoclasm.

9

The Role of Images

— —

9.1.1 Martin Luther, from *Receiving Both Kinds in the Sacrament (1522)*

The short extract clearly states Luther's view of images. Luther (1483–1546), founder of the Reformation, defended his views on images against Catholics on the one hand and the Reformer Karlstadt and his followers on the other. Luther opines that images are to be tolerated in churches, but they are not to be worshipped.

Some people have treated the images shamefully, without the knowledge or consent of their rulers and teachers. They really deserve a stiff punishment. But let Satan be Satan; we will address ourselves to the main subject. To have images is not wrong. God himself in the Old Testament commanded the bronze serpent to be lifted up [Num 21.8–9], and the cherubim to be placed on the golden ark [Exod 25.18]. But the worship of images God has forbidden [Exod 20.5]. It is true that they are dangerous, and I wish there were none of them on the altars. But we cannot prove it right to mutilate and burn them instead of tolerating them. I shall give you my reason for saying this: The devil and his papists want to appear quite nice, and to have done nothing wrong. Now if you argue that images are being greatly misused and therefore we should have none of them but should mutilate and burn them, they will say: We do not misuse them. And how will you refute them? They will point out that women and wine are also dangerous things and are being misused, and what is there that is not being misused? They will say that you have slandered not the misuse, however, but the images themselves, which could conceivably be used in a proper way. What will you say to this? You see, in this way they will have caught you. And if they break off a single leaf they will claim to have won the entire forest, for they are hungry and watching closely for each opportunity. So we must be wise in our struggle with the pretty devil. We must permit the images to remain, but preach vigorously against the wrong use of them. We must preach not merely against this particular misuse or danger, the worshipping of images. That is a very small matter.

(And they would probably say you are crazy to accuse people of worshipping stone and wood.) But we must preach against the worst misuse of all, of which the papists are guilty to overflowing. I refer to the fact that they place images in the churches because they think they are thereby doing a good work and a service to God. Of course none of them would acknowledge such disbelief, even though it must be present in the heart where real Christian faith is lacking. You see, with a word like that you have quickly done more damage to the images than all the world can do with rifles and swords. When the common man learns that it is not a service to God to place images in the churches, he will cease doing it of his own accord without your insistence. He will have pictures painted on the walls only because he likes them or for decoration or some other reason that does not involve sin. How did we ever get into this predicament, that men should forbid us to do what God has not forbidden, particularly they who are struggling against human teachings and ordinances? (pp. 258–60)

Source: *Luther's Works, vol. 38, Word and Sacrament II*, trans. and ed. Abdel Ross Wentz, general ed. Helmut T. Lehmann, Philadelpia, Fortress Press, 1959.

9.1.2 Martin Luther, from *A Sermon Preached by Martin Luther, Ecclesiastes (Wednesday 12 March 1522)*

Luther here reiterates the freedom of having or not having images.

Therefore, I have to admit that the images cannot help by themselves; they are neither good nor bad; we can have them or not have them. . . . For I cannot deny that there might be a man who uses images rightly. If I were asked, I should have to admit that images do not anger me [as such]. If there were only one man on earth who used images rightly, the devil would immediately urge against me: Why, oh why do you condemn that which may be used rightly? He would then have achieved his triumph and I would have to concede it. He should not have got nearly so far if I had been here. He drove us into this pride. But the word of God is not discredited. You meant to blacken the devil and forgot charcoal and took chalk instead. Therefore it is necessary to know the Scriptures well and to use them at the right time if one sets out to fence with the devil etc. (pp. 41–2)

Source: Helga Robinson-Hammerstein, *Faith, Force and Freedom, Translation of the Fourth Invocavit Sermon & Introduction*, A Navicula Publication, Dublin, Trinity College, School of History, 2001.

9.1.3 Martin Luther, from *Against the Heavenly Prophets in the Matter of Images and Sacraments (1525)*

Written three years after his Invocavit Sermons, this refutation of the followers of Karlstadt and of the enthusiasts is a more systematic discussion of images. The fundamental issue for Luther is the distinction between external images and internalized idols worshipped in the heart. If they are used in proper fashion for remembering Christ, Mary and the saints, images are to be tolerated. As a means of proclaiming the gospel images are welcome.

On the Destruction of Images I approached the task of destroying images by first tearing them out of the heart through God's Word and making them worthless and despised. This indeed took place before Dr Karlstadt ever dreamed of destroying images. For when they are no longer in the heart, they can do no harm when seen with the eyes. But Dr Karlstadt, who pays no attention to matters of the heart, has reversed the order by removing them from sight and leaving them in the heart. For he does not preach faith, nor can he preach it; unfortunately, only now do I see that. Which of these two forms of destroying images is best, I will let each man judge for himself. For where the heart is instructed that one pleases God alone through faith, and that in the matter of images nothing that is pleasing to him takes place, but is a fruitless service and effort, the people themselves willingly drop it, despise images, and have none made. But where one neglects such instruction and forces the issue, it follows that those blaspheme who do not understand and who act only because of the coercion of the law and not with a free conscience. Their idea that they can please God with works becomes a real idol and a false assurance in the heart. Such legalism results in putting away outward images while filling the heart with idols. I say this so that everyone may see the kind of a spirit that is lodged in Karlstadt. He blames me for protecting images contrary to God's Word, though he knows that I seek to tear them out of the hearts of all and want them despised and destroyed. It is only that I do not approve of his wanton violence and impetuosity. (pp. 84–5)

The meaning is not that I wish to defend images, as has been sufficiently indicated. Rather murderous spirits are not to be permitted to create sins and problems of conscience where none exist, and murder souls without necessity. For although the matter of images is a minor, external thing, when one seeks to burden the conscience with sin through it, as through the law of God, it becomes the most important of all. For it destroys faith, profanes the blood of Christ, blasphemes the gospel, and sets all that Christ has won for us at nought, so that this Karlstadtian abomination is no less effective in destroying the kingdom of Christ and a good conscience, than the papacy has become with its prohibitions regarding food and marriage, and all else that was free and without sin. For eating and drinking are also minor, external things. Yet to ensnare the conscience with laws in these matters is death for the soul. From this let every man note which of us two is the more Christian. I would release and free consciences and the souls from sin, which is a truly spiritual and evangelical pastoral function, while Karlstadt seeks to capture them with laws and burden them with sin without good cause. And yet he does this not with the law of God, but with his own conceit and mischief, so that he is not only far from the gospel, but also not even a Mosaic teacher. And yet he continually praises the 'Word of God, the Word of God', just as if it were therefore to become God's Word as soon as one could say the Word of God. Usually those who make great ado in praising God's Word do not have much to back them up, as unfortunately we have previously experienced under our papistic tyrants. However to speak evangelically of images, I say and declare that no one is obligated to break violently images even of God, but everything is free, and one does not sin if he does not break them with violence. One is obligated, however, to destroy them with the Word of God, that is, not with the law in a Karlstadtian manner, but with the gospel. This means to instruct and enlighten the conscience that it is idolatry to worship them, or to trust in them, since one is to trust alone in Christ. Beyond this let the external matters take their course. God grant that they may be destroyed, become dilapidated, or that they remain. It is all the same and makes no difference, just as when the poison has been removed from a snake. Now I say this to keep the conscience free from mischievous laws and fictitious sins, and not because I would defend images. Nor would I condemn those who have destroyed them, especially those who destroy divine and idolatrous images. But images for memorial and witness, such as crucifixes and images of saints, are to be tolerated. This is shown above to be the case even in the Mosaic law. And they are not only to be tolerated, but for the sake of the memorial and the witness they are praiseworthy and honourable, as the witness stones of Joshua [Josh 24.26] and of Samuel (1 Sam 7[.12]) (pp. 90–1)

Now we do not request more than that one permit us to regard a crucifix or a saint's image as a witness, for remembrance, as a sign as that image of Caesar was. Should it not be as possible for us without sin to have a crucifix or an image of Mary, as it was for the Jews and Christ himself to have an image of Caesar who, pagan and now dead, belonged to the devil? Indeed the Caesar had coined his image to glorify himself. However, we seek neither to receive nor give honour in this matter, and are yet so strongly condemned, while Christ's possession of such an abominable and shameful image remains uncondemned. (p. 96)

I have myself seen and heard the iconoclasts read out of my German Bible. I know that they have it and read out of it, as one can easily determine from the words they use. Now there are a great many pictures in those books, both of God, the angels, men and animals, especially in the Revelation of John and in Moses and Joshua. So now we would kindly beg them to permit us to do what they themselves do. Pictures contained in these books we would paint on walls for the sake of remembrance and better understanding, since they do no more harm on walls than in books. It is to be sure better to paint pictures on walls of how God created the world, how Noah built the ark, and whatever other good stories there may be, than to paint shameless worldly things. Yes, would to God that I could persuade the rich and the mighty that they would permit the whole Bible to be painted on houses, on the inside and outside, so that all can see it. That would be a Christian work. Of this I am certain, that God desires to have his works heard and read, especially the passion of our Lord. But it is impossible for me to hear and bear it in mind without forming mental images of it in my heart. For whether I will or not, when I hear of Christ, an image of a man hanging on a cross takes form in my heart, just as the reflection of my face naturally appears in the water when I look into it. If it is not a sin but good to have the image of Christ in my heart, why should it be a sin to have it in my eyes? This is especially true since the heart is more important than the eyes, and should be less stained by sin because it is the true abode and dwelling place of God. (pp. 99–100)

Source: *Luther's Works, vol. 40, Church and Ministry II*, trans. Bernhard Erling and Conrad Bergendoff, ed. Conrad Bergendoff, general ed. H. T. Lehmann, Philadelphia, Fortress Press, 1958.

9.2 Huldrych Zwingli, from *A Short Christian Instruction* (1523)

Zwingli (1484–1531) was a preacher and Reformer in Zürich. His strongly biblically based and rather extreme arguments concerning images differed from Luther. He categorically rejects the presence of any images in places of worship. Moreover, they must not be used as aids in teaching the Christian faith; the word of God alone will suffice.

Concerning images: it is reasonable for everyone to teach, as has been found, that images are forbidden by God – so that, after they have been instructed and strengthened, the unlearned and weak ones may soon accept what should be done with the images. For this purpose, the little book that recently came out, *On the Abolition of Images*, will serve well because it has much scriptural evidence. Whoever does not have this, let him read the following passages: Exodus 20.23 (at the end on the silver idols); Exodus 34.12–17; Leviticus 19.4; Leviticus 26.1; Deuteronomy 4.3, 23–28; Deuteronomy 5.7–9; 1 Samuel 7.3–6; Numbers 25.4f.; Deuteronomy 7.5, 25f.; Deuteronomy 11.16f.; Deuteronomy 13.6–18; Deuteronomy 27.15; Joshua 24.23; Judges 10.6–16; Psalm 96.5; Psalm 115.4–8; Isaiah 42.17; Isaiah 44.9–20; Jeremiah 10.2–16; Jeremiah 13.10; Ezekiel 14; Ezekiel 6; Micah 1.5–7; Habakkuk 2.18f.; II Kings 18.4, 33–35; II Kings 10.15–30; II Kings 23.4–23; II Chronicles 31.1–7; I Corinthians 5.10f.; Acts 15.20, 29; I Corinthians 8.4f.; I Corinthians 10.19–21; I Corinthians 12.2; Galatians 5.1, 20; I Thessalonians 1.9; I Peter 4.3; I John 5.21.

Of the passages noted, some forbid images or idols, some ridicule them, and some teach how one should abolish them. At the same time, however, one is to proceed carefully so that evil does not result. For until Christian people are instructed rightly, that one should not pay the images any honour, one may still have patience until the weak are also able to follow – so that the matter may be brought to a conclusion with unanimity. Some passages praise those who have got rid of images. Here some disagree in the following way: 'This command concerns only Jews and not Christians.' One should answer thus: the two parts, 'You shall not have foreign gods' [Exodus 20.3] and 'You shall have no image or likeness' [Exodus 20.4], are like a safeguard and explanation of the first commandment, 'You shall trust in one God.' Look at Deuteronomy 5.6, where God says: 'I am your Lord God, who has led you out of Egypt, etc.' Observe that this is the first commandment, wherein God has set himself forth as our God. Now he forbids the things which want to lead us away from him and says immediately thereafter, 'You shall not have other gods after me or in my sight' [Deut 5.7]. And that is a way through which the children of Israel were often led away – and we Christians the same. For whoever has sought help and confidence from a creature which the believer ought to seek only with God, has made a foreign god for himself. For that is forever one's god in which one takes refuge. Hence, that is one thing that may draw us from God: foreign gods. The other thing that may lead us away is images. For that reason, God forbids them first: 'You shall make no carved image, nor likeness or copy of the things which are in heaven, on the earth or in the water' [Deut 5.8]. See, one is simply not to make any. And if in some way we must have an image before us, as happened to Daniel and others in Daniel Chapter 3, then he says: 'You shall give them no honour' – neither genuflecting, bowing nor reverencing (for that is what the word *schahah* means), 'and render them no service either'. The Latin words also sufficiently point this out: 'You shall not worship them; also show them no honour.' If one has them in a church then one has already given the images honour. And, if one says 'I do not worship them; they teach and admonish me,' that is all a fable. God does not speak here of worship, which we want to understand: he is above that, for he knows well that no wise person worships an image. However, he forbids here all manifestations of honour, so that one may not bow, genuflect, kneel, light candles or burn incense before them. If one is not honouring them, then what are they doing on the altar? Indeed, one is honouring them no less than pagans do their images of idols when they have called them by the name of idols. We have done likewise. We name the pieces of wood with the names of the blessed. One piece of wood we name Our Lady and the Mother of God, the other we name St Nicholas, etc. And those who do this cry that we want to destroy the honour of the saints, but when they call idols by saints' names they are already dishonouring the saints. Moreover, it is also wrong that the pictures teach us. We should be taught solely by the word of God. Instead, the idle priests, who should have taught us unceasingly, have painted the teachings on the walls for us. And we poor simple people have therewith been deprived of the teaching and have fallen to images, and have honoured them. We have begun to seek from creatures what we should have sought only from God. And though they often should have taught us, they omitted teaching and held the Mass frequently instead. We simple ones have not understood the Mass, and also the majority of them also, until it has come to the point that by far the majority of Christian people have not known the essential point as to how a person is saved. Indeed, with their fables of the saints, some have pitiably turned us from the true word of God to the creature. But if one objects that images are not forbidden in the New Testament, this also is wrong. . . .

Now compare I John 5.21: 'Dear Children, be on your guard against images!' and other passages and see, therefore, whether or not images are also forbidden in the New Testament. Acts Chapter 15 is advice by the Christians at Jerusalem that Christians should be on guard against the defilement caused by images. Furthermore, if we say 'The saints' images show us what they have done and suffered so that we do likewise,' then one should ask us when our works are righteous. We must always say: if they are done in faith which is also the love for God, then they are pleasing to God according to I Corinthians Chapter 13. One asks us further: on what basis have the saints done such? We will say: out of true faith. Now let someone show us where they have painted or copied this faith. We cannot show it save in their hearts. Therefore it must always follow that we also must learn that faith is necessary in our hearts if we want to do anything pleasing to God. This we cannot learn from walls but only from the gracious pulling of God out of his own word. (pp. 68–70)

Source: *Huldrych Zwingli, Writings, vol. 2, In Search of True Religion: Reformation, Pastoral and Eucharistic Writings*, trans. H. Wayne Pipkin, Allison Park, PA, Pickwick Publications, 1984.

9.3 Jean Calvin, from *The Institutes of the Christian Religion*

Like Zwingli, Jean Calvin (1509–64), French theologian and second generation Reformer, differed in his radical iconoclasm from Luther. Calvin discusses the role of images at length. He disproves of any kind of use of images in sacred spaces. The only images allowed are those that picture visible objects, but only in the context of teaching or for pleasure. In parts his refutation is aggressive, polemical and condescending.

(It is unlawful to attribute a visible form to God, and generally whoever sets up idols revolts against the true God (Scriptural argument for rejecting images in worship)

We are forbidden every pictorial representation of God But as Scripture, having regard for men's rude and stupid wit, customarily speaks in the manner of the common folk, where it would distinguish the true God from the false it particularly contrasts him with idols. It does this, not to approve what is more subtly and elegantly taught by the philosophers, but the better to expose the world's folly, nay, madness, in searching for God when all the while each one clings to his own speculations. Therefore, that exclusive definition, encountered everywhere, annihilates all the divinity that men fashion for themselves out of their own opinion: for God himself is the sole and proper witness of himself. Meanwhile, since this brute stupidity gripped the whole world – to pant after visible figures of God, and thus to form gods of wood, stone, gold, silver, or other dead and corruptible matter – we must cling to this principle: God's glory is corrupted by an impious falsehood whenever any form is attached to him. Therefore in the law, after having claimed for himself alone the glory of deity, when he would teach what worship he approves or repudiates, God soon adds, 'You shall not make for yourself a graven image, nor any likeness' [Ex 20.4]. By these words he restrains our waywardness from trying to represent him by any visible image, and briefly enumerates all those forms by which superstition long ago began to turn his truth into falsehood. For we know that the Persians worshipped the sun; all the stars they saw in the heavens the stupid pagans also fashioned into gods for themselves. There was almost no animal that for the Egyptians was not the figure of a god. Indeed, the Greeks seemed to be wise above the rest, because they worshipped God in human form. But God does not compare these images with one another, as if one were more suitable, another less so; but without exception he repudiates all likenesses, pictures, and other signs by which the superstitious have thought he will be near them. (Book 1, Ch. 11, para. 1, pp. 99–100)

The doctors of the church, too, partly judged otherwise One ought, besides, to read what Lactantius and Eusebius have written concerning this matter, who do not hesitate to take as a fact that all whose images are seen were once mortals. Likewise, Augustine clearly declares that it is wrong not only to worship images but to set them up to God. Yet he says nothing else but what had been decreed many years before in the Council of Elvira, of which the thirty-sixth canon reads: 'It is decreed that there shall be no pictures in churches, that what is reverenced or adored be not depicted on the walls.' But especially memorable is what the same Augustine elsewhere cites from Varro, and confirms by his own subscription, that the first men to introduce statues of the gods 'removed fear and added error'. If Varro alone had said this, perhaps it would have had little authority, yet it deservedly ought to strike shame in us that a pagan man, groping so to speak in the dark, arrived at this light, that bodily images are unworthy of God's majesty because they diminish the fear of him in men and increase error. Facts themselves certainly testify that this was said no less truly than wisely; but Augustine, having borrowed from Varro, as it were, brings it forth from his own thought. And at the outset, indeed, he points out that the first errors concerning God in which men were entangled did not begin from images, but once this new element was added, errors multiplied. Next, he explains that the fear of God was diminished or even destroyed, because in the folly of images and in stupid and absurd invention his divinity could easily be despised. On the second of these points, would that we might not have experienced it to be so true! Whoever, therefore, desires to be rightly taught must learn what he should know of God from some other source than images.

The images of the papists are entirely inappropriate   Therefore, if the papists have any shame, let them henceforward not use this evasion, that pictures are the books of the uneducated, because it is plainly refuted by very many testimonies of Scripture. Even if I were to grant them this, yet they would not thus gain much to defend their idols. It is well known that they set monstrosities of this kind in place of God. The pictures or statues that they dedicate to saints – what are they but examples of the most abandoned lust and obscenity? If anyone wished to model himself after them, he would be fit for the lash. Indeed, brothels show harlots clad more virtuously and modestly than the churches show those objects which they wish to be thought images of virgins. For martyrs they fashion a habit not a whit more decent. Therefore let them compose their idols at least to a moderate decency, that they may with a little more modesty falsely claim that these are books of some holiness! *(There would be no 'uneducated' at all if the church had done its duty.)* But then we shall also answer that this is not the method of teaching within the sacred precincts believing folk, whom God wills to be instructed there with a far different doctrine than this trash. In the preaching of his Word and sacred mysteries he has bidden that a common doctrine be there set forth for all. But those whose eyes rove about in contemplating idols betray that their minds are not diligently intent upon this doctrine. Therefore, whom, then, do the papists call uneducated whose ignorance allows them to be taught by images alone? Those, indeed, whom the Lord recognizes as his disciples, 'whom he honours by the revelation of his heavenly philosophy, whom he wills to be instructed in the saving mysteries of his Kingdom. I confess, as the matter stands, that today there are not a few who are unable to do without such 'books'. But whence, I pray you, this stupidity if not because they are defrauded of that doctrine which alone was fit to instruct them? Indeed, those in authority in the church turned over to idols the office of teaching for no other reason than that they themselves were mute. Paul testifies that by the true preaching of the gospel 'Christ is depicted before our eyes as crucified' [Gal 3.1 p.]. What purpose did it serve for so many crosses – of wood, stone, silver, and gold – to be erected here and there in churches, if this fact had been duly and faithfully taught: that Christ died on the cross to bear our curse [Gal 3.13], to expiate our sins by the sacrifice of his body [Heb 10.10], to wash them by his blood [Rev 1.5], in short, to reconcile us to God the Father [Rom 5.10]? From this one fact they could have learned more than from a thousand crosses of wood or stone. For perhaps the covetous fix their minds and eyes more tenaciously upon gold and silver than upon any word of God. (Book 1, Ch. 11, para. 6–7, pp. 105–7)

(*Origin of the use of images, and consequent corruption of worship, although sculpture and painting are gifts of God.*)

Any use of images leads to idolatry Adoration promptly follows upon this sort of fancy: for when men thought they gazed upon God in images, they also worshipped him in them. Finally, all men, having fixed their minds and eyes upon them, began to grow more brutish and to be overwhelmed with admiration for them, as if something of divinity inhered there. Now it appears that men do not rush forth into the cult of images before they have been imbued with some opinion too crass – not indeed that they regard them as gods, but because they imagine that some power of divinity dwells there. Therefore, when you prostrate yourself in veneration, representing to yourself in an image either a god or a creature, you are already ensnared in some superstition. For this reason, the Lord forbade not only the erection of statues constructed to represent himself but also the consecration of any inscriptions and stones that would invite adoration [Ex 20.25]. For the same reason, also, in the precept of the law a second part is subjoined concerning adoration. For just as soon as a visible form has been fashioned for God, his power is also bound to it. Men are so stupid that they fasten God wherever they fashion him; and hence they cannot but adore. And there is no difference whether they simply worship an idol, or God in the idol. It is always idolatry when divine honours are bestowed upon an idol, under whatever pretext this is done. . . . Moreover, they daily consecrated new images, yet did not believe themselves to be making new gods. 'Read the excuses that Augustine refers to as having been pretended by the idolaters of his own age: when they were accused, the vulgar sort replied that they were not worshipping that visible object but a presence that dwelt there invisibly. Those who were of what he called 'purer religion' stated that they were worshipping neither the likeness nor the spirit; but that through the physical image they gazed upon the sign of the thing that they ought to worship. What then? All idolaters, whether Jews or pagans, were motivated just as has been said. Not content with spiritual understanding, they thought that through the images a surer and closer understanding would be impressed upon them. Once this perverse imitation of God pleased them, they never stopped until, deluded by new tricks, they presently supposed that God manifested his power in images. In these images, nevertheless, the Jews were convinced that they were worshipping the eternal God, the one true Lord of heaven and earth; the pagans, that they were worshipping their gods whom, though false, they imagined as dwelling in heaven.

Image worship in the church Those who assert that this was not done heretofore, and within our memory is still not being done, lie shamelessly. For why do they prostrate themselves before these things? Why do they, when about to pray, turn to them as if to God's ears? Indeed, what Augustine says is true, that no one thus gazing upon an image prays or worships without being so affected that he thinks he is heard by it, or hopes that whatever he desires will be bestowed upon him. Why is there so much difference among the images of the same God, that one is passed over or honoured in a common manner, but upon another is bestowed every solemn honour? Why do they tire themselves out with votive pilgrimages to see images whose like they have at home? Why do they take up the sword to defend these images today as if they were altars and hearth fires, even to the point of butchery and carnage, and more easily bear being deprived of the one God than of their idols? Nevertheless, I do not yet enumerate the crass errors of the multitude, which are well-nigh infinite, and which occupy the hearts of almost all men; I am only indicating what they profess when they especially wish to exculpate themselves of idolatry. We do not call them 'our gods', they say. Neither did Jews nor pagans of old so speak of them, and yet the prophets did not hesitate repeatedly to accuse them of fornications with wood and stone [Jer 2.27; Ezek 6.4ff.; cf. Isa 4.19–20; Hab 2.18–19; Deut 32.37] only for doing the very things that are daily done by those who wish to be counted Christians, namely, that they carnally venerated God in wood and stone. (Book 1, Ch. 11, para. 9–10, pp. 109–11)

The functions and limits of art And yet I am not gripped by the superstition of thinking absolutely no images permissible. But because sculpture and painting are gifts of God, I seek a pure and legitimate use of each, lest those things which the Lord has conferred upon us for his glory and our good be not only polluted by perverse misuse but also turned to our destruction. We believe it wrong that God should be represented by a visible appearance, because he himself has forbidden it [Ex 20.4] and it cannot be done without some defacing of his glory. And lest they think us alone in this opinion, those who concern themselves with their writings will find that all well-balanced writers have always disapproved of it. If it is not right to represent God by a physical likeness, much less will we be allowed to worship it as God, or God in it. Therefore it remains that only those things are to be sculptured or painted which the eyes are capable of seeing: let not God's majesty, which is far above the perception of the eyes, be debased through unseemly representations. Within this class some are histories and events, some are images and forms of bodies without any depicting of past events. The former have some use in teaching or admonition; as for the latter, I do not see what they can afford other than pleasure. And yet it is clear that almost all the images that until now have stood in churches were of this sort. From this, one may judge that these images had been called forth not out of judgment or selection but of foolish and thoughtless craving. I am not saying how wickedly and indecently the greater part of them have been fashioned, how licentiously the painters and sculptors have played the wanton here – a matter that I touched upon a little earlier. I only say that even if the use of images contained nothing evil, it still has no value for teaching.

As long as doctrine was pure and strong, the church rejected images But setting aside this distinction, let us in passing examine if it is expedient to have in Christian churches any images at all – whether they represent past events or the bodies of men. First, if the authority of the ancient church moves us in any way, we will recall that for about five hundred years, during which religion was still flourishing, and a purer doctrine thriving, Christian churches were commonly empty of images. Thus, it was when the purity of the ministry had somewhat degenerated that they were first introduced for the adornment of churches. I shall not discuss what reason impelled those who were the first authors of this thing; but if you compare age with age, you will see that these innovations had much declined from the integrity of those who had done without images. Why? Are we to think that those holy fathers would have allowed the church to go for so long without something they adjudged useful and salutary? Of course it was because they saw in it either no usefulness or very little, but very much danger, that they repudiated it out of deliberation and reason, rather than overlooked it out of ignorance or negligence. . . . And by the dreadful madness that has heretofore occupied the world almost to the total destruction of godliness, we have experienced too much how the ensign of idolatry is, as it were, set up, as soon as images are put together in churches. For men's folly cannot restrain itself from falling headlong into superstitious rites. But even if so much danger were not threatening, when I ponder the intended use of churches, somehow or other it seems to me unworthy of their holiness for them to take on images other than those living and symbolical ones which the Lord has consecrated by his Word. I mean Baptism and the Lord's Supper, together with other rites by which our eyes must be too intensely gripped and too sharply affected to seek other images forged by human ingenuity. Behold the incomparable boon of images, for which there is no substitute, if we are to believe the papists!

Childish arguments for images at the Council of Nicaea (787) Now, I believe, I should have said quite enough of this matter but for the fact that the Nicene Council commands my attention – not that most celebrated council called by Constantine the Great, but the one held eight hundred years ago at the command and under the auspices of the Empress Irene. For it decreed not only that there were to be images in churches but also that they were to be worshipped. For whatever I say, the authority of the Council will occasion a great prejudice in favour of the opposite side. Yet, to speak the truth, this does not move me so much as does the desire to inform my readers how far the madness went of those who were more attached to images than was becoming to Christians. But let us dispose of this first. Those who today defend the use of images allege the support of that Council of Nicaea. However, there exists a book in refutation under the name of Charlemagne, the style of which leads me to conclude that it was composed at the same time. In it are set forth the opinions of the bishops who participated in the Council and the proofs which they employed. John, the legate of the Easterns, said: 'God created man in his image' [Gen 1.27], and from this he therefore concluded that we must have images. The same man thought that images were commended to us by this sentence: 'Show me thy face, for it is beautiful' [Cant 2.14]. Another, to prove that images ought to be set upon altars, cited this testimony: 'No one lights a lantern and puts it under a bushel' [Matt 5.15]. Still another, to show us that looking upon them is useful to us, adduced a verse from

The Psalms: 'O Lord, the light of thy countenance has been sealed upon us' [Ps 4.7, Vg.; 4.6, EV]. Another seized upon this comparison: just as the patriarchs have used the sacrifices of the heathen, so ought saints' images for Christians to take the place of the heathens' idols. To the same end they twisted that verse: 'O Lord, I love the beauty of thy house' [Ps 25.5 . . .]. But pre-eminently ingenious is this interpretation: 'As we have heard, so also have we seen' [1 John 1.1 p.]. Therefore he implies that men know God not only by hearing his Word but also by looking upon images. Bishop Theodore speaks with similar penetration: 'Wonderful is God in his saints' [Ps 67.36, Vg.]; and elsewhere it is said, 'To the saints who are on earth' [Ps 15.3, Vg.; 16.3, EV]. Therefore this ought to refer to images. In short, so disgusting are their absurdities that I am ashamed even to mention them. (Book 1, Ch. 11, para. 12–14, pp. 112–15)

Source: *The Library of Christian Classics, vol. 20, Jean Calvin, The Institutes of the Christian Religion, Book 1*, ed. John T. McNeill, trans. Ford Lewis Battles, London, SCM Press, 1960.

9.4 The General Council of Trent, from *Decree on the Invocation, the Veneration and the Relics of Saints and on Sacred Images (1563)*

In the context of the Counter-Reformation, the Council of Trent (1545–63) reaffirmed the Second Council of Nicaea, i.e., the veneration of saints, relics and images, by pointing out that it is the 'original subjects' who are honoured.

(Veneration of saints) 1255 The holy Council, in accordance with the practice of the Catholic and apostolic Church from the early years of the Christian religion, and in accordance with the common teaching of the holy Fathers and the decrees of the sacred Councils, orders all bishops and others who have the official charge of teaching to instruct the faithful diligently, in particular as regards the intercession and the invocation of the saints, the honour due to their relics, and the lawful use of images. Let them teach the faithful that the saints, reigning together with Christ, pray to God for men and women; that it is good and useful to invoke them humbly and to have recourse to their prayers, to their help and assistance, in order to obtain favours from God through His Son, our Lord Jesus Christ, who alone is our Redeemer and Saviour. Those who deny that the saints enjoying eternal happiness in heaven are to be invoked; or who claim that saints do not pray for human beings or that calling upon them to pray for each of us is idolatry or is opposed to the word of God and is prejudicial to the honour of Jesus Christ, the one Mediator between God and humankind (cf. 1 Tim 2.5); or who say that

it is foolish to make supplication orally or mentally to those who are reigning in heaven; all those entertain impious thoughts. (pp. 361–2)

(Veneration of relics) 1256 The sacred bodies of the holy martyrs and of the other saints living with Christ, which have been living members of Christ and the temple of the Holy Spirit (cf. 1 Cor 3.16; 6.19; 2 Cor 6.16), and which are destined to be raised and glorified by Him unto life eternal, should also be venerated by the faithful. Through them many benefits are granted to human beings by God. For this reason, those who say that veneration and honour is not due to the relics of the saints, or that these relics and other sacred memorials are honoured in vain by the faithful, and that it is futile to visit the places where the martyrs have died to implore their assistance, are to be condemned absolutely, just as the Church has already condemned them and even now condemns them. (p. 362)

(Veneration of images) 1257 Further, the images of Christ, of the Virgin Mother of God and of other saints are to be kept and preserved, in places of worship especially; and to them due honour and veneration is to be given, not because it is believed that there is in them anything divine or any power for which they are revered, nor in the sense that something is sought from them or that a blind trust is put in images as once was done by the gentiles who placed their hope in idols (cf. Ps 135 (134).15ff); but because the honour which is shown to them is referred to the original subjects which they represent. Thus, through these images which we kiss and before which we kneel and uncover our heads, we are adoring Christ and venerating the saints whose likeness these images bear. That is what was defined by the decrees of the Councils, especially the Second Council of Nicaea, against the opponents of images. (p. 362)

Source: *The Christian Faith in the Doctrinal Documents of the Catholic Church*, 7th revised edition, ed. J. Neuner, SJ, and J. Dupuis, SJ, London, Collins, 2001

Next to the Word of God: Music

— —

10.1 Martin Luther, *Preface to the Wittenberg Hymnal (1524)*

With reference to the Old Testament and to Paul, Luther expresses his special love of music and how the arts and, especially, hymns should have a place in church life and in the education of young people.

That it is good and God pleasing to sing hymns is, I think, known to every Christian; for everyone is aware not only of the example of the prophets and kings in the Old Testament who praised God with song and sound, with poetry and psaltery, but also of the common and ancient custom of the Christian church to sing Psalms. St Paul himself instituted this in I Corinthians 14[.15] and exhorted the Colossians [3.16] to sing spiritual songs and Psalms heartily unto the Lord so that God's Word and Christian teaching might be instilled and implanted in many ways. Therefore I, too, in order to make a start and to give an incentive to those who can do better, have with the help of others compiled several hymns, so that the holy gospel which now by the grace of God has risen anew may be noised and spread abroad. Like Moses in his song [Exod 15.2], we may now boast that Christ is our praise and song and say with St Paul, I Corinthians 2[.2], that we should know nothing to sing or say, save Jesus Christ our Saviour. And these songs were arranged in four parts to give the young – who should at any rate be trained in music and other fine arts – something to wean them away from love ballads and carnal songs and to teach them something of value in their place, thus combining the good with the pleasing, as is proper for youth. Nor am I of the opinion that the gospel should destroy and blight all the arts, as some of the pseudo-religious claim. But I would like to see all the arts, especially music, used in the service of Him who gave and made them. I therefore pray that every pious Christian would be pleased with this [the use of music in the service of the gospel] and lend his help if God has given him like or greater gifts. As it is, the world is too lax and indifferent about teaching and training the young for us to abet this trend. God grant us his grace. Amen. (pp. 315–16)

Source: *Luther's Works, vol. 53, Liturgy and Hymns*, trans. Paul Zeller Strodach, rev. and ed. Ulrich S. Leupold, general ed. Helmut T. Lehmann, Philadelphia, Fortress Press, 1965.

10.2 Martin Luther, *Preface to Georg Rhau's Symphoniae iucundae (1538)*

In this extract Luther marvels about and praises music as a wonderful gift, being 'next to the Word of God'.

Greetings in Christ! I would certainly like to praise music with all my heart as the excellent gift of God which it is and to commend it to everyone. But I am so overwhelmed by the diversity and magnitude of its virtue and benefits that I can find neither beginning nor end or method for my discourse. . . .We can mention only one point (which experience confirms), namely, that next to the Word of God, music deserves the highest praise. She is a mistress and governess of those human emotions – to pass over the animals – which as masters govern men or more often overwhelm them. No greater commendation than this can be found – at least not by us. For whether you wish to comfort the sad, to terrify the happy, to encourage the despairing, to humble the proud, to calm the passionate, or to appease those full of hate – and who could number all these masters of the human heart, namely, the emotions, inclinations, and affections that impel men to evil or good? – what more effective means than music could you find? The Holy Ghost himself honours her as an instrument for his proper work when in his Holy Scriptures he asserts that through her his gifts were instilled in the prophets, namely, the inclination to all virtues, as can be seen in Elisha [II Kings 3.15]. On the other hand, she serves to cast out Satan, the instigator of all sins, as is shown in Saul, the king of Israel [I Sam 16.23]. Thus it was not without reason that the fathers and prophets wanted nothing else to be associated as closely with the Word of God as music. Therefore, we have so many hymns and Psalms where message and music join to move the listener's soul, while in other living beings and [sounding] bodies music remains a language without words. (pp. 321–3)

Source: *Luther's Works, vol. 53, Liturgy and Hymns*, trans. and ed. Ulrich S. Leupold, general ed. Helmut T. Lehmann, Philadelphia, Fortress Press, 1965.

Mystical Visions and Poetry

— —

11.1 Teresa of Avila, from *The Book of Her Life*

This Spanish mystic and Carmelite nun (1515–82) here describes her experi-ence of a vision of Christ as he appeared to her. She insists and argues that this is a real vision, one of incredible splendour and light granted by God. An internalized sense of intellectual inferiority is expressed, however, which she apparently felt towards her male confessors, who had left her in no doubt that 'intellectual' visions are superior to 'imaginative' ones.

[Ch. 28] Deals with the great favours the Lord granted her and how He appeared to her the first time . . .

To return to our topic, I passed some days – a few – in which I experienced this vision continually; it did me so much good that I never left prayer. No matter how much I did, I strove that it be done in such a way that it would not displease the One who I clearly saw was witnessing it. And although sometimes I was afraid on account of all the warnings they were giving, this fear didn't last long, because the Lord was giving me assurance. One day, while I was in prayer, the Lord desired to show me only His hands which were so very beautiful that I would be unable to exaggerate the beauty. This vision caused me great fear; any supernatural favour the Lord grants me frightens me at first, when it is new. After a few days I saw also that divine face which it seems left me completely absorbed. Since afterward He granted me the favour of seeing Him entirely, I couldn't understand why the Lord showed Himself to me in this way, little by little, until later I understood that His Majesty was leading me in accordance with my natural weakness. May He be blessed forever! So much glory would have been unbearable next to so lowly and wretched a subject as I; and as one who knew this, the merciful Lord was preparing me.

It will seem to your Reverence that strength like this wasn't necessary to see some hands and so beautiful a face. Glorified bodies have such beauty that the sight of so supernatural a beauty deriving from glory causes confusion. Thus the vision caused me a fear so great that I was completely agitated and disturbed, although afterward I remained so certain and secure and felt such other effects that I immediately lost the fear.

One feastday of St. Paul, while I was at Mass, this most sacred humanity in its risen form was represented to me completely, as it is in paintings, with such wonderful beauty and majesty; I have written about it in particular to your Reverence when you insistently ordered me to do so. And writing about it was very difficult for me to do because one cannot describe this vision without ruining it. But as best I could I have already told you about it, and so there is no reason to speak of it here again. I only say that if there were nothing else to provide delight for one's vision in heaven than the exalted beauty of glorified bodies, this vision would be very great glory, especially the vision of the humanity of Jesus Christ, our Lord. And if even here on earth His Majesty shows Himself according to what our wretchedness can bear, what will be the glory when such a blessing is enjoyed completely?

I never saw this vision – nor any other – with my bodily eyes, even though it is an imaginative one. Those who know more about these matters than I say that the intellectual vision is more perfect than this one and that this one is much more perfect than visions seen with the bodily eyes. These latter, corporeal visions, they say, are the lowest and the kind in which the devil can cause more illusions; although at that time I couldn't understand this. But since an imaginative vision was being granted to me, I desired that I might see it with my bodily eyes so that my confessor wouldn't tell me that I had imagined it. And after the vision passed away, it also happened to me – and this was at once – that I thought that I had imagined it; thinking I had deceived my confessor, I was bothered about having told it to him. This was another cause for tears, and I went and explained to him. He asked me whether it just seemed to me that I had deceived him or whether I had desired to deceive him. I told him the truth, for, in my opinion, I had not lied, nor had I intended to; nor for anything in the world would I say one thing for another. He well knew this, and so he tried to calm me. I felt so sorry for having gone to him with these things, for I don't know how the devil got me to torment myself with the thought that I had made up the vision. But so quickly did the Lord grant me this favour and declare this truth that very soon the doubt about my imagining it left me, and afterward I saw clearly my foolishness. If I should have spent many years trying to imagine how to depict something so beautiful, I couldn't have, nor would I have known how to; it surpasses everything imaginable here on earth, even in just its whiteness and splendour.

The splendour is not one that dazzles; it has a soft whiteness, is infused, gives the most intense delight to the sight, and doesn't tire it; neither does the brilliance, in which is seen the vision of so divine a beauty, tire it. It is a light so different from earthly light that the sun's brightness that we see appears very tarnished in comparison with that brightness and light represented to the sight, and so different that afterward you wouldn't want to open your eyes. It's like the difference between a sparkling, clear water that flows over crystal and on which the sun is reflecting and a very cloudy, muddy water flowing along the ground. This doesn't mean that the sun is represented or that the light resembles sunlight. It seems in fact like natural light, and the sunlight seems artificial. It is a light that has no night; nothing troubles it. In sum, it is of such a kind that a person couldn't imagine what it is like in all of life's days no matter how powerful the intellect. God gives it so suddenly that there wouldn't even be time to open your eyes, if it were necessary to open them. For when the Lord desires to give the vision, it makes no more difference if they are opened than if they are closed; even if we do not desire to see the vision, it is seen. No distraction is enough to resist it, nor is there power or diligence or care enough to do so. I have clearly experienced this, as I shall say.

What I should now like to speak of is the way in which the Lord reveals Himself by means of these visions. I don't mean that I shall explain how such a strong light can be put in the interior faculty and so clear an image put in the intellect – for it seems truly that that's where it is – because this is something for men of learning to explain. The Lord has not given me understanding of how this is done, and I am so ignorant and my intellect so dull that to no matter what extent these men of learning have desired to explain to me how this vision comes about, I have still not been able to understand. It is certain that even though it seems to your Reverence that I have a lively intellect, I do not. In many things I've experienced that I don't know any more than what is given me to eat, as the saying goes. Sometimes my confessors have been amazed at my ignorance. And I have never understood, nor have I desired to understand, how God causes this vision or how it could come about, nor did I ask, even though, as I have said, for many years now I've had contact with competent men of learning. Whether something was a sin or not – yes, this I did discuss with them. As for the rest, it wasn't necessary for me to think anything but that God did it all. I saw there was no reason for me to be startled but to praise Him. Indeed the difficult things He does cause more devotion in me; and the more difficult, the more devotion they cause.

I shall then say what I have come to see through experience. How the Lord does it, your Reverence will speak of better than I, and will explain what remains obscure and what I may not have known how to say. It seemed clear to me in some cases that what I saw was an image, but in many other instances, no; rather, it was Christ Himself by reason of the clarity with which He was pleased to reveal Himself to me. Sometimes the vision was so obscure that it seemed to me an image, not like an earthly drawing no matter how perfect it may be – for I have seen many good ones. It is foolish to think that an earthly drawing can look anything like a vision; it does so no more nor less than living persons resemble their portraits. No matter how good the portrait may have turned out, it can't look so natural that in the end it isn't recognized as a dead thing. But let us leave this example aside; it applies well here and is very exact.

I don't say this example is a comparison – for comparisons are never so exact – but the truth. The difference lies in that which there is between living persons and paintings of them – no more nor less. For if what is seen is an image, it is a living image – not a dead man, but the living Christ. And He makes it known that He is both man and God, not as He was in the tomb but as He was when He came out of the tomb after His resurrection. Sometimes He comes with such great majesty that no one could doubt but that it is the Lord Himself. Especially after receiving Communion – for we know that He is present, since our faith tells us this – He reveals Himself as so much the lord of this dwelling that it seems the soul is completely dissolved; and it sees itself consumed in Christ. O my Jesus! Who could make known the majesty with which You reveal Yourself! And, Lord of all the world and of the heavens, of a thousand other worlds and of number-less worlds, and of the heavens that You might create, how the soul understands by the majesty with which You reveal Yourself that it is nothing for You to be Lord of the world!

In this vision the powerlessness of all the devils in comparison with Your power is clearly seen, my Jesus; and it is seen how whoever is pleasing to You can trample all hell under foot. In this vision the reason is seen why the devils feared when You descended into limbo and why they would have preferred to be in another thousand lower hells in order to flee from such great majesty. I see that You want the soul to know how tremendous this majesty is and the power that this most sacred humanity joined with the Divinity has. In this vision there is a clear representation of what it will be like on Judgment Day to see the majesty of this King and to see its severity toward those who are evil. This vision is the source of the true humility left in the soul when it sees its misery, which it cannot ignore. This vision is the source of confusion and true repentance for sins; although the soul sees that He shows love, it doesn't know where to hide, and so it is completely consumed. I say that this vision has such tremendous power when the Lord desires to show the soul a great part of His grandeur and majesty that it would be impossible for any subject to endure it – unless the Lord should want to help it very supernaturally by placing it in rapture and ecstasy since in the enjoyment of that divine presence the vision of it is lost. Is it true that it is forgotten afterward? That majesty and beauty remain so impressed that they are unforgettable, except when the Lord wishes the soul to suffer a great dryness and solitude of which I shall speak further on; for then it seems it even forgets God. The soul undergoes a change; it is always absorbed; it seems that a new, living, high degree of love is beginning. For although the intellectual vision, of which I spoke, that represents God in an imageless way is more perfect, a wonderful thing happens when so divine a presence is represented in the imagination so that in conformity with our weakness this presence can last in the memory and keep the thought well occupied. These two kinds of vision almost always come together. This is the way they occur: with the eyes of the soul we see the excel-lence, beauty, and glory of the most holy humanity; and through the intellectual vision, which was mentioned, we are given an understanding of how God is powerful, that He can do all things, that He commands all and governs all, and that His love permeates all things.

This vision is very worthy of esteem and, in my opinion, there is no danger in it, because by its effects it is known that the devil has no power here. It seems to me he has wanted to represent the Lord Himself in this way three or four times by a false representation. He takes the form of flesh, but he can't counterfeit the image by giving it the glory that it has when it comes from God. He makes representations so as to destroy the true vision the soul has seen; but the soul of itself resists and is agitated, displeased, and disturbed since it loses the devotion and delight it had before and remains without any prayer. In the beginning this happened, as I said, three or four times. It is something so very different that even if one has experienced only the prayer of quiet, I believe that one will understand by the effects which were mentioned in speaking of locutions. This false representation is something very obvious; if the soul does not want to be deceived, and it walks in humility and simplicity, I don't think it will be deceived. Anyone who has had a true vision from God can tell the false almost immediately, for, although this false vision begins with pleasure and delight, the soul hurls it from itself; and even the delight, I think, must be different – it doesn't have the appearance of pure and chaste love. The devil very quickly shows who he is. So where there is experience, the devil, in my opinion, can do no harm.

That this vision from God could be the work of the imagination is the most impossible of impossible things; it is utter nonsense to think so, for the beauty and the whiteness of one hand alone is completely beyond our imagination. It's impossible to see in a moment, without thinking or ever having thought about them, things represented that in a long time could not have been put together by the imagination, because they go far beyond, as I said, what we can comprehend here on earth. And if we could imagine something of the vision, the difference could still be seen clearly by this other factor that I shall now mention. For if the vision were represented by means of the intellect, apart from the fact that it wouldn't produce any of the great effects that a true one produces, the soul would be left exhausted. Doing this would be like wanting to make oneself go to sleep and yet remaining awake because the sleep doesn't come. When people need sleep or feel a weakness in the head and desire sleep, they do what they can and at times it seems they are achieving something. But if it isn't true sleep that comes to them, they will not be sustained nor will they experience in their head a renewed feeling of strength; rather, they will feel more exhausted. Something similar would happen here; for if the intellect were to produce the vision, the soul would be left exhausted – not sustained and strong, but tired and displeased. One cannot exaggerate the richness that the true vision leaves; it even gives health to the body and leaves it comforted.

I gave this reason along with others when they told me that the devil was the cause or that I had fancied the vision – and this was often – and I made comparisons as I could, and the Lord gave me understanding. . . .

I said that since I was previously so wretched I couldn't believe that if the devil did this to deceive me and bring me to hell he would have taken a means as contrary as was that of removing vices and bestowing virtues and fortitude. For I saw clearly that by these experiences I was at once changed. (Ch. 28, para. 1–13, pp. 237–44)

Source: *The Collected Works of St Teresa of Avila, vol. 1, The Book of Her Life*, trans. Kieran Kavanagh, OCD and Ottilio Rodriguez, OCD, Washington, Institute of Carmelite Studies, ICS Publications, 1987.

11.2.1 John of the Cross, from *The Ascent of Mount Carmel*

In his commentary on his own poem, The Ascent of Mount Carmel, *the Spanish poet, mystic and doctor of the Church, John of the Cross (1542–91), points out that the senses are a help in growing in knowledge and in spirituality. Yet he emphasizes that ultimately full perfection in spirituality implies the disposal of all sensory perception.*

An answer to the proposed question. God's procedure and purpose in communicating spiritual goods by means of the senses.

In order that God lift the soul from the extreme of its low state to the other extreme of the high state of divine union, He must obviously, in view of these fundamental principles, do so with order, gently, and according to the mode of the soul. Since the order followed in the process of knowing involves the forms and images of created things, and since knowledge is acquired through the senses, God, to achieve His work gently and to lift the soul to supreme knowledge, must begin by touching the low state and extreme of the senses. And from there He must gradually bring the soul after its own manner to the other end, His spiritual wisdom, which is incomprehensible to the senses. Thus, naturally or supernaturally, He brings a person to the supreme spirit of God by first instructing him through discursive meditation and through forms, images, and sensible means, according to the individual's own manner of acquiring knowledge.

This is the reason God gives a person visions, forms, images, and other sensitive and spiritual knowledge – not because He does not desire to give spiritual wisdom immediately, in the first act. He would do this if the two extremes (human and divine, sense and spirit) could through the ordinary process be united by only one act, and if He could exclude the many preparatory acts, which are so connected in gentle and orderly fashion that, as is the case with natural agents, each is the foundation and preparation for the next. The first preparative acts serve the second; the second, the third; and so on. Therefore God perfects man gradually according to his human nature, and proceeds from the lowest and most exterior to the highest and most interior. He first perfects the corporal senses, moving one to make use of natural exterior objects that are good, such as:

hearing sermons and masses, looking upon holy objects, mortifying the palate at meals, and disciplining the sense of touch through penance and holy rigor. When these senses are somewhat disposed, He is wont to perfect them more by granting some supernatural favours and gifts to confirm them further in good. These supernatural communications are, for example: corporal visions of saints or holy things, very sweet odours, locutions, and extreme delight in the sense of touch. The senses are greatly confirmed in virtue through these communications and the appetites withdrawn from evil objects. Besides this the interior bodily senses, such as the imagination and fantasy, are gradually perfected and accustomed to good through considerations, meditations, and holy reasonings, and the spirit is instructed. When through this natural exercise they are prepared, God may enlighten and spiritualize them further with some supernatural imaginative visions from which the spirit, as we affirmed, at the same time profits notably. This natural and supernatural exercise of the interior sense gradually reforms and refines the spirit. This is God's method of bringing a soul step by step to the innermost good, although it may not always be necessary for Him to keep so mathematically to this order, for sometimes God bestows one kind of communication without the other, or a less interior one by means of a more interior one, or both together. The process depends on what God judges expedient for the soul, or upon the favours He wants to confer. But His ordinary procedure conforms with our explanation.

By this method, then, God instructs a person and makes him spiritual. He begins by communicating spirituality, in accord with the person's littleness and small capacity, through elements that are exterior, palpable, and accommodated to sense. He does this so that by means of the rind of those sensible things, in themselves good, the spirit making progress in particular acts and receiving morsels of spiritual communication may form a habit in spiritual things and reach the actual substance of spirit, foreign to all sense. A person only obtains this little by little, after his own manner, and by means of the senses to which he has always been attached. In the measure that a man approaches spirit in his dealings with God, he divests and empties himself of the ways of the senses, of discursive and imaginative meditation. When he has completely attained spiritual communion with God he will be voided of all sensory apprehensions concerning God. The more an object approaches one extreme, the further it retreats from the other; upon complete attainment of the one extreme, it will be wholly separated from the other. There is a frequently quoted spiritual axiom which runs: *Gustato spiritu, desipit omnis caro* (Once the taste and savour of the spirit is experienced, everything carnal is insipid). The ways of the flesh (which refer to the use of the senses in spiritual things) afford neither profit nor delight. This is obvious; if something is spiritual, it is incomprehensible to the senses, but if the senses can grasp it, it is no longer purely spiritual. The more knowledge the senses and natural apprehensions have about it, the less spiritual and supernatural it will be, as we explained above.

As a result the perfect spirit pays no attention to the senses; it neither receives anything through them, nor uses them principally, nor judges them to be requisite in its relationship with God, as it did before its spiritual growth. A passage from St Paul's epistle to the Corinthians bears this meaning: *Cum essem parvulus, loquebar ut parvulus, sapiebam ut parvulus, cogitabam ut parvulus. Quando autem factus sum vir, evacuam quae erant parvuli* (When I was a child, I spoke as a child, I knew as a child, I thought as a child. But when I became a man, I put away childish things). [1 Cor 13.11] We have already explained how sensible things and the knowledge the spirit can abstract from them are the work of a child. Should a person always have attachment to them and never become detached, he would never stop being a little child, or speaking of God as a child, or knowing and thinking of God as a child. In his attachment to the rind of sense (the child), he will never reach the substance of spirit (the perfect man). For the sake of his own spiritual growth, therefore, a person should not admit these revelations, even though God is the author of them, just as a child must be weaned in order to accustom its palate to a hardier and more substantial diet. (Ch. 17, para. 3–6, pp. 155–8)

In conclusion, a person must not fix the eyes of his soul upon that rind of the figure and object supernaturally accorded to him, whether the object pertains to the exterior senses (locutions and words to the sense of hearing; visions of saints and beautifully resplendent lights to the sense of sight; fragrance to the sense of smell; delightful tastes to the palate; and to the sense of touch other pleasures derived from the spirit, as is more commonly the case with spiritual persons), or whether it is an interior imaginative vision. He must instead renounce them all. He must fasten the eyes of his soul only upon the valuable spirituality they cause, and endeavour to preserve it by putting into practice and properly doing whatever is for the service of God, and pay no attention to those representations, nor desire any sensible gratification. By this attitude a person takes from these apprehensions only what God wants him to take, that is, the spirit of devotion, since God gives them for no other principal reason. And he rejects the sensory element which would not have been imparted had he possessed the capacity for receiving spirituality without the apprehensions and exercises of the senses. (Ch. 17, para. 9, p. 159)

Source: *The Collected Works of St John of the Cross*, trans. Kieran Kavanagh, OCD and Otilio Rodriguez, OCD, Washington, DC, Institute of Carmelite Studies, ICS Publications, 1973.

11.2.2 John of the Cross, *The Living Flame of Love*

In the poem John of the Cross praises Christ and his presence in this mystic's life.

O living flame of love
That tenderly wounds my soul
In its deepest centre! Since
Now You are not oppressive,
Now consummate! if it be Your will:
Tear through the veil of this sweet
Encounter!

O sweet cautery O delightful wound!
O gentle hand! O delicate touch
That tastes of eternal life
And pays every debt!
In killing You changed death to life.

O lamps of fire!
In whose splendours
The deep caverns of feeling,
Once obscure and blind,
Now give forth, so rarely, so
exquisitely,
Both warmth and light to their
Beloved.

How gently and lovingly
You wake in my heart,
Where in secret You dwell alone;
And by Your sweet breathing,
Filled with good and glory,
How tenderly You swell my heart
with love!

(pp. 717–18)

Source: *The Collected Works of St John of the Cross*, trans. Kieran Kavanagh, OCD and Otilio Rodriguez, OCD, Washington, Institute of Carmelite Studies, ICS Publications, 1973.

Part 4

Seventeenth to Nineteenth Centuries

— —

Introduction

The lasting impact of the Reformation and Counter-Reformation on theology and Christian life influenced the beginnings of the Enlightenment, i.e. the turn to the human subject from a formerly theocentric world-view, the radical stress on rationalism, and the critique of religion. The French Revolution, technological advances and industrialization, the degradation of countless humans to slave labour and living in slums, the Romantic movement partly in opposition to an over-emphatic rationalism, the philosophical-political ideas of thinkers such as Kant and Hegel, Feuerbach and Marx provided the background and challenge to church life and theology. It is during this time too that various academic disciplines and sub-disciplines developed, including that of theology and especially the historical-critical method in biblical studies.

After the great theological epoch of the Reformation, Protestants in the following centuries became preoccupied with orthodoxy with little theological development. Yet a few theologians, like Schleiermacher, saw the need to engage, at least to some extent, with the current thinking of the time. Roman Catholic theology stagnated altogether, with few interesting exceptions, and was content to employ the dullest of manuals and maintain its opposition to modernity until the late nineteenth century. This era, then, was to be one of the least creative in the history of theology, marked by doctrinal correctness and confessionalism. In the seventeenth and eighteenth centuries, Puritanism made itself felt in England and America. In Germany Pietism was exposed by Spener and Zinsendorf. Methodism developed in England under John Wesley, inspired by Zinsendorf's 'Herrenhuter Gemeine'. At the heart of these Protestant groups was an emphasis on a lived faith and a zeal for spreading the word of Christ.

Given the importance that the Reformers had attached to preaching the word, the iconoclasm that some of them had espoused, and the radical questioning of faith and the Church in philosophical circles in the Enlightenment, it is not surprising that during this period we witness the decline of art in churches. Up to the Baroque, Christian themes still provided the central subject matter among leading artists; now history themes, genre and portraiture increasingly featured in art. Church patronage declined, while the autonomy of the artist increased.

Annual exhibitions and an art market were established. The leading artists were largely interested in non-Christian themes, while Christian subjects and church art were left to second and third-rate painters and sculptors. The nineteenth century, with its sentimental religious art, often kitsch in fact, was a far cry from the artistic heights of Michelangelo, Caravaggio, van der Weyden, or Rembrandt. This decline in art thus reflected the current cultural and religious developments, especially the shift towards a humanist age, and the vast impact of the printed word. It was the human agent who increasingly decided on questions of knowledge and truth, while unquestioned faith in an almighty God and obedience to an authoritarian Church could no longer be taken for granted.

In the mid-eighteenth century Alexander Gottlieb Baumgarten wrote his seminal *Aesthetica* in which the term 'aesthetics' was employed for the first time. Baumgarten's intention was to continue the work of his teacher, the rationalist philosopher and mathematician Christian Wolff, who had undertaken a systematic separation of the sciences, including the separation of theology and philosophy. Baumgarten's aim was to place aesthetics, the *scientia cognitionis sensitivae*, the science concerned with sense knowledge, alongside logic as the science of theoretical knowledge. The aim of aesthetics, for Baumgarten, was to perfect sense knowledge, and this perfection he considered to be nothing less than beauty itself. In other words, beauty is not so much an attribute of things, or a feeling of what is pleasant, but rather an expression of perfecting one's attainment of knowledge in and through the realm of the senses (cf. M. Hauskeller, *Was das Schöne sei* (1994), p. 209).

However, aesthetics, as a sub-discipline of philosophy, generally came to be understood as synonymous with the philosophy of art. Significant contributions to philosophical aesthetics in the eighteenth and nineteenth centuries include those by Burke, Kant, Hegel, Schiller, Schelling, Schlegel, Schopenhauer, Nietzsche and Kierkegaard. The relative ebb in theology and in contributions pertaining to a specifically *theological* aesthetics from the seventeenth to the nineteenth centuries is partially reflected in the extracts selected here. In comparison to the other four epochs, the extracts are somewhat sparse and disparate. Some of the most relevant of these, in fact, were written by philosophers rather than by theologians.

One sphere which has played a significant role since the very beginning of the Church and of Christian theology is doxology, the theology of praise, in all its variety. It was mentioned earlier how all theology has a fundamental doxological aspect. Yet there are instances when this is more concretely expressed. For Luther, composing hymns was not only an important expression of his theology of the crucified God, of grace and justification, but also served the faithful as means of praise of the triune God. Given Luther's role as the foremost Reformer, it is not surprising that music became the central art form in Protestant churches in subsequent centuries. Here theology and music merge and become vibrant doxology; a theological aesthetics had come to birth. In the time after Luther, a number of pastors and theologians excelled in writing poetry and hymns. In these hymns they took up major 'Protestant' themes, such as the role of faith and grace, human sin and the redeeming love of the suffering Christ, the power of the Word of God, etc. Poet and divine George Herbert gave titles like 'Faith', 'Love' or 'Church-Musick' [sic] to his poems, while von Zinsendorf wrote one of the best-known Christian hymns, 'Jesus thy blood and righteousness'. Charles Wesley wrote a multitude of hymns, where the praise of Christ's marvellous love is captured, e.g. 'Love divine, all loves excelling'. In these hymns the main foci of Protestant theology, spirituality and pastoral concern found a creative, artistic mode of expression. Many of these hymns have become classics and play a vital part in the Protestant liturgical tradition to this day.

Possibly the outstanding thinker concerning a theological aesthetics during this time was the eighteenth-century New England Calvinist clergyman and philosopher Jonathan Edwards. Edward Farley even claims that there has been no other Christian theologian who was to occupy himself or herself as much with the question of beauty as Edwards did (Farley, 2001, p. 43). Given that Edwards is associated with American Puritanism and took some of his thinking from a rather extreme Calvinist position, emphasizing election, his extensive and passionate writing on the beauty of the world, the beauty of the human being, spiritual beauty, and the beauty of the triune God comes almost as a surprise. Edwards was influenced by English philosophers including John Locke, David Hume and Francis Hutcheson who, in the context of the Enlightenment turn to the human subject, relocated beauty primarily in the realm of the personal, i.e. in human sensibility. Still, with Edwards the medieval idea of beauty was not replaced altogether. This is obvious when he describes beauty in the world as a reflection of divine beauty. Edwards differs from other contemporary thinkers in his belief that what constitutes beauty is not primarily aesthetic sensibility, but 'sweet mutual consents' and 'union of heart', which are manifested in 'general good will'. For Edwards beauty is above all evident in a certain benevolence, in good will towards others. Beauty is 'true virtue'. In this way beauty attains a moral dimension, and it connotes human self-transcendence in reaching out to the other. For Edwards, beauty is ultimately both objective and subjective, sensibility and being (Farley, 2001, pp. 44–5, 47).

While in ancient and medieval times beauty had been understood as objective being, a radical shift took place during the Enlightenment. Kant's thought, in particular, was to influence aesthetic perceptions into the twentieth century. In his *Critique of Judgement* he asserted that aesthetic judgements are both necessary and subjective – as they are based on feeling – yet they claim universality, a universality that cannot be validated by concepts but only by consensus or common sense. Aesthetic judgements are made in terms of seeing in the object a 'purposiveness without purpose' (*Zweckmässigkeit ohne Zweck*). This oft-quoted idea was to anticipate the notion of 'l'art pour l'art', i.e. a concept of art which was no longer understood in relation to, and subordinate to, religious and moral references. Rather art now was to be enjoyed aesthetically for its own sake, beauty being in the eye of the beholder, in the imagination of the individual.

The Romantics, who opposed the Enlightenment overemphasis on Rationalism, stressed the importance of the human emotions, feeling and passion. This made itself felt in a variety of artistic and intellectual branches, in music – Liszt, Schumann and Chopin – in the visual arts – Turner, Blake and C. D. Friedrich – and in literature with poets such as Wordsworth and Shelley. During this time, too, the aesthetic dimension of the sublime finds expression in the arts, and is more theoretically reflected upon by contemporary thinkers, e.g. Kant and Burke. The sublime connotes what is awe-inspiring, overwhelming, threatening and mysterious. It is achieved by including into a work of art elements of the fantastic, of melancholy and sometimes of transience and morbidity. The works of the leading German Romantic artist Caspar David Friedrich, with their atmosphere of melancholy and of death and transience in nature, as also Turner's wild landscapes, are examples of the sublime in art. Indeed, in Romantic visual art, music, literature, theology, and in some strands of philosophy, an emphasis on human emotions and passions, as well as a sense of a longing for the infinite, the emphasis on the beauty and sublime of nature and on epiphanies in nature are apparent. Although 'secular' themes, such as genre and landscape painting, were now the major foci, there still remained a desire for religious expression in art. The first modern and foremost theologian of the epoch, Friedrich Schleiermacher, was in contact with Caspar David Friedrich. Schleiermacher wrote in his Speeches to the 'Cultured Despisers' of Religion that the essence of religion was 'neither thinking nor acting, but intuition and feeling'. Moreover he had what we might call today a holistic vision, where every individual thing is part of the whole, and everything limited a representation of the infinite. Such notions are directly reflected in Friedrich's works, e.g. 'Monk by the Seashore', or 'The Lonely Tree'. Blake echoes Schleiermacher and Friedrich when he writes in his 'Auguries of Innocence':

> To see a World in a Grain
> And a Heaven in a Wild Flower,
> Hold Infinity in the palm of your hand
> And eternity in an hour.

These are typical of the religious and aesthetic sentiments expressed in the various contemporary Romantic thinkers and artists. True religious sensibility meant to search for infinity and eternity in what is transient, in the small finite things. Beauty is discerned in panentheist terms, i.e. in nature in which the grandeur of the divine is displayed. In this way spiritual dimensions in the contemporary arts were increasingly perceived through non-explicit religious subject matter.

The idealist philosopher Hegel, a key thinker in this period, contributed what is arguably the most comprehensive aesthetic theory in modernity. Unlike Kant, who had deeply influenced his thinking, Hegel considered beauty in art as superior to beauty in nature, as it is 'born again of the mind'. Nor did he concentrate on what constitutes beauty or aesthetic experience, as Kant did, but was more concerned with the meaning and role of the work of art. He regarded art-works essentially as giving expression to world-views in certain historical and cultural periods. For Hegel, the beauty of art is the manifestation of the idea in sensuous form, the idea being the totality of human self-expression. That work of art is the finest which best and most fully expresses the idea. Like philosophy and religion, art is the place where the mind comes to know and to express itself. Yet Hegel thought that the history of art had in a certain sense come to an end with the advance and development of Romantic art, with its strong emphasis on inwardness and human subjectivity. Art works, he pointed out, are no longer worshipped as divine, they no longer satisfy the spiritual needs as in the past. Genuine life and truth was now expressed by the ideas, by 'thought and reflection [which] have spread their wings above fine art'. Certainly it is true that the nineteenth century with its Romantic and later its realist and impressionist art had long left behind the spiritual-aesthetic heights of religious art in earlier epochs.

Finally, Søren Kierkegaard, whose thought was to influence twentieth-century existentialist philosophy, insisted that the quest for truth and for authentic living is grasped existentially and is to be experienced. He regarded the aesthetic atti-tude as the first stage of existence in which the human being discovers the pow-ers of her or his imagination as infinite desire. Kierkegaard used to equate the aesthetic stage with that of romantic Idealism and pointed out that to remain in that stage of creative imagination means that one remains inauthentic as one does not face the 'either-or' experiences of daily life. Artists live an illusory exis-tence as they evade the suffering of reality. It is the ethical and religious stage which present limits to the aesthetic stage. The ethical stage demands responsi-bility of a person to another and to society. The religious stage, as the ultimate stage, while retrieving the subjective inwardness of the aesthetic stage, calls for a radical transformation comprising a leap of faith towards the absolute. This leap is existential, a leap into the dark, an absurd faith with risks and uncertainty since there is no objective evidence of a divine being. Kierkegaard did not deny the aesthetic attitude in favour of the religious attitude. The aesthetic attitude ought to be enjoyed and affirmed, but it should not be seen as a way of salvation.

This period, then, saw huge intellectual transformations, political revolutions, and the critique of religion, which have had a lasting effect on culture, the Church and the life of faith. Against this background it should not surprise that we are dealing with an epoch comprising diverse, if partly overlapping, aesthetic concerns: the composition of hymns in Protestant circles, Edwards' writing on beauty, the Romantic artists and intellectuals with their panentheist sensibilities, Schleiermacher's idea of religion as feeling and intuition, the decline of religious art, and the ground-breaking philosophical contributions of thinkers such as Burke, Baumgarten, Kant and Hegel.

This sense of growing diversity in the wider cultural sphere, and in the more narrowly defined development of philosophical and theological aesthetics, points us, in turn, towards the twentieth century, the age of pluralism.

Singing God's Praise

—–—

12.1 George Herbert, from *The Works of George Herbert*

George Herbert (1593–1633) was a British poet and divine. His collection of poems, The Temple, *includes well-known hymns that are still enjoyed by Christian worshippers world-wide, such as 'The God of love my shepherd is'. In the following three poems Herbert speaks of church music, the art of preaching and of love.*

Church-Musick

> *Sweetest of sweets, I thank you: when displeasure*
> Did through my bodie wound my minde,
> You took me thence; and in your house of pleasure
> A daintie lodging me assign'd.
>
> Now I in you without a bodie move,
> Rising and falling with your wings:
> We both together sweetly live and love,
> Yet say sometimes, *God help poore Kings.*
>
> Comfort, I'le die; for if you poste from me,
> Sure I shall do so, and much more:
> But if I travell in your companie,
> You know the way to heavens doore. (p. 81)

The Windows

> Lord, how can man preach thy eternall word?
> He is a brittle crazie glasse:
> Yet in thy temple thou dost him afford
> This glorious and transcendent place,
> To be a window, through thy grace.

But when thou dost anneal in glasse thy storie,
Making thy life to shine within
The holy Preachers; then the light and glorie
More rev'rend grows, and more doth win;
Which else shows watrish, bleak, and thin.

Doctrine and life, colours and light, in one
When they combine and mingle, bring
A strong regard and aw: but speech alone
Doth vanish like a flaring thing,
And in the eare, not conscience ring. (pp. 83–4)

Love I

Immortall Love, authour of this great frame,
Sprung from that beautie which can never fade;
How hath man parcel'd out thy glorious name,
And thrown it on that dust which thou hast made,

While mortall love doth all the title gain!
Which siding with invention, they together
Bear all the sway, possessing heart and brain,
(Thy workmanship) and give thee share in neither.

Wit fancies beautie, beautie raiseth wit:
The world is theirs; they two play out the game,
Thou standing by: and though thy glorious name
Wrought our deliverance from th' infernall pit,

Who sings thy praise? onely a skarf or glove
Doth warm our hands, and make them write of love. (p. 65)

Love II

Immortall Heat, O let thy greater flame
  Attract the lesser to it: let those fires,
  Which shall consume the world, first make it tame;
And kindle in our hearts such true desires,

As may consume our lusts, and make thee way.
  Then shall our hearts pant thee; then shall our brain
  All her invention on thine Altar lay,
And there in hymnes send back thy fire again:

Our eies shall see thee, which before saw dust;
  Dust blown by wit, till that they both were blinde:
  Thou shalt recover all thy goods in kinde,
Who wert disseized by usurping lust:

All knees shall bow to thee; all wits shall rise,
And praise him who did make and mend our eies. (p. 66)

Love III

Love bade me welcome: yet my soul drew back,
    Guiltie of dust and sin.
But quick-ey'd Love, observing me grow slack
    From my first entrance in,
Drew nearer to me, sweetly questioning,
    If I lack'd anything.

'A guest,' I answer'd, 'worthy to be here';
    Love said, 'You shall be he'.
'I the unkind, the ungratefull? Ah my dear,
    I cannot look on thee.'
Love took my hand, and smiling did reply,
    'Who made the eyes but I?'

'Truth, Lord, but I have marr'd them; let my shame
    Go where it doth deserve.'
'And know you not,' sayes Love, 'who bore the blame?'
    'My dear, then I will serve.'
'You must sit down,' sayes Love, 'and taste my meat.'
    So I did sit and eat. (p. 67)

Source: *George Herbert, The Poetical Works of George Herbert*, New York, D. Appleton and Co., 1857.

12.2 Angelus Silesius (Johann Scheffler), from *The Cherubinic Wanderer*

Of Lutheran descent, this mystical poet (1624–77) and controversial convert to Catholicism is best known for his poems 'Heilige Seelenlust' and 'Der Cherubinische Wanderer'. In the first poem he exclaims God's rapture at God's own transcendent beauty. In the second he applies rich analogical language in his doxology on the beauty of God.

Book 5, Eternally God Is in Love with His Beauty

God's beauty is so radiant, unutterably bright,
That He eternally feels rapture at its sight. (p. 114)

Book 6, How God Dwells in the Holy Soul

If you should ask how God the Word in you does dwell,
Know that it is like suns flooding the world with light
And like a bridegroom coming in the night
And like a king enthroned in his realm,
A father with his son, a master in his school,
And like a treasure hidden from our sight
And like an honoured guest in robes of white
And like a jewel in a crown of gold,
A lily in a flowery field,
And like sweet music at an evening meal.
And like the oil of cinnamon ignited
And like a host in a pure shrine,
A fountain in a garden of cool wine:
Tell me, where else clad in such beauty he is sighted? (p. 129)

Source: *Angelus Silesius, The Cherubinic Wanderer*, trans. Maria Shrady, ed. Josef Schmidt, New York, Mahwah, Toronto, Paulist Press, 1986.

12.3 Nikolaus L. von Zinzendorf, *Jesu thy Blood and Righteousness*

The founder of the Herrenhuter Brüdergemeine, von Zinzendorf (1700–60), who proclaimed a 'religion of the heart', reveals in this hymn rich imagery in a Christ-centred spirituality, clearly influenced by Luther's theologia crucis.

Jesu, thy blood and righteousness
My beauty are, my glorious dress;
Midst flaming worlds, in these arrayed,
With joy shall I lift up my head.

Bold shall I stand in thy great day;
For who aught to my charge shall lay?
Fully absolved through these I am
From sin and fear, from guilt and shame.

The holy, meek, unspotted Lamb,
Who from the Father's bosom came,
Who died for me, even me, to atone,
Now for my Lord and God I own.

Lord, I believe thy precious blood,
Which at the mercy-seat of God
For ever doth for sinners plead
For me, even for my soul, was shed.

Lord, I believe, were sinners more
Than sands upon the ocean shore,
Thou hast for all a ransom paid,
For all a full atonement made.

When from the dust of death I rise
To claim my mansion in the skies,
Even then this shall be all my plea –
Jesus hath lived, hath died for me!

Jesu, be endless praise to thee,
Whose boundless mercy hath for me,
For me and all thy hands have made,
An everlasting ransom paid.

Ah! give to all thy servants, Lord,
With power to speak thy gracious word,
That all who to thy wounds will flee
May find eternal life in thee.

Thou God of power, thou God of love,
Let the whole world thy mercy prove!
Now let thy word o'er all prevail;
Now take the spoils of death and hell.

O let the dead now hear thy voice,
Now bid thy banished ones rejoice,
Their beauty this, their glorious dress,
Jesu, thy blood and righteousness! (pp. 95–6)

Source: *A Rapture of Praise, Hymns of John and Charles Wesley*, ed. H. A. Hodges and A. M. Allchin, Hodder and Stoughton, 1966. Von Zinzendorf's hymn is translated by John Wesley.

12.4 John and Charles Wesley, from *A Rapture of Praise*

While John Wesley (1703–91) became the founder of Methodism, his brother Charles (1708–88) excelled in writing hymns. However, all their collections of hymns were published in their joint names. While the first hymn gives praise to the triune God, the second – one of the most well-known hymns – praises the perfect divine love and expresses the Christian commitment to serve that love.

Father, in whom we live,
In whom we are, and move,
The glory, power, and praise receive
Of thy creating love.
Let all the angel throng
Give thanks to God on high;
While earth repeats the joyful song,
And echoes to the sky.

Incarnate Deity,
Let all the ransomed race
Render in thanks their lives to thee
For thy redeeming grace.
The grace to sinners showed
Ye heavenly choirs proclaim,
And cry: Salvation to our God,
Salvation to the Lamb!

Spirit of Holiness,
Let all thy saints adore
Thy sacred energy, and bless
Thine heart-renewing power.
Not angel tongues can tell
Thy love's ecstatic height,
The glorious joy unspeakable,
The beatific sight.

Eternal, Triune Lord!
Let all the hosts above,
Let all the sons of men, record
And dwell upon thy love.
When heaven and earth are fled
Before thy glorious face,
Sing all the saints thy love hath made
Thine everlasting praise. (p. 76)

Love divine, all loves excelling,
Joy of heaven, to earth come down;
Fix in us thy humble dwelling,
All thy faithful mercies crown:
Jesu, thou art all compassion,
Pure unbounded love thou art;
Visit us with thy salvation,
Enter every trembling heart.

Come, almighty to deliver,
Let us all thy grace receive;
Suddenly return, and never,
Never more thy temples leave;
Thee we would be always blessing,
Serve thee as thy hosts above,
Pray, and praise thee, without ceasing,
Glory in thy perfect love.

Finish then thy new creation,
Pure and spotless let us be;
Let us see thy great salvation,
Perfectly restored in thee;
Changed from glory into glory,
Till in heaven we take our place,
Till we cast our crowns before thee,
Lost in wonder, love, and praise. (p. 120)

Source: *Rapture of Praise, Hymns of John and Charles Wesley*, ed. H. A. Hodges and A. M. Allchin, London, Hodder and Stoughton, 1966.

Divine Beauty and the Beauty of Creation

13.1 John Owen, from *The Glory of Christ*

The English Puritan divine, preacher and statesman, John Owen (1616–83), in his meditations on The Glory of Christ, *puts emphasis on Christ as the sole representative of God and examines the various aspects of his glory, humility, love, obedience, etc. Here he outlines the imperfect anticipatory and the perfect eschatological reality of our vision of Christ.*

The difference between faith's present view of the glory of Christ and our seeing it in heaven 'We walk by faith, not by sight' (2 Corinthians 5.7). In this life, faith; in the life to come, sight. They are the abilities of the soul which make it aware of the glory of Christ. Faith's view of the glory of Christ in this world is dark and hazy. As the apostle says: 'Now we see . . . dimly' (1 Corinthians 13.12). Our knowledge is not direct, but is like an imperfect reflection of the reality. The gospel, without which we could not discover Christ at all, is still very far from fully displaying the greatness of his glory. This is because we ourselves imperfectly understand it. Our faith is weak and imperfect. There is no part of his glory we can fully understand. In our present earthly state there is something like a wall between us and Christ. But sometimes we see him through the windows. 'Behold, he stands behind our wall; he is looking through windows, gazing through the lattice' (Song of Solomon 2.9). These windows are the opportunities we have of hearing and receiving the promises of the gospel in the means of grace and the ministry of the word. Such opportunities are full of refreshment to the souls of those who believe. But the view of his beauty and glory does not last. Then we cry: 'As the deer pants for the water brooks, so pants my soul for you, O God. My soul thirsts for God, for the living God. When shall I come and appear before God?' (Psalm 42.1, 2). When shall I see him again, even if it is only through a window? Sometimes, like Job, we cannot see him because he hides his face behind a cloud (see Job 23.8, 9). At other times he shows himself as the sun in all its strength and we cannot bear its brightness. Now, by comparison, let us consider how we will see the same glory of Christ when we are in heaven. Our sight will be immediate, direct and steady.

Christ himself with all his glory will be really and continually with us. We shall no longer have to be satisfied with the mere descriptions of him that we have in the gospel. We shall see him face to face (1 Corinthians 13.12) and as he is (1 John 3.2). We shall see him with our bodily eyes, for Job says: 'In my flesh shall I see God (my Redeemer), whom I shall see for myself, and my eyes shall behold' (Job 19.25–27). Our bodily senses will be restored and glorified in a way we cannot now understand, in order that we may be able to look at Christ and his glory forever and ever. We shall see not only his human nature but his divinity also in its infinite wisdom, love and power. That glory will be a thousand times more than anything we can imagine. This sight of Christ is what all the saints of God long for. It is their desire 'to depart and be with Christ, which is far better; to be absent from the body and to be present with the Lord' (Philippians 1.23; 2 Corinthians 5.8). Those who do not often have this longing are earthly and unspiritual people.

No-one in this life has the power, either spiritually or bodily, to see the glory of Christ as it really is. When some reflections of his divine glory were seen on the Mount of Transfiguration, the disciples were confused and very much afraid. If the Lord Jesus came to us now in his majesty and glory, we would be incapable of receiving any benefit or comfort from his appearance. The apostle John, whom he loved, fell at his feet as dead when he appeared to him in his glory (Revelation 1.17). Paul and all those who were with him fell to the earth when the brightness of his glory shone on them as they journeyed to Damascus (see Acts 26.13, 14). What an insult it is to God when foolish people try to make pictures and images of the Lord Christ in his present glory! The only way we can know him now is by faith, dimly. We cannot know him now as he truly is, full of indescribable glory. Because of our sinful natures, our minds were completely dark and evil, being unable to see spiritual things in a proper light. We have been partly restored by grace and have become light in the Lord (Ephesians 5.8). But our minds are still imprisoned in our natural bodies and many weaknesses and imperfections remain. These will be gone for ever in heaven (see Ephesians 5.27). After the resurrection our minds and bodies will be free from everything that has prevented us from enjoying a full view of the glory of Christ. Then one pure act of spiritual sight in looking on the glory of Christ, one pure act of love in clinging to God, will make us far happier and more satisfied than we could ever be with all our religious activities. We have a natural power to understand and judge things in this present earthly life. But this natural ability cannot help us to see and understand spiritual things, as the apostle shows us in 1 Corinthians 2.11, 14: 'What man knows the things of a man except the spirit of the man which is in him? Even so, no one knows the things of God except the Spirit of God . . . The natural man does not receive the things of the Spirit of God, for they are foolishness to him; nor can he know them, because they are spiritually discerned.' So God gives us the supernatural ability of faith and grace. We still have our natural understanding but it is only by spiritual ability that we see spiritual things. In heaven there will be the added ability to see glory.

1. As spirituality does not destroy but improves natural ability, so the ability to comprehend glory will not destroy the powers of faith and grace, but will perfect them absolutely. 2. By nature we cannot clearly understand the essence of grace which is seen only by those who receive it. So by grace we cannot fully understand the nature of glory, which is seen perfectly only when we are changed and living in glory. 3. The best idea we can get of the nature of glory is to consider that the moment it shines on us we shall be changed into the perfect likeness of Christ.

There is a progression from nature to glory. Grace renews nature, glory makes grace perfect and so finally the whole soul is brought to its rest in God. The blind man saw men as trees walking when the Saviour first touched his eyes. At the Saviour's second touch, he saw everything clearly (see Mark 8.22–25). This is like the difference between the sight of grace and the sight of glory.

Having thought of our minds, now let us think of our glorified bodies. After we are risen from the grave, we shall see our Redeemer. Stephen actually saw, 'the glory of God and Jesus standing at the right hand of God' (Acts 7.55). Who would not wish to have shared the privilege of the disciples who physically saw Christ while he was on earth? He told them that 'many prophets and righteous men desired to see what you see' (Matthew 13.17). If this was such a great privilege, how glorious it will be when, with our eyes purified and strengthened, we shall see Christ in the fullness of his glory! We cannot imagine what it will be like but we know he prayed to his Father that we should be where he is, to see the greatness and beauty of his glory (see John 17.24). While we are here in this world 'we ourselves groan within ourselves, eagerly waiting for the adoption, the redemption of our body' (Romans 8.23). Like Paul, we cry: 'O wretched man that I am! who will deliver me from this body of death?' (Romans 7.24). The nearer anyone is to heaven, the more earnestly he desires to be there, because Christ is there. Our thoughts of Christ are so confused and imperfect that they usually end in our longing to be able to know him better. But this is the best state of mind we can be in here! I pray God I may never be delivered from it and that the Lord would increase such desires more and more in all who believe.

The heart of a believer, affected by the glory of Christ, is like a needle touched by a magnet. It can no longer be quiet or satisfied at a distance, although its movements are weak and trembling. It is continually pressing towards him but will not come to its rest in this world. But there in heaven, with Christ continually before us, we shall be able to look steadily at him in all his glory. This constant view will bring an everlasting refreshment and joy to our souls. We cannot understand, however, what the final vision of God will be like. But we know that the pure in heart shall see God (Matthew 5.8), and even in eternity Christ will be the only means of communication between God and the church.

Let us look for a moment at the Old Testament saints. They saw something of the glory of Christ but only in the form of veiled symbols. They longed for the time when the veil would be removed and the symbols give place to reality. They looked for the fulfilment of all the divine promises about the coming of the Son of God into the world. There was often more of the power of true faith and love in their hearts than is found among most believers today. When Jesus actually came, old Simeon took the child in his arms and said: 'Now Lord let me depart, now let me die, this is what my soul has longed for' (see Luke 2.28, 29).

We have a clearer revelation of the unique nature of Christ and of his work than those saints of old. And the view we shall have of Christ's glory in heaven will be much clearer and far brighter even than the revelation we now have. If those old saints prayed so long for the removal of the veils and symbols and desired so earnestly to see the glory of Christ, how much more earnestly should we be praying to see his glory?

We have now thought of the glory of Christ as being shown in three degrees. The Old Testament saints under the law had the symbols. In the gospel we have the perfect likeness. But we must wait for heaven where Christ is, to enjoy the reality.

Let us examine ourselves to see whether we are pressing forward continually towards the perfect view of the glory of Christ in heaven. If we are not, it is a sure sign that our faith is not real. If Christ is in us, he is 'the hope of glory' (Colossians 1.27). Many love the world too well to wish to get through it quickly to a place where they may see the glory of Christ. Their interest is in their possessions, their business, or family. Such people see the beauty of this world in the mirror of self-love and their minds are changed into the same selfish image. On the other hand, true believers, delighting to see the glory of Christ in the gospels, are changed into his image.

Our Lord Jesus Christ alone perfectly understands the eternal blessedness which will be enjoyed by those who believe in him. He prays that they may 'be with me where I am, that they may behold my glory' (John 17.24). If we can at present understand only a little of what glory means, at least we ought to trust the wisdom and love of Christ that it will be infinitely better than anything we can enjoy here. Should we not be continually desiring to be included in his prayer? (Ch. 12, pp. 57–62)

Source: *John Owen, The Glory of Christ*, ed. Hervey Mockford, general ed. J. K. Davies, London, Grace Publications Trust, 1987.

13.2.1 Jonathan Edwards, from *Images or Shadows of Divine Things*

This North-American Calvinist philosopher, theologian and minister (1703–58) made an important contribution to theological aesthetics, especially to the theology of beauty. In this extract he praises the beauty in and of nature, colours, skies, flowers, sunrays, etc. Yet, in line with the Platonic and Christian tradition, he points out that ultimately spiritual, hidden beauty is the supreme beauty.

The Beauty of the World

The beauty of the world consists wholly of sweet mutual consents, either within itself or with the supreme being. As to the corporeal world, though there are many other sorts of consents, yet the sweetest and most charming beauty of it is its resemblance of spiritual beauties. The reason is that spiritual beauties are infinitely the greatest, and bodies being but the shadows of beings, they must be so much the more charming as they shadow forth spiritual beauties. This beauty is peculiar to natural things, it surpassing the art of man. Thus there is the resemblance of a decent trust, dependence and acknowledgment in the planets continually moving round the sun, receiving his influences by which they are made happy, bright and beautiful: a decent attendance in the secondary planets, an image of majesty, power, glory, and beneficence in the sun in the midst of all, and so in terrestrial things, as I have shown in another place. It is very probable that that wonderful suitableness of green for the grass and plants, the blues of the skie [sic], the white of the clouds, the colours of flowers, consists in a complicated proportion that these colours make one with another, either in their magnitude of the rays, the number of vibrations that are caused in the atmosphere, or some other way. So there is a great suitableness between the objects of different senses, as between sounds, colours, and smells; as between colours of the woods and flowers and the smells and the singing of birds, which it is probable consist in a certain proportion of the vibrations that are made in the different organs. So there are innumerable other agreeablenesses of motions, figures, etc. The gentle motions of waves, of [the] lily, etc., as it is agreeable to other things that represent calmness, gentleness, and benevolence, etc. the fields and woods seem to rejoice, and how joyful do the birds seem to be in it. How much a resemblance is there of every grace in the field covered with plants and flowers when the sun shines serenely and undisturbedly upon them, how a resemblance, I say, of every grace and beautiful disposition of mind, of an inferior towards a superior cause, preserver, benevolent benefactor, and a fountain of happiness. How great a resemblance of a holy and virtuous soul is a calm, serene day. What an infinite number of such like beauties is there in that one thing, the light, and how complicated an harmony and proportion is it probable belongs to it. There are beauties that are more palpable and explicable, and there are hidden and secret beauties. The former pleases, and we can tell why; we can explain the particular point for the agreement that renders the thing pleasing. Such are all artificial regularities; we can tell wherein the regularity lies that affects us. [The] latter sort are those beauties that delight us and we cannot tell why. Thus, we find ourselves pleased in beholding the colour of the violets, but we know not what secret regularity or harmony it is that creates that pleasure in our minds. These hidden beauties are commonly by far the greatest, because the more complex a beauty is, the more hidden is it. In this latter fact consists principally the beauty of the world, and very much in light and colours. Thus mere light is pleasing to the mind. If it be to the degree of effulgence, it is very sensible, and mankind have agreed in it: they all represent glory and extraordinary beauty by brightness. The reason of it is either that light or our organ of seeing is so contrived that an harmonious motion is excited in the animal spirits and propagated to the brain. That mixture we call white is a proportionate mixture that is harmonious, as Sir Isaac Newton has shown, to each particular simple colour, and contains in it some harmony or other that is delightful. And each sort of rays play [sic] a distinct tune to the soul, besides those lovely mixtures that are found in nature. Those beauties, how lovely is the green of the face of the earth in all manner of colours, in flowers, the colour of the skies, and lovely tinctures of the morning and evening. Corollary: Hence the reason why almost all men, and those that seem to be very miserable, love life, because they cannot bear to lose sight of such a beautiful and lovely world. The ideas, that every moment whilst we live have a beauty that we take not distinct notice of, brings a pleasure that, when we come to the trial, we had rather live in much pain and misery than lose. (pp. 135–7)

Source: *Images or Shadows of Divine Things by Jonathan Edwards*, ed. Perry Miller, Westport, CT, Greenwood Press [Yale University Press], 1948.

13.2.2 Jonathan Edwards, from *Experiencing God*

In this passage Edwards defends the power of the imagination as something which may well be a sign of the work of the Holy Spirit since it helps us to perceive the invisible and is closely linked to contemplation, affection, as well as to the intellectual and spiritual sphere.

The distinguishing marks of a work of the Spirit of God; Part 1 – The effect on people's imagination

It is no argument that an operation on people's minds is not the work of the Spirit of God, that many who are subject to it have great impressions made on their imaginations. That people have many impressions on their imaginations does not prove that they have nothing else. It is easy to account for there being much of this nature among a people, where a great many, of all kinds, have their minds engaged with intense thought and strong feelings about invisible things. Indeed, it would be strange if this did not happen. Such is our nature that we cannot think about invisible things without a degree of imagination. I dare appeal to any man, of the greatest powers of mind, whether he is able to fix his thoughts on God or Christ, or the things of another world, without imaginary ideas attending his meditations? And the more engaged the mind is, and the more intense the contemplation and affection, still the more lively and strong the imaginary idea will ordinarily be; especially when attended with surprise. And this is the case when the mental prospect is very new, and takes strong hold of the passions, such as fear or joy; and when the state and views of the mind suddenly changes from a contrary extreme, such as from that which was extremely dreadful to that which is extremely delightful. And it is no wonder that many people do not easily distinguish between that which is imaginary and that which is intellectual and spiritual; and that they are apt to lay too much weight on the imaginary part, and are most ready to speak of that in the account they give of their experiences, especially people of less understanding and distinguishing capacity. As God has given us such a faculty as the imagination, and so made us that we cannot think of things spiritual and invisible without some exercise of this faculty; so it appears to me that such is our state and nature that this faculty is really subservient and helpful to the other faculties of the mind, when a proper use is made of it; though often, when the Imagination is too strong, and the other faculties weak, it overbears, and disturbs them in their exercise.

It seems clear to me, in many instances with which I have been acquainted, that God has really made use of this faculty to truly divine purposes; especially in some that are more ignorant. God seems to condescend to their circumstances, and deal with them as babes; as of old he instructed his church, whilst in a state of ignorance and minority, by types and outward representations. I can see nothing unreasonable in such a position. Let others who have much occasion to deal with souls in spiritual concerns, judge whether experience does not confirm it. It is no argument that a work is not of the Spirit of God, that some who are the subjects of it have been in a kind of ecstasy, in which they have had their minds transported into a train of strong and pleasing imaginations, and a kind of visions, as though they were rapt up to heaven, and there saw glorious sights. I have been acquainted with some such instances, and I see no need of bringing in the help of the devil into the account that we give of these things, nor yet of supposing them to be of the same nature as the visions of the prophets, or St Paul's rapture into paradise. Human nature, under these intense exercises and affections, is all that need be brought into the account. If it may be well accounted for, that people under a true sense of the glorious and wonderful greatness and excellence of divine things, and soul-ravishing views of the beauty and love of Christ, should have the strength of nature overpowered, as I have already shown that it may; then I think it is not at all strange that amongst great numbers that are thus affected and overborne, there should be some persons of particular constitutions that have their imaginations affected like this. The effect is no other than what bears a proportion and analogy to other effects of the strong exercise of their minds. It is no wonder, when the thoughts are so fixed, and the affections so strong – and the whole soul so engaged, ravished, and swallowed up – that all other parts of the body are so affected as to be deprived of their strength, and the whole frame ready to dissolve. Is it any wonder that, in such a case, the brain in particular (especially in some constitutions), which we know is most especially affected by intense contemplations and exercises of mind, should be so affected that its strength and spirits should be diverted for a while, and taken off from impressions made on the organs of external sense, and wholly employed in a train of pleasing delightful imaginations, corresponding with the present frame of the mind? Some people are ready to interpret such things wrongly, and to lay too much weight on them, as prophetic visions, divine revelations, and sometimes indications from heaven of what is to happen (which, in some instances I have known, have been disproved in the event).

But yet it appears to me that such things are evidently sometimes from the Spirit of God, though indirectly; that is, their extraordinary frame of mind, and that strong and lively sense of divine things which is the occasion of them, is from his Spirit; and also as the mind continues in its holy frame, and retains a divine sense of the excellence of spiritual things even in its rapture; which holy frame and sense is from the Spirit of God, though the imaginations that attend it are only accidental, and therefore there is commonly something or other in them that is confused, improper, and false. (pp. 29–31)

Source: *Experiencing God, Jonathan Edwards, Selected Readings from His Spiritual Classics*, ed. Robert Backhouse, London, Marshall Pickering, 1995.

13.2.3 Jonathan Edwards, from *The Philosophy of Jonathan Edwards, From His Private Notebooks*

Edwards develops his ideas on the Trinity by analysing the meaning of Christ as the image of God and the meaning of 'delight' – an aesthetic term – which marks the relations between the persons of the Trinity.

Trinity . . . Again, that which is the express and perfect image of God is God's idea of His own essence. There is nothing else can be an express and fully perfect image of God, but God's idea. Ideas are images of things and there are no other images of things in the most proper sense but ideas, because other things are only called images as they beget an idea in us of the thing of which they are the image – so that all other images of things are but images in a secondary sense. But we know that [the] Son of God is the express and perfect image of God, and His image in the primary and most proper sense. (2 Corinthians 4.4, 'lest the light of the glorious gospel of Christ, who is the image of God, should shine unto them.'

Philippians 2.6, 'who being in the form of God.' Coloss. 1.15, 'who is the image of the invisible God.' Hebrews 1.3, 'who being the brightness of his glory, and the express image of his person.')

Again, that image of God which God infinitely loves, and has His chief delight in, is the perfect idea of God. It has always been said that God's infinite delight consists in reflecting on Himself and viewing His own perfections or, which is the same thing, in His own perfect idea of Himself; so that 'tis acknowledged that God's infinite love is to, and His infinite delight [is] in, the perfect image of Himself. But the Scriptures tell us that the Son of God is that image of God which He infinitely loves. Nobody will deny this: that God infinitely loves His Son (John 3.35, 'The Father loveth the Son'; 5.20). So it was declared from Heaven, by the Father at His baptism and transfiguration, 'this is my beloved Son in whom I am well pleased'. So the Father calls Him His elect, in which His soul delighteth (Isai. 42.1). He is called the beloved (Ephesians 1.6). The Son also declares that the Father's infinite happiness consisted in the enjoyment of Him; Proverbs 8.30, 'I was daily His delight, rejoicing always before Him.' Now none, I suppose, will say that God enjoys infinite happiness in two manners, one in the infinite delight He has in enjoying His Son, His image, and another in the view of Himself different from this. So if not, then these ways wherein God enjoys infinite happiness are both the same; that is, His infinite delight in the idea of Himself is the same with the infinite delight He has in His Son, and if so His Son and that idea He has of Himself are the same.

Again, that which is the express image of God, in which God enjoys infinite happiness, and is also the word of God is God's perfect idea of God. The word of God, in its most proper meaning, is a transcript of the divine perfections. This word is either the declared word of God or the essential. The one is the copy of the divine perfections given to us, the other is the perfect transcript thereof in God's own mind. But the perfect transcript of the perfections of God in the divine [mind] is the same with God's perfect idea of His own perfections. But I need tell none, how the Son of God is called the word of God.

Lastly, that which is the express image of God, in which He infinitely delights and which is His word and which is the reason or wisdom of God, is God's perfect idea of God. That God's knowledge or reason or wisdom is the same with God's idea, none will deny. And that all God's knowledge or wisdom consists in the knowledge or perfect idea of Himself is shown before and granted by all. But none needs to be told that the Son of God is often called in Scripture by the names of the wisdom and logos of God. Wherefore God Himself has put the matter beyond all debate, whether or no His Son is not the same with His idea of Himself; for it is most certain that His wisdom and knowledge is the very same with His idea of Himself. How much does the Son of God speak in proverbs under that name of wisdom!

There is very much of image of this in ourselves. Man is as if he were two, as some of the great wits of this age have observed. A sort of genie is with man, that accompanies him and attends wherever he goes, so that a man has conversation with himself. That is, he has a conversation with his own idea, so that, if his idea be excellent, he will take great delight and happiness in conferring and communing with it. He takes complacency in himself, he applauds himself. And wicked men accuse them [selves], and fight with themselves as if they were two. And man is truly happy then, and only then, when these two agree. And they delight in themselves and in their own idea and image as God delights in His.

The Holy Spirit is the act of God between the Father and the Son, infinitely loving and delighting in each other. Sure I am that, if the Father and the Son do infinitely delight in each other, there must be an infinitely pure and perfect act between them, an infinitely sweet energy which we call delight. This is certainly distinct from the other two. The delight and energy that is begotten in us by an idea is thus distinct from the idea, so it cannot be confounded in God, either with God begetting, or His idea and image – or Son. It is distinct from each of the other two, and yet it is God. The pure and perfect act of God is God, because God is a pure act. It appears that this is God, because that which acts perfectly is all act and nothing but act. There is image of this in created beings that approach to perfect action. How frequently do we say that the saints of Heaven are all transformed into love and dissolved into joy – become activity itself, changed into pure ecstasy! I acknowledge these are metaphorical in this case; but yet it is true that, the more perfect the act is, the more it resembles those infinitely perfect acts of God in this respect. And I believe it will be plain to one that thinks intensely, that the perfect act of God must be a substantial act. We say that the perfect delights of reasonable creatures are substantial delights; but the delight of God is properly a substance, yea, an infinitely perfect substance, even the essence. It appears by the Holy Scriptures that the Holy Spirit is the perfect act of God. The name declares it, (1) the spirit of God denotes to us the activity, vivacity, and energy of God, and (2) it appears that the Holy Spirit is the pure act of God and energy of the deity, by His office, which is to activate us and quicken all things, and to beget energy and vivacity in the creature. And it also appears that the Holy Spirit is this act of the deity, even love and delight, because from eternity there was no other act in God but thus acting with respect to Himself, and delighting perfectly and infinitely in Himself as that infinite delight that is between the Father and the Son. For the object of God's perfect act must necessarily be Himself because there is no other. But we have shown that the object of the divine mind is God's Son and idea. And what other act can be thought of in God from eternity, but delighting in Himself, the act of love which God is (1 John 4.8, 'he that loveth not; knoweth not God: for God is love')? And if God is love, and he that dwelleth in love dwelleth in God, and God in him, doubtless this intends principally that infinite love God has to Himself; so that the Scripture has told us that that love which is between the Father and Son is God. The Holy Spirit's name is the Comforter. But no doubt but 'tis the infinite delight God has in Himself is that Comforter, that is, the fountain of all delight and comfort. (pp. 254–7)

Source: *The Philosophy of Jonathan Edwards, From His Private Notebooks*, ed. Harvey G. Townsend, Westport, CT, Greenwood Press, 1972 (University of Oregon Monographs, 1955).

14

Feeling, Imagination and Contemplation

— ·—

14.1 Friedrich D. E. Schleiermacher, from *On Religion: Speeches to Its Cultured Despisers*

Against the Enlightenment critique of religion and in the context of Romanticism, Schleiermacher (1768–1834), the first modern theologian, tried to situate and defend the role of religion. According to him, religion is located neither in metaphysics nor in morals, but above all in feeling and intuition. This emphasis on feeling is reflected in all strands of writing and the arts during the Romantic epoch. It is interesting to note the close correspondence, for example, between Caspar David Friedrich's art and the thought expressed in Schleiermacher, especially his idea of religion as the feeling of absolute dependence.

I wish I could present religion to you in some well-known form so that you might immediately remember its features, its movements, and its manners and exclaim that you have here or there seen it just this way in real life. But I would deceive you. For it is not found among human beings as undisguised as it appears to the conjurer, and for some time has not let itself be viewed in the form peculiar to it. The particular disposition of various cultivated peoples no longer shows itself so purely and distinctly in individual actions, since their commerce has become more many-sided and what they have in common has increased through all sorts of connections. Only the imagination can grasp the entire idea behind these qualities, which are encountered only singly as dispersed and mixed with much that is foreign. This is also the case with spiritual things, and among them with religion. It is well known to you how everything is now full of harmonious development; and precisely this has caused such a completed and extended sociability and friendliness within the human soul that none of the soul's powers in fact now acts among us distinctly, as much as we like to think of them as distinct. In every accomplishment each is immediately precipitated by polite love and beneficial support of the other and is somewhat deflected from its path. One looks around vainly in this cultured world for an action that could furnish a true expression of some capacity of spirit, be it sensibility or understanding, ethical life or religion.

Do not, therefore, be indignant and explain it as disdain for the present if, for the sake of clarity, I frequently lead you back to those more childlike times where, in a less perfected state, everything was still, distinct and individual. If I begin at once with that theme, and in some way or other meticulously come back to it, this is to warn you emphatically about the confusion of religion with things that sometimes look similar to it and with which you will everywhere find it mixed.

If you put yourselves on the highest standpoint of metaphysics and morals, you will find that both have the same object as religion, namely, the universe and the relationship of humanity to it. This similarity has long since been a basis of manifold aberrations; metaphysics and morals have therefore invaded religion on many occasions, and much that belongs to religion has concealed itself in metaphysics or morals under an unseemly form. But shall you, for this reason, believe that it is identical with the one or the other? I know that your instinct tells you the contrary, and it also follows from your opinions; for you never admit that religion walks with the firm step of which metaphysics is unable and you do not forget to observe diligently that there are quite a few then it must be set off from those in some manner, regardless of the common subject-matter. Religion must treat this subject-matter completely differently, express or work out another relationship of humanity to it, have another mode of procedure or another goal; for only in this way can that which is similar in its subject-matter to something else achieve a determinate nature and a unique existence. I ask you, therefore, What does your metaphysics do – or, if you want to have nothing to do with the outmoded name that is too historical for you, your transcendental philosophy? It classifies the universe and divides it into this being and that, seeks out the reasons for what exists, and deduces the necessity of what is real while spinning the reality of the world and its laws out of itself. Into this realm, therefore, religion must not venture too far. It must not have the tendency to posit essences and to determine natures, to lose itself in an infinity of reasons and deductions, to seek out final causes, and to proclaim eternal truths. . . . Let us deal honestly with one another. You do not like religion; we started from that assumption. But in conducting an honest battle against it, which is not completely without effort, you do not want to have fought against a shadow like the one with which we have struggled. Religion must indeed be something integral that could have arisen in the human heart, something thinkable from which a concept can be formulated about which one can speak and argue. I find it very unjust if you yourselves stitch together something untenable out of such disparate things, call it religion, and then make so much needless ado about it. . . . In order to take possession of its own domain, religion renounces herewith all claims to whatever belongs to those others and gives back everything that has to determine and explain the universe according to its nature as does metaphysics; it does not desire to continue the universe's development and perfect it by the power of freedom and the divine free choice of a human being as does morals. Religion's essence is neither thinking nor acting, but intuition and feeling. It wishes to intuit the universe, wishes devoutly to overhear the universe's own manifestations and actions, longs to be grasped and filled by the universe's immediate influences in childlike passivity. Thus, religion is opposed to these two in everything that makes up its essence and in everything that characterizes its effects. Metaphysics and morals see in the whole universe only humanity as the centre of all relatedness, as the condition of all being and the cause of all becoming; religion wishes to see the infinite, its imprint and its manifestation, in humanity no less than in all other individual and finite forms. Metaphysics proceeds from finite human nature and wants to define consciously, from its simplest concept, the extent of its powers, and its receptivity, what the universe can be for us and how we necessarily must view it. Religion also lives its whole life in nature, but in the infinite nature of totality, the one and all; what holds in nature for everything individual also holds for the human being; and wherever everything, including man, may press on or tarry within this eternal ferment of individual forms and beings, religion wishes to intuit and to divine this in detail in quiet submissiveness. Morality proceeds from the consciousness of freedom; it wishes to extend freedom's realm to infinity and to make everything subservient to it. Religion breathes there where freedom itself has once more become nature; it apprehends man beyond the play of his particular powers and his personality, and views him from the vantage point where he must be what he is, whether he likes it or not.

Thus religion maintains its own sphere and its own character only by completely removing itself from the sphere and character of speculation as well as from that of praxis. Only when it places itself next to both of them is the common ground perfectly filled out and human nature completed from this dimension. Religion shows itself to you as the necessary and indispensable third next to those two, as their natural counterpart, not slighter in worth and splendour than what you wish of them. (pp. 204–7)

Source: *Friedrich D. E. Schleiermacher, On Religion: Speeches to Its Cultured Despisers*, trans. Richard Crouter, Cambridge, Cambridge University Press, 1988, pp. 97–9, 101–2, reprinted in P. Helm, ed., *Faith and Reason*, Oxford, Oxford University Press, 1999.

14.2 Samuel Taylor Coleridge, from *Biographia Literaria*

British poet, conversationalist and philosopher, Coleridge (1772–1834) was influenced first by Berkeley and then by Kant, Fichte and Schelling. His thought on the imagination – in particular his distinction between fancy and imagination – and his views on the nature of perception had considerable influence on nineteenth-century literary and religious thought.

The imagination then I consider either as primary, or secondary. The primary imagination I hold to be the living power and prime agent of all human perception, and as a repetition in the finite mind of the eternal act of creation in the infinite I AM. The secondary I consider as an echo of the former, co-existing with the conscious will, yet still as identical with the primary in the kind of its agency, and differing only in degree, and in the mode of its operation. It dissolves, diffuses, dissipates, in order to re-create; or where this process is rendered impossible, yet still, at all events, it struggles to idealize and to unify. It is essentially *vital*, even as all objects (as objects) are essentially fixed and dead.

Fancy, on the contrary, has no other counters to play with but fixities and definites. The fancy is indeed no other than a mode of memory emancipated from the order of time and space; and blended with, and modified by that empirical phaenomenon of the will which we express by the word *choice*. But equally with the ordinary memory it must receive all its materials ready made from the law of association. (Vol. 1, Ch. 13, p. 167)

But if this should be admitted as a satisfactory character of a poem, we have still to seek for a definition of poetry. The writings of Plato, and Bishop Taylor, and the *Theoria Sacra* of Burnet, furnish undeniable proofs that poetry of the highest kind may exist without metre, and even without the contradistinguishing objects of a poem. The first chapter of Isaiah (indeed a very large proportion of the whole book) is poetry in the most emphatic sense; yet it would be not less irrational than strange to assert that pleasure, and not truth, was the immediate object of the prophet. In short, whatever specific import we attach to the word poetry, there will be found involved in it, as a necessary consequence, that a poem of any length neither can be, nor ought to be, all poetry. Yet if a harmonious whole is to be produced, the remaining parts must be preserved in *keeping* with the poetry; and this can be no otherwise effected than by such a studied selection and artificial arrangement as will partake of one, though not a peculiar, property of poetry. And this again can be no other than the property of exciting a more continuous and equal attention than the language of prose aims at, whether colloquial or written.

My own conclusions on the nature of poetry, in the strictest use of the word, have been in part anticipated in the preceding disquisition on the fancy and imagination. What is poetry? is so nearly the same question with, what is a poet? that the answer to the one is involved in the solution of the other. For it is a distinction resulting from the poetic genius itself, which sustains and modifies the images, thoughts and emotions of the poet's own mind. The poet, described in ideal perfection, brings the whole soul of man into activity, with the subordination of its faculties to each other, according to their relative worth and dignity. He diffuses a tone and spirit of unity that blends and (as it were) fuses, each into each, by that synthetic and magical power to which we have exclusively appropriated the name of imagination. This power, first put in action by the will and understanding and retained under their irremissive, though gentle and unnoticed, controul [sic] (*laxis effertur habenis*) reveals itself in the balance or reconciliation of opposite or discordant qualities: of sameness, with difference; of the general, with the concrete; the idea, with the image; the individual, with the representative; the sense of novelty and freshness, with old and familiar objects; a more than usual state of emotion, with more than usual order; judgement ever awake and steady self-possession, with enthusiasm and feeling profound or vehement; and while it blends and harmonizes the natural and the artificial, still subordinates art to nature; the manner to the matter; and our admiration of the poet to our sympathy with the poetry. . . . Finally, good sense is the body of poetic genius, fancy its drapery, motion its life, and imagination the soul that is every where, and in each; and forms all into one graceful and intelligent whole. (Vol. 2, Ch. 14, pp. 173–4)

Source: *Samuel Taylor Coleridge, Biographia Literaria*, ed. George Watson, London, J. M. Dent & Sons Ltd / New York, E. P. Dutton & Co. Inc., 1975.

14.3 John Henry Newman, from *A Grammar of Assent*

In A Grammar of Assent *Newman (1801–90), member of the Oxford Movement, convert to Catholicism and Cardinal, examines how conscience plays a role in our knowledge of God. Here he discusses how imagination leads to action only in an indirect way and also in what regard conscience and the sense of the beautiful, or of taste, correspond to and differ from each other.*

Real Assents . . . Next, Assent, however strong, and accorded to images however vivid, is not therefore necessarily practical. Strictly speaking, it is not imagination that causes action; but hope and fear, likes and dislikes, appetite, passion, affection, the stirrings of selfishness and self-love. What imagination does for us is to find a means of stimulating those motive powers; and it does so by providing a supply of objects strong enough to stimulate them. The thought of honour, glory, duty, self-aggrandisement, gain, or on the other hand of Divine Goodness, future reward, eternal life, perseveringly dwelt upon, leads us along a course of action corresponding to itself, but only in case there be that in our minds which is congenial to it. However, when there is that preparation of mind, the thought does lead to the act. Hence it is that the fact of a proposition being accepted with a real assent is accidentally an earnest of that proposition being carried out in conduct, and the imagination may be said in some sense to be of a practical nature, inasmuch as it leads to practice indirectly by the action of its object upon the affection. (pp. 82–3)

Apprehension and Assent in Religion, Belief in One God . . . Let us then thus consider conscience, not as a rule of right conduct, but as a sanction of right conduct. This is its primary and most authoritative aspect; it is the ordinary sense of the word. Half the world would be puzzled to know what was meant by the moral sense; but everyone knows what is meant by a good or bad conscience. Conscience is ever forcing on us by threats and by promises that we must follow the right and avoid the wrong; so far it is one and the same in the mind of everyone, whatever be its particular errors in particular minds as to the acts which it orders to be done or to be avoided; and in this respect it corresponds to our perception of the beautiful and deformed. As we have naturally a sense of the beautiful and graceful in nature and art, though tastes proverbially differ, so we have a sense of duty and obligation, whether we all associate it with the same certain actions in particular or not. Here, however, Taste and Conscience part company: for the sense of beautifulness, as indeed the Moral Sense, has no special relations to persons, but contemplates objects in themselves; conscience, on the other hand, is concerned with persons primarily, and with actions mainly as viewed in their doers, or rather with self alone and one's own actions, and with others only indirectly and as if in association with self. And further, taste is its own evidence, appealing to nothing beyond its own sense of the beautiful or the ugly, and enjoying the specimens of the beautiful simply for their own sake; but conscience does not repose on itself, but vaguely reaches forward to something beyond self, and dimly discerns a sanction higher than self for its decisions, as is evidenced in that keen sense of obligation and responsibility which informs them. And hence it is that we are accustomed to speak of conscience as a voice, a term which we should never think of applying to the sense of the beautiful; and moreover a voice, or the echo of a voice, imperative and constraining, like no other dictate in the whole of our experience. And again, in consequence of this prerogative of dictating and commanding, which is of its essence, Conscience has an intimate bearing on our affections and emotions, leading us to reverence and awe, hope and fear, especially fear, a feeling, which is foreign for the most part, not only to Taste, but even to the Moral Sense, except in consequence of accidental associations. No fear is felt by anyone who recognises that his conduct has not been beautiful, though he may be mortified at himself, if perhaps he has thereby forfeited some advantage; but, if he has been betrayed into any kind of immorality, he has a lively sense of responsibility and guilt, though the act be no offence against society, – of distress and apprehension, even though it may be of present service to him, – of compunction and regret, though in itself it be most pleasurable, – of confusion of face, though it may have no witnesses. These various perturbations of mind which are characteristic of a bad conscience, and may be very considerable, – self-reproach, poignant shame, haunting remorse, chill dismay at the prospect of the future, – and their contraries, when the conscience is good, as real though less forcible, self-approval, inward peace, lightness of heart, and the like, – these emotions constitute a specific difference between conscience and our other intellectual senses, – common sense, good sense, sense of expedience, taste, sense of honour, and the like, – as indeed they would also constitute between conscience and the moral sense, supposing these two were not aspects of one and the same feeling, exercised upon one and the same subject-matter.

So much for the characteristic phenomena, which conscience presents, nor is it difficult to determine what they imply. I refer once more to our sense of the beautiful. This sense is attended by an intellectual enjoyment, and is free from whatever is of the nature of emotion, except in one case, viz. when it is excited by personal objects; then it is that the tranquil feeling of admiration is exchanged for the excitement of affection and passion. Conscience too, considered as a moral sense, an intellectual sentiment, is a sense of admiration and disgust, of approbation and blame: but it is something more than a moral sense; it is always, what the sense of the beautiful is only in certain cases; it is always emotional. No wonder then that it always implies what that sense only sometimes implies; that it always involves the recognition of a living object, towards which it is directed. Inanimate things cannot stir our affections; these are correlative with persons. If, as is the case, we feel responsibility, are ashamed, are frightened, at transgressing the voice of conscience, this implies that there is One to whom we are responsible, before whom we are ashamed, whose claims upon us we fear. If, on doing wrong, we feel the same tearful, broken-hearted sorrow which overwhelms us on hurting a mother; if, on doing right, we enjoy the same sunny serenity of mind, the same soothing, satisfactory delight which follows on our receiving praise from a father, we certainly have within us the image of some person, to whom our love and veneration look, in whose smile we find our happiness, for whom we yearn, towards whom we direct our pleadings, in whose anger we are troubled and waste away. These feelings in us are such as require for their exciting cause an intelligent being: we are not affectionate towards a stone, nor do we feel shame before a horse or a dog; we have no remorse or compunction on breaking mere human law: yet, so it is, conscience excites all these painful emotions, confusion, foreboding, self-condemnation; and on the other hand it sheds upon us a deep peace, a sense of security, a resignation, and a hope, which there is no sensible, no earthly object to elicit. 'The wicked flees, when no one pursueth;' then why does he flee? whence his terror? Who is it that he sees in solitude, in darkness, in the hidden chambers of his heart? If the cause of these emotions does not belong to this visible world, the Object to which his perception is directed must be Supernatural and Divine; and thus the phenomena of Conscience, as a dictate, avail to impress the imagination with the picture of a Supreme Governor, a Judge, holy, just, powerful, all-seeing, retributive, and is the creative principle of religion as the Moral Sense is the principle of ethics. (pp. 106–10)

Source: J. H. Newman, *An Essay in Aid of A Grammar of Assent*, London, New York, Bombay, Calcutta, Longmans, Green and Co., 1909.

14.4 John Ruskin, from *Modern Painters*

Ruskin (1819–90) was an influential English art critic and social reformer who came to recognition through his multi-volume work Modern Painters. *He became the first professor of fine arts in Oxford University in 1870. Ruskin developed a spiritual interpretation of art whereby he emphasized that a people's architecture and art are expressive of its ethical views and its religion. In this extract on the theoretic faculty he concludes that believers often endeavoured to earn their own salvation. Instead they ought to let God work on them. The true service of God will be* theoria, *the contemplation and vision of God.*

General Conclusions Respecting the Theoretic Faculty

At present it would be useless to enter on an examination for which we have no materials; and I proceed, therefore, to notice that other and opposite error of Christian men in thinking that there is little use or value in the operation of the theoretic faculty, not that I at present either feel myself capable, or that this is the place for the discussion of that vast question of the operation of taste (as it is called) on the minds of men, and the national value of its teaching, but I wish shortly to reply to that objection which might be urged to the real moral dignity of the faculty, that many Christian men seem to be in themselves without it, and even to discountenance it in others.

It has been said by Schiller, in his letters on aesthetic culture, that the sense of beauty never farthered the performance of a single duty. Although this gross and inconceivable falsity will hardly be accepted by anyone in so many terms, seeing that there are few so utterly lost but that they receive, and know that they receive, at certain moments, strength of some kind, or rebuke from the appealings of outward things; and that it is not possible for a Christian man to walk across so much as a rood of the natural earth, with mind unagitated and rightly poised, without receiving strength and hope from some stone, flower, leaf, or sound, nor without a sense of a dew falling upon him out of the sky; though, I say, this falsity is not wholly and in terms admitted, yet it seems to be partly and practically so in much of the doing and teaching even of holy men, who in the recommending of the love of God to us, refer but seldom to those things in which it is most abundantly and immediately shown; though they insist much on his giving of bread, and raiment, and health, (which he gives to all inferior creatures,) they require us not to thank him for that glory of his works which he has permitted us alone to perceive: they tell us often to meditate in the closet, but they send us not, like Isaac, into the fields at even, they dwell on the duty of self-denial, but they exhibit not the duty of delight.

Now there are reasons for this, manifold, in the toil and warfare of an earnest mind, which, in its efforts at the raising of men from utter loss and misery, has often but little time or disposition to take heed of anything more than the bare life, and of those so occupied it is not for us to judge, but I think, that, of the weaknesses, distresses, vanities, schisms, and sins, which often even in the holiest men, diminish their usefulness, and mar their happiness, there would be fewer if, in their struggle with nature fallen, they sought for more aid from nature undestroyed. It seems to me that the real sources of bluntness in the feelings towards the splendour of the grass and glory of the flower, are less to be found in ardour of occupation, in seriousness of compassion, or heavenliness of desire, than in the turning of the eye at intervals of rest too selfishly within; the want of power to shake off the anxieties of actual and near interest, and to leave results in God's hands; the scorn of all that does not seem immediately apt for our purposes, or open to our understanding, and perhaps something of pride, which desires rather to investigate than to feel.

I believe that the root of almost every schism and heresy from which the Christian church has ever suffered, has been the effort of men to earn, rather than to receive, their salvation; and that the reason that preaching is so commonly ineffectual is, that it calls on men oftener to work for God, than to behold God working for them. If, for every rebuke that we utter of men's vices, we put forth a claim upon their hearts; if for every assertion of God's demands from them, we could substitute a display of his kindness to them; if side by side with every warning of death, we could exhibit proofs and promises of immortality; if, in fine, instead of assuming the being of an awful Deity, which men, though they cannot and dare not deny, are always unwilling, sometimes unable, to conceive, we were to show them a near, visible, inevitable, but all beneficent Deity, whose presence makes the earth itself a heaven, I think there would be fewer deaf children sitting in the market-place.

At all events, whatever may be the inability in this present life to mingle the full enjoyment of the Divine works with the full discharge of every practical duty, and confessedly in many cases this must be, let us not attribute the inconsistency to any indignity of the faculty of contemplation, but to the sin and the suffering of the fallen state, and the change of order from the keeping of the garden to the tilling of the ground. We cannot say how far it is right or agreeable with God's will, while men are perishing round about us, while grief, and pain, and wrath, and impiety, and death, and all the powers of the air, are working wildly and evermore, and the cry of blood going up to heaven, that any of us should take hand from the plough; but this we know, that there will come a time when the service of God shall be the beholding of him; and though in these stormy seas, where we are now driven up and down, his Spirit is dimly seen on the face of the waters, and we are left to cast anchors out of the stern, and wish for the day, that day will come, when, with the evangelists on the crystal and stable sea, all the creatures of God shall be full of eyes within, and there shall be 'no more curse, but his servants shall serve him, and shall see his face.' (Ch. 15, para. 9–12, pp. 138–41)

Source: John Ruskin, *Modern Painters*, vol. 2, part 3, sections 1 and 2, New York, John Wiley & Sons, 1889.

15

Art and Aesthetics:
Philosophical–Theological Perceptions

— ▬ —

15.1 Immanuel Kant, from *Critique of Judgement*

This pre-eminent German philosopher of the Enlightenment (1724–1804),
whose thought on aesthetics has been influential to this day, here discusses
the sublime. The sublime as an aesthetic category was conceived by the
Romantics and features in the works of contemporary artists, musicians and
writers, such as J. M. W. Turner, C. D. Friedrich, Franz Liszt, etc. and in the
writings of theologians and philosophers such as Burke, Kant and Schleier-
macher. Kant, who in his aesthetics concentrated on the nature of aesthetic
experience, argues that the sense of the sublime is not present in nature as
such but is aroused in the mind by perceiving the might of nature. In
contemplating the 'effects of might' one may also become aware of God's
sublimity on condition that one is sincerely tuned towards God's will.

On the Dynamically Sublime in Nature

On Nature as a Might Might is an ability that is superior to great obstacles. It is
called *dominance* [*Gewalt*] if it is superior even to the resistance of something
that itself possesses might. When in an aesthetic judgment we consider nature as
a might that has no dominance over us, then it is *dynamically sublime*. If we are
to judge nature as sublime dynamically, we must present it as arousing fear. (But
the reverse does not hold: not every object that arouses fear is found sublime
when we judge it aesthetically.) For when we judge [something] aesthetically
(without a concept), the only way we can judge a superiority over obstacles is by
the magnitude of the resistance. But whatever we strive to resist is an evil, and it
is an object of fear if we find that our ability [to resist it] is no match for it. Hence
nature can count as a might, and so as dynamically sublime, for aesthetic judgment only insofar as we consider it as an object of fear. We can, however, consider an object *fearful* without being afraid *of* it, namely, if we judge it in such a
way that we merely *think* of the case where we might possibly want to put up

resistance against it, and that any resistance would in that case be utterly futile. Thus a virtuous person fears God without being afraid of him. For he does not think of wanting to resist God and his commandments as a possibility that should worry *him*. But for every such case, which he thinks of as not impossible intrinsically, he recognizes God as fearful. Just as we cannot pass judgment on the beautiful if we are seized by inclination and appetite, so we cannot pass judgment at all on the sublime in nature if we are afraid. For we flee from the sight of an object that scares us, and it is impossible to like terror that we take seriously. That is why the agreeableness that arises from the cessation of a hardship is *gladness*. But since this gladness involves our liberation from a danger, it is accompanied by our resolve never to expose ourselves to that danger again. Indeed, we do not even like to think back on that sensation, let alone actively seek out an opportunity for it. On the other hand, consider bold, overhanging and, as it were, threatening rocks, thunderclouds piling up in the sky and moving about accompanied by lightning and thunderclaps, volcanoes with all their destructive power, hurricanes with all the devastation they leave behind, the boundless ocean heaved up, the high waterfall of a mighty river, and so on. Compared to the might of any of these, our ability to resist becomes an insignificant trifle. Yet the sight of them becomes all the more attractive the more fearful it is, provided we are in a safe place. And we like to call these objects sublime because they raise the soul's fortitude above its usual middle range and allow us to discover in ourselves an ability to resist which is of a quite different kind, and which gives us the courage [to believe] that we could be a match for nature's seeming omnipotence.

For although we found our own limitation when we considered the immensity of nature and the inadequacy of our ability to adopt a standard proportionate to estimating aesthetically the magnitude of nature's *domain,* yet we also found, in our power of reason, a different and nonsensible standard that has this infinity itself under it as a unit; and since in contrast to this standard everything in nature is small, we found in our mind a superiority over nature itself in its immensity. In the same way, though the irresistibility of nature's might makes us, considered as natural beings, recognize our physical impotence, it reveals in us at the same time an ability to judge ourselves independent of nature, and reveals in us a superiority over nature that is the basis of a self-preservation quite different in kind from the one that can be assailed and endangered by nature outside us. This keeps the humanity in our person from being degraded, even though a human being would have to succumb to that dominance [of nature]. Hence if in judging nature aesthetically we call it sublime, we do so not because nature arouses fear, but because it calls forth our strength (which does not belong to nature [within us]), to regard as small the [objects] of our [natural] concerns: property, health, and life, and because of this we regard nature's might (to which we are indeed subjected in these [natural] concerns) as yet not having such dominance over us, as persons, that we should have to bow to it if our highest principles were at stake and we had to choose between upholding or abandoning them. Hence nature is here called sublime [*erhaben*] merely because it elevates [*erhebt*] our imagination, [making] it exhibit those cases where the mind can come to feel its own sublimity, which lies in its vocation and elevates it even above nature.

This self-estimation loses nothing from the fact that we must find ourselves safe in order to feel this exciting liking, so that (as it might seem), since the danger is not genuine, the sublimity of our intellectual ability might also not be genuine. For here the liking concerns only our ability's *vocation* revealed in such cases, insofar as the predisposition to this ability is part of our nature, whereas it remains up to us, as our obligation, to develop and exercise this ability. And there is truth in this, no matter how conscious of his actual present impotence man may be when he extends his reflection thus far.

I admit that this principle seems farfetched and the result of some subtle reasoning, and hence high-flown [*überschwenglich*] for an aesthetic judgment. And yet our observation of man proves the opposite, and proves that even the commonest judging can be based on this principle, even though we are not always conscious of it. For what is it that is an object of the highest admiration even to the savage? It is a person who is not terrified, not afraid, and hence does not yield to danger but promptly sets to work with vigour and full deliberation. Even in a fully civilized society there remains this superior esteem for the warrior, except that we demand more of him: that he also demonstrate all the virtues of peace-gentleness, sympathy, and even appropriate care for his own person – precisely because they reveal to us that his mind cannot be subdued by danger. Hence, no matter how much people may dispute, when they compare the statesman with the general, as to which one deserves the superior respect, an aesthetic judgment decides in favour of the general. Even war has something sublime about it if it is carried on in an orderly way and with respect for the sanctity of the citizens' rights. At the same time it makes the way of thinking of a people that carries it on in this way all the more sublime in proportion to the number of dangers in the face of which it courageously stood its ground. A prolonged peace, on the other hand, tends to make prevalent a mere[ly] commercial spirit, and along with it base selfishness, cowardice, and softness, and to debase the way of thinking of that people. This analysis of the concept of the sublime, insofar as [sublimity is] attributed to might, may seem to conflict with the fact that in certain situations – in tempests, storms, earthquakes, and so on – we usually present God as showing himself in his wrath but also in his sublimity, while yet it would be both foolish and sacrilegious to imagine that our mind is superior to the effects produced by such a might, and is superior apparently even to its intentions. It seems that here the mental attunement that befits the manifestation of such an object is not a feeling of the sublimity of our own nature, but rather submission, prostration, and a feeling of our utter impotence; and this mental attunement is in fact usually connected with the idea of this object when natural events of this sort occur. It seems that in religion in general the only fitting behaviour in the presence of the deity is prostration, worship with bowed head and accompanied by contrite and timorous gestures and voice; and that is why most peoples have in fact adopted this behaviour and still engage in it. But, by the same token, this mental attunement is far from being intrinsically and necessarily connected with the idea of the *sublimity* of a religion and its object. A person who is actually afraid and finds cause for this in himself because he is conscious that with his reprehensible attitude he offends against a might whose will is at once irresistible and just is not at all in the frame of mind [needed] to admire divine greatness, which requires that we be attuned to quiet contemplation and that our judgment be completely free. Only if he is conscious that his attitude is sincere and pleasing to God, will these effects of might serve to arouse in him the idea of God's sublimity, insofar as he recognizes in his own attitude a sublimity that conforms to God's will, and is thereby elevated above any fear of such natural effects, which he does not regard as outbursts of God's wrath. Even humility, as a strict judging of our own defects which, when we are conscious that our own attitudes are good, could otherwise easily be cloaked with the frailty of human nature [as an excuse], is a sublime mental attunement, namely, voluntary subjection of ourselves to the pain of self-reprimand so as gradually to eradicate the cause of these defects. This alone is what intrinsically distinguishes religion from superstition. The latter establishes in the mind not a reverence for the sublime, but fear and dread of that being of superior might to whose will the terrified person finds himself subjected but without holding him in esteem; and this can obviously give rise to nothing but ingratiation and fawning, never to a religion based on good conduct.

Hence sublimity is contained not in any thing of nature, but only in our mind, insofar as we can become conscious of our superiority to nature within us, and thereby also to nature outside us (as far as it influences us). Whatever arouses this feeling in us, and this includes the *might* of nature that challenges our forces, is then (although improperly) called sublime. And it is only by presupposing this idea within us, and by referring to it, that we can arrive at the idea of the sublimity of that being who arouses deep respect in us, not just by his might as demonstrated in nature, but even more by the ability, with which we have been endowed, to judge nature without fear and to think of our vocation as being sublimely above nature. (para. 28, pp. 119–23)

Source: *Immanuel Kant, The Critique of Judgement (1790)*, trans. Werner S. Pluhar, Indianapolis, Hackett Publishing Company, 1987.

15.2 Georg W. F. Hegel, from *Aesthetics – Lectures on Fine Art*

The immensely influential German Idealist philosopher Hegel (1770–1831) arguably wrote the most comprehensive and systematic aesthetics in modernity. Still relevant, it has impacted on literary theory, art history, philosophical and theological aesthetics. Hegel concentrates on the content and meaning of works of art and their expression of ideas. He considered art in the context of history and was both a proponent and critic of Romantic aestheticism. In this extract he writes about art's power of expressing truth and at the same time predicts the end of art, i.e. the priority of philosophy/ science over art in expressing the true and the real. He comments on the spiritual and religious dimension of art and on the depiction of the Christ event in Romantic art.

Introduction Art liberates the true content of phenomena from the pure appearance and deception of this bad, transitory world, and gives them a higher actuality, born of the spirit. Thus, far from being mere pure appearance, a higher reality and truer existence is to be ascribed to the phenomena of art in comparison with [those of] ordinary reality.

Neither can the representations of art be called a deceptive appearance in comparison with the truer representations of historiography. For the latter has not even immediate existence but only the spiritual pure appearance thereof as the element of its portrayals, and its content remains burdened with the entire contingency of ordinary life and its events, complications, and individualities, whereas the work of art brings before us the eternal powers that govern history without this appendage of the immediate sensuous present and its unstable appearance.

But if the mode in which artistic forms appear is called a deception in comparison with philosophical thinking and with religious and moral principles, of course the form of appearance acquired by a topic in the sphere of *thinking* is the truest reality; but in comparison with the appearance of immediate existence and of historiography, the pure appearance of art has the advantage that it points through and beyond itself, and itself hints at something spiritual of which it is to give us an idea, whereas immediate appearance does not present itself as deceptive but rather as the real and the true, although the truth is in fact contaminated and concealed by the immediacy of sense. The hard shell of nature and the ordinary world make it more difficult for the spirit to penetrate through them to the Idea than works of art do.

But while on the one hand we give this high position to art, it is on the other hand just as necessary to remember that neither in content nor in form is art the highest and absolute mode of bringing to our minds the true interests of the spirit. For precisely on account of its form, art is limited to a specific content.

Only one sphere and stage of truth is capable of being represented in the element of art. In order to be a genuine content for art, such truth must in virtue of its own specific character be able to go forth into [the sphere of] sense and remain adequate to itself there. This is the case, for example, with the gods of Greece. On the other hand, there is a deeper comprehension of truth which is no longer so akin and friendly to sense as to be capable of appropriate adoption and expression in this medium. The Christian view of truth is of this kind, and, above all, the spirit of our world today, or, more particularly, of our religion and the development of our reason, appears as beyond the stage at which art is the supreme mode of our knowledge of the Absolute. The peculiar nature of artistic production and of works of art no longer fills our highest need. We have got beyond venerating works of art as divine and worshipping them. The impression they make is of a more reflective kind, and what they arouse in us needs a higher touchstone and a different test. Thought and reflection have spread their wings above fine art. Those who delight in lamenting and blaming may regard this phenomenon as a corruption and ascribe it to the predominance of passions and selfish interests which scare away the seriousness of art as well as its cheerfulness; or they may accuse the distress of the present time, the complicated state of civil and political life which does not permit a heart entangled in petty interests to free itself to the higher ends of art. This is because intelligence itself subserves this distress, and its interests, in sciences which are useful for such ends alone, and it allows itself to be seduced into confining itself to this desert.

However all this may be, it is certainly the case that art no longer affords that satisfaction of spiritual needs which earlier ages and nations sought in it, and found in it alone, a satisfaction that, at least on the part of religion, was most intimately linked with art. The beautiful days of Greek art, like the golden age of the later Middle Ages, are gone. The development of reflection in our life today has made it a need of ours, in relation both to our will and judgement, to cling to general considerations and to regulate the particular by them, with the result that universal forms, laws, duties, rights, maxims, prevail as determining reasons and are the chief regulator. But for artistic interest and production we demand in general rather a quality of life in which the universal is not present in the form of law and maxim, but which gives the impression of being one with the senses and the feelings, just as the universal and the rational is contained in the imagination by being brought into unity with a concrete sensuous appearance. Consequently the conditions of our present time are not favourable to art. It is not, as might be supposed, merely that the practising artist himself is infected by the loud voice of reflection all around him and by the opinions and judgements on art that have become customary everywhere, so that he is misled into introducing more thoughts into his work; the point is that our whole spiritual culture is of such a kind that he himself stands within the world of reflection and its relations, and could not by any act of will and decision abstract himself from it; nor could he by special education or removal from the relations of life contrive and organize a special solitude to replace what he has lost.

In all these respects art, considered in its highest vocation, is and remains for us a thing of the past. Thereby it has lost for us genuine truth and life, and has rather been transferred into our *ideas* instead of maintaining its earlier necessity in reality and occupying its higher place. What is now aroused in us by works of art is not just immediate enjoyment but our judgement also, since we subject to our intellectual consideration (i) the content of art, and (ii) the work of art's means of presentation, and the appropriateness or inappropriateness of both to one another. The *philosophy* of art is therefore a greater need in our day than it was in days when art by itself as art yielded full satisfaction. Art invites us to intellectual consideration, and that not for the purpose of creating art again, but for knowing philosophically what art is. (pp. 9–11)

The Religious Domain of Romantic Art

The Redemptive History of Christ   The reconciliation of the spirit with itself, the absolute history, the process of the truth, is brought to our view and conviction by the appearance of God in the world. The simple heart of this reconciliation is the coalescence of absolute essentiality with the individual human subject; an individual man is God, and God an individual man. This implies that the human spirit, in its Concept and essence, is *implicitly* true spirit, and every individual subject, therefore, as man, has the infinite vocation and importance of being one of God's purposes and being in unity with God. But on this account man is all the same faced with the demand that he give actuality to this his Concept which at first is purely implicit, i.e. that he make union with God the goal of his being, and achieve it. If he has fulfilled this vocation, then in himself he is free infinite spirit. This is possible for him only because that unity is the original fact, the eternal basis of human and divine nature. [In the first place] this goal is at the same time the absolute beginning, the presupposition of the romantic religious consciousness that God himself is man, flesh, that he has become this individual person in whom therefore the reconciliation does not remain something implicit (in which case it would be known only in its *Concept*) but stands forth *objectively* existent for human senses and conscious contemplation as this individual actually existing man. It is on account of this moment of individuality that in Christ every individual has a vision of his own reconciliation with God which in its essence is no mere possibility; it is actual and therefore has to appear in this one man as really achieved. But, secondly, since this unity, as the spiritual reconciliation of opposed moments, is no mere *immediate* coalescence into one, it follows that in this *one* man the process of spirit too, through which alone consciousness is truly spirit, must attain existence as the history of this man. This history of the spirit, consummated in one individual, contains nothing except what we have already touched on above, namely that the individual man casts aside his individuality of body and spirit, i.e. that he suffers and dies, but conversely through the grief of death rises out of death, and ascends as God in his glory, as the actual spirit which now has indeed entered existence as an individual, as this subject, yet even so is essentially truly God only as Spirit in his Church.

Apparent Superfluity of Art This history provides the fundamental topic for religious romantic art, and yet for this topic art, taken purely as art, becomes to a certain extent something superfluous. For the chief thing lies here in the inner conviction, feeling, and conception of this eternal truth, in the *faith* which bears witness to itself of the absolute truth and thereby imparts it to the inner life of mind. A developed faith, in other words, consists in the immediate conviction that the conception of the factors in this history suffices to bring truth itself before consciousness. But if it is a matter of the consciousness of *truth*, then the *beauty* of the appearance, and the representation, is an accessory and rather indifferent, for the truth is present for consciousness independently of art.

Necessary Emergence of Art Yet, on the other hand, the religious material contains in itself at the same time a factor whereby it is not only made accessible to art but does in a certain respect actually *need* art. In the religious ideas of romantic art, as has been indicated more than once already, this material involves pushing anthropomorphism to an extreme, in that it is precisely this material (i) which has as its centre the coalescence of the Absolute and Divine with a human person as actually perceived and therefore as appearing externally and corporeally, and (ii) which must present the Divine in this its individuality, bound as it is to the deficiency of nature and the finite mode of appearance. In this respect, for the appearance of God art provides to the contemplative consciousness the special presence of an actual individual shape, a concrete picture too of the external features of the events in which Christ's birth, life and sufferings, death, Resurrection, and Ascension to the right hand of God are displayed, so that, in general, the actual appearance of God, which has passed away, is repeated and perpetually renewed in art alone.

The Details of the External Appearance are Accidental But in so far as in this appearance the accent is laid on the fact that God is essentially an individual person, exclusive of others, and displays the unity of divine and human subjectivity not simply in general but as *this* man, there enter here again, in art, on account of the subject-matter itself, all the aspects of the contingency and particularity of external finite existence from which beauty at the height of the classical Ideal had been purified. What the free Concept of the beautiful had discarded as inappropriate, i.e. the non-Ideal, is here necessarily adopted and brought before our vision as a factor emerging from the subject-matter itself.

While therefore the Person of Christ as such is frequently chosen as a subject, every time those artists have proceeded in the worst possible way who have attempted to make out of Christ an ideal in the sense and in the manner of the classical ideal. For although such heads and figures of Christ do display seriousness, calm, and dignity, Christ should have on the one hand subjective personality and *individuality*, and, on the other, inwardness and purely *universal* spirituality; both these characteristics are inconsistent with the imprint of bliss on the visible aspect of the human form. To combine both these extremes in expression and form is of supreme difficulty, and painters especially found themselves in perplexity every time they depart from the traditional type.

Seriousness and depth of consciousness must be expressed in these heads, but the features and forms of the face and the figure must neither be of purely ideal beauty nor deviate into the commonplace and the ugly or rise to pure sublimity as such. The best thing in relation to the external form is the mean between natural detail and ideal beauty. To hit this due mean correctly is difficult, and so in this matter what may be especially conspicuous is the skill, sense, and spirit of the artist.

In general, in the case of representations throughout this whole sphere, we are referred, independently of the subject-matter, which belongs to faith, to the matter of the artist's subjective creation, more than is the case in the classical ideal. In classical art the artist aims at presenting the spiritual and the Divine directly in the forms of the body itself and in the organization of the human figure, and therefore the bodily forms in their modifications, when these diverge from the customary and the finite, afford a principal part of the interest. In the sphere now under consideration the shape remains the customary and familiar one; its forms are to a certain extent indifferent, something particular, which may be thus or otherwise, and may in this respect be treated with great freedom. Therefore the preponderating interest lies on the one hand in the manner in which the artist still makes the spiritual and the most inward content shine, as this spiritual element itself, through this customary and familiar material; on the other hand, in the artist's execution, in the technical means and skills whereby he has been able to breathe spiritual vitality into his shapes and make the most spiritual things perceptible and comprehensible.

As for the further subject-matter, it lies, as we have seen already, in the absolute history which springs from the Concept of spirit itself and which makes objective the conversion of bodily and spiritual individuality into its essence and universality. For the reconciliation of the individual person with God does not enter as a harmony directly, but as a harmony proceeding only from the infinite grief, from surrender, sacrifice, and the death of what is finite, sensuous, and subjective. Here finite and infinite are bound together into one, and the reconciliation in its true profundity, depth of feeling, and force of mediation is exhibited only through the magnitude and harshness of the opposition which is to be resolved. It follows that even the whole sharpness and dissonance of the suffering, torture, and agony involved in such an opposition, belong to the nature of spirit itself, whose absolute satisfaction is the subject-matter here.

This process of the spirit, taken in and by itself, is the essence and Concept of spirit in general, and therefore it entails the characteristic of being for consciousness the universal history which is to be repeated in every individual consciousness. For consciousness, as a multiplicity of individuals, is precisely the reality and existence of the universal spirit. At first, however, because the Spirit has as its essential factor reality in the individual, that universal history itself proceeds only in the shape of *one* individual in whom it happens as his, as the history of his birth, his suffering, his death, and his return from death, though in this individual it preserves at the same time the significance of being the history of the universal absolute Spirit.

The real turning-point in this life of God is the termination of his individual existence as *this* man, the story of the Passion, suffering on the cross, the Golgotha of the Spirit, the pain of death. This sphere of portrayal is separated *toto caelo* from the classical plastic ideal because here the subject-matter itself implies that the external bodily appearance, immediate existence as an individual, is revealed in the grief of his negativity as the negative, and that therefore it is by sacrificing subjective individuality and the sensuous sphere that the Spirit attains its truth and its Heaven. On the one hand, in other words, the earthly body and the frailty of human nature in general is raised and honoured by the fact that it is God himself who appears in human nature, but on the other hand it is precisely this human and bodily existent which is negative and comes into appearance in its grief, while in the classical ideal it does not lose undisturbed harmony with what is spiritual and substantial. Christ scourged, with the crown of thorns, carrying his cross to the place of execution, nailed to the cross, passing away in the agony of a torturing and slow death – this cannot be portrayed in the forms of Greek beauty; but the higher aspect in these situations is their inherent sanctity, the depth of the inner life, the infinity of grief, present as an eternal moment in the Spirit as sufferance and divine peace.

The wider group around this figure is formed partly of friends, partly of enemies. The friends are likewise no ideal figures but, in accordance with the Concept, particular individuals, ordinary men whom the pull of the Spirit brings to Christ. But the enemies are presented to us as inwardly evil because they place themselves in opposition to God, condemn him, mock him, torture him, crucify him, and the idea of inner evil and enmity to God brings with it on the external side, ugliness, crudity, barbarity, rage, and distortion of their outward appearance. In connection with all these there enters here as a necessary feature what is unbeautiful in comparison with the beauty of Greek art.

But the process of death is to be treated in the divine nature only as a point of transition whereby the reconciliation of the Spirit with itself is brought about, and the divine and human sides, the sheerly universal and the subjective appearance, whose mediation is in question, close together affirmatively. This affirmation is in general the basis and the original foundation [of the divine history] and must therefore also be made evident in this positive way. For this purpose the most favourable events in the history of Christ are supplied especially by the Resurrection and the Ascension, apart from the scattered moments at which Christ appears as teacher. But here there arises, especially for the visual arts, a supreme difficulty. For *(a)* it is the spiritual as such which is to be portrayed in its inwardness, *(b)* it is the absolute Spirit which in its infinity and universality must be put affirmatively in unity with subjectivity [i.e. in Christ] and yet, raised above immediate existence, must in the bodily and external shape bring before contemplation and feeling the entire expression of its infinity and inwardness. (Section III, Ch. 1, pp. 534–9)

Source: *Georg F. W. Hegel, Aesthetics – Lectures on Fine Art*, trans. T. M. Knox, vol. 1, Oxford, Clarendon Press, 1975.

15.3.1 Søren Kierkegaard, from *Journals and Papers*

The Danish Lutheran existentialist philosopher-theologian Kierkegaard (1813–55) wrote extensively on aesthetics. In short observations, he reflects in these passages primarily on the relationship between aesthetics, ethics and religion. Here, as in his Either/Or, *he emphasizes the primacy of truth over beauty and momentary aesthetic enjoyment in the context of religion and its ceremonies.*

Art, artists, artistry, the artistic

The Christian must not lack the eye, in a human sense the illuminating light, which for me makes it easier to comprehend a painted landscape than nature; there and in history he meets God's eye. (para. 134, p. 55)

Estheticism, the Esthetic

Christianity does not at all emphasize the idea of earthly beauty, which was everything to the Greeks; on the contrary, in a flight of genuine humour Paul speaks about the earthenware pots in which the spirit dwells. It is a real problem: to what extent should Christ be portrayed as an ideal of human beauty – and strangely enough, although many other kinds of similarities have been discerned between Christ and Socrates, no one has thought at all about this aspect, for Socrates was, as is well known, uglier than original sin. (para. 797, p. 368)

The relation between esthetics and ethics – the transition – pathos-filled, not dialectical – there a qualitatively different dialectic begins. To what extent are poetry and art reconcilable with life – something is true in esthetics – something else in ethics? (para. 808, p. 371)

By and large it is the most disastrous notion in the world that 'eloquence' has become the medium for the proclamation of Christianity. Sarcasm, irony, humour lie far closer to the existential in Christianity. (para. 818, p. 373)

Christianity-Eloquence All the ancients (Plato – many places in *Phaedrus, Gorgias*, etc.; Aristotle in *Rhetoric*; the later ancients after Plato and Aristotle) were unanimous, as were other later ones who thought about the matter, that the potency of eloquence is based upon probability. Christianity is the paradox. When it came into the world there was no eloquence (for the apostles and martyrs were far from being eloquent speakers; their lives were paradoxes and their words paradoxes just as Christianity is). But now Christianity has produced an effect in this world. This effect, whatever else it is, should not be confused with Christianity itself, is not Christianity itself. This effect (the shadow of the paradox of Christianity) comes within the category of probability. Christianity is now made probable – and so *eo ipso* the rhetoricians flourish. With reasons upon reasons, they are able to depict and depict and bellow and make all Christianity so probable, so probable – that it most likely is no longer Christianity. At first it happened *bona fide*, with good intentions – in our time the rhetoricians know well enough that it is wrong, but they think, let us just keep on. Christianity as probability – and served by rhetoricians – thus Christianity is abolished. (para. 824, p. 376)

Symptom When something is about to go out of life or has gone out, the change is recognizable by the fact that the passing actuality evokes another kind of interest – for example, speculative, esthetic, artistic. Thus it is characteristic of our age that a more and more common theme for novels . . . is the struggle of the genius with actuality. This indicates that no one ever thinks of realizing these things in actuality (Goethe, for example, openly adulterated his genius into talent). But just the same, we have to have the struggles of genius around, and the novels supply them. Shortsighted people make the mistake of thinking that it nevertheless is always a good thing that something is introduced this way; they even believe that in this manner it comes nearer to us or that we draw closer to it – ah, they are mistaken, this mode signifies that the actuality is becoming more distant. Thus the more artistically finished the novel becomes, the less it enters into life, the more it merely pampers and coddles people by dealing enjoyably with such things in the realm of the imagination. To believe that the artistic helps one into actuality is just as mistaken as to believe that the more artistically complete the sermon, the more it must influence the transformation of life – alas, no, the more it influences life esthetically, the more it influences away from the existential. (para. 827, p. 378)

Hypocrisy A hymn, after all, is the production of a poet, and the process no doubt goes something like this: the poet is seized by a mood, and he surrenders to it. Let us now assume that the content of such a hymn is love for his Saviour, how the soul loves him, gives up the whole world to have him, etc., and this is set forth in the most glowing expressions. That may be enough. But this hymn is supposed to be sung by the congregation. It always says *I* in the hymn; consequently, it is I who am singing. Am I able to say such a thing about myself – even in the remotest manner? No; therefore either I must sit without thinking so that I notice nothing at all, or I must be forced into hypocrisy. Generally the law for all religious communication is that it be true. Why? Because religiously there should be a turning in the direction of acting, doing accordingly, and it is precisely this turning which distinguishes the religious from the esthetic. The esthetic leads into the wild blue yonder, comes like a sneeze and goes like a sneeze. The esthetic is the moment and is in the moment; religiously, it is precisely the next moment which is decisive, for then I am supposed to act, and if I do not attend to that, I have changed that moment in the church or in the hymn singing into esthetic enjoyment. Therefore it is very important that everything that is said and sung in church should be true, not that it should be beautiful, great, glorious, ravishing, etc., not that I start to cry while my heart beats violently – no, the question is whether I am primarily related to all this in terms of acting accordingly. In church there is rarely straightforward talk of how things go in actuality. 'But it is improper' – what? – the way things go in actuality? – this I admit. But this is precisely why it should be talked about in church, in order that things may be different. The law is always: the truer, the better – not, the more ceremonious, the better. Religiously, ceremony is 'doing accordingly'; ceremony with trombone and trumpet, or ceremony in silk and velvet is, religiously, a misunderstanding, a ceremoniousness which seems to be neither a product of nor an aid to an understanding of the fact that God is spirit. As soon as we move in the direction of getting a ceremony appropriate for what is fitting to talk about in church or, more correctly, for expressions which are suitable in church, expressions ceremonious enough to be used in church, we very easily end in shadow-boxing or in hypocrisy. For God knows that life outside does not proceed very ceremoniously at all, and nevertheless this is what should be aimed at. (para. 829, pp. 379–80)

Source: *Søren Kierkegaard, Journals and Papers, vol. 1*, trans. and ed. Edna H. Hong and Howard V. Hong, Bloomington, London, Indiana University Press, 1967.

15.3.2 Søren Kierkegaard, from *Either/Or, Part 2*

In this extract Kierkegaard discusses the difference between the ethical individual and the aesthetic individual. He emphasizes that the person must move to the ethical stage. The person who lives ethically makes a choice, knows herself and is able to distinguish between the accidental and the essential.

Balance between the Esthetic and the Ethical in the Development of the Personality

On the whole, to choose is an intrinsic and stringent term for the ethical. Wherever in the stricter sense there is a question of an Either/Or, one can always be sure that the ethical has something to do with it. The only absolute Either/Or is the choice between good and evil, but this is also absolutely ethical. The esthetic choice is either altogether immediate, and thus no choice, or it loses itself in a great multiplicity. For example, when a young girl follows her heart's choice, this choice, however beautiful it is otherwise, is no choice in the stricter sense, because it is altogether immediate. If a man esthetically ponders a host of life tasks, then he, as is the case with you in the preceding portion, does not readily have one Either/Or but a great multiplicity, because the self-determining aspect of the choice has not been ethically stressed and because, if one does not choose absolutely, one chooses only for the moment and for that reason can choose something else the next moment. . . .

The person who chooses only esthetically never reaches this transfiguration, this higher dedication. Despite all its passion, the rhythm in his soul is only a *spiritus lenis* [weak aspiration]. . . . But choose, and you will see the validity inherent in so doing; indeed, no young girl can be as happy with her heart's choice as a man who has known how to choose. Consequently, either a person has to live esthetically or he has to live ethically. Here, as stated, it is still not a matter of a choice in the stricter sense, for the person who lives esthetically does not choose, and the person who chooses the esthetic after the ethical has become manifest to him is not living esthetically, for he is sinning and is subject to ethical qualifications, even if his life must be termed unethical. You see, this is, so to speak, the *character indelebilis* of the ethical, that the ethical, although it modestly places itself on the same level as the esthetic, nevertheless is essentially that which makes the choice a choice. And this is what is sad when one contemplates human life, that so many live out their lives in quiet lostness; they outlive themselves, not in the sense that life's content successively unfolds and is now possessed in this unfolding, but they live, as it were, away from themselves and vanish like shadows. Their immortal souls are blown away, and they are not disquieted by the question of its immortality, because they are already disintegrated before they die. They do not live esthetically, but neither has the ethical become manifest to them in its wholeness; nor have they actually rejected it, and therefore they are not sinning either, except insofar as it is a sin to be neither one thing nor the other. Nor do they doubt their immortality, for the person who deeply and fervently doubts it on his own behalf is sure to find what is right. I say 'on his own behalf', and it certainly is high time that someone warns against the magnanimous, gallant objectivity with which many thinkers think on behalf of all others and not on their own. If anyone calls what I am claiming here self-love, then I shall answer: That comes from having no idea of what this 'self' is and from the futility of a person's gaining the whole world but losing himself, and also it is bound to be a poor argument that does not first and foremost convince the person who presents it. Rather than designating the choice between good and evil, my Either/Or designates the choice by which one chooses good and evil or rules them out. Here the question is under what qualifications one will view all existence and personally live. (pp. 166–9)

Let us now compare an ethical and an esthetic individual. The primary difference, the crux of the matter, is that the ethical individual is transparent to himself and does not live *ins Blaue hinein* [in the wild blue yonder], as does the esthetic individual. This difference encompasses everything. The person who lives ethically has seen himself, knows himself, penetrates his whole concretion with his consciousness, does not allow vague thoughts to rustle around inside him or let tempting possibilities distract him with their juggling; he is not like a 'magic' picture that shifts from one thing to another, all depending on how one shifts and turns it. He knows himself. The phrase *gnothi seauton* [know yourself] is a stock phrase, and in it has been perceived the goal of all a person's striving. . . .

The esthetic individual considers himself in his concretion and makes distinctions *inter et inter* [between the one and the other]. He sees something as belonging to him in an accidental way, something else as belonging essentially. Yet this distinction is very relative, for as long as a person lives only esthetically, everything really belongs to him equally accidentally, and when an esthetic individual maintains this distinction, it merely shows a lack of energy. The ethical individual has learned this in despair and thus has another distinction, for he also makes a distinction between the essential and the accidental. Everything that is posited in his freedom belongs to him essentially, however accidental it may seem to be; everything that is not posited in his freedom is accidental, however essential it may seem to be. But for the ethical individual this distinction is not a product of his arbitrariness so that he might seem to have absolute power to make himself into what it pleased him to be. To be sure, the ethical individual dares to employ the expression that he is his own editor, but he is also fully aware that he is responsible, responsible for himself personally, inasmuch as what he chooses will have a decisive influence on himself, responsible to the order of things in which he lives, responsible to God. Regarded in this way, the distinction is correct, I believe, for essentially only that belongs to me which I ethically take on as a task. If I refuse to take it on, then my having refused it essentially belongs to me. When a person considers himself esthetically, he may make distinctions as follows. He says: I have a talent for painting – this I regard as an accidental trait; but I have a keen wit and a keen mind – this I regard as the essential that cannot be taken away from me without my becoming somebody else. To that I would answer: This whole distinction is an illusion, for if you do not take on this keen wit and keen mind ethically, as a task, as something for which you are responsible, then it does not belong to you essentially, and primarily because as long as you live merely esthetically your life is totally inessential.

To a certain degree, the person who lives ethically cancels the distinction between the accidental and the essential, for he takes responsibility for all of himself as equally essential; but it comes back again, for after he has done that, he makes a distinction, but in such a manner that he takes an essential responsibility for excluding what he excludes as accidental. Insofar as the esthetic individual, with 'esthetic earnestness', sets a task for his life, it is really the task of becoming absorbed in his own accidental traits, of becoming an individual whose equal in paradoxicality and irregularity has never been seen, of becoming a caricature of a human being. The reason we rarely meet such characters in life is that we rarely meet people who have a notion of what it is to live. But since many people have a decided penchant for chattering, we encounter on the street, at parties, and in books a great amount of chatter that has the unmistakable stamp of the *Originalitets-Wuth* [mania for originality] that, carried over into life, would enrich the world with a host of artificial products, one more ridiculous than the other.

The task the ethical individual sets for himself is to transform himself into the universal individual. Only the ethical individual gives himself an account of himself in earnest and is therefore honest with himself; only he has the paradigmatic decorum and propriety that are more beautiful than anything else. But to transform himself into the universal human being is possible only if I already have it within myself *kata dunamin* [potentially]. In other words, the universal can very well continue in and with the specific without consuming it; it is like that fire that burned without consuming the bush. If the universal human being is outside me, there is only one possible method, and that is to take off my entire concretion. This striving out in the unconstraint of abstraction is frequently seen. . . .

Every person, if he so wills, can become a paradigmatic human being, not by brushing off his accidental qualities, but by remaining in them and ennobling them. But he ennobles them by choosing them. By now you have easily seen that in his life the ethical individual goes through the stages we previously set forth as separate stages. He is going to develop in his life the personal, the civic, the religious virtues, and his life advances through his continually translating himself from one stage to another. As soon as a person thinks that one of these stages is adequate and that he dares to concentrate on it one-sidedly, he has not chosen himself ethically but has failed to see the significance of either isolation or continuity and above all has not grasped that the truth lies in the identity of these two. (pp. 258–62)

Source: *Søren Kierkegaard, Either/Or, Part 2*, trans. and ed. Edna H. Hong and Howard V. Hong, Princeton, Princeton University Press, 1987.

Part 5

The Twentieth Century

— —

Introduction

The twentieth century was marked by a rapid growth of pluralism, fragmentation and by disillusionment with the high hopes of modernity. Indeed, pluralism has become a hallmark of late modernity, whether in theology, the arts or other cultural and intellectual domains. This includes an apparent loss of agreed ultimate values which has made itself felt in all cultural spheres.

The belief in human progress and the confidence in technology and science based solely on reason ended abruptly and disastrously with World War One. After World War Two and the Holocaust, the question theologians had to face was how to engage at all in theology after Auschwitz. Had the belief in a powerful God not been rendered absurd with the slaughter of millions of innocent people? Such concerns, as well as the effects of imperialism in the southern hemisphere, the two world wars, the Hiroshima bomb, the unparalleled explosion of information through mass media and the awareness of suffering, not only on one's doorstep but on a global scale, were to affect the development of theology, philosophy and the arts. Theology has had to grapple with secularization and nihilism, but now, with the arrival of postmodernity, it also needs to respond to the renewed interest in all sorts of religious phenomena.

In this context one might recall that from the turn of the century, with the momentous contributions of the Post-Impressionists van Gogh, Cézanne, Seurat and Gauguin, the foundations had been laid for the simultaneous development of different styles in art. Up to the Impressionists one style had basically grown out of another. The Post-Impressionists once again sought to integrate form and substance into their works, whereas the Impressionists' aim had been to capture the fleeting moment. The Post-Impressionists became the forerunners of Expressionism, Cubism and Fauvism. From then on various styles in the visual arts developed simultaneously, including abstract art and conceptual art. In fashion, music and literature similar diversification of styles occurred, culminating in the late twentieth century with its typically postmodern artistic features, such as pastiche, irony and even cynicism. In theology this plurality was perhaps not yet as noticeable at the beginning of the century. However, in the latter half, local theologies, ecumenism, and theology in dialogue with other disciplines, especially with the sciences and the arts, were to become central issues.

It is in the face of these cultural, intellectual and historical trends that themes relating to a theological aesthetics are addressed. Obviously, the extracts chosen for this final section are far more numerous than those for the previous epochs. The difficulty here, unlike in earlier centuries, is the fact that the authors and texts which one might classify as 'classics' have not yet been quite established. Even if central texts on our theme, by thinkers such as Tillich, Barth, von Balthasar and Burch Brown, are likely to be remembered in future centuries, it is not clear yet which contributions to theological aesthetics of the twentieth century will finally be judged to be of seminal importance.

But we might see this difficulty in a more positive light. The publications on theological aesthetics, especially in the last twenty years, have expanded on an unprecedented scale. The dialogue between theology and the arts is now not only conducted by individual scholars, but by whole sub-departments, research centres within faculties, and conferences are also devoted to the theme. While in part this dialogue may echo something of the general trend towards aestheticization in all realms of everyday life in postmodern culture, it also reflects something of the actual state of theology, a discipline now struggling for its place in the academy. How can theology be relevant in an age when, in Europe, at any rate, church attendance is the exception rather than the rule? One way of tackling this issue is the trend towards interdisciplinary studies, which includes the arts. Moreover, for some of the educated middle classes, the museum or art gallery has become the modern temple, providing spiritual nourishment and meditative experiences.

In this final part, then, the aim is to give a representative, if not exhaustive, selection of the authors and themes emerging in recent theological aesthetics. Considering the range of texts included, one might at first be overwhelmed by their thematic diversity. Yet it is interesting to note that, despite such variety, certain basic themes recur.

In Chapter 16, Art as a 'locus theologicus', we find Tillich, Rahner, Dillenberger and Pattison amongst others. A common thread in these texts is the question how art can function as a source of and in theology. This is expressed in various contexts, from a personal memoir, like Sölle's, to more comprehensive and systematic analyses, as in Dillenberger or Tillich.

Tillich's role here is fundamental; he was the first theologian to appreciate autonomous modern art as a source of and for theology. His great love of the visual arts is witnessed in the many articles he wrote on the subject. While he has been criticized by subsequent scholars of theology and the arts for his somewhat problematic methodology and for his lack of interpreting works of art in detail, his pioneering stature remains unquestioned. Little recognized is Rahner's important contribution on the theme. His – like Tillich's – insistence that a work of art, as a genuine source of human self-expression, must not only be seen as an *ancilla theologiae* but can be a relevant locus of theology remains pertinent to this day. Hence his view that theology cannot be regarded as complete until it integrates the arts as an intrinsic moment of itself.

In the mid-century, French priest and man of vision Pie-Raymond Régamey devoted a whole book to the relationship between religion and the arts. He concluded, as Tillich, Rahner and Dillenberger would also argue, that even the atheist or Communist artist and those who have no connection with the Church must be allowed to work for the Church. In this way he raised a central issue: it is not necessarily the religiosity of the artist that matters in creating a spiritual or even a sacred work of art, but 'strictly speaking sacred art only requires a sacred character of the actual artistic creation, of the artist's exercise of his [or her] art'. This insight was in stark contrast to what had been the practice in the nineteenth century, when works with Christian subject matter intended for sacred spaces were frequently carried out by third-rate pious artists. No doubt they were sincere, but their art lacked in imagination, intellectual rigour, artistic brilliance, skill and originality, i.e. those aspects that make good art, and thus good theology.

Recognition of the abiding role of the arts not only in theology, but especially in the life of the church, in liturgy and places of worship was affirmed by Vatican II as well as by John Paul II in his Letter to Artists in 1999. It is regrettable, however, that the Council's clearly stated recommendation that the clergy ought to be trained in the 'history and development of sacred art' has often been ignored. This in turn may account for the lack of imagination and inspiring art in many church buildings to this day.

In Chapter 17, Truth, Meaning and Art, the writers' questions pertain to the art work as a shaper of meaning in today's culture. This includes the possibility of finding truth in a world that no longer adheres to a commonly agreed set of truths. The issue of meaning and truth, moreover, is driven by the apparent meaninglessness in so much of current culture. Harvey Cox argues here that the theologian must avoid the danger of being concerned merely with 'high' culture, but must engage with the realities of mass media and popular culture. He recommends adopting a balance between an uncritical reception of TV and popular culture, and the danger, not least among academics, of remaining in the ivory tower of high culture. Küng too calls for balance. The artist, he argues, must continue to address questions of meaning. In this way Küng opposes the Kantian defence of *l'art pour l'art* and opines, echoing Aquinas, that the beautiful must not be an 'innocuous sedative' but an evocation of the 'good made visible'. The artist, as well as the Church and the individual believer, must look deep and oppose the banal and the superficial. In similar fashion, Gilkey comments on the critical, prophetic, moral and political role of art against the backdrop of a spiritual vacuum in a technical, skill and money oriented culture. Art, like religion, can raise people's social and religious awareness. In their healing and critical dimensions both are essential to culture. In this way the experience of art, especially of a 'classic', is a 'disclosure of truth', as Tracy puts it. One of the most remarkable works in the field to appear in the last quarter of the twentieth century is Frank Burch Brown's *Religious Aesthetics, A Theological Study of Making and Meaning* (1989). In his excellent study, this theologian and musician occupies himself with issues such as the aesthetic dimensions in religious experience, the connections between sin and bad taste, artistic imagination and religious meaning, and the underestimated role of classic works of art in church life and Christian identity. While most writers implicitly or explicitly locate theological aesthetics in the realm of fundamental theology, due to the revelatory aspect in the arts, Burch Brown observes that it can play a role in all branches of theology. Thus theological aesthetics is not an option but a 'must', in recognition of the fact that religious experience and faith have an aesthetic dimension. In this way, theological aesthetics can build bridges among the theological disciplines.

Related to these two sections is the group of extracts in Chapter 18, Imagination, Creativity and Faith. Included here are writers who focus on these aspects from various angles, yet some of whom, in particular Brunner and Wolterstorff, might easily have been grouped under the previous sections too. According to Brunner, art contributes to finding meaning and is a manifestation of 'the longing for something else', i.e. the longing for an other, better world. Therefore art has a soteriological dimension. Yet, Brunner also notes the 'dangers' of art. His arguments echo Kierkegaard when he warns against adopting an aestheticist attitude, as it promotes being content with a life of illusion and discards the responsibility and decision involved in the life of faith.

Noteworthy here is the Russian Christian existentialist philosopher Berdyaev, who wrote extensively and at times with some brilliant insights on the creative aspect in the human person. He stressed that creativity, like freedom, is 'God's summons' to the human being and the human being's 'duty towards God'. Creativity needs no justification and is of religious significance as it constitutes woman's and man's relationship and response to God. Both creativity and freedom are therefore manifestations of grace. This is not only asserted by Berdyaev but also, in a different context, by liberation theologian Leonardo Boff. Indeed creativity pertains to Christian life itself and to a theology of creation and grace. Here too Moltmann-Wendel's article is of interest when she invites her readers to imagine and put into practice a holistic theology that integrates the whole person, spirit, mind and body. David Ford also takes what might be called a holistic view when he discusses feasting in its Christian, aesthetic, ethical and ultimately transformative dimensions.

The essential role of the imagination in theology has been examined by William Lynch, John McIntyre and Garrett Green. The latter two note the integrative and constructive function of the imagination, its ability to creatively think the possible. The imagination and images thus have an eschatological-soteriological, transcending dimension. Moral theologian Enda McDonagh makes this more concrete in his treatment of the relationship between poetry, prayer and politics as instances of the imagination and creativity at work. He concludes that in order to develop, a theologian must be both critical and creative.

What may come as a surprise is that in the twentieth century a considerable number of theologians with diverse theological frameworks and backgrounds have focused their attention not only on divine revelation but, in particular, on the beauty of God. In recent philosophical debates, beauty as an aesthetic category has played a minor role and has sometimes been challenged as having little relevance in the face of the ugliness and suffering of world wars, nuclear weapons, hunger and human alienation. In one way or another, the classic idea of God, however, as supreme beauty, has remained – even if marginally at times – of interest to theologians to this day. In fact, one might even speak of something of a 'renaissance of beauty' in recent years.

In the Introduction to Part I, we saw how, for the Greeks, beauty was a propaedeutic to the good; the transcendental of the beautiful was seen as being closest to, and connected with, the good. Later, the idea of God as supreme beauty and the analogical idea of God as the divine artist, or supreme creator, and the human artist as the always limited co-creator, is found in patristic thought, notably in Ambrose and Augustine. More or less overtly, we notice these ideas again in the later writings included in Chapter 19. In the early part of the twentieth century, the relationship of the divine and the beautiful was taken up by, among others, Dutch theologian van der Leeuw. He noted that whoever truly serves beauty serves God. For him, as for most theologians in the East or West, the unity of art and religion is founded essentially on the doctrine of the incarnation. Yet, he also commented that religion never quite coincides with art, since 'religion, in faith, becomes worship', while beauty must be served, not worshipped. Paradoxically, before the face of God all art becomes nothing; yet it is in the work of art that glimpses of the beauty of God may be revealed.

Barth and von Balthasar also write on the beauty of God, both in the context of a theology of glory. According to Barth, God is beautiful in God's love and freedom and in the radiation of joy. Von Balthasar conceived his work *The Glory of the Lord*, one of the major contributions to theology in the twentieth century, in terms of a theological aesthetics, to accompany a theological dramatics and a theological logics, which refer respectively to the *pulchrum, bonum* and *verum*. He argued that a theological aesthetics must be conceived in two stages as a theory of vision (i.e. fundamental theology) and as a theory of rapture (i.e. dogmatic theology). Von Balthasar pointed out that the beauty of God never radiated more brightly than in *the* beautiful form, Christ, in pouring out his redeeming love for humankind on the Cross.

Echoes of Aquinas' ideas of the unity of the beautiful, the good and the true are also reflected in the neo-Thomist philosopher Maritain, in Navone, as well as in one of the most significant modern Catholic moral theologians, Bernard Häring. Häring, like Balthasar, was intensely aware that the ethical without a sense of beauty becomes joyless, lifeless, and descends into dull regulations. In this way, he argued that beauty is as much a transcendental dimension as goodness, truth, and oneness. Moltmann, likewise, points out that the ethical and the aesthetic intrinsically belong to one another in the life of faith and in our ideas of the divine. Joy and the beauty of God are essential to living in Christ and to our vision of God. The glory of God is manifested in the Crucified. It transforms the world, and, as Moltmann writes, reflecting the tradition of Paul and the Fathers, we will see such glory, when we die into God and are born to new life. That beauty is a way of coming to know God is also reflected in very recent writers, such as Richard Viladesau, Alejandro Garcia-Rivera, and Joan Chittister. Beauty may be encountered in poetry, the visual arts, in music, etc., that is in finite existence. Beauty is thus made apparent by human acts of creation, which are the work of the Spirit, the source of all beauty, as Patrick Sherry affirms in his pneumatological approach to a theology of beauty.

Charles Hartshorne, writing on 'man's vision of God', also includes a section on God and beauty. He argues that as feeling and quality are 'positive excellences' and are as such addressed by philosophers under the realm of aesthetics, so theology ought to incorporate these insights into thinking of God. Being in itself involves feeling; feeling cannot be reduced to a certain way of thinking or willing, but belongs to being as such. Hence, he asserts, we cannot think of God as being without feeling but on the contrary 'as more rich in feeling than any other being'. Just over twenty years later, Sallie McFague, from a more ecological and feminist angle, also speaks of the God who feels. She notes that we do not hesitate referring to the God of love, but are afraid to call God lover. God loves the world intensely and intimately; therefore, it is essential to speak of eros and passionate love and feeling in God, a lover who needs the beloved, the God who, as the mystics affirmed, desires us, and whom we desire in return.

In a long tradition, thus, from Plato to the early Fathers, Augustine, Aquinas, Edwards to the late twentieth-century writings, we find the notion that the reality and revelation of God cannot be contemplated without the dimension of beauty, that God is beauty in Godself and the source of all beauty. Indeed, one would suggest that a sense of beauty in God and in the world makes our theologizing more whole, more exciting, more colourful and vibrant. Beauty as the splendour of truth and goodness, supremely revealed in the trinitarian God, is an idea, it seems, that has 'stood the test of time', and will be glimpsed wherever the Spirit of the divine fills creation, both human and divine.

Art as a 'locus theologicus'

— —

16.1 Paul Tillich, from 'Art and Ultimate Reality'

Tillich (1886–1978) was the first theologian to open up and examine modern art as a locus theologicus. *Of the numerous articles he wrote on the subject, 'Art and Ultimate Reality' (1960) has probably been the most influential one. Tillich here outlines five types of religious experience and their corresponding stylistic elements in art. He favours the expressionist style, which he relates to the ecstatic-spiritual type of religious experience.*

Ultimate reality underlies every reality, and it characterises the whole appearing world as non-ultimate, preliminary, transitory and finite. These are philosophical terms, but the attitude in which they originally have been conceived is universally known. It is the awareness of the deceptive character of the surface of everything we encounter which drives one to discover what is below the surface. But soon we realise that even if we break through the surface of a thing or person or an event, new deceptions arise. So we try to dig further through what lies deepest below the surface – to the truly real which cannot deceive us. We search for an ultimate reality, for some thing lasting in the flux of transitoriness and finitude. All philosophers searched for it, even if they called change itself the unchanging in all being. They gave different names to ultimate reality expressing in such names their own anxieties, their longing, their courage, but also their cognitive problems and discoveries about the nature of reality. The concepts in which ultimate reality is expressed, the way philosophy reached them and applied them to the whole of reality fills the pages of the history of philosophy. It is a fascinating story just as is the history of the arts in which ultimate reality is expressed in artistic forms. And actually, they are not two histories. Philosophical and artistic expressions of the experience of ultimate reality correspond to each other. But dealing with such parallels would trespass the limits of my subject.

The term 'ultimate reality' is *not* another name for God in the religious sense of the word. But the God of religion would not be God if he were not first of all ultimate reality. On the one hand, the God of religion is more than ultimate reality. Yet religion can speak of the divinity of the divine only if God *is* ultimate reality. If he were anything less, namely, *a* being – even the highest – he would be on the level of all other beings. He would be conditioned by the structure of being like everything that is. He would cease to be God.

From this follows a decisive consequence. If the idea of God includes ultimate reality, everything that expresses ultimate reality expresses God whether it intends to do so or not. And there is nothing that could be excluded from this possibility because everything that has being is an expression, however preliminary and transitory it may be, of being-itself, of ultimate reality.

The word 'expression' requires some consideration. First, it is obvious that if something expresses something else – as, for instance, language expresses thought – they are not the same. There is a gap between that which expresses and that which is expressed. But there is also a point of identity between them. It is the riddle and the depth of all expression that it both reveals and hides at the same time. And if we say that the universe is an expression of ultimate reality, we say that the universe and everything in it both reveals and hides ultimate reality. This should prevent us from a religious glorification of the world as well as from an anti-religious profanisation of the world. There is ultimate reality in this stone and this tree and this man. They are translucent toward ultimate reality, but they are also opaque. They prevent it from shining through them. They try to exclude it.

Expression is always expression for someone who can receive it as such, for whom it is a manifestation of something hidden, and who is able to distinguish expression and that which is expressed. Only man within the world we know can distinguish between ultimate reality and that in which it appears. Only man is conscious of the difference of surface and depth.

There are three ways in which man is able to experience and express ultimate reality in, through and above the reality he encounters. Two of these ways are indirect; one of them is direct. The two indirect ways of expressing ultimate reality are philosophy – more specifically, metaphysics – and art. They are indirect because it is their immediate intention to express the encountered reality in cognitive concepts or in esthetic images.

Philosophy in the classical sense of the word seeks for truth about the universe as such. But in doing so, philosophy is driven towards explicit or implicit assertions about ultimate reality. We have already pointed to the manifoldness of such concepts, and 'ultimate reality' is itself one of them. In the same way, while trying to express reality in esthetic images, art makes ultimate reality manifest through these images – the word image, taken in its largest sense, which includes lingual and musical figures. To be able to show this concretely is the main purpose of my lecture, and here I feel supported by the self-interpretation of many artists who tell us that their aim is the expression of reality.

But there is the third and direct way in which man discerns and receives ultimate reality. We call it religion – in the traditional sense of the word. Here ultimate reality becomes manifest through ecstatic experiences of a concrete-revelatory character and is expressed in symbols and myths. Myths are sets of symbols. They are the oldest and most fundamental expression of the experience of ultimate reality. Philosophy and art take from their depth and their abundance. Their validity is the power with which they express their relation of man and his world to the ultimately real. . . .

Usually secular philosophy is called simply philosophy, and art simply art; while in connection with the sacred, namely, the direct symbols of ultimate reality, philosophy is called theology, and art is called religious art. The creative as well as destructive consequences of this conflict dominate many periods of man's history, the most significant for us being the five hundred years of modern history. The reduction of these tensions and the removal of some of their destructive consequences would certainly come about if the decisive point in the following considerations were established.

That decisive point is this: the problem of religion and philosophy, as well as that of religion and art, is by no means confined to theology and religious art; it appears wherever ultimate reality is expressed through philosophical concepts and artistic images, and the medium through which this happens is the stylistic form of a thought or an image. Styles must be deciphered. And for this one needs keys with which the deciphering can be done, keys which are taken from the very nature of the artistic encounter with reality. It is not my task to point to such keys for the deciphering of styles in general, or of the innumerable collective and personal styles which have appeared in history. Rather, I shall indicate those stylistic elements which are expressive for ultimate reality. The best way to do this is to look at the main type in which ultimate reality is shown in the great manifestations of man's religious experience. They express in a direct way the fundamental relation of man to ultimate reality, and these expressions shine through the artistic images and can be seen in them. On this basis, I suggest distinguishing five stylistic elements which appear, in innumerable mixtures, in the great historic styles in East and West, and through which ultimate reality becomes manifest in works of art. After the description of each of these elements, I want to show pictures as examples, without discussing them concretely, and with the awareness of the contingent, almost casual, character in which they were chosen, for many technical reasons.

The first type of religious experience, and also the most universal and fundamental one, is the sacramental. Here ultimate reality appears as the holy which is present in all kinds of objects, in things, persons, events. In the history of religion, almost everything in the encountered world has become a bearer of the holy, a sacramental reality. Not even the lowest and ugliest is excluded from the quality of holiness, from the power of expressing ultimate reality in the form of here and now. For this is what holiness means, not moral goodness – as moralistically distorted religions assume. There is actually no genuine religion in which the sacramental experience of the divine as being present does not underlie every other religious utterance. This enables us to discover the first stylistic element which is effective in the experience of ultimate reality. It appears predominantly in what often has been called magic realism. But because of the non-religious meaning of the term, magic, I prefer to call it *numinous* realism. The word numinous is derived from the Latin *numen* (appearing divinity with a divine-demonic quality). It is *realism* that depicts ordinary things, ordinary persons, ordinary events, but it is numinous realism. It depicts them in a way which makes them strange, mysterious, laden with an ambiguous power. It uses space-relations, body stylisation, uncanny expressions for this purpose. We are fascinated and repelled by it. We are grasped by it as something through which ultimate reality mysteriously shines. Much primitive art has this character. It does not exclude other elements, and this is most conspicuous, for its greatness has been rediscovered by our contemporary artists who have been driven to similar forms by the inner development of their artistic visions. These visions have received different names. In the development of cubism from Cézanne to Braque, at least one element of numinous realism is present. It is present in the stylo-metaphysics of De Chirico and in the surrealism of Chagall. It appears in those contemporary painters and sculptors who unite the appreciation of the particular thing with cosmic significance they ascribe to it.

All this is the correlate to religious sacramentalism. It shows ultimate reality as present here and now in particular objects. Certainly, it is created by artistic demands, but intended or not, it does more than fulfill these demands. It expresses ultimate reality in the particular thing. Religiously and artistically, however, it is not without dangers. The religious danger of all sacramental religion is idolatry, the attempt to make a sacramentally consecrated reality into the divine itself. This is the demonic possibility which is connected with all sacramental religion. The artistic danger appears when things are used as mere symbols, losing their independent power of expression. It is difficult to draw the line between an artificial symbolism and the symbolic power of things as bearers of ultimate reality. Perhaps one could say that wrong symbolism makes us look away from one thing to another one for which it is a symbol; while genuine symbolic power in a work of art opens up its own depths, and the depths of reality as such. . . .

Related to the sacramental type of religion and at the same time radically going beyond it is the mystical type. Religious experience tries to reach ultimate reality without the mediation of particular things in this religious type. We find this type actualised in Hinduism and Buddhism, in Taoism and Neo-Platonism. And, with some strong qualifications, in some places in later Judaism, Islam and Christianity. It can undergo a transformation into a monistic mysticism of nature under the famous formula of the God of Nature. In it God is equated with nature – with the creative ground of nature which transcends every particular object. We find this in ancient Asia as well as in modern Europe and America. Correlate to this religious type is that stylistic element in which the particularity of things is dissolved into a visual continuum. This continuum is not a grey in grey: it has all potentialities of particular beings within itself, like the Brahman in Hinduism and the One in Neo-Platonism or the creating God in Christianity as they include within themselves the possibility of the whole world. The continuum contains tensions, conflicts, movements. But it has not yet come to particular things. They are hidden in a mere potential state. They are not yet actual as distinguishable objects; or if so, they shine through form afar as before creation. We find this in Chinese landscapes in which air and water symbolise the cosmic unity, and individual rocks or branches hardly dare emerge to an independent existence. We find it in the background of Asiatic and Western paintings, even if the foreground is filled with figures. It is a decisive element in the impressionist dissolution of particulars into a continuum of light and colours. Most radically it has been carried through in what is called today, non-objective painting. For instance, the latest decade of American painting is dominated by it. Of course, one cannot show ultimate reality directly, but one can use basic structural elements of reality like line, cubes, planes, colours, as symbols for that which transcends all reality – and this is what the non-objective artists have done. In the same period in which Eastern mysticism powerfully enters the American scene, American artists have deprived reality of its manifoldness, of the concreteness of things and persons, and have expressed ultimate reality through the medium of elements which ordinarily appear only in unity with concrete objects on the surface of reality. Here also the dangers must be seen. The sacred emptiness can become mere emptiness, and the spatial emptiness of some pictures indicates merely artistic emptiness. The attempt to express ultimate reality annihilating reality can lead to works in which nothing at all is expressed. It is understandable that as such a state in religion has led to strong reactions against the mystical type of religion, it has led in art to strong reactions against the non-objective stylistic elements. . . .

Like mysticism, the prophetic-protesting type of religion goes beyond the sacramental basis of all religious life. Its pattern is the criticism of a demonically distorted sacramental system in the name of personal righteousness and social justice. Holiness without justice is rejected. Not nature, but history becomes the place of the manifestation of ultimate reality. It is manifest as personal will, demanding, judging, punishing, promising. Nature loses its demonic as well as its divine power. It becomes subject to man's purposes as a thing and a tool. Only on this religious basis could there arise an industrial society like that in which we are living.

If we now ask what stylistic element in the visual arts corresponds to such an experience of ultimate reality, we must answer that it is 'realism' both in its scientific-descriptive and in its ethical-critical form. After nature has been deprived of its numinous power, it is possible for it to become a matter of scientific analysis and technical management: The artistic approach to this nature is not itself scientific but it deals with objects, prepared as mere things by science. Insofar as it is artistic creation, it is certainly not imitation of nature, but it brings out possibilities of seeing reality which enlarge our daily life encounter with it, and sometimes antecedes scientific discoveries.

The realistic element in the artistic styles seems far removed from expressing ultimate reality. It seems to hide it more than express it. But there is a way in which descriptive realism can mediate the experience of ultimate reality. It opens the eyes to a truth which is lost in the daily-life encounter with reality. We see as something unfamiliar what we believed we knew by meeting it day by day. The inexhaustible richness in the sober, objective, quasi-scientifically observed reality is a manifestation of ultimate reality, although it is lacking in directly numinous character. It is the humility of accepting the given which provides it with religious power.

Critical realism is predominantly directed to man – personally, socially, and historically, although the suffering in nature is often taken into the artistic expression of the ugliness of encountered reality. Critical realism, as, for instance, given by Bosch and Brueghel, Callot and Goya, Daumier and Ensor, by Grosz and Beckmann, shows ultimate reality by judging existing reality. In the works of all those enumerated, it is the injustice of the world which is subject to criticism. But it is done in works of art, and this very fact elevates critical realism above mere negativity. The artistic form separates critical realism from simple fascination with the ugly. But of course if the artistic form is lacking, it is distorted reality and not ultimate reality that appears. This is the danger of this stylistic element as it also is of some kinds of merely intellectual pseudo-criticism, to succumb to a negativity without hope. . . .

The prophetic-critical type of religion has in itself the element of hope. This is the basis of its power. If the element of hope is separated from the realistic view of reality, a religious type appears which sees in the present the anticipation of future perfection. What prophetic hope expects is affirmed as given in forms of perfection which the artist can produce in the world of images. The self-interpretation of the Renaissance as society reborn was particularly conducive to this attitude. But it had predecessors, for instance, in the classical period of Greece, and has been followed in our modern period by attempts to renew this stylistic element.

As a religious attitude it can be called religious humanism which sees God in man and man in God here and now, in spite of all human weakness. It expects the full realisation of this unity in history and anticipates it in artistic creativity. The artistic style expressing it is usually called idealism, a word which is in such disrepute today that it is almost impossible to use. It is worse than criminal if you are called an idealist. But not only the word, the concept itself was under harsh criticism. In the period in which the numinous, the descriptive and the critical-realistic element dominated the whole development, the idealistic tradition was despised and rejected. In spite of the innumerable religious pictures that it produced, it was seen as unable to mediate ultimate reality. I myself shared this mood. The change occurred when I realised that idealism means anticipation of the highest possibilities of being; that it means remembrance of the lost, and anticipation of the regained, paradise. Seen in this light, it certainly is a medium for the experience of ultimate reality. It expresses the divine character of man and his world in his essential, undistorted, created perfection.

But more than in the other stylistic elements, the danger which threatens artistic idealism must be emphasised: confusing idealism with a superficially and sentimentally beautifying realism. This has happened on a large scale, especially in the realm of religious art, and is the reason for the disrepute into which idealism, both word and concept, has fallen. Genuine idealism shows the potentialities in the depths of a being or event, and brings them into existence as artistic images. Beautifying realism shows the actual existence of its object, but with dishonest, idealising additions. This danger must be avoided as we now come to attempts to create a new classicism. I am afraid that this warning is very much apropos. . . .

Now I come to my fifth and last stylistic element. The great reaction against both realism and idealism (except numinous realism) was the expressionistic movement. To which religious type is it correlated? Let me call it the ecstatic-spiritual type. It is anticipated in the Old Testament, it is the religion of the New Testament and of many movements in later Church history; it appeared in sectarian groups again and again in early Protestantism, in religious Romanticism. It appears in unity and conflict with the other religious types. It is marked by its dynamic character both in disruption and creation. It accepts the individual thing and person but goes beyond it. It is realistic and at the same time mystical. It criticises and at the same time anticipates. It is restless, yet points to eternal rest. It is my conviction as a Protestant theologian that this religious element, appearing everywhere as a ferment – and in many places highly developed – comes into its own within Christianity. But our problem is, how does this type express itself in the visual arts? Which stylistic element corresponds to it? I believe the expressionist element is the artistic correlative to the ecstatic-spiritual type of religious experience. Ultimate reality appears 'breaking the prison of our form', as a hymn about the Divine Spirit says. It breaks to pieces the surface of our own being and that of our world. This is the spiritual character of expressionism – using the word in a much larger sense than the German school of this name.

The Church was never happy with ecstatic movements. They seemed to destroy its sacramental foundation. Society today has not been happy with the great expressionist styles in past and present because they have broken and are still breaking through the realistic and idealistic foundations of modern industrial society. But it is just this that belongs to the manifestation of ultimate reality. Expressionist elements are effective and even dominating in many styles of past and present. In our Western history they determine the art of the catacombs, the Byzantine, the Romanesque, most of the Gothic and the Baroque style, and the recent development since Cézanne.

There are always other elements cooperating, but the expressionistic element is decisive in them. Ultimate reality is powerfully manifest in these styles, even if they disregard symbols of the religious tradition. But history shows that styles which are determined by the expressionist element are especially adequate for works of art which deal with the traditional religious symbols.

But we must also mention the dangers of the expressionist elements in our artistic styles. Expression can be understood as the expression of the subjectivity of the artist, just as in the religious field, the spirit can be understood as an ecstatic-chaotic expression of religious subjectivity. If this happens in religion, ecstasy is confused with over-excitement; and over-excitement does not break through any form and does not create anything new. If a work of art expresses only the subjectivity of the artist, it remains arbitrary and does not penetrate into reality itself. And now let us recall some examples in a final group of pictures. Van Gogh – 'Hills at St Remy'. Munch – 'The Scream'. Derain – 'The London Bridge'. Marc – 'Yellow Horses'. . . . – Heckel's 'Prayer'. Nolde – 'Pentecost'. And I must confess that some of my writings are derived from just this picture, as I always learned more from pictures than from theological books. And, finally, Nolde – 'Prophet'.

The main point in the discussion of the five stylistic elements which can become mediators of ultimate reality has been to show that the manifestation of the ultimate in the visual arts is not dependent on the use of works which traditionally are called religious art. I want to conclude with a few remarks about the nature of such works and their relation to the five stylistic elements discussed.

If art expresses reality in images and religion expresses ultimate reality in symbols then religious art expresses religious symbols in artistic images (as philosophical concepts). The religious content, namely a particular and direct relation of man to ultimate reality, is first expressed in a religious symbol, and secondly, in the expression of this symbol in artistic images. The Holy Virgin or the Cross of the Christ are examples. In this relation it can happen that in the work of art as well as in the encounter with it, the one of two expressions may prevail over the other one: The artistic form may swallow the religious substance, objectively or in personal encounter. This possibility is one of the reasons for the resistance of many religious groups against religious art, especially in a devotional context. Or the religious substance may evoke pictorial products which hardly can be called works of art, but which exercise a tremendous religious influence. This possibility is one of the reasons for the easy deterioration of religious art in its use by the churches.

The avoidance of both shortcomings is a most demanding task for religious artists. Our analysis of the five stylistic elements may be useful in this respect.

Obviously, the stylistic element which we have called numinous realism is an adequate basis for religious art. Wherever it is predominant in the primitive world, the difference between the religious and the secular is often unrecognisable. In the recent forms of numinous realism the cosmic significance of works under the control of this element is obvious, but it is hard to use them for the highly personalistic stories and myths of the religions of the prophetic type.

The mystical-pantheistic element of artistic styles resists radically the attempt to use it for the representation of concrete religious symbols. Non-objective art like its mystical background is the elevation above the world of concrete symbols, and only symbols of this elevation above symbols can be expressed in artistic images.

Descriptive and critical realism, if predominant in a style, have the opposite difficulty. They can show everything concretely religious in its concreteness, but only if united with other elements can they show it as religious. Otherwise, they secularise it and, for example, make out of Jesus a village teacher or a revolutionary fanatic or a political victim, often borrowing sentimental traits and beautifying dishonesty from the distortions of the idealistic style. This is the seat of most religious *Kitsch*.

Another problem is religious art under the predominance of the fourth stylistic element, the anticipating one. Anticipation of fulfillment can, of course, most easily be expressed through figures of the religious legend and myth. But one thing is lacking. The estrangement of the actual human situation from the essential unity of the human with the divine, the reality of the Cross which critical realism shows in its whole empirical brutality, and which expressionism shows in its paradoxical significance. Because this is lacking even in the greatest works under the predominance of the idealistic style, it can become the other source of *Kitsch* in religious art.

The expressionistic element has, as already indicated, the strongest affinity to religious art. It breaks through both the realistic acceptance of the given and the idealistic anticipation of the fulfilled. And beyond both of them it reaches into the depth of ultimate reality. In this sense it is an ecstatic style-element, expressing the ecstatic character of encountered reality. Nobody can overlook this ecstatic element in the great religious art, however different the combination of this element with the other stylistic elements may be. To show the ecstatic-spiritual character in the expression of ultimate reality in the many great periods of religious art in East and West is a task to which the ideas of this lecture could only lay the foundation. It is enough if they have done this and made somehow visible the manifestation of ultimate reality through the different stylistic elements which appear in different relation to each other in all works of the visual arts. (pp. 317–29)

Source: *Paul Tillich, Writings in the Philosophy of Culture, Kulturphilosophische Schriften*, ed. Michael Palmer, Berlin, New York, De Gruyter, 1990.

16.2 Karl Rahner, from 'Theology and the Arts'

Rahner (1904–84), a German Jesuit and one of the leading theologians of the twentieth century, concentrated in his numerous writings on the revelation of God as mystery in the world. In this article he raises issues that are fundamental to the theology of art. He points out that theology must integrate the verbal and non-verbal arts since they are authentic means of human self-expression, of religious experience, of God's self-communication. They are therefore essential sources of and for theology.

I shall begin by asking just what art really is, for it is a difficult question whether the individual arts – sculpture, painting, music, poetry and so on – can really be subsumed under a single concept of 'art'. Let us leave aside for the moment the literary arts like poetry or drama whose medium is the human word. For by the very nature of the case these 'verbal arts' are very closely related to theology, which also comes to expression in word. Focusing for the moment just on those arts which do not employ words, like architecture, sculpture, painting and music, we can say that all of these arts too are meant to be expressions, human self-expressions which embody in one way or another the process of human self-discovery. Looking at it this way, our question then is whether these human self-expressions in the various non-verbal arts have the same value and significance as the verbal arts. A musician will certainly say that his music is not just a lesser form of human self-expression, but is a unique and irreplaceable mode of expression which cannot be substituted for by words or by some form of verbal art. We could say the same for painting and sculpture. When one stands before a painting of Rembrandt's, one can try to say in words what the painting is expressing. But however much one art can be translated into another art, ultimately, sculpture, painting and music (prescinding here from architecture, since it is far more functional than the others) have their own independent validity as forms of human self-expression which cannot be completely translated into verbal statements. Presupposing that all the arts cannot ultimately be reduced to verbal art, then our question is: How is theology related more precisely to these non-verbal arts? Insofar as man expresses himself in all of these arts as well as in theology, each in its own unique way, all these different arts and theology are mutually interconnected and related. But the situation is more difficult than we tend to imagine. If and insofar as theology is man's reflexive self-expression about himself in the light of divine revelation, we could propose the thesis that theology cannot be complete until it appropriates these arts as an integral moment of itself and its own life, until the arts become an intrinsic moment of theology itself. One could take the position that what comes to expression in a Rembrandt painting or a Bruckner symphony is so inspired and borne by divine revelation, by grace and by God's self-communication, that they communicate something about what the human really is in the eyes of God which cannot be completely translated into verbal theology. If theology is not identified a priori with verbal theology, but is understood as man's total self-expression insofar as this is borne by God's self-communication, then religious phenomena in the arts are themselves a moment within theology taken in its totality. In practice, theology is rarely understood in this total way. But why should a person not think that when he hears a Bach oratorio, he comes into contact in a very unique way with God's revelation about the human not only by the words it employs, but by the music itself? Why should he not think that what is going on there is theology? If theology is simply and arbitrarily defined as being identical with verbal theology, then of course we cannot say that. But then we would have to ask whether such a reduction of theology to verbal theology does justice to the value and uniqueness of these arts, and whether it does not unjustifiably limit the capacity of the arts to be used by God in his revelation.

Theology, Art and Experience Presupposing this distinction between the verbal and non-verbal arts, and focusing now on the verbal or literary arts like poetry, drama and the novel which share with theology the medium of the human word, we could perhaps characterise these arts from a theological point of view by saying that they succeed, each in its own unique way, in putting a person in touch with those depths of human existence wherein religious experience takes place. When I say, for example, that a person should love God, I have said something very deep in this simple statement. But uttered amidst all the superficial routine of daily life, it does not generate much understanding or appreciation of what the statement really means. But if I read some of the lyric lines of a John of the Cross or perhaps a novel by someone like Graham Greene, which, to be sure, cannot simply 'contain' an immediate and genuine religious experience, for that is quite impossible, but which perhaps evokes in me my own experience of the religious, then this literature has accomplished something which reflexive, purely conceptual and rational theology is not able to accomplish. There are, of course, theologians in the narrower, stricter sense like Augustine or Thomas Aquinas in some of his Eucharistic poems where religious experience and reflexive, conceptual theology are closely joined. But these are exceptions, and they represent something which is rarely found in the theology of modern times. Maybe something like this can be found in some of Newman's sermons. But in general it is a rare occurrence any more. Hans Urs von Balthasar once said that what we lack in modern times is a 'theology on its knees'. We could perhaps add to that we also lack a 'poetic theology', and I see that as a defect in our theology. But, of course, we have to be reasonable and balanced about this. There is also a kind of theology which is perfectly justified in taking a deep breath and proceeding patiently through the long and arduous reflections of conceptual theology which cannot be expected to lead immediately to some kind of religious or mystical experience. It is, nevertheless, perfectly justified. But however much it must be left to the individual theologian to what extent he evokes or does not evoke religious experience in his theology, nevertheless it is perhaps fair to admit that one of the consequences and deficiencies of a rationalistic theology working exclusively with 'scientific' methods is that theology has lost so much of its poetry. Moreover, theology faces a task especially today which is not new, but has been greatly neglected in recent centuries, namely, that it be in some way a 'mystagogical' theology. By this I mean that it must not speak only in abstract concepts about theological questions, but must also introduce people to a real and original experience of the reality being talked about in these concepts. To this extent what I have called 'poetic theology' could be understood as one of the ways, although not the only way, of doing this kind of mystagogical theology. In this sense and understanding the following statement correctly, we can say that all Christian theology has to be 'subjective'. It cannot speak about objects which lie outside the realm of the personal, spiritual and free reality of human existence itself. There is no such thing as a theological statement about a beetle. Hence all the objects of the natural sciences considered just in themselves lie outside the realm of theology. We could say, then, that theology does not begin until it really begins to be subjective. But subjective in this sense does not mean arbitrary or maintaining that black is white. Christian theology must be subjective insofar as it has to speak of faith, hope and love and about our personal relationship with God. It must be subjective insofar as ultimately, whether directly or indirectly, it must describe, evoke and introduce one mystagogically to this personal and spiritual relationship between man and God. In other words, theology as revelation theology is the mediation of God's call precisely to human subjectivity. When theology can no longer accomplish this, when it becomes 'objective' in a false sense, this is not good theology, but bad theology.

The Unity of Sensibility If indeed, as we have said, the arts play a role in this mediation, what do we mean when we speak of 'seeing' or 'hearing' God in a work of art? . . . If it is not the ears alone which hear, but the whole person, then something is religious or not religious depending on what kind of a person the hearer is and on the total concrete situation in which he is doing the hearing. Whether this melody is religious or not depends quite simply on whether you base your judgment on the melody taken exclusively in a purely acoustical context, or whether you situate it in a total human context. For then the acoustical phenomenon becomes something different, not in view of itself, but in view of the situation. But the relationship between the artistic realm and the religious realm is not easy to define. God is, indeed, everywhere with His grace, as we would want to maintain in theology, but this does not mean that every reality has the same relationship to me or to God. God is not present in a chemical change in my stomach in the same way that He is when I act with trust or love or responsibility towards my neighbour. Hence the question about the possible religious significance of non-religious art is a difficult question. . . .

[R]eligious painting is not simply identical with painting which represents some explicitly religious content. If someone paints a Nativity scene with Jesus, Mary and Joseph and explains by means of halos and the like what the painting is supposed to mean, then this is a religious painting in the objective sense. Maybe it is not an especially religious painting at all because it cannot evoke a genuine and radical religious response in the viewer. There is, after all, religious 'kitsch' as we say in German. Some 'religious art' is well intended and painted by pious people, but it is not genuine religious art because it does not touch those depths of existence where genuine religious experience takes place. Conversely, it could be that a painting of Rembrandt's, even if it is not religious in its thematic, objective content, nevertheless confronts a person in his total self in such a way as to awaken in him the whole question of existence. Then it is a religious painting in the strict sense. It can be religious in this sense even if it does not have an explicit, thematic religious content. This touches on another difficult question. One could conceivably maintain that the truly holy person is identical with the person who has developed fully all the dimensions of his human existence. To put it another way, I could say that when a person's sensibility, his capacity to see and hear are fully developed, his experiences are identical with his religious sense. In other words, I could take the viewpoint that the fully developed human being and the real saint are identical, and only when a person is fully developed in all the dimensions of his human existence can he be a saint in the fullest sense. One could hold this because apparently in heaven one is not only going to be very pious, but also fully human in the complete development of all human capacities. That is one side of the question. But if we proceed empirically, we could easily reach the opposite conclusion. Are there not persons who are really and genuinely holy, who selflessly love God and their neighbour in a radical way, but, nevertheless, their artistic sensibility is hardly developed at all? They would be considered boors in the realm of art because they can respond to artistic things only in a very rudimentary way. And vice-versa, there are people whose artistic sensibility is developed to an extraordinary degree, but are, nevertheless, not holy. I suppose we have to make a distinction here between the offer of an opportunity for a religious response and one freely accepted. . . .

The Eternal in Historical Particularity . . . I would like to conclude with some final remarks on our central topic. A poet, as we say, speaks in images and likenesses. The possibility of this kind of poetic language is rooted ultimately in the analogy of being, insofar as all realities are intrinsically interrelated, are somehow interconnected and related to one another and therefore can ultimately be conceived only by moving beyond them as individual realities to the whole of reality. This analogy of being makes it possible for the poet to speak in images and likenesses, and enables him to understand particular human experiences as mysteriously pointing beyond themselves to God. For example, he can represent love between human beings in its hidden depths as pointing analogously to the love of God. Even when such human realities as fidelity, responsibility and acceptance of the mystery of life are not expressed in any explicitly religious way, they point ultimately to the reality about which theology does speak explicitly. It seems questionable to me whether today there really is so much less Christian and religious literature in poetic and artistic form. It would be quite possible that the analogous symbols in which a real poet expresses himself today have changed so much that they are no longer intelligible to people brought up in the traditional piety. But it is nevertheless possible that the poet is basically giving expression to religious statements in this different set of analogous symbols. Such a situation calls for careful scrutiny of the language of the poet. In any case, analogy makes possible the understanding of one reality as the mysterious disclosure of another, higher and more comprehensive reality. Everything which comes to expression in art is a particular actualisation of that human transcendence through which a person, as a spiritual and free being, is oriented to the fullness of all reality. Only because the human person is a being who by his very nature pushes beyond every given boundary, a being for whom every end is a new beginning, a being who encounters the unfathomable mystery of things, only because and insofar as the human person is a transcendent being can there be both art and theology in their real senses. Both art and theology are rooted in man's transcendent nature. But it is important to see why and how this human transcendence is always represented in art in a quite definite, particular and historical way. True art always embodies a very definite, particular and historical instance of human transcendence. To this extent, art can and must be thoroughly historical. There is a real history of art, artists do not always say the same thing. The artist by his very nature is necessarily the discoverer of a concrete situation in which man concretely actualises his transcendent being in a new and different way. But what follows from this is not that there is an opposition between man's historical and transcendent nature, but rather that there is a mutual and necessary interrelationship of dependence between the two. The true artist, to be sure, proclaims what is eternal in truth, in love, in man's endless quest and boundless desire. But he is an artist and not just a conceptualist and rationalist only when he creates this proclamation of the eternal in a new and unique way. In real art the absolutely historical particularity of the artist and the eternal in his proclamation are one. It is precisely this which constitutes the essence of a work of art. I can understand Dürer's 'The Hare' as a *concretissimum*, as an utterly concrete and definite given in an innocuous human experience. But if I really look at it with the eyes of an artist, there looks out at me, if I can put it this way, the very infinity and incomprehensibility of God. (pp. 24–9)

Source: Karl Rahner, 'Theology and the Arts', *Thought*, vol. 57, no. 224, 1982.

16.3 Pie-Raymond Régamey, from *Religious Art in the Twentieth Century*

Régamey, a French Catholic priest and writer, was one of the first and most outspoken proponents of an inclusion of modern works in sacred spaces by artists who do not necessarily consider themselves Christian believers or who are not churchgoers. Here he argues why such artists and their art must be recognized by the Church.

The Non-Christian Artist in the service of the Church Among the most interesting questions arising from the previous discussion are three which we will now consider in turn. First, what are the chances of a non-Christian artist's producing work suitable for a church? Second, is there a place for non-objective art in church? Third, what use can church architecture make of present day building techniques? The first question is an important one because at the moment some of our best artists are outside the Church, and even hostile to it. And when it is suggested that these artists should be commissioned for church decoration, a common Catholic reaction is to consider them as complete outsiders whose work, of whatever kind it may be, must be rigidly barred from churches. Joseph Samson's answer to the problem is to consider it from the point of view of the works produced rather than to generalise about the unsuitability of non-Christian artists or argue from a determined notion of faith as a *sine qua non* of acceptance by the Church. If, he claims, a work is Christian in tone, it qualifies for acceptance by the Church, since this proves that there is sufficient faith in the artist who produced it. This is a very reasonable approach, if only because we have plenty of good Christian work by non-Christian artists on which to base our judgment.

Of all the pictures of St Francis de Sales, none captures the saint's spirit in quite the way that Bonnard's has. Whatever criticism we may have of Lurcat's tapestries, he has undeniably helped produce something at Assy just as sacred as anything left us by the Middle Ages. Leger's mosaic on the façade of this same church, in which we can all find minor faults, has the immediate effect of breaking off our contact with the everyday world, calling on us to transcend it, as everything truly sacred must. Then we have the windows at Audincourt, also by Leger, which have been called 'some of the most overpowering work that Christian art has given us for five centuries'. The works speak for themselves. Matisse's chapel at Vence has such an atmosphere in it that priests saying mass there have remarked that they have not offered the sacrifice with more fervour since their ordination. Therefore, it seems only reasonable to admit that the non-Christian artist can give us works of true magnificence which amply fulfill their function in the church – by which we mean the atmosphere they create for the faithful who are preparing to take part in the mass. This seems infinitely more constructive than decreeing from the start that no 'unbeliever' will be allowed to create a work of art for the Church. (Ch. 10, pp. 177–9)

It soon becomes apparent that the arguments regarding the non-Christian artist are on two different levels. On one side it may be argued that faith, in the abstract, is the essential issue. On the other side are those who consider faith not as an abstraction but as a state of things manifested here and now. It is all very well to envisage faith as living, balanced, integrated, and soundly equipped for correcting even any deviations in an artist's feelings. But in practice, what do we find? What is the faith of our contemporaries, in fact? And what is that faith really capable of? If we are honest, we must admit that the faith of the present day is riddled with ignorance, error, and vague, muddled thinking. Instead of grasping the invisible world boldly and bringing it to us with absolute conviction, today's faith appears as a rather negative, servile form of obedience, preoccupied essentially with not going against what the Church teaches. It is theoretical, and yet it is far from finding a meeting ground with current ways of thinking, even on the theoretical plane. Its attempts to provide artistic themes savour too much of system and the catechism. The artists who profess Christianity are, as often as not, the most sentimental. It is not surprising if the works that the pious artist produces for pious people manifest clearly the dull, dispirited devotion that belongs to the common faith of many today. This judgment is not made of people's inner lives, of course, but simply of the external manifestations of their lives. All sorts of historical factors are involved, and they explain how a real, heroic faith could – as in the case of St Theresa of Lisieux – be inextricably bound up with the most appalling mawkishness. We may talk all we want to about art on the ideal level, but when we examine the valid works we have today and the conditions of their achievement, we cannot overlook facts. We have to conclude that in certain cases a 'non-Christian' will have a deeper, more genuine, and more effective feeling for the theme or function of a work than will a 'Christian'. The abstract notions of faith and unbelief are of little avail. And even when the outward manifestation of the artist's faith is beyond reproach and has no ill effect on his creative expression, he is still likely to be dominated by the idealistic notion of the supremacy of faith over all the means at his disposal, and thus committed to translating the ideal world into works of art. This, as Bazaine said, is the reason the artists who produce 'religious art' so often fail in their task. To begin with an act of faith and then adapt a given reality of ordinary life to it is to bring together two independent entities which will never meet. This is the reason why all 'committed' art fails, as we have already observed. When bound to such a scheme, art cannot take its normal course. It is artificially manipulated for the good of the cause. The artists who engage in such activity are betraying that cause whenever they set out to serve it. Whereas the faith of many Christian artists has absolutely no effect on their work, there are non-believers whose Christian reaction to Christian themes is very striking indeed, just as we find far higher religious ideals among some non-Catholics than among some Catholics. Instead of dull conformity, we find the pure spontaneity of unerring instinct. Therefore, it may well be argued, let the Church profit by the work of the unbeliever when it is clearly the product of his whole being, fundamentally attuned to the realities of our faith. How often we find among such artists a truly vital aspiration toward the sacred, far more intense and demanding than is found among many Christians! A further argument, often pushed rather too far, follows the conception advanced by the German Romantics and Kierkegaard, of the 'ironic' character of art. The plastic arts, it is agreed, are wholly inadequate to depict supernatural mysteries. Therefore, the imagination of the artist is a kind of substitute for faith, and the non-believer can thus produce valid work for the Church. Art is the opposite of life, in the sense that it follows the artist's inner voice in order to produce an expression, and nothing more. Another argument is that art is merely decorative (here the Classical and Baroque traditions influence the theory) and need not be taken too seriously. True faith is unnecessary when art is a matter of adaptations and suitabilities. A work of art, for many critics, is sufficiently sacred if it is good painting or sculpture. There is, for them, no specifically Christian or sacred art. Art is only Christian or sacred when it submits to laws of appropriateness for its destined place. Any gifted, intelligent, sensitive artist can appreciate what is fitting, and be sufficiently influenced by it to produce the work required. This is a superficial conception, perhaps, but it does at least present a serious view of art, although the value offered is only that of a work honestly executed. Every good painting, Michelangelo said, is noble and devotional in itself and therefore is able to honour God, whether or not the artist is a believer. Then there are those who feel that the inner flame of the artist is necessarily sacred of its nature. If inspiration is profound, the work of art is *ipso facto* religious and therefore worthy of being put in a church. This is a sufficient faith, they say; supernatural faith is not essential. The principal argument is closely akin to this last one, and may easily be confused with it. The difference between the two is that the argument above is purely naturalistic; its proponents are not concerned with supernatural faith, and so its necessity does not arise for them. But those who maintain the line of argument we will consider next state quite clearly that supernatural faith is the more or less immediate principle in virtue of which a work will be worthy of the Church. What they ask of the unbelieving artist, and what they find in him, is the aptitude to be somehow affected by the living faith of the Church. This aptitude is found precisely in the 'inner flame', the depth of the artist's inspiration. . . .

It is not so much the presence or absence of faith that we can discern in works of art as the precise qualities of that faith or the particular degree in which it is insufficient. This amounts to saying that we cannot tell whether it is faith that is involved or some substitute for faith. For the Christian artist, faith makes him sensitive to the supernatural as well as to all the data of everyday life. If an artist does not have faith, he cannot be completely attuned to the whole Christian out-look, but he will be partially attuned, in certain tendencies and on certain points. Theoretically, one could say that the Christian artist is like a wireless receiver that can pick up all wavelengths, whereas the non-Christian can receive only a few. But in practice, all artists, whether Christian or otherwise, tend to be much the same. The area in which they partake of the *sensus Ecclesiae* seems to be rather limited for both. An artist finds perceptible equivalents for the mysterious facts of faith; and as far as this goes, there seems to be very little difference between what the Christian and the non-Christian can find. There is, in other words, hardly any difference at this stage between real faith and its substitutes or equivalents. What difference is there, after all, between actual faith in the mysteries of Christianity and a vivid comprehension of them without actual belief? The only difference is an assent which does not affect this comprehension of the mysteries, at least in their material expression in art. Therefore, it is almost impossible to say whether any artist judged by his work alone has or has not true faith. It is probably better to leave such judgments to God. Supernatural faith and the non-believing artist's substitute for faith are both a share in the faith of the Church. Real faith and substitute faith function in the sphere of art in the same way. Both the believer and the unbeliever, in virtue of some vital attraction to a point of faith, are open to the Church's teaching on that point. Normally, of course, the believer is privileged in his understanding, but here again it is impossible to generalise, for it is spiritual sensitivity more than faith that influences the artist's reaction and is expressed in plastic form. In either case, the extreme complexity of our present problems breaks down the accepted theory that supernatural faith in the artist affects the sacred value of his work. Of course, all works of sacred art are sacred in virtue only of the supernatural faith by which the Church lives, but it is perfectly possible that a substitute for faith in one artist's soul can achieve more than the supernatural faith of another. And we may well find many cases of this anomaly; but these will serve as exceptions that prove the rule, for a substitute for faith still only acts in accordance with the demands of faith. At this juncture we can perhaps rectify whatever was too partial in our two opposing views, and this will help us at the same time to make one or two doctrinal points clear. For those who deny that an unbeliever can produce a work of sacred art, I would like to suggest that strictly speaking sacred art only requires a sacred character of the actual artistic creation, of the artist's exercise of his art. The most truly sacred artist in the Church, I would say, is the one who puts the most sacred quality in the forms of his creation. Artists who profess to be materialists can very well be the best equipped for certain tasks in the Church. A true artist is not a logician. His apparent materialism may quite conceivably be the result of a thirst for justice or an extreme altruism. Each case must be considered on its own merits, and of course the whole question would be unthinkable in a really Christian society. But society today is not Christian, and we have to take the world as it comes. . . . And it is evident, if we examine their work, that artists of today are far from sentimental in their treatment of sacred themes. On the contrary, they react against sentimentality very strongly.

It seems, then, that non-Christian artists should be allowed to work for the Church. The imaginative intuition must be understood as being a sort of artistic faith which is so deeply rooted in the creator's soul that it is present in all his powers. (Ch. 10, pp. 182–90)

Source: Pie-Raymond Régamey, *Religious Art in the Twentieth Century*, New York, Herder and Herder, 1963.

16.4 Vatican Council II, from *Constitution on the Sacred Liturgy*

The Second Vatican Council (1962–65) aimed to foster reforms and renewal in the Roman Catholic Church, in its theology and church life. In this section on liturgy, the documents advise that and how music and visual art must be fostered in the Church.

Sacred Music The musical tradition of the universal church is a treasure of inestimable value, greater even than that of any other art. The main reason for this pre-eminence is that, as a combination of sacred music and words, it forms a necessary, or integral part of the solemn liturgy. Sacred scripture, indeed, has praised sacred song (see Eph 5.19; Col 3.16). So have the Fathers of the church and the Roman pontiffs who in more recent times, led by St Pius X, have explained more precisely the ministerial function of sacred music in the service of the Lord. Therefore sacred music is to be considered the more holy, the more closely connected it is with the liturgical action, whether making prayer more pleasing, promoting unity of minds, or conferring greater solemnity on the sacred rites. The church, indeed, approves of all forms of true art which have the requisite qualities, and admits them into divine worship. Accordingly, the sacred council, keeping to the norms and precepts of ecclesiastical tradition and discipline and having regard to the purpose of sacred music, which is the glory of God and the sanctification of the faithful, decrees as follows:

Liturgical worship takes on a more dignified character when the rites are celebrated solemnly in song, with sacred ministers taking part and with the active participation of the people. . . .

The treasury of sacred music is to be preserved and cultivated with great care. Choirs must be diligently developed, especially in cathedral churches. Bishops and other pastors of souls must do their best to ensure that whenever a liturgical service is to be accompanied by chant, the whole body of the faithful may be able to take that active part which is rightly theirs, as laid down in articles 28 and 30.

Much emphasis should be placed on the teaching of music and on musical activity in seminaries, in the novitiates and houses of studies of religious of both sexes, and also in other Catholic institutions and schools. To impart this instruction teachers are to be carefully trained and put in charge of the teaching of sacred music. It is desirable also that higher institutes of sacred music be established whenever possible. (Ch. 6, para. 112–15, pp. 152–4)

In some places, in mission lands especially, there are people who have their own musical tradition, and this plays an important part in their religious and social life. For this reason their music should be held in due esteem and should be given a suitable role, not only in forming the religious sense but also in adapting worship to their native genius, as indicated in articles 39 and 40. Therefore, in the musical training of missionaries, special care should be taken to ensure that they will be capable of encouraging the traditional music of those peoples both in the schools and in sacred services, as far as may be practicable. (Ch. 6, para. 119, p. 154)

Composers, animated by the Christian spirit, should accept that it is part of their vocation to cultivate sacred music and increase its store of treasures. Let them produce compositions which have the qualities proper to genuine sacred music, and which can be sung not only by large choirs but also by smaller choirs, and which make possible the active participation of the whole congregation. The texts intended to be sung must always be in conformity with catholic doctrine. Indeed, they should be drawn chiefly from the sacred scripture and from liturgical sources. (Ch. 6, para. 121, p. 155)

Sacred Art and Furnishings The fine arts are rightly classed among the noblest activities of human genius; this is especially true of religious art and of its highest achievement, sacred art. Of their nature the arts are directed toward expressing in some way the infinite beauty of God in works made by human hands. They are dedicated to God, they praise him and extend his glory to the extent that their only purpose is to turn people's spirits devoutly toward God. For that reason the church has always been a friend of the fine arts, has ever sought their noble ministry and has trained artists. Its chief purpose has been to ensure that all things set apart for use in divine worship should be worthy, becoming, and beautiful, signs and symbols of things supernatural. In fact the church has, with good reason, always seen itself as an arbiter of the arts, deciding which of the works of artists are consistent with faith, piety and the traditional laws of religion, and are to be considered suitable for sacred use. The church has been particularly careful to ensure that sacred furnishings should be dignified and beautiful and thus contribute to the decorum of worship. It has admitted changes in material, style, or ornamentation prompted by the progress of artistic technique with the passage of time. The fathers have therefore decided to issue the following decrees on these matters:

The church has not adopted any particular style of art as its own, but guided by people's temperaments and circumstances, and the needs of the various rites, it has admitted styles from every period. Thus in the course of the centuries it has brought into existence a treasury of art which must be very carefully preserved.

The art of our own times from every race and country should also be given free scope in the church, provided it bring to the task the reverence and honour due to the sacred buildings and rites. Thus it is enabled to join its voice to that wonderful chorus of praise sung by the great masters in past ages of catholic faith.

Ordinaries are to take care that in encouraging and favouring truly sacred art, they should look for noble beauty rather than sumptuous display. The same principle applies also to sacred vestments and ornaments. Bishops should be careful to ensure that works of art which are repugnant to faith, morals, and Christian piety, and which offend true religious sense either by depraved forms or through lack of artistic merit or because of mediocrity or pretence, be kept well away from the house of God and from other sacred places. And when churches are to be built, let great care be taken that they are suitable for the celebration of liturgical services and for the active participation of the faithful. (Ch. 7, para. 122–4, pp. 156–7)

Bishops, either personally or through suitable priests who are gifted with a knowledge and love of art, should have a special concern for artists, so as to imbue them with the spirit of sacred art and of the sacred liturgy. It is also desirable that schools or academies of sacred art should be established in those parts of the world where they would be useful for the training of artists. All artists who, prompted by their talents, desire to serve God's glory in the church should always bear in mind that they are engaged in a kind of holy imitation of God the Creator and that the works they produce are destined to be used in Catholic worship, for the edification of the faithful and to foster their piety and religious formation. (Ch. 7, para. 127, p. 158)

During their philosophical and theological studies, clerics are to be taught about the history and development of sacred art, and about the basic principles which govern the production of its works. Thus they will be able to appreciate and preserve the church's ancient monuments, and be able to aid by good advice artists who are engaged in producing works of art. (Ch. 7, para. 129, p. 159)

Source: *Documents Vatican Council II, Constitutions, Decrees, Declarations*, ed. Austin Flannery, OP, rev. ed. Northport, NY, Costello Publishing Company / Dublin, Dominican Publications, 1996.

16.5 Aidan Nichols, from *The Art of God Incarnate*

In this passage, British Dominican theologian and Balthasar scholar Aidan Nichols expounds a phenomenological understanding of art and suggests how the experience and understanding of the work of art is significantly similar to the perception of divine revelation.

The Shape of the Artwork

What we enjoy in art is, rather, some aesthetically moving form. When we are looking at a Sisley landscape the object of our enjoyment is the painting itself, not the visual sensations. The pleasantness of the looking is logically prior to the pleasantness of the sensations. The feelings we have, when these are other than a joy of the mind in the form embodied sensuously in the canvas, are extrinsic and posterior to that enjoyment which makes the experience an experience of the beautiful.

I have now introduced a further but familiar concept, that of the *beautiful*. Familiar it may be, dangerous it certainly is, for the temptation is perennial to use the concept for some specifiable quality defined by a rule of artistic making like the celebrated 'Golden Number' in the science of proportion. All such definitions of the beautiful prove otiose because sooner or later they rule out of court artworks which speak powerfully to us while lacking the essential claimed for the beautiful. But this does not mean that the language of the beautiful should be abandoned. According to the phenomenological school, in calling a work of art beautiful we are doing two things. First, we are recommending it as an object which meets the criterion of any aesthetic object, the power to communicate with us through a configuration of matter. Mikel Dufrenne, the leading writer of this school, could hardly go further in freeing artists from an *a priori* concept of the *stylistically* beautiful when he declares that,

> The norm of the aesthetic object is invented afresh by each such object, and each has no other law than the one it makes for itself.

Second, in calling the artwork beautiful we describe it by echoing a judgement made 'within' the artwork, rather than by us. Meaning is not projected on to an arrangement of paints or of masses of stone. It is already embodied and communicated there through its creator's handling of the sensuous. We can recognise beauty therefore, without creating a theory of the beautiful. Indeed, there is no such theory to create. There is the stating of what aesthetic objects are, and to the degree that they are, they are beautiful.

This enables us to clear away one major misapprehension. The judgement that makes the aesthetic experience what it is should be distinguished from the judgements which express our special tastes by affirming our preferences. Taste is not the inner organisation of aesthetic perception but merely something which sharpens or dulls it. We can acknowledge that a canvas is a work of art without appreciating it personally. We can, and perhaps more commonly do, appreciate an artwork without giving it properly aesthetic acknowledgement. For instance, you may be hugely appreciative of Holman Hunt's *The Light of the World*, but the appreciation may be directed to memories of childhood religiosity which it awakens. Our special preferences in art may dictate the breadth or narrowness of our vision, our errors and failures of appreciation. Their consequences may be enormous, as when neo-Classical observers failed to 'see' the English Gothic cathedrals. Hence the need to examine them and re-examine. It is in the moment that our aesthetic judgement ceases to specify such preferences and simply registers in the presence of the beautiful that it is wholly, universally valid and not simply valid 'for me'. This is so because at such a moment, it lets the object speak and show itself for what it is. The historical conditioning of taste is no argument against aesthetic judgement of this kind. We need not fear that we are indulging in a piece of concealed solipsism when we describe an artwork, 'really' chatting away about ourselves. We are doing something mercifully more interesting than re-arranging our pleasurable sensations.

The artwork is rightly judged beautiful or, otherwise expressed, itself, if it embodies the meaningful in the sensuous. The sensuous element is responsible for the artwork's peculiar plenitude and its uniquely imposing form of presence. It 'speaks to' us or 'strikes' us through the glory of the sensuous realm to which it belongs. R. G. Collingwood was mistaken in thinking that the primary reality of the artwork was an idea in the mind of the artist, only secondarily extruded more or less successfully into some material medium. The 'weight' of the sensuous, rendered communicative by the artist's creative talent, accounts for the ability of the artwork to take an initiative with us and to be experienced by us as a kind of address. This sensory matrix necessarily remains an integral aspect of its being and its value to the perceiver. . . .

The meaning embodied in the artwork is communicated, then, in a unique, *sui generis* manner. It is found in the very organisation of the sensuous and lies in the spatial schemata of the canvas. This meaning defies translation into the clarity of prose, not because it is vacuous but because it is inexhaustible. Unlike other sorts of sign, the traffic-light, the flag of the nation, the linguistic signs of literal prose, we can set no limit to the plurality of readings that express the artwork. The multiple points of view spectators and critics find themselves taking up before a work of art, if they truly represent an effort to grasp its real character, testify to what Dufrenne would call the 'depth' of the aesthetic object. No artwork can be taken in at a single glance. It must be lived with, and in the living will show us a multitude of faces, and an unlimited power to illuminate our experience.

As an embodiment of meaning in the sensuous order, the artwork communicates with us through two essential means. First of all, it is part of an *iconology*, a pattern of images and motifs in an artist's work or in a wider artistic tradition. A network of visual images forms in art a sign-system which is a kind of visual analogue to a language. Just as a language provides the articulation for the basic

set of perceptions available to the people who speak the language, so an iconology forms a possible world of aesthetic perceptions. Language in its rich
metaphorical development takes up the literal sense of the world of natural
objects and transforms the meanings we find ready made about us into a new
world which is distinctively human. An artistic iconology likewise makes 'the
world to which man belongs become the world which belongs to man'. It
depends on 'natural' meanings for the source of its forms, whether these are
representational and figurative or abstract and formalistic. Just as a particular
poet will rely on certain established metaphorical transformations of the literal
in speech, so too an artist in his iconology will presuppose a background of
stylistic convention from which his own creative innovation stands out. An
iconology is always in debt to a particular cultural setting. At the same time, in
the hands of a great artist, it has a power to communicate its new world of
significance in a way which transcends that limited cultural setting from which it
emerged. (Ch. 6, pp. 91–4)

The second means whereby the artwork communicates with us is this. The world
of meaning constituted by the iconology of the painting is always a world shot
through with a singular affective quality. This quality of feeling is what makes
the world of the artwork as we would say 'expressive' to us. In looking at a
picture we should be first of all disinterested. To allow the artwork to speak we
must not muffle it by a barrage of our own prior feelings, memories and mental
habits. When on achieving this suspension of egoism we succeed in seeing the artwork in the pregnant aesthetic sense of 'to see' we find that the feeling-quality of
disinterestedness gives way to fresh and original feelings called forth by the artwork itself. These feelings lead on in good art appreciation to a type of reflection
which is sympathetic, rather than objectifying. Feelings do not become irrelevant
to seeing, as when we have a thing taped and are content to let it be 'out there'.
On the contrary, the role of reflection, in the best art-criticism whether our own
made to ourselves or other people's offered in print, is to clarify and support the
feelings we have before the artwork. A response of this kind is not emotional in
the sense of vapid and vacuous. It is a precise, appropriate response because it is
a right reading of the 'singular affective quality' which characterises the canvas
before our eyes. Our feeling-response to the contours, colours, and painterly
technique of Van Gogh's canvases, for example, *is* our reading of the tragic
world he portrays in his paintings. Dufrenne goes so far as to call such feeling a
kind of knowledge rather than a kind of emotion. By means of it the painting
reveals a world to us, an experience comparable to the 'Got it!' of knowing.
Emotion, on the other hand, is merely a reaction to a world already given.

    The artwork, therefore, has a revelatory power. We have already noted in
looking at St Nicephorus' theology of the icon that the image is, at its heart, an
intentional reality. It is a 'being towards', a sign. It is this capacity of the image
to point beyond itself while remaining the absolutely necessary and wonderful
medium of what it signifies that we refer to when we speak of its 'revelatory'

capacity. The artwork is essentially part of the real in which we are interested. It never becomes superfluous. Yet at the same time our attention is drawn to it not for its own sake but for the content it embodies. It is never surpassed as a medium of the peculiar knowledge it leads to, but it is in its nature to lure us on, away from itself. . . .

Indirectly, but no less genuinely, the artwork also reveals its creator. Except by accident it does not of course offer us information about the artist, the kind of data that the historian gathers. It does something more. It places us in communion with him, ushering us into a presence which the historian could not hope to communicate. The biography of an artist can only tell us about a man precisely as artist if it has first been instructed by his art. The artwork speaks of its creator by what is called *style* . . . To attain a style is 'to do what we want to do'. Whenever a particular way of treating matter, or arranging colour, line, and mass, can be seen as enabling some vision of things there we have style and there the artist himself appears in his work.

The artwork as the shaper of existence   To hold that there is a genuine issue of knowing from aesthetic experience is not to deny that looking at a painting is a different sort of cognitive experience from reading about painting, or devouring a theological treatise. There is no detachable conclusion in the experience of a work of art which can be acquired and used apart from the work itself. The yield of the experience is not an instrument, a fact or a truth. But the experience of the artwork is not for that reason a nugatory one. It can be powerful enough to alter the meaning and weight of all the rest of my experience, before and after it. Art requires and releases an askesis or discipline of vision so that we learn how to look with a purity of insight into the heart of human life. Such looking shifts our whole way of reading the significance of the world. In its wake we find our own existence reshaped from the experience of what we have seen. (Ch. 6, pp. 98–100)

The Artwork and Christian Revelation

It seems that we need to be able to articulate the character of revelation in terms of an interplay of fact and significance, or of event and interpretation. Second, we need to show how through the mediation of signals or signs in this interplay the human capacity for self-transcendence towards the divine is realised. Third, a satisfactory account must show how man is led thereby to an awareness of the ultimately personal values in existence as these might be manifested in fully concrete historical reality, in a quite specific form of life. In such a revelatory form, the evidence for the light of revelation would be open to our perception without our 'subjecting that light to the standards and laws of those perceiving it'.

It is remarkable that a number of the features of the artwork that we have considered in the last chapter, and, obliquely, throughout this essay, seem to stand out as a pattern reflecting this constellation of demands in the search for a model in the theology of revelation. Firstly, in the artwork the configured materials of the object as it leaves the artist's hands are certainly fact, yet the artwork is only constitutive of the aesthetic experience when the perceiver approaches it with that sympathy which allows him to 'read' its affective world. Similarly, an adequate account of revelation must show the grounding of revelation in the historical – and therefore embodied and sensuous – order, where an event may strike us as expressing the divine 'speaking' to us through the peculiar plenitude of some experience. The 'disinterested' looking in which a man temporarily suspends the systematically interpretative function of his own presuppositions and convictions, tastes, and interests in order to let the artwork stand forth in its own integrity releases, through the affective intensity of the inner 'world' of the artwork, a new set of feelings. Through this experience he comes to inhabit that world of meaning it carries, by means of a communion of sympathy. Likewise, before the event which is the given, historical foundation of the revelatory event as an encounter between God and man, not just any kind of scrutiny is apt to let the event yield its full significance. It requires a suspension of the screening process by which we determine what is or is not possible within the imaginative borders of reality we occupy, what is or is not compatible with God or man as we have theorised them. Not less important, the 'disinterested' perceiver must lay aside the tendency to exploit events in terms of his own fears and aspirations, for these will project on to them a character not their own. Once this discipline has been achieved, he may find that the event in question discloses to him an unsuspectedly rich source of meaning, a whole new world into which he is attracted by the weight of evident truth and goodness it bears.

The revelatory event breaks in on a man, as the aesthetic experience arises in a moment of communion from the art object in gallery or church, and he finds himself reorganising his own world of meaning, what counts for him as 'the real', in its light. In the course of that, just as the artwork can shape an existence, moving us to the suppression of self so that fidelity to ultimate values may replace the distortions of the relentless ego, so the revelatory event proves able to place us in touch with an absolutely satisfying and complete hold on the reality that blesses us with its own truth, even if it calls on us for a painful reshaping of our lives. The revelatory event satisfies our nisus towards transcendence by disclosing to us the inexhaustibly satisfying reality we call 'God' drawing near to meet us.

This it does, secondly, through the mediation of signs. Just as the artwork communicates its full meaning only in the context of iconology, an interrelating set of images, so the reciprocities and echoes between events that we may suspect to be revelatory in force – their *typological* connections – are what give us the full meaning of the revelatory event, which is never to be looked at in isolation, as a lone image uncontextualised in its iconology. (Ch. 7, pp. 112–13)

How may the model of the artwork satisfy those demands for a sound theology of revelation that are made by the model of personal encounter? Surely by provoking us to see in the figure of Christ disclosure of his personal source, 'the Father', analogous to the style's disclosure of the artist in the artwork: The characteristic qualities of Jesus' acting and response to others, especially that abiding and unmistakable feature of self-emptying obedience from love and unto death which marks his activity, forms the style of the artwork of Christ. We do not look for the Father behind this style, as though it were a mere material integument which had to be laid aside: this style simply is the disclosure of the artist, the Father of Christ. 'He who has seen me, has seen the Father; how can you say, "Show us the Father"?' In the world opened up to us by Christ, therefore, we are established in a unique personal communion with the Father, before a presence and countenance that no other materials could yield us.

Finally, this personal encounter is mediated in a quite specific, concrete, and particular form of life, that of Jesus Christ. We shall turn in a moment to consider the christological possibilities of the model of the artwork. Here it will perhaps suffice to say that the combination of sharpened sense of particularity and deepened sense of the mystery of being that the artwork gives us should enable us to place satisfactorily the respective roles of cataphatic or affirmative knowing and apophatic or negative knowing in the knowledge proper to awareness of the self-revealing God. Natural theology does not offer an epistemology that can do justice to this mystery. Its traditional arguments for God's existence express a 'demand of reason' that reality must be a whole. This claim would defeat itself if we supposed it could be wholly met at the rational level: the furthest we may go without undermining the argument for transcendence itself is a purely formal knowledge of some ultimate ground or principle of reality of whose nature we can form no proper conception. . . . No satisfactory epistemological basis here for our grasp of the living God as one who enters into communication with man. Yet on the other hand, to claim that we have some strictly immediate knowledge of God seems futile. It seems absurd to claim a transcendent experience of God, for part of the meaning of 'transcendent' is precisely 'what goes beyond experience'. But if there can be no strictly immediate knowledge of God, how can some direct but mediate knowledge of him be claimed without presupposing such a power to determine his nature as would deny his transcendence? Once again, the aesthetic model may assist us.

What the artwork mediates to us is a particular reality in its depth. It sheds light on that reality exactly in the mystery of its being. (Ch. 7, pp. 115–16)

Source: Aidan Nichols, OP, *The Art of God Incarnate, Theology and Image in Christian Tradition*, London, Darton, Longman and Todd, 1980.

16.6 Thomas Franklin O'Meara, from 'The Aesthetic Dimension in Theology'

This North American Dominican and theologian of the University of Notre Dame has written on topics bridging philosophy and theology, e.g. Romantic Idealism and Roman Catholicism: Schelling and the Theologians (1982). Here he argues what role the aesthetic plays in fundamental theology.

There are several consequences for fundamental theology when it takes seriously the quality of access found through the aesthetic experience.

First, fundamental theology sees in art a sustenance of two domains: subjectivity and objectivity. The aesthetic act is productive. The forms of art are not the object of perception, but the medium. Similarly, in faith and theology, the text, the law, the liturgy, and the church building are not the object but the medium. Art's particular relationship to cognition and emotion allows it to lay claim to immediacy. Religious immediacy may be an aspect of consciousness, not of analysis, and mature awareness of revelation invites the objectless pondering of grace. The realm of immediacy as found in mysticism is traditionally seen as a development of faith, grace, and life. So both revelation and theology follow an aesthetic pattern. Therefore, the goal of theology is not model-substitution but contemplation as openness to disclosure through life and presence.

Second, fundamental theology explains how areas of Christian faith and life can be enterprises of the imagination. As productive consciousness gives structure to knowledge, theology arranges and draws out the new, creative correlations of revelation within culture. Although the medium can be legal, logical, and verbal forms, it is primarily intuitive. Theological creativity is neither an emptying of language nor an arbitrary projection of meanings. Like revelation, art aims at the transcendent but is realized in history. Art is ultimately not theoretical; it withers under too intense a hermeneutic. Theology is the discernment of the presence of the 'More' amid sin and grace. Like art, when theology is only a symbolism, it is empty – devoid of prophetic, existential, and spontaneously transcendent dimensions, and ready to be passed over quickly. While finite form is the medium for both grace and art, the identification of meaning with symbol spells not the birth but the death of art and faith in the contemporary world.

Third, in the arts, we find a presentation of the fundamental pattern, of our existence: joy mixed with tragedy. There is a negative aesthetic: pain and limitation. The scriptural theme of life out of death is also an artistic truth. The ultimate critique of everything is suffering, and each suffering is ultimately the messenger of death. Contradiction and negation are presence and glory. Every human life, not just Jesus Christ's, like every art-work, has the quality of chiaroscuro: the beautiful is glimpsed with the sharp lines of finitude, the limits of negation, and the shadows of apophasis.

In their union of the aesthetic-mystical and the real-divine, these ideas about the aesthetic dimension in theology stand in a long tradition reaching from Origen to Pseudo-Dionysius to Meister Eckhart to Schelling to Heidegger. For them, human finitude and change are not hopeless and punishing shipwrecks but clearings for revelation. Even nothingness – which in our century seems at times to be the lord of the world – has its own dignity, reality, and dark glory. (pp. 214–16)

Source: Thomas Franklin O'Meara, 'The Aesthetic Dimension in Theology', in Diane Apostolos-Cappadona (ed.), *Art, Creativity, and the Sacred, An Anthology in Religion and Art*, New York, Crossroad, 1988.

16.7 John Dillenberger, from *A Theology of Artistic Sensibilities, The Visual Arts and the Church*

Dillenberger, a theologian and cultural historian, was President of Hartford Seminary. He has written on the Reformation and also on the relationship of theology and visual art. In this passage he advocates the necessity of a discipline of seeing and discusses the contribution the arts can make to culture and to the life of faith and to theology.

Towards a Theology of Wider Sensibilities

Sense, Sensibility, and the Visual ... Modern art confronts us in such a way that we cannot be indifferent; we are somehow different as a result. It deliberately tries to lead us into new territories. It has not always succeeded, for it has led many to believe that, since the recognizable patterns have disappeared, they could themselves do as well as the artists did. So many even today believe that children can do as well. But all one needs to do is to take a child's drawing or painting and place it alongside one of the modern artists and, if one has eyes at all, one sees the difference. That a child can do as well as a trained modern artist is one of those unexamined ideas that disappears the moment one places the respective works side by side. In the past, similar theories were held about the work of Jackson Pollock. Any careful examination makes it clear that the apparent chaos is at once one that involves pattern and randomness, a control and an openness to accident. In a marvellous way, the randomness and accident do not overcome the structure, nor does the structure become so dominant and all-controlling that accident and openness are eliminated. How close this is to nature and life – a structured indeterminateness, an indeterminate structuredness.

Of course, some modern art is poor; in that regard it is not unlike other disciplines. But modern art has probably been more consistently ignored, decried, or found amusing than the other approaches to our world. It takes a discipline of seeing to find more than that in modern art. Indeed, calling for a new discipline of seeing may be one of its major contributions to our life. The statement 'I don't know anything about art, but I know what I like' also testifies to a view of the visual that one would not accept in any other area of life. Where else would one use ignorance as a claim for validating one's opinion? There is a discipline in seeing, just as there is a discipline in everything else that we do well, whether it is reading or writing or making something or listening to significant music, or even loving someone. A discipline of seeing does not come by being told how to see, though that may be helpful, even necessary; it comes primarily by seeing and seeing and seeing over and over again. In the realm of music we assume that it takes discipline and repeated hearing to find one's way into the appreciation of a symphony. Such a discipline stands in marked contrast to the lure of a popular melody, which demands little of us. Frequently the same people appreciate both; yet in terms of the stretching of our sensibilities, a symphony rates above a popular tune. With respect to the visual arts, people are not generally willing to grant a similar distinction, that is, between naive and high art. (Ch. 9, pp. 241–2)

Precisely because art has a seductive character, sensuous to the core, a discipline of seeing is essential in order for one to be illumined beyond the sensory embodiment. The discipline of seeing, learned by repeated seeing and essentially in no other way, forms the seductive into a discriminating sensuousness that is more than itself. Horizons are stretched, formed, and filtered, as creation's images are regained in their sensuousness, in their seductive aspects, precisely for their Creator.

Why should we leave seduction only to the devil? The devil has the monopoly on seduction because the demonic requires no discipline of seeing. God's seductive creation requires the appropriate discipline of seeing. The choice is not between innocent, uplifting objects, on the one hand, and sensuous, seductive art, on the other – as moralists like to describe it. The choice is in how one sees the sensuous, for art is sensuous by nature.

When the church arrests cultural vitality for fear that demons may be present, life and humanity are stifled, and the visual powers degenerate to the detriment of humanity. We live in a time of new opportunity. The gamut has been run from the domination of faith, to its material and secular denial, to new forms of perception, diverse and open to new-forming constellations. All art is not religious, and the museum is not its temple, but the artist today represents, to use the language of the late Paul Tillich, a manifestation of one form of the latent church. Such a recognition means that we do not expect the artist to utilize the subject matter in forms of the past, but, rather, to represent the new forms and perceptions that can become the source of transfiguration and transformation. This view of art places it in the realm of affirmation. Art may have a prophetic function, laying bare perceptions we would otherwise have missed – but prophetic in the sense that, like prophetic disclosures through other media, it arises out of a vision of reality that reflects its negation. The visual arts thus have a double character, disclosing a vision with which we may or may not agree but simultaneously purveying a shared vision through nuances unique to itself.

The Visual Arts and the Other Arts   The arts other than the visual made their way back into Protestantism in a way in which painting and sculpture did not. Perhaps they were considered safer than the visual, for dance, music, and literature by definition come and go. They are not continually present like painting or sculpture. A dance is gone, for example, except in memory, once the dance is over. Moreover, dance, music, literature, and liturgy itself are sometimes magnificent and more often tame and folksy. David may have danced on the altar before the Lord, but sometimes dances – for example, those of the Lord's Prayer – become poor art, merely illustrating the prayer. There seems to be something intimidating when the church is involved, so that artists of every stripe lose much of their passion in the church. Music, once also excluded from the Reformed tradition, has become the dominant Protestant art form. Again, music is not present unless it is being performed, except in the mind of a composer or one well trained in music. Moreover, when music is combined with words, as in a chorale, one has the best of both worlds with no special problems. The music overcomes the archaic nature of the language, while the language gives intelligibility to the music. Frequently, however, the words hide the depth of the music, what the music alone may bring. Beyond the ordinary level in which music seems to please us, the structure of music may also affect, address, stretch, confirm, trouble the depths of our being in ways no other discipline does, not because it is better but because it represents a unique sensibility, analogous to but not identical with other sensibilities.

Because literature is verbal, it has had an easier time in the church than have the other arts. But in a time when the verbal is not known for its own distinctive style, through which indeed what it says could not be said in another way in order to express a specific perception or reality, it is too easily assumed that the substance of a specific literature can be translated into other forms of speech. There is a tremendous difference between an essay, for example, and a literary creation of another order such as a poem or a novel. The latter conveys many features, a complex of nuances that no declarative prose could convey. That is why discussions of the meaning of a poem or a novel do not always enhance what one has witnessed but frequently reduce the meaning to levels of comprehension well beneath the level of the work itself. The delight of great literature is that talk may help us to understand it more, but talk never exhausts what one has read or seen. It does not permit a full conveyance of what is disclosed in another form. In theological work, the literary arts are incorporated in order to make vivid what has and is being said. Literature is used because it discloses facets and nuances of theological meaning analogous to but different from what ordinary or philosophical discourse might provide.

There is nothing wrong with this use of literature, provided that illustration is not considered the only or uniquely special character of literary art. Poetry and drama are unique both because they are a special genre and because their style discloses what another style cannot. Poetry takes us into a world in which style conveys more than the subject that is present. David Daiches has put it well: 'Great poetry carries beliefs into its language in such a way that it can achieve a communication transcending the bounds of those beliefs,' and then he adds, 'but we must learn to read it.' That is why talking about a poem should only be an act of honouring that does not transgress the boundaries. A literary art may be said to have facility and discipline when, in an imaginative suggestiveness, it creates resonances in our being that would be violated by overexplication.

In this sense the literary and the visual arts are identical. Indeed, the literary arts can be said to stand closer to the visual arts than to the disciplines that share the verbal in ordinary and philosophical discourse as we usually encounter it. As in the case of the literary arts, so in the visual, the verbal has its place, its way of talking about, of suggesting, of pointing to, but in such a way that the painting or sculpture speaks to us – if one may use the expression – in its own way. Thus, seeing conveys more and in ways different from saying. Respecting the boundaries, avoiding transgression, is important to both the literary and the visual arts.

This delineation of the literary and the visual implies that positive affirmations are as important to these arts as is the critical, allegedly prophetic nature of the arts. It may be true that the arts convey more quickly than other disciplines the seismographic shifts in a society, perhaps because sensitivity is so central to the nature of the discipline, though one wonders why it should be less true in others. Nevertheless, the value of the arts does not rest simply in either their pleasing or their prophetic functions, but also in their affirmations about life. Precisely this shift from the prophetic to the affirmative is to be found in the literary writing of Nathan A. Scott, Jr.

Certainly the primary agenda of the abstract expressionists was to present the world anew to us, freed of forms that once had power but had become banal. From their different orientations, they strove to present the mystery of the grandeur of humanity. Mark Rothko evokes the mystical tradition; Robert Motherwell a humanistic stance in the grand classical sense; Jackson Pollock the visions of one who, though he descended into hell, saw new realities glimpsed from afar; Barnett Newman the grand sublime in rigorous, demanding form. The arts, like other disciplines, can be trivial and, with respect to religious issues, banal. But they can also convey facets of life and truth in religious or non-religious subject matter. Significant art, as classic, to use David Tracy's phrase, purveys more than what transpires in a given time; from a particular time, it carries us into perceptions suggestive and illuminating of humanity in other times.

Theology Today . . . Except for the repristination of fundamentalism and conservative theologies, theologians today are interested in symbols and literary forms, as well as in psychology and the social sciences. Theology is thus moving toward a view of language and reality that is closer to the arts than has been the case at any time thus far in the twentieth century. Inversely, the arts, though not fully accepted in their own right, may also have made an impact on theology. Predominantly theology was closer to the social and psychological sciences, originally modelled on the philosophy of science, in the first half of the century than it has been since. In that earlier phase, theology was like the scholastic disciplines in which analysis, classification, prediction, and clarification played a major role. Today the analogy is closer to the more contemporary views of science and to the literary and the visual arts. We do, therefore, live in a time of new opportunity, one that must be seized. Theologians by and large do not yet know the extent to which their own disciplines may be enriched, if not transformed, by a deeper exposure to the arts, including the visual arts.

We live in a pluralistic world, a world with many convictions and many sensibilities. For some, that may be incapacitating. For others, an understanding of this diversity may also be a new opportunity, a way of understanding cultural diversity as also an expression of a split within humanity. Because our sensibilities are diverse, each offering something the other does not even when it centres on the same reality, we have the choice of taking one at the expense of the others or of counting on all of them, even when we know that we will not be able to cultivate all in equal ways. There is a division in our very nature, an affinity with a difference among our sensibilities – sight, touch, taste, hearing, speaking. These modalities, understood from the standpoint of creation, define our full humanity in relation to God. Understood from the standpoint of our actual state – from the perspective of the fall, if you will – the unity does not come naturally. Understood from the standpoint of redemption, we need the discipline of each sensibility in order to express a full humanity eschatologically oriented to its fulfillment. (Ch. 9, pp. 244–9)

Source: John Dillenberger, *A Theology of Artistic Sensibilities, The Visual Arts and the Church*, London, SCM Press, 1987.

16.8 George Pattison, from *Art, Modernity and Faith*

Theologian and philosopher, Pattison (University of Oxford) has widely published on theology and the arts. In this extract he makes rather relevant observations why icons cannot function as models for a contemporary theology of art. Further, he notes that, due to the eschatological dimension of art, a theology of art must not only be conceived in terms of a natural theology but a theology of redemption.

Icons of Glory

It [the icon] is, we may say, a manifestation of the eschatological world, the redeemed and deified world, the divine life itself, reaching out into the world of the 'spectator', transforming and transfiguring it into the reality which is 'represented' there.

To a considerable extent then the claim is justified that the painterly technique is throughout determined by its theological conception, or, rather, that the method of painting itself is theologically conceived, without the use of allegory or extrinsic and obtrusive symbolism.

Yet there is a paradox here. Although the tradition and practice of eastern iconography may in this way offer a more immediate blending of visual form and theological meaning than in much of the religious art of the West (and therewith a more robust affirmation of the theophanous potentialities of matter) it nonetheless treats its material, visual element in a distinctive way. The icon in one sense deconstructs the given sensuous, material world. In particular the use of inverse perspective and stylisation ('spiritualisation') of figure and gesture seems to imply an abstract rather than a concrete engagement with the world of matter and sense. The 'matter' of the icon is not the 'matter' of the world of sensuous experience and activity. It is not the world as seen by the physical eye but the world as seen by the spiritual eye. Its matter is a different kind of matter. Matter is reassembled on a different plane, within the horizon of another (eschatological) plane. The flesh which it reveals is a flesh whose desires and passions have been vanquished and subjugated. Despite Lazarev's comment that there is no call for the mortification of the flesh in Rublev's work, and despite the claims made by commentators that there is nothing here of the kind of world-denying 'spiritualism' of the Augustinian-Platonic tradition of ascetic spirituality, there is nonetheless a kind of Platonism and a kind of asceticism in these pictures.

We may recall, as John Baggley emphasises, that this is essentially a monastic art produced under strict ascetical traditions. Its spiritual context is that of the *Philokalia* (a collection of monastic and eremetical texts collected in the eighteenth century) and of the hesychasts (practitioners of the mantra-like repetition of the sacred name of Jesus). Baggley gives many extracts from the *Philokalia* which give something of the flavour of its spiritual attitude. For example: 'If, then, you wish to behold and commune with Him who is beyond sense-perception and beyond concept, you must free yourself from every impassioned thought'. And: 'You cannot attain pure prayer while entangled in natural things and agitated by constant cares'. It is, in short, a spirituality of ascesis, of solitude, of the celibate undistracted life, of a life of total conversion and sanctification. It is in this context that the tendency towards abstraction, the stylisation and the conventionalism of much icon-painting is to be understood. The icon-painters and their defenders are, at the end of the day, no less – perhaps more – suspicious of the body and the visible world than their western counterparts. It is perhaps simply that they have ascended so far up the ascetical ladder that they are confident of being able to re-order matter on their own terms. I do not mean to suggest that such a spirituality is worthless and I certainly do not want to imply that its art is devoid of beauty or sublimity. But there are dimensions which are totally absent from it. Its world is a thoroughly religious world.

There is no attention to the human figure, to worldly situations, to natural forms and colours as being of interest and value in themselves. Its world is a sacred world, turned away from the concerns of secular living and the common life in the world. There is no sign of either artistic or spiritual existence having been risked in the dangers and delights of the sensuous phenomenality of life.

But all this is precisely the starting-point for the theology of art which we are seeking here, since our theology respects (because it knows in the experience of those who write it) the truth of the modern affirmation of autonomy and world-liness both in life and in art. And our theology knows that it cannot hope to respond to the crisis of modernism and post-modernism by simply turning its back on the whole development which has led us to this point.

There has been an astonishing flowering of interest in icons over the last twenty years. This may simply be an accident resulting from the opening up of previously little-known cultural traditions. Yet, as Sartre said, there are no accidents in life. If this interest has flowered, at this time it may be precisely because the world of icons seems to offer one kind of way out from the present confusion of religious and cultural values, a way out of the complexity, darkness and flux of human affairs into the abstract clarity of a heavenly order. But it is unlikely that any theological response to the present will stick unless it addresses the concrete historical form of the present. It may be both refreshing and stimulating to step sideways out of our own situation into the realm of another cultural tradition but neither Orthodoxy (nor any other tradition) can resolve questions which have arisen within the very specific horizons of western thought and culture. Yet as we return to the West and its concern for, 'creation's images . . . in their sensuousness' we may take with us something of the Orthodox conviction that images may attain an equal dignity with words in the communicating of divine things, and, following from this, that in doing so they do not need to be reduced to symbols or allegories. (Ch. 7, pp. 130–2)

Restoring the Image

At the start of this chapter I suggested that a contemporary theology of art should not be content to find a place for itself within the field of natural theology but should instead see itself in terms of a theology of redemption. We are now in a position to see why this should be so. For the implication of my argument is that there is an unsurpassable meaning and value to be found in the pursuit of those desires which draw us towards the world, and which enable or inspire us to affirm the goodness of that world in which we find ourselves. It should be clear by now that I regard art as having its unique place in the economy of human life precisely among such desires: arising from them, shaped by them and revealing them. It is in this context that we can recognise the force of Hans Küng's remark that art is an 'anticipation' of the 'still-awaiting humanizing of man'. For art anticipates – perhaps in a fuller sense than that intended by Küng – the messianic kingdom itself, the return of the world to that created fulness in which we may declare, with God, that it is all 'very good'. In this way the activity of art, and of all good looking, proclaims that our desire towards the world is neither wasted nor futile. This desire rises from the eye of the flesh and sees in what it sees the presence of a good creation and the beginning of a more perfect consummation. Peter Fuller subtitled his study of Ruskin's ultimately sad vision 'art and the absence of grace'. Our argument has brought us to the point where we may, on the contrary, declare the presence of a 'structural grace in things', a grace revealed to the rightly desiring heart and which we appropriate in our own acts of seeing and of shaping the visible things of this visible world. . . .

The theology of art does not require artists to become overtly religious in their work (though it does not exclude this). Rather it points them back into their own work, back to the figural space of desire and the play within it of its dance and travail with the world. It does not demand the surrender of artistic autonomy but declares the seriousness of art – though seriousness here does not, of course, mean ponderousness: there is a serious humour, a serious tenderness, a serious play and a serious joy as well as a serious doubt and a serious despair. Seriousness is not opposed to lightness but to triviality. In this respect the theology of art is open both to the dark vision of Rothko's final works and to the Neo-Romantic quest for a new unitary vision. All that is excluded is triviality, cynicism and the wanton or careless exercise of the creative gift. For these are not the principles of art but of kitsch. (Ch. 8, pp. 153–4)

Source: George Pattison, *Art, Modernity and Faith, Restoring the Image*, London, Macmillan, 1991.

16.9 Dorothee Sölle, from *Against the Wind, A Memoir of a Radical Christian*

Sölle (1929–2003) was a leading, politically engaged and often controversial voice in German theology. In her memoir she reflects on how poetry and literature influenced her own way of doing theology, and how the poetic word as such is a place of theology.

Theology and literature are a *cantus firmus*, a leading theme in my life. In my judgment, the two have to be in relation one to the other. I examined the relation in a formal, scholarly manner in my habilitation dissertation which was published as a book in 1973 and titled *Realization: Studies in the Relation between Theology and Fiction since the Enlightenment*. The study originated in my theological interest in literature. My interest was aroused by the numerous traces of religious language in fiction-writing that does not regard itself as religious at all; I refer to quotations from and allusions to the Bible and to figures and motifs, images and personalities of the world of religion. In the course of a process of secularization, the language of Christian faith has come to be at the disposition of indirect, metaphorical speech and has taken on most diverse functions anywhere between blasphemy and sacralization.

It is the emancipative use of religious language in fiction-writing that justifies not only the theologians but also the literary scholars asking about the theological implications of such acceptance and appropriation. What role does the linguistic domain of the Bible or of general religiosity play in a text constructed in accordance with different rules? For what did the writer need that linguistic domain? What part does theology then have in the different text? What perspective did it bring to that text? On what can a theological interpretation base itself, and what would it look like? Such were my questions as I studied interpretations of the writings of Georg Büchner, William Faulkner, Thomas Mann, Karl Philipp Moritz, Jean Paul, and Alfred Döblin. . . .

The separation of the domains of aesthetics, politics, and religion is the dogma of modernity that I could never completely agree to. An allegedly politics-free religion ends up venerating power and its idols, whereas poetry creates a boundary-dissolving freedom, a kind of oceanic feeling. I really do not believe in the modern program of *poésie pure*: Wherever it happens successfully that the unmixed purity of the beautiful becomes sound and language, poetry is no longer 'pure' and 'for itself'. Paul Celan's lyrical work serves as an example of how precisely, in most sparse, often hermetic language, the reality of the world of the extermination camp enters and the promises of tradition shine forth.

When I learned Greek, the concept *kalonkagathon* became very dear to my heart. In my seventeen-year-old unintelligence, I wondered how the Greeks could take two words that for us have nothing to do with each other, and turn them into the one word, beauty-good. Where on earth would one find aesthetics and ethics in the same dish? My amazement was deepened even more when I found out that medieval theology taught that God touches us through beauty, changes us, and draws us Godward. This thought meets us in many a tradition of mysticism, including those of Islam; it has taken deep root in me now. In order really to do theology, we need a different language. Poetry and liberation are topics central to my life. Something is lacking when, for an extended period of time, I have written no poetry.

I try to say in poems what annoys me and what gives me joy, what makes me suffer and what comforts me. In more recent literature, there is a great deal of self-pity; and I find that disquieting, because I find that one needs to praise God, if such pious language is at all appropriate. Without giving praise, we do not really breathe. And the only way of sharing the experience of liberation is by naming what is good and freeing. . . . For me it is like taking a breath, as well as an imperative, to speak of something besides misfortune. It is the experience of hearing and the process of speaking that govern my poetry writing. I try to work on linguistic precision and conviction.

The German writer Friedrich Gottlieb Klopstock (1724–1803) wrote beautifully about religion and poetry. 'There are ideas that can hardly be expressed except in poetry; or, rather, it is appropriate to the nature of certain subjects to reflect on them poetically and to make clear that too much would be lost were they to be thought about in any other way. In my judgment, contemplations on God's omnipresence belong essentially in this category.' It strikes me that Klopstock is pleading for a bit of pantheism here. The presence of God can be articulated neither in the language of everydayness, of triviality, nor of science.

When one tries to communicate God, that is, to say something that goes beyond the language of everyday life, one has to search. Unlike many theologians who actually want to do scholarship, my own search does not take the scholarly path. I do not believe that searching that way will lead us on. Instead, I believe that theology is much more an art than a science. It has to understand itself as an attempt to cross the bounds of everyday language, oriented toward art rather than to the abstract, rational, and neutral. Why is it that in the world of the West only theology developed and not theopoetry? . . .

For me, praying and writing poetry, prayer and poem, are not alternatives. The message I wish to pass on is meant to encourage people to learn to speak themselves. For example, the idea that every human being can pray is for me an enormous affirmation of human creativity. Christianity presupposes that all human beings are poets, namely, that they can pray. That is the same as seeing with the eyes of God. When people try to say with the utmost capacity for truthfulness what really concerns them, they offer prayer and are poets at the same time. To discover this anew, to bring it into reality or to make it known, is one of the goals I pursue in my poems. (pp. 150–3)

Source: Dorothee Sölle, *Against the Wind, Memoir of a Radical Christian*, trans. Barbara and Martin Rumscheidt, Minneapolis, Fortress Press, 1999.

16.10 Gesa Elsbeth Thiessen, from *Theology and Modern Irish Art*

The author here discusses the work of art as a locus theologicus, *as well as the relationship between the image and the word.*

Conclusion: Towards a Theology of Art

What is fundamental to a theology of and through art, as to other current theological approaches, is the conviction that theology must be radically based in and draw its inspiration from life, from the experience of people. It cherishes the central place and makes use of the classical *loci theologici* and asserts at the same time that the theologian, in order to be credible and relevant to contemporary life, especially Christian life, and to the task of theology, must firmly place herself or himself in and operate from the reality of our existence in which surprising new *loci* can be found.

During the course of our study, painted images were not only discovered and discussed as such sources of theology, but it was possible, moreover, to uncover sometimes remarkable parallels, convergences and mutual illumination between the painted image and the written theological word. However, it was also pointed out that theology conveyed in art, unlike in traditional theological writing, tends to be less defined, unsystematic, more visionary, imaginative and metaphorical in character. Yet, the image can be intensely direct, shocking, even confrontational, due to its visual immediacy, the freedom of the artist's imagination and expression. It is precisely here that the artistic image can make its relevant contribution to theological endeavour. . . .

Theology based on the visual image is an embodied theology; it is located in particularity and matter, i.e. in a concrete painting, sculpture, installation etc. To make the image the source of one's theological engagement implies a radical 'yes' to creation, to creativity, and to the capacity of the imagination. It is a positive affirmation of our life-giving senses, of the sensuous and sensual, of the aesthetic, of eros, of the fact that spirit, even the divine Spirit, can be perceived in and through the material. It is the seemingly paradoxical assertion that ultimate reality or, more especially, the invisible face of the always-greater God, is glimpsed and known in the bits and pieces of earthly existence, which is at the centre of this theology. It acknowledges eros in the profoundest sense, God's deepest desire, love and yearning for us as created beings and our desire for the divine and for union with one another. This is what pictorial images, poetry, music or the writings of mystics can powerfully reveal. Doing theology through art affirms and takes as its basis the very fact that the human being experiences and learns through the senses. Body, soul, mind and spirit, all that makes up our being, is intimately related, connected and sacred.

Everything is in God and God is revealed in everything the panentheist would suggest, or, in other words, it is the belief that, as McFague notes, the world is the body of God which pertains to a theology of art. Thus it shares a central concern with what has been stressed in recent years, especially in feminist thinking, namely that life is, and theology therefore needs to be, embodied or, as one might put it, 'enmattered'. As we trust in an incarnate God, our theology and Christian living must be concerned with the earth, with both the physical and spiritual wellbeing and healing of people and of creation. Such faith in the Word-made-flesh allows us to delight in visual images of the divine, to celebrate the wonder and beauty of the sensuous, even if and because we perfectly know that the face of God will never be fully revealed in our earthly life. In fact, it is essentially the incarnation that allows for a theology through the material visual image. Since the belief that we are made in the image of God is at least as old as the first chapter of Genesis, there is nothing new in this basic assertion of the goodness and sacredness of creation. But it is the radical insistence on and contemplation of an embodied theology – mainly from an eco-feminist perspective – against the history of a dualistic outlook on matter and spirit, body and soul, natural and supernatural, which places it in the forefront of contemporary theological thinking. A theology focused on the image supports and is situated therefore in close proximity to such current theological concerns. Of course, while ecological theology deals mainly with organic, living matter, with good stewardship of and care for the earth, the embodied or 'en-mattered' theology of art looks at a cultural product, something created by a person. Nevertheless, both eco-feminist and theology through art are related as they both challenge and strive to replace a dualistic perception of the world with a more holistic one, each from its own angle. Moreover, both have a contextual dimension. As a theology of art is centrally inspired by individual works of art, by the life experience of the artists and the context in which their works are produced, it thus takes seriously particularity and abstains from absolute claims. Or, in other words, *if* more universal claims are made, they arise from and through the particular. In this manner and through its dialogical nature, a theology like this one enjoys a certain freedom and humility and knows itself as being *one* way of discovering glimpses of ultimate reality.

In [art] . . . feelings and expressions ranging from deepest pain and suffering to exuberant, ecstatic joy are encountered. Prophetic and visionary, the work of art 'speaks' of life in all its aspects, including death. In this way it may also 'speak' of the divine, whether directly through Christian iconography or in less obvious fashion. Naturally, the written word does the same. However, there is a difference. While a text *describes* the beauty or ugliness, happiness or suffering of a human being, for example, which the reader has to image in her or his mind, the painting *visually shows* that figure which can be glanced in one moment. It is this – at times confrontational and shocking – immediacy which provokes instant reactions of repulsion or attraction, disgust or delight, wonder and awe. This is its beauty and danger. Real engagement with visual art demands more than a glance, it demands to go beyond one's immediate reactions. What is required, precisely because of the sensuous, seductive nature of art, is a discipline of seeing. Disciplined, intensive seeing is essential in order to appreciate the work of art not merely in terms of its sensuous quality on the one hand or its moral dimension, for example, on the other, but rather to be illumined by what it conveys as a whole, i.e. its intertwined aesthetic, spiritual, intellectual and ethical dimensions. Moreover, ultimately true seeing and genuine understanding happens through affection and love, a love free of naivety or sentimentality. The old notion that one must love a person or something to really know him, her or it, is pertinent. In this way seeing becomes profound, creative and a possibility for healing or transformation.

Visual images, positive and often negative, confront the human being daily and have become and are becoming increasingly more powerful through the media of television, advertisement and computers. It is high time then for the theological world and the churches to treat and value the artistic image – paintings, sculptures, installations, films – as a relevant source of and in theology. It is both paradoxically and obviously in the concrete materiality of the work of art that human beings may continue to glimpse the incomprehensible, unimaginable Other, the God of creation, 'the glory of Christ who is the image of God' (2 Cor 4.4), the God of freedom and love.

In this way, art, especially contemporary art, will not only play an increasingly important role in theology, but hopefully it will gain and regain its place and importance in church life, i.e. in places of worship. In opposition to the many destructive images that surround us, art, like theology, may yet offer something different, something life-giving and life-affirming, a critical view of our existence, a call to change, a glimmer of hope, an anticipation of what may be and could be.

Nevertheless, in all our efforts to truly see and to treat and acknowledge the work of art as a *locus theologicus*, it is vital to be aware of the tension that exists between the artistic image and the written word. The tension lies in the very fact that, as Rahner rightly observed, the arts cannot be translated entirely into other modalities. It is precisely this tension that provides the ground for and gives life to doing theology through art. But tension in this context is not negative, and distinction does not mean separation. As long as the written word and the visual work of art can be distinguished, and as long as they *both* express reality and ultimate reality, intimate relations and infinite bridges between the two can be discovered, built and enlarged. . . . It is in this way that a theology based on images takes its place in the colourful palette of our polyphonic and symphonic reflection on the divine, in our search for meaning, in our faith seeking understanding. (Ch. 4, pp. 280–3)

Source: Gesa E. Thiessen, *Theology and Modern Irish Art*, Dublin, Columba Press, 1999.

16.11 Jeremy Begbie, from *Beholding the Glory, Incarnation through the Arts*

This musician and theologian (University of Cambridge) has widely written on the relationship between theology and music. In this extract he explores how today we may understand and, indeed, enjoy the triune God in terms of a 'three part polyphony'.

What could be more apt than to speak of the Trinity as a three-note-resonance of life, mutually indwelling, without mutual exclusion and yet without merger, each occupying the same 'space', yet recognisably and irreducibly distinct, mutually enhancing and establishing each other? . . . Perhaps a large part of our chronic tendency to treat the Trinity as essentially a problem to be solved rather than a reality to be enjoyed – a mathematical puzzle about threeness and oneness to be agonised over on Trinity Sunday – has been fuelled by giving pride of place to the eye in telling us what is possible and impossible. Then it is hard to escape imagining God as blandly one (unitarianism), or a celestial committee of individuals (tritheism), or three manifestations of the 'one' God who has no distinctions in himself ('modalism'). (The next time we hear a Trinity Sunday sermon, there is a good chance that the illustrations will all be visual.) Not only that, many depictions of the Trinity have been essentially static and still, whereas to speak of three strings mutually resonating instantly introduces a dynamism which is arguably far truer to the trinitarian, living God of the New Testament.

A number of writers have recently been pressing that if we started being more unashamedly trinitarian in our approach to the incarnation, we would have far fewer problems. All too easily, 'divinity' becomes an abstraction – a 'nature' – which must be somehow fitted together with an equally abstract notion of 'humanity'. The New Testament writers do not seem to be very interested in 'divinity' – they do seem to be captivated by a living God, the God of Israel, now decisively identifying himself in and through the life, death and rising of Jesus, the authentic and ultimate human being. By the time John's Gospel is written (c. AD 90), this God is spoken of as including an eternal relationship. The relation between Jesus and the one he calls 'Father' is being traced to a relation within the heart of God – that between Father and Son. 'Divinity' is not the focus of attention, but the eternal love-relation of Son and the Father, into which we are adopted by the Holy Spirit. Likewise, in the New Testament, 'humanity' in some abstract sense does not seem to be the centre of interest, but (especially in Luke and Paul's writings) the particular Spirit-filled representative humanity of Jesus in which we can now share.

Conceiving 'God' as the eternally resonating chord of Father, Son and Spirit encourages us to be far more faithful to these biblical currents. Instead of thinking of Christ possessing a 'divine nature', we can imagine an eternal lively resonance between Father and Son, mediated by the Spirit, into which we can be caught up. Instead of thinking of Christ possessing a 'human nature', we can conceive him as the one in whom humanity has been restored to its created destiny, 'tuned' to the Father through the Spirit, and of you and me being 'tuned in' to his humanity by the same Spirit.

Of course, if we were to expand on this, we would need to make many qualifications. The relations within the Trinity are not identical to those between Son and the humanity of Christ, nor, indeed, between us and Christ. Also, we would need to insist that we are not attacking visual modes of thinking in themselves – a chronic and much-discussed Protestant tendency – or ignoring the fact that there have been some magnificent visual renderings of the Trinity, and, of course, of the incarnation. The main point here, however, is to suggest that serious difficulties arise if we rely too heavily or exclusively on one sense at the expense of others, and that the world of simultaneously sounding notes offers underdeveloped resources, not least when we want to explore the incarnation.

Musical Drama . . . Returning to the Trinity, instead of a chord, might it not be more appropriate to speak of God's life as three-part polyphony, even, as

Robert Jenson intriguingly suggests, a fugue? This more readily suggests response, giving and receiving, particularity of the persons, even the joy of God. Jenson can write: 'our enjoyment of God is that we are taken into the triune singing' and this by virtue of the incarnation. Certainly, applied directly to the incarnation, polyphony highlights another and often forgotten feature of it, which (as I have already hinted) can be all too easily eclipsed by Chalcedon. The incarnation is not a theory, or a picture, or a concept – but essentially a drama of interpenetration between the triune God and humanity, extending from Bethlehem to Jerusalem, a story with shape, struggle and direction, and a glorious climax: Christ, as fully human, established in the life of God, humankind and God at last *together* as they were meant to be. Music can remind us that all the extraordinary patterns of interpenetration and resonance we have been tracing – within God, between the Son and the humanity of Jesus, and between us and God – all participate in a magnificent multi-voiced symphony of salvation, with the incarnate Son at its heart. It is a symphony which has embraced dissonance at its most destructive, including the arresting dissonance and silence of Good Friday and Holy Saturday. Like all music, it is played out *for us* objectively in time, in the incarnate life of Christ, and now by virtue of the Spirit, it is played *in* and *through* us, catching us up in its manifold resonances – 'you are the music/While the music lasts' (Eliot).

Sounding Together   There is another dimension of the incarnation to mention which music, through its dynamic mixtures of sounds, can disclose with special potency. If it is typical of western modernity to see people as self-determining, isolated agents, sovereign over their carefully bounded 'space', the same is true of much thinking about the goal of the incarnation, which all too often is seen as the rescue of solitary individuals for heaven. But the true human goal of the incarnation is the creation of a new people, a community sustained by the Spirit, bound with that love which binds the incarnate Son to the Father (John 17.22). Models of people occupying mutually exclusive spaces (of the sort we saw earlier) will not help here. For we will likely begin to say: 'the more I can preserve my distance from you and others, the more likely I am to flourish and be free.' 'The more of me, the less of you' could well stand as a motto over a large amount of contemporary writing on human freedom. . . .

To explore the incarnation through music might well mean that even our most ingrained individualism is challenged. A rich theology of the Church spills out with comparative ease. The resonances we enjoy through the Spirit with the Son and Father, made possible by the cross, catch others up and bind us to them, even those who are 'out of tune'. The miracle of the incarnation eventually makes possible a kind of ensemble, a 'pure concert' in which we find that in 'being ourselves we're more capacious'. We expand and we are able to accommodate others we have previously shunned. This is the harmony of 'cross-purpose' – the harmony purposed in the crucifixion of the incarnate Lord. When it is turned into music, it can, at best, be a foretaste of heaven – not the sterile bliss of so many portrayals, but an abundant, dynamic multiplicity:

I heard the voice of many angels surrounding the throne and the living creatures and the elders; they numbered myriads of myriads and thousands of thousands, singing with full voice, 'Worthy is the Lamb that was slaughtered to receive power and wealth and wisdom and might and honour and glory and blessing.' (Rev. 5.12)

(Ch. 8, pp. 147–53)

Source: Jeremy Begbie (ed.), *Beholding the Glory, Incarnation through the Arts*, London, Darton, Longman and Todd, 2000.

17

Truth, Meaning and Art

— —

17.1 Harvey Cox, from *The Seduction of the Spirit, The Use and Misuse of People's Religion*

North American theologian Harvey Cox argues here that it is essential for scholars of religion to pay attention not only to the written word and 'high' culture, but to the widespread visual, electronic mass media, to popular culture, and to the religious ceremonies in different faiths and cultures.

The Image and the Icon

Ideally I suppose I should have a special interest in the mass media because they are so powerful, so mythogenic and so pervasive, and as a theologian it would be a dereliction of duty not to give them attention. My actual motivation, however, is not nearly so virtuous. The truth is I enjoy most of the mass media thoroughly. I have never outgrown my adolescent crush on movies, and although I prefer good ones, I even relish bad ones. . . .

In thinking theologically about the mass media I have come to disassociate myself from two groups, both of whom also have strong views on the subject. I disagree on the one hand with the anti-media defenders of 'high culture', many of them fellow inhabitants of the academic world; but I also disagree with the media pros and buffs, the celebrants of popular culture and especially of TV. . . .

Western society now stands in desperate need of something like a cultural rebirth or renaissance. But for anything like such a spiritual renewal to have even a chance of occurring we must release the vast cultural capital now controlled by the ruling institutions of industrial states. This liberating of the cultural bastille must happen both politically and technically if the hoarded heritage is to be made available to the 'masses' in such a way that they can both draw on it and contribute to it. I believe the electronic media contain within themselves one of the ingredients of a cultural revolution, the technical one. To ignore or dismiss them is to turn one's back on the most salient cultural fact of our era. No theologian with a serious interest in how the study of religion might be delivered from academic bondage to help spark the renewal of culture can afford such a back turning. . . . [U]ntil the pattern of power in the society itself changes, the control of the media will remain in the hands of those who will not permit their use for political or cultural renewal. Conceding the hours of exposure and the changing modes of consciousness to the media buffs does not prove their case. Media may broaden our purview and supply us with more data. But under present conditions of control and technology, if they do alter our consciousness, it is to make us feel more helpless and overwhelmed.

Still there is enormous promise in television, film and other new media. *In principle* they are more universal, equalitarian and accessible than previous modes of communication ever could be. Unlike books, for example, TV and film do not require the long expenditure of time required to learn to read or the even longer period required to learn how to write effectively. There are no *technical* reasons to prevent every TV or radio receiver from being a transmitter also, and this is just not true of books. Film is also *in principle* a radically equalising medium. It has already been proven that illiterate Andes Indians and ten-year-old children can be taught to make films in a few weeks. This makes me ask whether there is something indispensable about writing, and whether print is necessarily a way human beings will always communicate with one another, store memories and information, or tell stories. This raises the even more basic question of whether everyone everywhere has to learn to read. As awful as it may sound to book readers (and even more to book writers), the new media may eventually help move us beyond a culture dominated by print with its inherently elitist characteristics. Eventually books may become a marginal mode of communication, while oral and visual modes, made universally accessible by new social forms and electronic technology, once again become dominant. . . .

The electronic media *could*, given the needed changes in control and technology, facilitate a more democratic and more participatory society than we now have. Print cannot. I love books, but as one who has read and written many of them, I know how awkward and cumbersome they are as modes of communication. They take too long to write, cost too much to publish, encourage a certain snobbish reliance on a pretty style and vocabulary, and clutter up houses and libraries to a degree that is already becoming nearly impossible to handle. Also it takes a long time to reply to printed matter and it is not easily altered when you change your mind. Print does not reproduce the full range of human communicative sonorities and gestures the way tapes and especially films do. The readers of the world would do well to agree that we can save writing for *something* only if we stop trying to make it do *everything*. Writing will have an important place in the pluralistic communications culture of the future; alone, however, it cannot produce the cultural transformation we need. Films and TV, despite their present authoritarian structure, are inherently more capable of facilitating that revolution than writing could ever be.

This coming cultural revolution, from print to images, will have a shattering impact on the 'religions of the book', those faiths that were spawned during that relatively brief period of human history during which writing assumed such prominence. It will also completely alter the authority structure of those faiths. Experts on Holy Writ will no longer hold such sway. Meanwhile, as a teacher of religion I am often made uncomfortably aware of the distortions introduced into our learning about religion by virtue of the fact that those who teach and study it not only came into consciousness within religions and cultures dominated by writing, but also presently live and work on tiny rafts of written pages adrift in an ocean of images. The inevitable bias this creates reveals itself in our study of religious history, where we rely mainly on texts – with a little welcome help from the pottery shards and temple lintels shovelled out by archaeologists. It also distorts our study of 'non-Western' religions, where we concentrate too much on merely reading the Vedas or the Gita when we could also be learning from these faiths by chanting, fasting, praying or meditating. Our book-print mentality also lures us into spending too much time reading what other theologians write and not enough examining what the vast majority of simple people, who never write about their faith, actually do.

We should prepare ourselves for the changes it will entail in our whole way of life when the coming culture transformation sets in. But it will not, given present prospects, be utopia; and I do not think we should liquidate our paperback collections too quickly. Sadly, the electronic media, like the 'high culture' establishment from which they are so separated, are also in a state of captivity. Before they can facilitate any cultural change they have to be liberated themselves. But the prospect of *both* 'high culture' *and* the new media being freed and then finding each other is a dizzying one. Such a combination might make possible the emergence of a worldwide spiritual community, one in which billions of persons and millions of groups could tell one another their stories, listen, respond and refashion in a thousand unimagined permutations. Only then would we truly have a 'global village', something which, despite all the talk, we do *not* have today. A village is a place of instantaneous buzzing mutual communication among all villagers. We do not have that. Instead of a global village we have a global cluster of pyramids, a complex of vertical skyscrapers where signals come down from the tower tops but there is no way to answer back from the bottom. As long as this high rise stands, the electronic icon's spell will stupefy us. Its hypnotic power will tear us ever further from our inner selves and from the communities that keep us alive. But neither electrons nor icons are essentially evil, and we must never stop imagining a world where all pyramids are dismantled and we can use new technologies to see and hear one another on a scale never before possible. (Ch. 10, pp. 275–9)

Source: Harvey Cox, *The Seduction of the Spirit, The Use and Misuse of People's Religion*, New York, Simon and Schuster, 1973.

17.2 Hans Küng, from *Art and the Question of Meaning*

This Swiss Catholic theologian (b. 1928) and former director of the Institute for Ecumenical Research at Tübingen University, argues here that artists ought to work in a manner which properly cherishes past, present and future concerns, without becoming ideologically fixed on any one of these.

Art as Heritage, Anticipation, Elucidation of Meaning

Certainly, we are not taking anything back. Art may not be overtaxed, may not be identified with religion, to become a religion of art; art cannot produce and today does not seek directly to produce a meaning of life. But now think of the counterpoint: even though art may not be overtaxed, it may nevertheless be challenged. For every great painter transcends the visible in his own way, makes visible the invisible. And if art assists self-representation and experience of the world, serves to open up, interpret, and lay bare our reality, is it then to remain simply dumb in regard to the ultimate questions concerning this reality? Should it not again become more clearly involved precisely in the great questions of the sense or nonsense of life? Perhaps also it should become more powerfully involved in virtue of a critically acquired orientation of life, of a tried and tested assent: in virtue not only of the courage to depict negative experiences, the ugly, the meaningless, but also of the courage to depict positive contents of meaning, values, feelings, the 'beautiful' in this sense – the beautiful, that is, not as an innocuous sedative, but as a challenging evocation of the good made visible.

I do not mean of course that art should again become religious. Nor do I mean that art should deal mainly with religious themes and make use of the traditional symbols for transcendence. No, it is not possible to go back from autonomy to heteronomy and dependence. But should not the art of the future again become *open to religion*? Should it not mean going forward completely autonomously and independently to a new rootedness, to a new basic certainty, to a new firmly established basic trust? Not then an ideological-secularist art, which is constantly threatened by nihilism. But certainly a completely secular art with its hidden basis in an absolute ground of meaning, which – whether representationally as with Beckmann and Schlemmer or nonrepresentationally as with Kandinsky and Mondrian – perhaps by the arrangement of light and space would allow us to perceive something of the all-embracing dimension of the mystery of all things; which might indirectly throw some light on 'what involves me unconditionally', as Paul Tillich used to describe it.

Whatever the attitude of the artist to religion, to the question of God, to belief or unbelief, the opportunities offered to him by a basic trust rooted in particular in belief in God are immense. Particularly for the artist it should be of the utmost importance not to leave unanswered the great questions of ground and meaning, whither and whence, which would otherwise become constant occasions of doubt, acquiescence, or rebellion. Also and particularly for the work of the artist it should be of the utmost importance to know *whence we come, whither we are going, who we are* (parallels between art and theology may be noted marginally here).

For the artist who knows *whence we come* a new relationship to the *past* is possible. This is a *first* point.

Anyone, that is, who knows in a completely justified trust that the world and man do not come from the nothingness that explains nothing, but from that ground of grounds which as primal ground is also primal goal of man and the world, will not make an idol of the past: tradition will not be his God; history will be important for his art, but will not become an ideology, will not become historicism. (Ch. 5, pp. 37–9)

What is to be expected today from both state and Church, from both artists and viewers of art, is not an unreserved commitment to some part of the past, but a freely and critically discriminating attitude to our own history. Only in this way are we immune against that paralysing myth of 'decline' according to which in art also we have been going downhill ever since the Golden Age.

Anyone who believes in a first and last ground of meaning of the world and man can never believe in the ultimate decadence of man and his art; on the contrary, by looking back to the past, he can create a better orientation of life, can give greater meaning to life for himself, for his work, and also for other human beings. The great art of the past thus becomes for him an incomparably precious *heritage of meaning*.

For the artist *who* knows *whither we are going* a new relationship to the *future* is possible. This is a *second* point.

Anyone, that is, who relies in completely justified trust on the fact that human life and human history do not end in a nothingness that explains nothing, but are fullfilled in that goal of all goals which as primal goal is also itself the primal ground of the world and man, will not make an idol of the future: progress will not be his God; the future will be important for his art, but will not become an ideology, will not become futurism. . . .

What I want to warn against is only *ideological futurism* (certainly not propagated only in Italy and in art). I mean any kind of *religiosity centred on the future*: as if God had come only through technological evolution or politicosocial revolution and as if art (or theology) had nothing to do with the past; as if a new beginning had to be made again and again rigidly at zero and as if every revolt were itself a great renewal; as if the very latest art were not only the first available, but the very first and best of all. . . .

No, 'newness' or 'novelty' can never be the supreme law in art (or in theology); a radical break with all tradition is by no means a guarantee of anything better. Continually, rapidly increasing change of fashion trends and 'isms' – brought about less by the immanent development of art than by the constraints of exhibiting, of competition between galleries, of the art market, of the mass media

– is the expression of a craving for novelty which sometimes promotes outlets for art products but kills true art.

What is to be expected from both state and Church, from both artists and viewers of art, is not an irresponsible commitment inspired by a utopian sense of mission to any kind of programmed future, but a frankly and soberly realistic attitude also toward the different utopias of our age. Only in this way are we immune against the seductive myth of 'progress', according to which in art also the Golden Age is immediately at hand.

Anyone who believes in a first and last ground of meaning of the world and man can scarcely believe in the automatic ascent of man and his art; but, without fear of the future, precisely by his trust in an art of the future, he can create a better orientation of life, can give greater meaning to life for himself, his work, and also for other human beings.

The ever newly possible, always living art thus becomes for him a hope-inspiring *anticipation of meaning*.

For the artist who knows *who we are* a new relationship to the *present* becomes possible. This is a *third* point.

Anyone who in a completely justified trust admits that we are finite, defective beings and yet beings of infinite expectation and yearning, that we do not find an ultimate support in ourselves but only in that primal support which is also primal ground and primal goal of the world and man, will not make an idol of the present: the present moment will not be his God; the momentary impression will be important for his art, but will not become an ideology, will not become impressionism.

No, I am not attacking *impression*, concentration on the immediate present, an art which, without drawing pictures in the conventional sense, tries to capture and shape the fleeting impression of the moment, making use of 'chance' as an artistic method in individuality, subjectivity, and spontaneity. This is how French impressionism carried out its artistic experiments with light, sun, and colour, becoming increasingly detached from the object.

What I am criticizing is only *ideological impressionism* (also manifesting itself in a completely different form in modern American art). I mean any kind of *religiosity centred on the present* in art (or theology): as if God worked only through the momentary happening and as if history, looking both backward and forward, had no part to play; as if only the unhistorical 'eternal' present counted and history could be denied, the linkage with past and future ignored.

Anyone who stands up for the impressionist idea of art for art's sake too easily sacrifices art to its superficially beautiful semblance, lacking depth, substance, and detailed elaboration. This at any rate was the reproach of the postimpressionists who at an early stage feared a draining of meaning and content. This too is the reproach made against certain forms of American pop art, which took their sculptural themes and methods largely from show business and advertising, alienating these only slightly with the aid of screen printing processes and the like. . . .

No, 'objective quality' or 'actuality' cannot be the supreme law in art. Photographic fidelity, reliance on comic strips, environment, montage of real elements to form a picture – none of these in themselves guarantee the artistic mastery of reality. Not everything that is interesting is for that reason art, not every happening is an art event. The metamorphosis of signs, signals, and symbols of advertising, traffic regulations, and the mass media can certainly convey aesthetic experiences. But occasionally all it can do is to reveal boldly and simply our modern philistinism, superficiality, sex obsession, and the banality of modern slogans and appeals, happenings and idol figures.

What is to be expected from both state and Church, both artists and viewers of art, is not a passive acceptance of prevailing conditions, but a critical attitude, aware of our temporality, particularly toward the banal, commonplace present state of our mass culture: an attitude which must include both the remembrance of the past and looking ahead to the future . . . . Only in this way are we immune in our cheap 'wear out and throwaway' society against the myth of the 'eternal return of the same', which Nietzsche saw as the reverse side of nihilism (admittedly, a nihilism of which many are not yet aware).

Anyone who believes in a first and last ground of meaning of the world and man, even at a time of the obsolescence of fashions and the disintegration of 'isms', can scarcely believe in a definitive chaos of art; on the contrary, precisely out of his deeper understanding of the art of the present time, he can create a better orientation of life, can give greater meaning to life for himself, his work, and also for other human beings.

Art that is relevant particularly today, with all its enormous tensions and inconsistencies, then appears to him as an up-to-date *elucidation of meaning*. (Ch. 5, pp. 41–7)

Source: Hans Küng, *Art and the Question of Meaning*, London, SCM Press, 1981.

17.3 David Tracy, from *The Analogical Imagination*

The Chicago theologian David Tracy (b. 1939), who has concerned himself with theology's role in contemporary pluralist culture, discusses in this extract the meaning of 'the classic' in the realm of art. He emphasizes the need for an experience of art free from a preconceived aesthetics of taste or art theories, as well as the aspect of truth in art.

The Classic

The Normative Role of the Classics: Realized Experience

We all find ourselves compelled both to recognize and on occasion to articulate our reasons for the recognition that certain expressions of the human spirit so disclose a compelling truth about our lives that we cannot deny them some kind of normative status. Thus do we name these expressions, and these alone, 'classics'. Thus do we recognize, whether we name it so or not, a normative element in our cultural experience, experienced as a realized truth.

Yet what does it mean to find a normative element in cultural experience? My thesis is that what we mean in naming certain texts, events, images, rituals, symbols and persons 'classics' is that here we recognize nothing less than the disclosure of a reality we cannot but name truth. With Whitehead, here we find something valuable, something 'important'; some disclosure of reality in a moment that must be called one of 'recognition' which surprises, provokes, challenges, shocks and eventually transforms us; an experience that upsets conventional opinions and expands the sense of the possible; indeed a realized experience of that which is essential, that which endures. The presence of classics in every culture is undeniable. Their memory haunts us. Their actual effects in our lives endure and await ever new appropriations, constantly new interpretations. Their existence may be trusted to time, to the generations of capable readers and inquirers who will check our enthusiasms and ensure the emergence of some communal sense of the importance of certain texts, images, persons, events, symbols. . . .

When in the presence of any classic work of art, we do not, in fact, experience ourselves as an autonomous subject possessing certain tastes for certain qualities confronting the expression of someone else's taste, some easily controlled qualities hidden in the work by the artistic 'genius'. Instead the authentic experience of art is quite the opposite: We find ourselves 'caught up' in its world, we are shocked, surprised, challenged by its startling beauty *and* its recognizable truth, its instinct for the essential. In the actual experience of art we do not experience the artist *behind* the work of art. Rather we recognize the truth of the work's disclosure of a world of reality transforming, if only for a moment, ourselves: our lives, our sense for possibilities and actuality, our destiny.

When we ignore the actual experience of art by imposing alien aesthetic theories of taste upon it, we are tempted to misinterpret the experience as a purely, indeed, merely 'aesthetic' one. In a manner analogous to our attempted alienation of ourselves and our own effective history into the realm of historicist privacy masked as autonomy, we may deny that the work of art has anything to do with what we name knowledge, truth, reality. In an earlier and more homogeneous culture, training, education and cultivation were designed to aid everyone to experience the tested communal sense of the disclosive and transformative power and truth of the work of art. Now we seem too often content to cultivate a new form of alienation, the aesthetic sensibility. What is the popular understanding of an aesthetic sensibility but the controlled cultivation of an autonomous subject's taste for qualities in objects that exist in their own brittle autonomy over against that same subject? For publicness and truth, the autonomous subject will look elsewhere: to those forms of thinking guaranteed as scientific and technical. . . .

The work of art, sometimes even for the understanding of the artist, becomes simply the self-expression of a particularly complex, probably alienated, certainly idiosyncratic private self. The work of art, sometimes understood as possessing its own absolute autonomy by some formalist critics, is kept at a distance from our own cherished autonomy. It is always interesting, sometimes even fascinating. For art always provides new qualities to appreciate, new methods to understand how it works its fascination and, in Kierkegaard's sense of the aesthetic, new possibilities for our interesting Don Juan sensitivities to explore. But art does not provide an encounter with anything we can call truth about ourselves or reality. Art, too, is finally private.

Yet it remains worth inquiring whether this familiar, indeed popular understanding of 'aesthetic' experience accords with our actual experience of any authentic work of art. In fact it does not. Rather, as Hans-Georg Gadamer among others insists, the actual experience of the work of art can be called a realized experience of an event of truth. More exactly, when I experience any classic work of art, I do not experience myself as an autonomous subject aesthetically appreciating the good qualities of an aesthetic object set over against me. Indeed, when I reflect after the experience upon the experience itself, shorn of prior theories of 'aesthetics', I find that my subjectivity is never in control of the experience, nor is the work of art actually experienced as an object with certain qualities over against me. Rather the work of art encounters me with the surprise, impact, even shock of reality itself. In experiencing art, I recognize a truth I somehow know but know I did not really know except through the experience of recognition of the essential compelled by the work of art. I am transformed by its truth when I return to the everyday, to the whole of what I ordinarily call reality, and discover new affinities, new sensibilities for the everyday.

I do not experience a subject over against an object with my subjective consciousness in complete control. Rather I experience myself caught up in a relationship with the work of art in such manner that I transcend my everyday self-consciousness and my usual desires for control. In experiencing that actual internal relationship (no longer the external relationships of theories about the aesthetic subject or aesthetic object), I experience the impact of a realized experience, an event character of truth as a glimpse into the essential that is the real. I find I must employ words like 'recognize' to describe that impact. Such actual self-transcendence, I also recognize, is not my own achievement. It happens, it occurs, I am 'caught up in' the disclosure of the work. I am in the presence of a truth of recognition: recognition of what is important, essential, real beyond distractions, diversions, conventional opinions, idle talk, control and use of objects, techniques of distancing myself and manipulating others, the realm of publicness where only the lowest common denominator will count. . . .

Do I wish to discover how this work manages to work its power of disclosure through its form? I may study the best formalist and objective critics. Do I wish to know more about the workings of the artistic process? . . . All these methods, as we shall see below, really do aid an appropriation of the experience of art. Yet it remains the realized experience which must serve as the first word and the final criterion of relative adequacy in any attempt at both understanding and explanation. For only a realized experience and its disclosure of some recognition of the event-character of truth in the work of art will finally count for each as evidence. Only classic works of art, whatever their period, whatever their culture, can be counted on to allow, indeed to compel, that kind of experience and that kind of paradigmatic recognition. . . .

In allowing ourselves to experience art we are transformed, however briefly, into the mode of being of the work of art where we experience the challenge, often the shock, of a reality greater than the everyday self, a reality of the paradigmatic power of the essential that transforms us. Here the back-and-forth movement of every game becomes the buoyant dialectic of true freedom: surprise, release, confrontation, shock, often reverential awe, always transformation. In our actual experience of the work of art, we move into the back-and-forth rhythms of the work: from its discovery and disclosure to a sensed recognition of the essential beyond the everyday; from its hiddenness to our sensed rootedness; from its disclosure and concealment of truth to our realized experience of a transformative truth, at once revealing and concealing. . . .

When a work of art so captures a paradigmatic experience of that event of truth, it becomes in that moment normative. Its memory enters as a catalyst into all our other memories and, now subtly, now compellingly, transforms our perceptions of the real. It becomes a classic: always retrievable, always in need of appreciative appropriation and critical evaluation, always disclosive and transformative with its truth of importance, always open to new application and thereby new interpretation. That science reaches truth – the truths of verification and falsification – only an obscurantist would deny. That the work of art discloses an event not merely of taste, genius or beauty, but truth only a philistine, even an 'aesthetic' one, will finally deny. We can, to repeat, refuse to enter into the game of the work of art where the usual subject-object relationship of both ordinary experience and science is broken where a realized experience of the relationship itself, the back-and-forth movement of the event of disclosure and concealment, actually happens. We can refuse to enter the game of conversation where the subject matter produced through the form, not the formless ego, controls the questioning and the responding. We *can* make all these refusals. Yet somehow the classics endure as provocations awaiting the risk of reading: to challenge our complacency, to break our conventions, to compel and concentrate our attention, to lure us out of a privacy masked as autonomy into a public realm where what is important and essential is no longer denied. Whenever we actually experience even one classic work of art we are liberated from privateness into the genuine publicness of a disclosure of truth. It seems foolish, therefore, to develop theories of aesthetics which effectively deny the truth-character of the experience of art as a realized experience of the essential. It seems fatal to hand over the classics to the levelling power of a technical reason disguised as publicness, to consign them to the privacy of a merely entertaining, tasteful, interesting aesthetic realm of temporary refreshment. Instead we need, I believe, a rehabilitation of the notions of the normative, the authoritative – in a word, the classical – now freed from the private domain of elitist classicists and welcomed again as the communal and public heritage of our common human experience of the truth of the work of art. (Ch. 3, pp. 107–15)

Source: David Tracy, *The Analogical Imagination, Christian Theology and the Culture of Pluralism*, London, SCM Press, 1981.

17.4 Langdon Gilkey, from 'Can Art Fill the Vacuum?'

This Lutheran theologian of the University of Chicago has concerned him-self with the relationship of the sacred and society, and of theology and the sciences. In this passage he examines the prophetic, moral and political role of art and artist. Art can play a vital part in raising critical awareness in a 'cold' technical culture where skills and capital matter more than humans and faith; it can provide means of finding meaning.

A technical culture is voracious, devouring; it consumes all the other nontechnical aspects of culture by turning everything into a skill, a knowledge of how to do it, a *means*. Only art remains resistant – and then finds itself bought to decorate a gadget so as to sell the gadget better, or bought as an investment, better and safer than prime real estate!

What we are to do, and *why* we are to do it are queries thus pushed far to the side or left quite out of account. What all these instruments are *for*, what the *worth* of all this doing is, are forgotten matters, unpondered as if they were no longer questions at all. Our society generates tremendous rational and spiritual power, vast energies of thought, tons of words. But the highly trained and very expert *rational* power of the society, and the *spiritual* power of the society, its morals and religion, all seem bent on the production and glorification of instruments, creating effective, efficient, and competent *means* for doing something. If, however, all our joint energies, brains, and work are given to produce or refine some means for some further end, and if that future end never comes, or if, when it comes, it turns out to be worthless, *then* these energies, this thinking, and this work have been misspent, and a culture devoted entirely to them has a vacuum at its heart.

One significant role, or gift, of art is to enhance direct, immediate experience. It so reshapes immediate experience as to make it suddenly an end, an end in itself, as Aristotle put it; or as modern reflection has put it, an *event* of intrinsic worth, that is an event which, in and of itself, in and through its own taking place, creates immediate and experienced *meaning*. Artistic talent can, to be sure, be used also as an instrument – to beautify an object or spruce up an ad so as to sell something else – as can religious piety. But for art in itself, in its role as *art,* the 'meaning stops here'. It is a reality in itself, for itself. Whether it be a classic painting or sculpture, an ordinary object rendered into art, an assemblage of stray objects, we look at it as it *is,* as it presents itself. The event of our encounter is for itself, a significant enjoyment, an experience of seeing, here, at this moment. And we are deepened, refreshed, challenged to reorder ourselves, to see in a new way our world and ourselves – we are recreated. Here is a point, an end, a stopping place.

This event of enhancement is not 'subjective' any more than a technical instrument is subjective; for, after all, every means is a means only as an instrument of our subjective purposes. An encounter with a work of art is an interaction, an interaction of the presence of that work and of ourselves into this new creative event, the enhancement of our experience, of our being, and of our world. Without these events of enhancement, the enhancement of direct experience, nothing we do makes sense. Instruments and means, preparing and making ready, fixing it up, getting it set, tuning it up, even of the finest stereos and autos, *all* are means to enhanced experience or else they are worthless. This is the first and utterly essential role of art and the artistic: to re-create ordinary experience into value, into enhanced experience; to provide the ends – the deep, immediate, present enjoyments – for which all instruments exist and from which alone they receive their point. When an event that we label art thus stops the heedless flow of time in an enhanced moment, a moment of new awareness or understanding, a moment of intense seeing and of participation in what is seen, then (as the Zen tradition has taught us) the transcendent appears through art, and art and religion approach one another.

Probably unintentionally art has, or frequently has had, a quite other but equally significant role. Sometimes this is intentional, sometimes not; but when it is there, it is of vast creative power. This is the role of art in making us see in *new* and *different* ways, below the surface and beyond the obvious. Art opens up the truth hidden behind and within the ordinary; it provides a new entrance into reality and pushes us through that entrance. It leads us to what is really there and really going on. Far from subjective, it pierces the opaque subjectivity, the *not* seeing, of conventional life, of conventional viewing, and discloses reality.

The most obvious example of this is what we can only call *outrage* in works of art: outrage at the *dehumanization* of persons, at the *emptiness* of persons and of their roles in life, at the *inhumanity* of men and women to others, at the grotesque *misshapenness* of people and of their behaviour, at the wanton *suffering* that is universal. Here art is not so much providing the ends essential to a technical culture; rather is it uncovering the emptiness, the distortion, and the demonic cruelty of such a culture. Quite possibly artists feel subjectively that they are merely being 'hard', 'honest', 'realistic', or possibly ironic and humorous – 'laughing at the absurdity of life', as we like to put it – and they probably are right. But the work itself and the event it creates in relation to us, *itself* manifests outrage, and this shines through every line and colour – as, for example, in German Expressionism, Picasso's *Guernica*, in a lot of Chicago imagists, and in much punk art. Art enhances direct experience; it also tears off the mask covering ordinary experience to expose its disarray, its disastrous waywardness, its betrayals, its suffering. Here it has – possibly unconsciously – a 'prophetic role', denouncing the culture it lays bare. And inescapably this is a *moral* and often a *political* role. An example from recent experience has been the unexpected power that folk music exhibited in the civil rights and the anti-Vietnam movements. Here a form of passionate art – *not* political or moral theory or even reformist preaching – led this mighty moral movement to political victory. What was revealed in and by those songs, and by the events of their being sung and being heard, was not subjective at all: what was revealed or exposed was the *reality* of a segregated, bloated, and imperialist culture that called for exposure and transformation. The need for that same role exists as much now as then – and art can be its most effective warrior, which is, incidentally, why Russia – and much of the American moral majority – is so afraid of contemporary art. When art thus condemns present reality in the name of humanity and justice and seeks for its transformation, it becomes itself the vehicle of the transcendent and approaches the religious.

Art, however, provides more than negative images of ordinary reality. It gives us most of our creative images of ourselves, our world and our relations to one another. Human life is lived in and through symbols that shape and guide us in all we are and do: symbols of nature, symbols of ourselves – who we are, what we can be, what we ought to be – symbols of our community and society, symbols of the sacred that permeates all. Works of art set these symbols into images; through them we can *see* ourselves and our world, possibly for the first time. 'In art we find ourselves and lose ourselves at the same time,' said Thomas Merton.

Art is bitterly iconoclastic; it opposes the phony, the empty, and the outrageous in life; thus does it ruthlessly demolish the dead wood of convention – and thus does it search for new images of the strange reality of nature, of ourselves, and of the sacred amid which we live. It fills the vacuum of our present vague and empty images of ourselves and of reality. Like religion, it recreates by offering a set of symbols of our own being, of community, and of the sacred. Like religion, it heals and re-creates as well as cuts and cauterizes; it is essential to every culture, and especially to a technical culture.

If all of this – and this is a lot – makes up the role of the artist in a technical culture, one can understand the inevitability of the artist as an *outsider*, as condemned to be on the boundary rather than in the comfortable, powerful, or acclaimed center of a culture's life. Artists have few of the traits that the culture emphasizes, applauds, or rewards: they are not experts; their importance is not that they know how to do anything useful to anyone but other artists; they don't make instruments for anyone else's use, or even make money or jobs for others. They say: Stop, look and *see* what is real, and *be*. In our rushing world, no one has time for this. Moreover they must and do participate in the suffering of the culture, live themselves within its sense of loneliness, emptiness, and aimlessness, experience outrage at its inhumanity, its infinite pain and despair – *if* they are to uncover, under its conventional and smooth surfaces, the stark reality of alienation. . . . The artist must be inside the culture to feel its wounds and its hurt, and yet enough outside, alien from it, to recognize these as *outrages* and to shape them creatively into *new* images less untrue to our reality. (pp. 188–92)

Source: Langdon Gilkey, 'Can Art Fill the Vacuum?', in Diane Apostolos-Cappadona (ed.), *Art, Creativity, and the Sacred, An Anthology in Religion and Art*, New York, Crossroad, 1988.

17.5 Frank Burch Brown, from *Religious Aesthetics, A Theological Study of Making and Meaning*

In one of the most significant works on theological aesthetics in the late twentieth century, the author, a North American theologian, musician and composer at Virginia State University, examines the significance of art as a source of divine revelation, of meaning, as well as the difference between the two modes of theological writing and of artistic expression in communicating something of the transcendent.

Artistic Makings and Religious Meanings

This artistic capacity to envision, and in vision to transfigure this world or some hypothetical counterpart, evidently responds uniquely to an abiding human need. That is the need to discover, imagine, and come to grips with a world that can be thought and felt to matter, both in its goodness and beauty and in its evil and horror. The fact that art can in various ways address this need is one thing that distinguishes it from mere play or sport, which even at their most exciting and involving are rarely said to be deeply meaningful or revealing. Art, too, has its games, thrills, and spectacles. Art, too, provides moments of sheer escape from a life that threatens to become unbearably hard or abusively boring. But we need art for more than that. Precisely because we are embodied, thinking, passionate beings who want meaning and meaningfulness, truth and emotional satisfaction, we cannot be engaged wholly except through forms that imaginatively encompass and orient us within something like a world: something, moreover, as purposeful in its apparent purposelessness as we hope and trust life itself can be.

The *body* gains from artistic world-making because it is partly through the fiction of a world and its embodiment that the body itself is able to speak to the mind of which it is a part and which it partly transcends. The world of the body, in short, is mediated in part by the worlds of art, which become the body's self-disclosure.

The *mind* gains from art's imagined worlds because, although they prompt it to 'think more', its thinking does not exhaust them. Because the worlds of art represent things felt to matter (even while distanced from immediate concerns) and amounting to more than what is strictly logical, quantifiable, and measurable, the mind that thinks through the alternate worlds of works of art reconsiders even this present world in terms of qualities and values and purposes. If the mind's processes of reasoning remain as before, the sense of things with which they begin and to which they finally must appeal is changed. In addition the blurring of the lines of distinction between real and unreal in art causes the mind to re-examine its assumptions about what makes for reality and unreality. In all these ways the artistic affects and expands our sense of truth itself, giving rise to what Kant calls 'thinking more'.

From this the *heart* itself benefits; for the worlds it is given in art are ones to which willing and feeling belong. Where the worlds of art and of actuality converge, and yet in converging do not conform to the heart's desire, there it becomes the heart's will to transform or be transformed. Art then can become prophetic in mode, showing what is unjust or senseless, and possibly what is required in response. In this way as in others, art potentially can render, in Barzun's words, a 'massive blow' that 'leaves one changed'. For the heart, the world of the prophetic work is morally or politically or perhaps religiously charged.

Because a world so charged is the sort of world that one enters or inhabits religiously, we can conclude that the worlds of artistic imagination can at times serve to reveal the realities significant to religion and *soul*. Nothing less is implied in Tillich's assertion that through the beauty of the Botticelli painting 'something of the divine source of all things' came through to him, and in a way that affected his whole life. If the theologian objects to anyone's making such a claim with respect to art, arguing instead that it is God and not art that reveals, then there are two counter-arguments that theological aesthetics might make. First, since Scripture is counted by most Christians as in some way revealed, and since a significant portion of Scripture is artistic, then it follows that art can play a part in divine revelation. Second, it seems plain that however illuminated the human mind may be by what some theologians term 'special' revelation, one still is human and usually responds most fully to those media that speak most vividly to the human being as a whole. And since nothing – even if revealed – is meaningful unless discerned and in some way understood, it makes sense that the meaning even of 'special' revelation should be mediated in part by aesthetic and artistic forms that can engage one wholly.

Our discussion of the visionary and prophetic dimension of the arts indicates that, like religion as a whole, art is widely engaged in the transformation of life and world and, indirectly, of what we have referred to as the embodied soul. Even if one concludes that the world revealed and envisioned through the deepest works of artistic imagination is the world that somehow or in some way was there all along, one nevertheless must recognize that it was not already there in just that way for oneself or for the human community. Mimesis in art is always in some degree metamorphosis. From this it follows that through artistic imagination and metaphoric representation our human world and religion itself undergo continual transformation and reformation. While what the Church terms the 'Word of God' calls into question the absolute validity of any human expression and vision, there is no reason why that 'Word' cannot sound – and in a distinctive tone – in the prophetic, visionary, and revelatory artistic expressions found within the community of Christian faith. It also may sound from without. The art that has the greatest religious significance is not necessarily the art of institutional religion but rather that art which happens to discern what religion in its institutional or personal forms needs most to see.

What we have ended up claiming, then, is that at points religion takes the form of art, and art the form of religion; that whatever is considered ultimate in being and meaning can speak through both forms, and can call both into question; and, finally, that even outside the realm of formal religion, art in the various aspects we have discussed can become religiously significant, though without some of the meanings supplied by the institutional religious milieu. Through many such arts the health and wholeness of the self and of the human community come into question; yet they also come into a condition of new possibility. (Ch. 4, pp. 109–11)

Questioning the Classics: Norms and Canons in Religion and Art

To include aesthetic works in the canon of Christian classics is entirely consistent with the integralist theories of art and religion which we have supported and presumably advanced. Like other religious classics, these are works of exceptional quality that deeply and repeatedly reward attention and that can be valued similarly over a long period of time by a wide range of perceptive and receptive people.

To claim certain artworks as religious classics, however, is by no means to assume that they exist in perpetual harmony with other Christian classics or that they always give rise to compatible interpretations and evaluations. . . .

Although the 'languages' spoken by Christian art and theology are related to each other not only in what they say but also to some extent in how they say it, they nonetheless cannot be translated without remainder one into the other. This is clear from the norms by which they are to be evaluated, from the aims they can rightly be expected to fulfil, and finally from the manner in which they exercise their influence as classic religious works.

Theological discourse in its most typical classical mode strives to be logically consistent, coherent, comprehensive, conceptually precise, and propositional. To be sure, even theology of this kind is rooted in symbol and metaphor and must be responsive to the norms of prayer and practice. This is reflected in the maxim *lex orandi, lex credendi* (the law of praying [is] the law of believing). Moreover, theology as a mode of explanation and understanding that works with the pre-understandings of the tradition must guard against explaining away what the tradition affirms as inexplicable mystery. Yet for faith to seek the understanding that theology itself can provide is for faith to seek expression, in so far as possible, in rational and intellectual form.

Clearly the expectations and criteria for artistic success are very different from those for theology, in addition to differing in some measure from one kind of art to another. It is true that the arts involve certain kinds of rationality and that even non-verbal religious art can sometimes present a particular doctrine with theological precision. This might be said of Masaccio's painting of 1425 entitled *The Holy Trinity with the Virgin and St John* (Santa Maria Novella, Florence). It might also be said of the Trinitarian symbolism in Monteverdi's setting of the 'Gloria Patri' in the 'Magnificat' that concludes his *Vespers of the Blessed Virgin* (1610). But the special gift of art is not doctrinal precision, conceptual clarity, or the ability to 'think straight'. Art's gift, when not given over simply to a delight that is almost sheerly aesthetic, is rather to explore fictively, metaphorically, and experientially what formal theology cannot itself present or contain. When certain works of Rembrandt, for instance, make divine forgiveness and grace 'visible', they are far more than theological illustrations, and their peculiar profundity cannot therefore simply be absorbed directly into theological discourse, although it may penetrate in ways that ultimately affect the theologian's own vision and reflection.

Precisely because the means and ends of art diverge in many respects from those of theology and indoctrination, it often happens that the effect and meaning of an artwork exist in some tension with theological norms as these inform normal religious and liturgical practice. In Mozart's great but unfinished Mass in C Minor (K.427), the setting of the 'Et Incarnatus Est' for soprano, three wind instruments, and strings is extraordinarily florid and sensuous. (Not coincidentally, it may have been intended to be sung by Mozart's new bride Constanze.) Accordingly, this work has aptly been described as not only 'the quintessence of the art of sound' but also 'ravished music in ecstasy before God made man'. It would not occur to a theologian to imagine the Incarnation in quite the mode one imagines here. And no one would want to claim that here one finds *the* meaning of the Incarnation. Yet this beauty is not that of sheer carnality; its sensuality is transfigured. The peculiar tension between the doctrine of Word made flesh and the experience of musical ravishment creates a religious as well as – aesthetic wonder – a Christian classic that courts heterodoxy only thereby to enrich the tradition itself.

In view of such contrasts between the characteristic language of theology and the languages of art, the arts cannot but differ from theology in the ways in which they establish their classics. Because art does not 'speak' theology *per se*, the judgment as to whether some style or work of art is a classic Christian 'statement' cannot responsibly be left simply to the theologian *qua* theologian any more than it can be left to the art connoisseur alone. Credible judgments as to the classic or non-classic status of religious aesthetic works, like judgments regarding their possible liturgical function, can only arise out of repeated experience and dialogue among representatives of a cross-section of Christianity, including those specially trained in the making and criticism of art. (Ch. 7, pp. 165–8)

Source: Frank Burch Brown, *Religious Aesthetics, A Theological Study of Making and Meaning*, Princeton, NJ, Princeton University Press, 1989.

17.6 Mark C. Taylor, from *Disfiguring: Art, Architecture, Religion*

Operating from a specifically postmodern perspective, the author argues that while an a/theoesthetics allows for the creation of a postmodern theology, it does not altogether abandon theoesthetics, a parameter for modern theology. Rather it subverts theoesthetics in a context of a world in which the human being is permanently dislocated and has no hope of resurrection.

A/theoesthetics

In the work of artists and architects who strive to figure the unfigurable in a disfiguring that is neither modern nor modernist postmodern, a previously unthought a/theoesthetic is beginning to emerge. A/theoesthetics does not involve the outright rejection of the program of theoesthetics. Any such direct opposition merely repeats the binary or dialectical structure that theoesthetics presupposes. Rather, in a manner similar to Kierkegaard's critique of Hegel, a/theoesthetics attempts to undo theoesthetics as if from within by figuring what it leaves unfigured. Thus a/theoesthetics does not break with theoesthetics in order to introduce something that is supposed to be totally new. To the contrary, a/theoesthetics borrows artistic strategies from the theoesthetic tradition to recall something that is terribly old. Though neither eternal nor divine, this immemorial borders on what might be refigured as the religious.

While theoesthetics defines the parameters of modern theology, a/theoesthetics creates the possibility of a postmodern a/theology. A/theology explores the space *between* the alternatives that define the Western ontotheological tradition. Thus, a/theology is neither theistic nor atheistic; it can be encompassed by neither positive nor negative theology. If it must be described in classical terms, it might be defined as something like a nonnegative negative theology that nonetheless is not positive. A/theology pursues or, more precisely, is pursued by an altarity that neither exists nor does not exist but is beyond both Being and nonbeing. This unthought and unthinkable beyond is suspended between the poles that constitute twentieth-century theology. . . .

Part of the burden of the foregoing chapters is to suggest that artistic and architectural practices running throughout the twentieth century parallel the dominant tendencies in modern theology. The disfiguring of abstract painting and modern architecture seeks a purity of form that transcends the vicissitudes of sensual and historical experience. The disfiguring of pop art and postmodern architecture, by contrast, attempts to escape the vacuity of pure form and abstract structure by total immersion in the immanence of the image. Though the tactics of abstraction and figuration differ significantly, they both remain utopian. For the abstract artist and modern architect, the Kingdom is *present* elsewhere. For the pop artist and postmodern architect, the Kingdom is *present* here and now. What neither of these alternatives confronts is the possibility of the impossibility of the Kingdom – here or elsewhere, now or then. This impossibility is figured in a/theoesthetics and refigured in a/theology.

A postmodernism that is no longer modernist must give up the hope of utopia. In theological terms, this means that we must let go of the dream of salvation. This is no easy task, for the denial of utopia can become utopian and the loss of the dream of salvation can become a salvation. The impossibility of reconciliation means that there is no resurrexit here or elsewhere, now or in the future. The door is closed, closed tightly; there is no upper room.

Postmodernism that is not a disguised modernism does not involve a return to traditional religion or the emergence of a secular religion that would make it possible to bind back together everything that has fallen apart. To the contrary, postmodernism *sensu strictissimo* creates the possibility of thinking religion otherwise. In the absence of reconciliation, we discover that we are caught in a double bind from which there is no escape. We are bound to and by structures – religious, psychological, political, social, cultural, and historical – that are both inescapable and forever deficient. The inadequacy of structures is a function of their unavoidably repressive character. A structure that does not repress is not a structure. Not all structures, of course, are equally repressive or repress in the same way. And yet, repression, regardless of its form, must be resisted. To resist, however, is not merely to negate. Simply rejecting repressive structures is as utopian as merely embracing them. . . .

A/theology involves an aesthetic education that subverts theoesthetics. This education does not teach the resignation to what is, nor does it promote transcendent spirituality. There is nothing beyond the unfigurable figured in the disfiguring work of art. A/theological aesthetic education does not disfigure this disfiguring by repeating the classical religio-philosophical gesture of translating figures and images into ideas and concepts. To the contrary, traditional religious and philosophical concepts must be disfigured by refiguring the disfiguring of postmodern art and architecture. Altarity can be rendered – if at all – only in a text that is rent. The wounded word is the bleeding trace in and through which altarity approaches by withdrawing and withdraws by approaching. Fragments within fragments are not unified or synthesized but come together by being held apart in their differences. The text woven from these traces is an *allograph*, which, in its failure – in its gaps and fissures, its faults and lacks – inscribes an Other it cannot represent. Though never present, the unrepresentable is unavoidable. It is the unsaid in all our saying that undoes all we do.

To live in the wake of modernity is to live without the hope of resurrexit. We need not travel far to find the desert, for it always approaches us where we are, to dislocate us as if from within. In the desert that has become our world, there is only exile – chronic exile – without beginning and without ending. Beginning never begins and ending never ends. Thus, all time is the meantime of the always already, and all space is the nonsite of the between that is no where. Forever under way in the absence of the Way, every arrival is a departure and every location a dislocation. (Ch. 9, pp. 316–19)

Source: Mark C. Taylor, *Disfiguring: Art, Architecture, Religion*, Chicago, London, University of Chicago Press, 1992.

18

Imagination, Creativity and Faith

— —

18.1 Emil Brunner, from *The Divine Imperative*

Brunner (1889–1966) was a Swiss theologian who, like Barth, advocated dialectical theology, but sharply differed from Barth in accepting the analogy of being. In this extract he discusses the positive contribution art can make to the life of faith in its striving for transcendence and in its eschatological dimensions. He also presents art's dangers, as he takes up Kierkegaard's critique and emphasizes responsibility of decision over aestheticism.

From time immemorial the relation between art and religion has been friendly rather than hostile, therefore the problem of faith versus art possesses none of that disjunctive sharpness which has so often characterized the discussion between faith and science. From both sides art and religion seem to be intended to come together; at almost all periods of history religion has sought artistic expression for her own life, above all in the form of poetry – even the Bible, as is well known, is no exception to this rule; art, too, has evinced a particular interest in religion, and especially in its greatest works of art, and in the case of the great masters it has made use of 'religious material'. We simply cannot imagine Western Art apart from Christianity. It is our duty to reflect on this remarkable relation between art and religion. For even art is a form of conduct: it, too, penetrates deeply into the life of man and determines the form it takes, both outwardly and inwardly; hence it, too, is a problem of ethics.

The living foundation of art is not so much in the existing world as in something which, without losing contact with it, transcends it. It is true, of course, that the power to shape things in an artistic manner is a gift from the Creator, like all other capacities. But its attention is not directed towards the created universe, as such, like science, but to a sphere which lies above and beyond it. The mere 'representation' of reality is not art, and the element of representation is entirely absent from that form of art in which the nature of art becomes most evident: music. Thus the origin of art does not lie in the perception of something which is present, but in an impulse to go beyond that which already exists. Art is always the child of the longing for something else. It shapes something which is not present, for and through the imagination, because that which is present does not satisfy man. In this sense it has more to do with Redemption than with Creation. It is an expression of the fact that man is conscious of his need for Redemption – otherwise, how is it that he cannot be content with the world as it is? and it shows that he has a dim premonition and a vision of the possibility of a better world. It is, therefore, an indication, given with the created order, even to fallen man, of man's knowledge of his origin, which he has never lost, of its restoration and its consummation. Art seeks unrealized Perfection. Even where the 'material' does not give any suggestion of this Vision of Perfection, the form – which in art is the essential thing – is always born out of the striving after unrestricted freedom and unlimited perfection. It is in the artistic form that man seeks release from the accidental, meaningless, weak, and imperfect aspects of reality; this aspiration becomes particularly clear where apparently all that art reproduces is something already present in the visible world. The process of 'ennobling', of intensification, which the existing world undergoes at the hands of the artist, betrays this origin. The influence of art also shows this. It 'elevates', it 'frees', it 'releases', but this process of emancipation, of elevation, and of release, is always accompanied by a shade of melancholy. For this process is not really present, it is only present in the imagination. It is indeed not formative reality, but merely an illusion on the fringe of reality. Its beneficent power may accompany man into life, but it is not able to change it; the power of the real world is too much for it.

Therefore, in spite of the fact that art and religion have so much in common, art contains an element of danger which produces a certain hostility towards religion: the danger, namely, of taking the reflection for the reality, or at any rate of resting content with it. Thus art becomes a substitute for faith, which is sought because it does not demand decision, as faith does, but merely the attitude of a spectator, or of one who is swayed hither and thither by the artistic influences around him; that is, it is not a real devotion, it is merely aesthetic. Just as intellectualism accompanies science, so does aestheticism accompany art, and this means that even within this sphere there appears the challenge to decision. For aestheticism – being satisfied with the freedom of illusion – is just as impossible to combine with faith as intellectualism. Both adopt the attitude of a spectator; both mean flight from responsible decision; both therefore destroy that community which is based on responsibility. Aestheticism makes man a creature who enjoys everything and seeks nothing but enjoyment. The man who is entangled in the net of aestheticism feels no responsibility for his fellow-men and *odi profanum vulgus et arceo*. He is an aristocrat, he is self-sufficient; he flees from the world of practical action where there is so much to disturb his inner repose and upset his balance. True, he desires to have a group of people round him, but he does not wish to serve them, but through their enjoyment he desires to intensify his own, indeed, if they are beautiful or interesting, he wants to enjoy *them*. Therefore, the aesthete may know friendship, or something like it – that is, enjoyment of the individuality of the other person – but not real unity; the union is dissolved as soon as the possibilities of enjoyment have been exhausted. Aestheticism is no more an essential part of art than intellectualism is of science. But in the actual reality of human life, in some way or another they are always connected, though this is certainly more frequent among the members of the art-loving 'public' than it is with the creative artist, to whom his work is often a confession of faith, a conflict, and a deed. Even to him, however, it will be a constant danger and temptation, unless he have special grace; hence it is not surprising that faith, where it is not itself subject to an aesthetic misinterpretation, but is fully aware of the demand for decision, does not adopt such an unambiguously positive attitude towards art as, at first sight, might have been expected. It is true, of course, that religion possesses such an attraction for art that it almost amounts to compulsion; but, as a rule, this religion will be pantheism and mysticism, and not the Christian Faith. The prohibition of 'images' in the Old Testament, which was necessary as a means of conflict against the pantheism of heathenism, is indeed removed in the New Testament; but the warning which it contains against a solution of contradictions by means of the imagination still remains, and the critical attitude, at a period when art and aestheticism can no longer be separated, may lead to open conflict. Fundamentally, however, in spite of all this, the Christian Faith is aware that, in some way or another, art foreshadows and awakens a longing for that which is to come. A Christian hostility to art can only exist where the Faith is misunderstood; here once for all we ought to correct the widespread and erroneous impression that Protestantism, especially in its Reformed (or Calvinistic) form, has been unfavourable to art, and has proved a barren field for art. When we think of Lutheran (Protestant) music in Germany, and of Calvinistic (Protestant) painting in Holland, and also of the importance of the Protestantism of both confessions in poetry and literature, we feel that it is time this assertion should cease. This does not mean that we dispute the fact that Puritanism manifested as little understanding of art as of nature, but this means very little for those who know how deep, at all points, is the gulf between the Reformed Faith and Puritanism.

Once the independent value of art has been recognized, however, it may also be valued on account of its influence. In the economy of human affairs it is that function by which the bodily nature of man is united with his psychical and spiritual nature. It corporealizes the spirit and spiritualizes the body. Therefore, especially where, in a false abstractness, the spiritual element is separated from the bodily element, it exercises an incomparably salutary influence, since it re-unites the elements which had been sundered. In this function, too, it gives a hint of the Redemption, which, according to the Christian Faith, will be not release from the body but a spiritualized bodily nature. This spiritualization in art is certainly *only* a suggestion, for it does not take place in reality, but only in a 'picture'; but from the 'picture' it also has a reflex influence upon the real man, and in so doing it exercises an influence which, though it may not be redeeming, is certainly releasing and preparatory, which the Church at all times has recognized and been able to use for her own purposes. It is true that the opinion often expressed at the present day that art – for instance, music – can become the means of expressing the Word of God as well as, and indeed better than, the human word, is based upon an error. Whoever asserts this does not mean by the Word of God the message of the God who is manifest in Jesus Christ. The message of what God has done for our redemption certainly cannot be expressed as music, and what God wills to say to us in Jesus Christ cannot be painted. In this respect the human word is not simply one method among others, for human speech alone can indicate quite unambiguously God's thought, Will, and Work. But music may very well support the word of the proclamation as an expression of the feeling aroused by the Word, and the art of painting may suggest in a pictorial manner what the Word means. This is no small service, and the truly great Christian artists have never wished it otherwise. Wordless art may awaken mysticism but never real faith. Even poetry must give way to simple prose because by the very fact of its beautiful form it only too easily transforms the decision of faith into the enjoyment of art. Where faith speaks directly in the prophetic message and in prayer it will never choose the actual art form, but often by the energy of its feeling and the earnestness of its reality (which is peculiar to all real faith) it will elevate language likewise to a great power of artistic expression. To the extent, however, in which the artistic intention becomes apparent, the Word will cease to be a message which awakens faith. (Ch. XL, pp. 499–503)

Source: Emil Brunner, *The Divine Imperative, A Study in Christian Ethics*, trans. Olive Wyon, London, Lutterworth Press, 1937.

18.2 Nicolas A. Berdyaev, from *Dream and Reality*

The influential Russian philosopher Berdyaev (1874–1948), who was expelled from the USSR in 1922 due to his critical stance towards totalitarianism and settled in Paris, developed a Christian existentialism. Influenced by neo-Kantian idealism, he asserted the importance of the spirit as that which truly exists and he focused on the creative aspect in the human being in achieving personhood, and on human freedom. In this extract he reflects on creativity, on the relationship of creativity, sin and redemption, on freedom and creativity, on the tragic element in the creative act, and on imagination and the contemplation of beauty.

The Domain of Creativity . . . The matter of creativity and of the creative vocation of man is not only a facet or one of the facets of my outlook, reached as a result of philosophical reasoning, but a source of my whole thinking and living – an initial inner experience and illumination. But it has also proved a cause of the greatest misunderstandings. Creativity, as a rule, is understood as an aesthetic or cultural concept denoting the sphere of science and the arts: knowledge and the production of works of art. In the religious or Christian context it is often discussed in terms of the somewhat trivial question of the relation of Christianity to cultural activities, in other words, of the question whether Christianity is or is not obscurantist. But the problem of creativity can be approached on a different and deeper level. Creativity stands in no need of justification from the religious or any other point of view: it is its own justification in virtue of the very existence of man; it is that which constitutes man's relation and response to God. The question of culture, of cultural values and of the products of culture, on the other hand, is a secondary and derivative one.

I have been deeply disturbed by the problem of the relation between creativity, sin and redemption. I have experienced moments of acute awareness of the sinfulness of man; and such moments probably marked the points of my closest approximation to Orthodoxy. But I also came to realize that to remain fixed in that position, to surrender oneself entirely to the sense of sin, spells frustration and a disablement of life. The consciousness of sin may be a stage on the way towards spiritual renewal and illumination; but it may also prove an omen of unrelieved darkness. There can be no creativity and no illumination if life is reduced to the consciousness of man's misery, wretchedness and possible salvation. If regeneration is to come, the sense of sin must be transformed into another and loftier experience. How are we to overcome the *vis inertiae*, the lameness and impotence of the sense of sin, and to reach out to a more ardent and more creative attitude? The counsels of current religious spirituality invite us to deepen the awareness of our sinful and unworthy condition, thereby making us susceptible of divine grace and illumination. But the source of grace is in God: grace proceeds from on high, whilst the realization of our sinful condition proceeds from below. My question then is this: can we ascribe to grace, which redeems the frustrations and the insignificance of human existence, a quality which is not only divine but also human, which is from 'below' as well as from 'above'. Is man justified solely by obedience to a higher divine power, or is he also justified by his human endeavour and creative ecstasy?

It is imperative to bear in mind that human creativity is not a claim or a right on the part of man, but God's claim on and call to man. God awaits man's creative act, which is the response to the creative act of God. What is true of man's freedom is true also of his creativity: for freedom too is God's summons to man and man's duty towards God. God does not reveal to man that which it is for man to reveal to God. In Holy Scripture we find no revelation concerning man's creativity – not on account of its implied denial of human creativity, but because creativity is a matter for man to reveal. God is silent on this matter and expects man to speak. I have frequently been asked to justify my idea of the religious significance of human creativity by quotations from Scripture. I may or I may not be able to provide such justification – but in any case such a demand is evidence of a fundamental misunderstanding of the problem under discussion. It is, in fact, the concealed, rather than the revealed, will of God that man should dare and create, and such daring and creativity are a token of man's fulfilment of the will of God.

It is absurd to charge me with an attempt to defy God. Creativity for me is implied in the fundamental Christian truth of God-manhood, and its justification is the theandric theme of Christianity. God's idea of man is infinitely loftier than the traditional orthodox conceptions of man, which are as often as not an expression of a frustrated and stunted mind. The idea of God is the greatest human idea, and the idea of man is the greatest divine idea. Man awaits the birth of God in himself, and God awaits the birth of man in himself. It is at this level that the question of creativity arises, and it is from this point of view that it should be approached. The notion that God has need of man and of man's response to him is, admittedly, an extraordinarily daring notion; yet in its absence the Christian revelation of God-manhood loses all meaning. The drama of God and his Other One, Man, is present and operative in the very depths of divine life. This is revealed not in theological doctrines but in spiritual experience, where the divine drama passes into a human drama and that which is above is converted into that which is below. But this is in no way inconsistent with redemption: rather it is another moment on the same spiritual path and another act in the mystical drama of God and man. . . .

Creativity, in my view, is not an 'insertion' in the finite, not a mastery over the medium, or the creative product itself: rather it is a flight into the infinite; not an activity which objectifies in the finite but one which transcends the finite towards the infinite. The creative act signifies an *ek-stasis*, a breaking through to eternity. This conception laid open to me the tragic character of creativity as it is displayed in the products of culture and society, viz., the continuous but unavailing effort and the ensuing painful disparity between the creative idea and its embodiment in the world. . . .

It is only in the creative act that man prevails over the oppression and enslavement of extraneous influences. The creative act reveals the absolute priority of the 'self', the subject, over the 'non-self', the object; but, at the same time, it strikes at the root of the egocentric, for it is eminently a movement of self-transcendence, reaching out to that which is higher than oneself. Creative experience is not characterized by absorption in one's own perfection or imperfection: it makes for the transfiguration of man and of the world; it foreshadows a new Heaven and a new Earth which are to be prepared at once by God and man. It is individual and indeed rebellious in nature, involving conflict between man and his environment, yet it is, in its liberating power, at the opposite pole of self-sufficiency, raising man to a vision of boundless and infinite reality.

This experience underlies my book *The Meaning of the Creative Act, An Essay in the Justification of Man*, which was written at a time of well-nigh intoxicating ecstasy, a book in which my thoughts and the normal course of philosophical argument seemed to dissolve into vision. It is an impulsive, unpremeditated and unfinished work (I am least of all satisfied with the section on Art), but it contains in that raw form all my dominant and formative ideas and insights. My misfortune is that, owing partly to the distraction provided by other themes and problems and partly to my unsystematic manner of thinking, I was never able to work out the principal thesis of this work. . . .

The problem of creativity was for me always one with the problem of freedom. The creative act of man and the emergence of new things and new values in the world are inconceivable within the closed cycle of Being, subject as it is to all kinds of determination, causal and otherwise. Creativity is possible only on account of Freedom, which is not determined by anything, not even by Being. The source of Freedom is in the void of non-being. Freedom, as I have repeatedly tried to show, is indeterminate, uncaused, gratuitous. But my original formulation of this idea, as found, for instance, in *The Philosophy of Freedom* and, to some extent, even in *The Meaning of the Creative Act*, was unsatisfactory because I was still beset by the associations of Idealist ontology and used the terminology characteristic of this philosophy.

My critics charged me with a refusal to admit the need of any given 'material' for the creative act of man. This charge was, of course, completely unfounded. I have never denied that man cannot create without a medium, that he cannot dispense with the world of external reality, and that he cannot perform anything in a vacuum. And yet the basic characteristic of a creative act consists in not being wholly determined by its medium, and that it comprises something new, something which cannot be derived from the external world in which it is embodied, or indeed from some fixed repository of ideal forms which press upon the creator's imagination. This, then, is the point where Freedom comes in – an untraceable, undetermined and unpredictable movement from within outwards. Creation is, in this sense, out of nothing. Without such freedom creativity would merely present a re-distribution of the given elements constituting the world, and the appearance of anything new and original would be pure illusion. . . .

I acknowledged that the gift of creativity proceeds from God; but man intervenes by virtue of his freedom, and, in his capacity of creator, he is no mere passive object in the hands of God. It is fruitless and absurd to ask whether creativity is justifiable from the point of view of the religion of redemption, because, though man be degraded and defiled by sin, there can be no redemption and no salvation without man's response to God. Redemption and salvation are, therefore, also acts of divine-human creativity. Similarly, the ultimate fulfilment of redemption and the coming of God's Kingdom comprises a creative act on the part of man. I have never failed to emphasize the religious, rather than the merely aesthetic or cultural, significance of creativity. My object has been not to justify creativity but to show that, in its divine-human character, it is itself justification, inseparable from all the other acts which characterize God's relation to man and to the world.

But there is another element in creativity which was very much in my mind when I wrote *The Meaning of the Creative Act*, namely the element of tragedy. Man's creative act is doomed to fail within the conditions of this world. It is a tremendous effort which is destined never to succeed. Its initial impulse is to bring forth new life, to transfigure the world and usher in a new heaven and a new earth; but in the conditions of the fallen world the effort turns out to be unavailing: it comes up against the inertia, the laws and compulsions of the external world, pervaded as it is by inexorable necessities. The attempt gives place to the production of aesthetic and cultural objects of a greater or lesser perfection. These objects, however, are symbols of reality rather than reality itself: a book, a symphony, a picture, a poem or a social institution; but all these are evidence of the painful disparity between the creative impulse and its partial and fragmentary embodiment in the objective world.

I will not repeat here what I have already said many times on this subject. But I should like to avert any possible misunderstanding, to which I seem frequently to have given occasion. I am far from denying the validity of culture and the value of its creative function in this world. Man is committed by virtue of his mundane destiny to the making of culture and civilization. And yet such making must not blind us to the fact that it is but a token of real transfiguration, which is the true, though unattainable, goal of creativity. 'Realistic' creativity, as distinct from 'symbolic' creativity, would, in fact, bring about the transfiguration and the end of this world, and the emergence of a new heaven and a new earth. The creative act, alike in its power and impotence, is eschatological – a prefiguration of the end of the world. (Ch. 8, pp. 207–14)

The link between creativity and a 'pessimistic' attitude towards life as it is given, with all its necessities, compulsions and conventions, made me attach a great importance to imagination, since without imagination there can be no creative activity. A creative act always rises above reality; it means imagining something other and better than the reality around us. But just as there may be evil imagination, calling up before us evil images and phantasms, so there may be false or illusory creative acts. Man is capable of responding not only to the call of God but also to the call of Satan.

And yet can we really speak of evil creativity? An artist may be driven by demonic powers or may have a demonic imagination (Leonardo da Vinci is a case in point), but, inasmuch as it is given to him to perform a truly creative act, his demonism is consumed in the fire of that creativity. These things are not susceptible of moralization. I have frequently come into conflict with traditional religious beliefs on this account. The universe of discourse characteristic of religious orthodoxy is forced to deny creativity altogether, or at best only to tolerate it in a superficial way, because it is to a large extent the expression of an organized social collective, with its norms, taboos, prohibitions and conventions. The creative impulse, on the other hand, is absolutely unique, unbidden and lawless. The stuff of art is inner conflict, conflict between man and the society in which he lives, man and his moral conscience. It is impossible to write a play, a novel or a lyrical poem without coming into conflict with the accepted norms and standards of moral and social behaviour, unless one is satisfied with quasi-artistic pieces glorifying social, moral or religious puppets. Similarly, creative philosophical thought cannot exist if conflict and tragedy are ruled out, if all things are certain and well-defined, if no new questions can arise and the human mind is put at rest. Orthodox systems, whether social or religious, however, do not want to hear of these problems; their attitude to creative unrest, to the searchings and wrestlings of the spirit, is, quite consistently, one of suspicion and hostility.

Most Orthodox theologians either regarded my views on creativity as heretical or thought that I was just beating about the bush, although some conceded that I had raised an important problem. I met with exactly the same attitude among the representatives of Western, Catholic and Protestant, theological thought. (Incidentally it was curious to observe that people in the West wavered in their reactions to my thought between labelling me a 'gnostic' and representing me as an 'Orthodox theologian'!) Indeed, the more closely I became acquainted with the modern Catholic and Protestant world, the more I realized how uncongenial the problem of creativity (or, for that matter, many other problems raised in Russian thought) was to the majority of its spokesmen. . . .

Only in the white heat of creative ecstasy, when none of the divisions and differentiations into subject and object had yet arisen, did I experience moments of fulfilment and joy. Creative *works* are within time, with its objectifications, discords and divisions, but the creative *act* is beyond time: it is wholly within, subjective, prior to all objectification.

There is an intimate link between creativity and contemplation, although the current tendency is to oppose them. Contemplation must not be understood as a state of sheer passivity or receptiveness: it comprises a distinctly active and creative element. Thus the aesthetic contemplation of natural beauty is more than a state: it is an act, a breaking through to another world. Beauty is indeed that other world revealing itself in our own. And in contemplating beauty man goes out to meet its call. A poet who is possessed by his vision of beauty is not engaged in passive observation but in an activity whereby he creates for himself and re-creates in his imagination the image of beauty. Contemplation does, admittedly, preclude the experience of struggle, conflict and opposition. But it supplies that background against which struggle, conflict and opposition acquire significance. Man ought to be able from time to time to fall back on contemplation in order to obtain relief from the activism of existence which, as we know too well to-day, can tear him to pieces. (Ch. 8, pp. 218–21)

Source: Nicolas Berdyaev, *Dream and Reality, An Essay in Autobiography*, London, Geoffrey Bles, 1950.

18.3 Dietrich Bonhoeffer, from *Letters and Papers from Prison*

Bonhoeffer (1906–45) signed the Barmen Declaration in 1934 and sided with the Confessing Church. He was executed by the Nazis. Bonhoeffer was concerned with how one could live a Christian life in the age of secularization. He was a cultured man, educated in the arts. In the Letters, *he occasionally comments on music, art and artists. Here he reflects on human eros and our love for God by use of the analogy of music.*

20 May 1944 There's always the danger in all strong, erotic love that one may love what I might call the polyphony of life. What I mean is that God wants us to love him eternally with our whole hearts – not in such a way as to injure or weaken our earthly love, but to provide a kind of *cantus firmus* to which the other melodies of life provide the counterpoint. One of these contrapuntal themes (which have their own complete independence but are yet related to the *cantus firmus*) is earthly affection. Even in the Bible we have the Song of Songs; and really one can imagine no more ardent, passionate, sensual love than is portrayed there . . . . It's a good thing that that book is in the Bible, in face of all those who believe that the restraint of passion is Christian (where is there such restraint in the Old Testament?). Where the *cantus firmus* is clear and plain, the counterpoint can be developed to its limits. The two are 'undivided and yet distinct', in the words of the Chalcedonian Definition, like Christ in his divine and human natures. May not the attraction and importance of polyphony in music consist in its being a musical reflection of this Christological fact and therefore of our *vita christiana*? This thought didn't occur to me till after your visit yesterday. Do you see what I'm driving at? I wanted to tell you to have a good, clear *cantus firmus*; that is the only way to a full and perfect sound, when the counterpoint has a firm support and can't come adrift or get out of tune, while remaining a distinct whole in its own right. Only a polyphony of this kind can give life a wholeness and at the same time assure us that nothing calamitous can happen as long as the *cantus firmus* is kept going. Perhaps a good deal will be easier to bear in these days together, and possibly also in the days ahead when you are separated. Please, Eberhard, do not fear and hate the separation, if it should come again with all its dangers, but rely on the *cantus firmus*. – I don't know whether I have made myself clear now, but one so seldom speaks of such things. (pp. 162–3)

Source: Dietrich Bonhoeffer, *Letters and Papers from Prison, The Enlarged Edition*, ed. Eberhard Bethge, London, SCM Press, 1971.

18.4 William F. Lynch, from *Images of Faith, An Exploration of the Ironic Imagination*

The North American Catholic theologian William F. Lynch who has concerned himself with the role of imagination in theology, here discusses as to how human imagination and faith relate to and struggle with the reality of existence.

Reimagining Faith

The embodying action of faith (and the imagination) has the most elemental beginnings. The first is the struggle to reach into existence itself.

An important point to start from in any serious attempt to explore the role of imagination in theology (or in life for that matter) is the relationship of faith and the imagination to existence. Let us suppose that it is the imagination which finds or makes what we call 'reality', that visual-conceptual image of our finite, our objective, our existent world. In saying that, we are at the centre of the life of the imagination and of the physiology of faith. Then we must realize that finding or making existence is a difficult task. How to fit all things together in some way that is even *partly* understandable? It involves a struggle and a wrestling, like Jacob wrestling with the angel. We cannot decide: I will struggle with God and not with the earth. That is really no decision at all, or at best a decision not to wrestle. But where we do make the decision to deal with existence, then epistemology and faith can best meet at the initial point of finite reality itself. I hypothesize that without faith the mind cannot enter into existence at all, even at the most elementary point.

We have reason now to know that the mind leaves what seems paradise when it first engages in real thought with the world, much less with God. The new sciences of the mind tell us we leave omnipotence. The specific thought whereby, leaving *this* paradise, the mind wrestles with anything less than omnipotence has faith carved into the very guts of this act by which it lays hold of the precise density of any actual thing. The very weight and shape and form not only *take* faith to lay hold of, but it *is* a faith. It gives up the feeling of omnipotence to acknowledge the existence of this other limited thing. It is the beginning of the body of faith. We are first coaxed into it, as infants, by those who love us. We enter, in thought and action, because we trust them.

Faith, therefore, is required to move into the step after step processes of rational knowledge. And all rational and scientific knowledge follows faith in sequence. . . .

We must only suppose, recalling our childhood – but can be reasonably sure of it – that reality comes as a shock when we first enter it, and it is a shock that it is heavy, has corners and edges, shines, glows, burns, tastes, and can ache and give great pain. Above all, it is resistant, you cannot go through it, it will not go away. A good deal of our thinking about God wants to make these qualities of really

being there go away; at least he is not that way! We say we abstract from limitation and call it God. We have often abstracted from the actual existence of things
and called it God. So we say that God is not heavy like iron. But suppose I say
that he is even more actual than iron, meaning that if you think the iron is really
there, that is the direction to take to imagine that God is there. But as the mind
often does now, in its search for God, there is only a ghost at the end of the
process, and very little existence or faith. We should reverse this process and
keep the stress on the existence of things. This is where the imagination comes in.
The task of the imagination is to imagine the real. At the end of tragedy man
comes in contact with existence, with the real thing. What I call the realistic
imagination always does. (Ch. 2, pp. 60–3)

Source: William F. Lynch, SJ, *Images of Faith, An Exploration of the Ironic Imagination*, Notre
Dame, London, University of Notre Dame Press, 1973.

18.5 Leonardo Boff, from *Liberating Grace*

*In the context of his theology of grace, the Brazilian Leonardo Boff, widely
recognized for his contribution to liberation theology, speaks of the importance of fantasy, imagination and creativity in the life of humans and, in
particular, in relation to the work of artists.*

Experiencing Grace in the Life of the Individual

Experiencing Grace in the Realm of Creativity The realm of spontaneous
creativity is certainly one of the areas of human experience where gratuitousness
shows up most clearly. We stand in wonder at an uneducated poet who can
string verses together in a wondrous succession of original thoughts and images.
Idea and rhyme flow with what seems to be absolute spontaneity. The agile brush
of a painter or the fingers of a violinist create a whole new universe of colours or
sounds in a matter of moments. This creativity seems to well up like a fountain.
It cannot be forced or produced by a sheer act of will. The person seems to be the
locale where a daimon or a genie is at work. That is why we commonly refer to
people of great spontaneous creativity as geniuses.

   The poet, the musician, and the writer feel overtaken by inspiration. On the
one hand, it is they who do the work. Their energy and their deepest selves are
totally involved. The effort to express themselves often leads to complete exhaus-
tion. On the other hand, they feel possessed by something that is above them,
outside them, or within them. It drives them to create, compelling them to
express their inner experience to the outside world. The poet exclaims that he is
overtaken by words. The painter explains that forms and colours take possession
of him. It is an experience of gratuitousness.

   Artistic creativity does not dispense us from effort, serious preparation, and discipline. But these things merely pave the way for inspiration. Inspiration itself cannot be produced. It breaks in unexpectedly. This explains the importance of the right moment, when a host of imponderable factors come together to allow for the explosive emergence of creativity. That is why people make a distinction between technique and creativity. Technique can be exercised anytime. Creativity has its own time, and it cannot be compelled to show itself whenever one wills it. The sheer exercise of willpower produces work. The result of creativity is a masterwork. The latter, as we noted above, does not dispense us from work; but our effort and work is to give shape to the creative impulse, to channel it, to subject it to the rigor of an ascetic ordering process. Through this process artists succeed in expressing all that they can, without losing themselves in dionysiac enjoyment of the impulse that has seized them. Through effort and assiduous work people of genius can rise to an authentic universality and somehow speak for all human beings and all ages.

Linked to creativity is fantasy and creative imagination. Modern studies have shown convincingly that fantasy is not mere fancifulness or a mechanism for escaping from conflict-ridden reality. It is the key to explaining authentic creativity even in science. Creative imagination enables us to break away from things that are taken for granted, to abandon accepted presuppositions and begin to think in unorthodox ways. It enables us to set off on a different road or head in a different direction. Fantasy enables us to unmask the limitations of reality. The latter is the concrete embodiment of one possibility, as we noted above. But all the other infinite possibilities are not thereby squelched. With them human beings can dream about and even construct what has not yet been experienced in reality before. They can be turned into reality because life is stronger than the structures that serve as its support and framework.

Thus the last and decisive word does not go to bare facts. The truly creative word has not yet been pronounced. Liberation has not yet been completely effected. Fantasy preserves the primacy of the future and of hope over the brutal reality of facts and the heavy weight of the present. Through it human beings manifest their innermost essence, their capacity to transcend and to keep on living above and beyond all limits. As Harvey Cox has pointed out, fantasy is the soil in which humanity's capacity for invention and innovation flourishes. Fantasy is the richest source of human creativity. Theologically speaking, fantasy is the image of the creator God in human beings. With fantasy human beings, like God, create entire worlds out of nothing. It is fantasy that nourishes the principle of hope in human beings and the utopian dimension that keeps history moving forward. It keeps opening humanity to the future and revitalising history, liberating both from the sclerotic hold of their own prior constructions. It is within the horizon of imagination and fantasy that gratuitousness shows up for what it truly is. (Ch. 9, pp. 95–7)

Source: Leonardo Boff, *Liberating Grace*, trans. John Drury, Maryknoll, NY, Orbis Books, 1979.

18.6 Nicholas Wolterstorff, from *Art in Action, Toward a Christian Aesthetic*

Wolterstorff, a North American philosopher and theologian, has taught at Calvin College and Yale University. He has written on the philosophy of religion, aesthetics, and on faith and reason. Here he makes a strong plea for the Christian artist to take responsibility in his or her life and work, both with regard to their own integrity and in the context of the church community. Art is not simply intended for contemplation in the secular sphere and for its own sake, but can be an instrument of commitment to God and to the Church.

Participation

I have suggested that at the very centre of the institution is a passionate commitment to the importance of perceptual contemplation of works of art, and more particularly, to *aesthetic* contemplation. And I have argued that the delight attained in aesthetic contemplation is good. It constitutes, so far forth, a facet in the attainment of our human destiny. The attainment of that delight typically requires, I suggested, certain modes of separation of art from ordinary life. But even those modes of separation are not bad. There is nothing inherently wrong about concert halls and art galleries, about having the leisure available for contemplating art, about blocking out for a time one's other concerns and focussing on the work of art. So the Christian has no difficulties with the determinative centre of our institution of high art. On the contrary, he affirms its importance.

But three things especially will concern him, as I see it.

(1) In the first place, he cannot divorce art from responsibility. He recognizes that responsibility belongs to the constitutive texture of human existence. Accordingly, he acknowledges that his participation in art must be an implementation of his responsibility.

What does this mean in practice? First, a good deal of what it means in practice is that the Christian artist must constantly be engaged in the difficult, precarious task of assessing priorities as he (or she) determines the direction of his endeavours – of assessing relative importance. He recognizes that art for contemplation can serve human fulfillment. But equally he recognizes that art for other purposes can serve human fulfillment. He refuses automatically to give priority to either of these over the other. Aesthetic contemplation is not always the best use to which art can be put; neither is it always the worst. And so the Christian artist must constantly be weighing his potential contribution to high art over against his potential contribution to art in one of its other manifestations.

But even when he is operating *within* the institution of high art, he must assess priorities as he determines the direction of his endeavours. He cannot simply go along with the trends and fads, nor can he simply do whatever happens to catch his fancy at the moment. Some movements in art are significant. They open up the future in promising ways and yield works of great significance. Others are insignificant. They are innovative, but trivially so; or they tread paths already so heavily trod that no living thing grows there. The Christian artist must constantly be making such judgments of relative importance.

I know, of course, that artists become nervous and skittish when one speaks of some movements in art as important and some as trivial, and of the need to choose by reference to one's judgments of importance. Yet in spite of their skittishness, artists themselves, when sitting on evaluation panels for, say, the National Endowment for the Arts, do in fact make such judgments of relative importance.

One point must be added to this discussion on responsibility in art. I have said that the artist who acknowledges his responsibility to God, to his neighbour, to himself, to nature, will find that he must constantly assess priorities as a way of determining the direction in which he turns his endeavours. It would be irresponsible, though, to determine these priorities by reference simply to what the public wants – to judge that what they want is always what is most important to do. Being a responsible artist is not the same as being a pandering artist. The two are in fact incompatible. Sometimes the artist must strike out on paths of exploration which, at the time, his public does not like, in the conviction that eventually his path will yield results more rewarding and enriching to his fellow human beings than would come by his simply giving them what at the moment they desire. The responsible philosopher does not determine what to say simply by reference to what people want him to say. Neither does the responsible artist determine what to make simply by reference to what people want him to make. He strives to serve the needs and enrichment of his fellows, not necessarily their wants.

(2) Secondly, the Christian artist will constantly be struggling to achieve wholeness, integrity, in his life. He will not be content to let his life fall apart into pieces – religion as one piece, art as another. For he knows that to answer the call to be a disciple of Jesus Christ is to commit his life as a whole, not just some fragments thereof, to God's cause in the world.

What we have seen, many times over in this discussion, is that the artist does not simply gush forth works of art in a subhuman, irrational flow. Be it granted that images, harmonies, tunes, situations, come to him from he-knows-not-where. Yet always he works with artistic *goals* and aims – sifting through the images that come to mind, discarding some, keeping others, moulding, shaping and revising them, encouraging yet others to come to mind. Though the wellsprings of images remain mysteriously hidden from us, yet composing a work of art is a deliberate action.

What can be said, then, is that the Christian artist will seek to bring his artistic goals into conformity with his Christian commitment. And he may indeed go the next step of seeking goals which are *appropriate* to his commitment, not just in conformity with it – as John Cage chose musical goals which he judged appropriate to his westernized form of Zen Buddhism, as Michelangelo in his middle period chose artistic goals he judged appropriate to his Platonism. In the case of the Christian artist, the world behind his work, the world of which his work is an expression, will incorporate his Christian commitment. In this way his art will not be separated from life. It will be of a piece with it.

A few paragraphs above I said that our Western institution of high art is a profoundly secularized institution. With that in mind, someone might wonder whether it is *possible* to participate as an artist in our institution of high art and yet adopt artistic goals which conform, or are appropriate, to one's Christian convictions. The answer is clearly Yes. T. S. Eliot and W. H. Auden are examples, as is Georges Rouault; or to come up to our own day, Olivier Messiaen and Krzysztof Penderecki. For our institution of high art is secularized not primarily in the sense that it does not tolerate artistic goals selected because they conform or are appropriate to the Christian gospel, but rather in the sense that it makes no difference to the influence and esteem of the artist within the institution whether or not he thus selects his goals. The institution does provide at least some amount of open space for the religiously, committed artist. . . .

(3) Thirdly – and this goes almost without saying – the Christian must resist the claims of ultimacy which repeatedly erupt from our institution of high art. Art does not provide us with the meaning of human existence. The Gospel of Jesus Christ does that. Art is not a way of rising toward God. It is meant instead to be in the service of God. Art is not man's glory. It displays man's degradation as well as his dignity. The community of artists is not the new humanity. The community of Christ's disciples is that. Art is not man's liberating saviour. Jesus Christ is that.

The church, the band of Christ's disciples, is the community of those who have taken up the call of God to work on His behalf in His cause of renewing human existence. The Christian knows indeed that God has never confined His mode of working to the church. And conversely, he knows with painful vividness that the church, with its splotches and blotches, often retards God's work. Yet he believes that when our stretch of history is seen whole, the disciples of Jesus will be seen to have played a decisive role in the coming of the righteous shalom, that is, in the coming of what the New Testament calls the Kingdom of God, where God is acknowledged as Lord. This Kingdom he sees not as *escape* from our creaturely status. He sees it rather as the situation where men acknowledge God's sovereignty and carry out the responsibilities awarded them at creation. He does not think of this merely as the *restoration* of some Edenic situation. For he believes that what has taken place in history will play its constructive role in the character of life in the Kingdom. He sees it rather as the renewal of human existence, so that man's creaturely vocation and fulfillment may be attained, now already and in the future.

The task in history of the people of God, the church, the followers of Jesus Christ, is in the first place to witness to God's work of renewal, to the coming of His Kingdom – to speak of what God has done and is doing for the renewal of human existence. Its task is, secondly, to work to bring about renewal by serving all men everywhere in all dimensions of their existence, working for the abolition of evil and joylessness and for the incursion into human life of righteousness and shalom. Thirdly, it is called to give evidence in its own existence of the new life, the *true*, authentic life – to give evidence in its own existence of what a political structure without oppression would be like, to give evidence in its own existence of what scholarship devoid of jealous competition would be like, to give evidence in its own existence of what a human community that transcends while yet incorporating national diversity would be like, to give evidence in its own existence of what an art that unites rather than divides and of what surroundings of aesthetic joy rather than aesthetic squalor would be like, to give evidence in its own existence of how God is rightly worshipped. And then lastly it is called to urge all men everywhere to repent and believe and join this people of God in the world. To be a Christian participating in this fourfold task of the church in the world is not to repudiate one's creational responsibilities before God. Those responsibilities have not been abrogated. One remains a human being, called to master nature, called to love one's neighbour as oneself, called to render praise to God. But those responsibilities have now all been set in a different context and have acquired a new dimension. The Christian now lives and works as member of a community which has said Yes to God's call to be His agent of renewal, a community sadly alienated from those of mankind who do not acknowledge Jesus Christ as Lord. That community now renders honour to God not only as creator but also as redeemer. That community now serves its fellow men not only with food and knowledge and political liberation but also with the message that in Jesus Christ there is freedom from bondage in all its forms.

It is in the context of this community that the Christian artist is also now called to do his work. He is called as artist to share in his people's task of being witness to God's work of renewal, its task of serving all men everywhere by working to bring about righteousness and peace, its task of giving evidence in its own existence of what the renewed life is like, its task of inviting all men everywhere to join the ranks of the people of renewal. Sharing in the task of this community is now the particular form which the artist's responsibility to God takes. . . .

We long for those bygone days of wholeness – for those days when the religious substance of society was unified, when the artist saw it as his calling to give expression to that substance rather than to stand in prophetic, agonized opposition to it, and when, accordingly, the art of the tribe was art at its most profound instead of what so often it is today – mindless pandering drivel. But those days are gone; and there is nothing you and I can do to bring them back. Better to protect our religious pluralism than to lament our loss of religious unity. Better to respect the artist's integrity than to lament his alienation.

But though we cannot recover the wholeness of our predecessors, what we can do is shed our parochialism. We can remove the blinkers which have led us to see only the arts as they operate in our institution of high art. And though we cannot recover an art of the tribe as a whole which has profundity and imagination, what we can do is repent ourselves of our elitism, dropping the assumption, so deeply ingrained in us by our institution of high art, that perceptual contemplation, and in particular aesthetic contemplation rewarding to the intellectual, is per se the noblest use to which a work of art can be put.

For those of us who are Christians one more thing lies within our reach: In the community of Christians as a whole, and more particularly in the liturgy of the church, it is still possible to have an art of the tribe which expresses rather than alienates itself from our deepest convictions, and which does not pander to us but rather ennobles us by its self-conscious dedication *ad maiorem gloriam Dei*. Paradise is forever behind us. But the City of God, full of song and image, remains to be built. (Ch. 2, pp. 193–9)

Source: Nicholas Wolterstorff, *Art in Action, Toward a Christian Aesthetic*, Grand Rapids, Michigan, Eerdmans, 1980.

18.7　John McIntyre, from *Faith, Theology and Imagination*

In the conclusion of his book, British theologian John McIntyre provides a detailed analysis of the nature and role of the imagination and of images, especially in faith and in theology. (Due to the scope of this anthology only the most relevant sections can be presented here.)

An Analytic of Imagination and Images

Imagination While it may have been the practice in medieval philosophy to regard imagination as an isolable faculty of the mind, and, while even a writer as circumspect as Mary Warnock refers to it as a 'power of the mind'; nevertheless, what has now emerged is that the imagination is the whole mind working in certain ways, which we shall in due course itemise. In much the same way, I would not regard 'reason', as I have said, as a separate faculty of the mind, but rather as the whole mind working in identifiable ways – arguing from general principles to specific conclusions, or from collections of cases to universal judgments, or assessing the relevance of alleged evidence, or the validity of conclusions, and so on. Therefore, on the basis of the different areas in which in the course of our study we have encountered imagination at work in religion and theology, in faith and in moral activity, let us now summarise our results in an analytic of the different characteristics of, first, imagination, and then, images. These items, though understandably similar, nevertheless are distinguishable.

One, imagination is sensitive to, and *perceptive* of, features in the world and in persons which the ordinary observer passes unnoticed. . . .

Two, imagination is *selective* from the mass of material with which the mind is ordinarily confronted, and from among which it concentrates upon the salient and we might add, the significant features. . . . Therefore, at any time, imaginative thinking has to take something, and leave something; and always it operates at the risk of distortion or caricature. At its best, it gets to the root of the matter, in much the same way as a portrait is able to do what no photographic copy ever can.

Three, because it is selective of the significant features of a situation, or a piece of history or of literature, imagination is also *synoptic and integrative.* Having selected the salient and load-bearing feature, it proceeds to arrange and systematise the material around it and in terms of it. . . .

Four, such systematising and integrating we must not regard as a kind of intellectual cabinet-making or joinery. It requires a high level of *creative and constructive* thought to put together the diverse elements of a story or pieces of literature into unitary form. It is not creative in the sense that it takes off from substantial material into flights of fancy. It has its feet very much on the ground, and it takes reality, the text or history very much as its starting-point. . . .

Five, another characteristic which we cannot omit from explicit mention, though it is implicit in all that has gone before, is the interpretative capacity of imagination. Though it is impossible to give any simple logical account of the nature of interpretation, nevertheless it is inalienable from any situation in which the human intellect understands any subject, and endeavours to explain it to itself or to others. The interpretative role is fulfilled through the imagination observing analogical connections between entities which less perceptive intellects miss. . . .

Six, at this point we must have the courage of our convictions and assert that imagination has a *cognitive* role to play in our intellectual lives. In other words, there are things that we would not know about the world around us, about other persons, about our obligations, about ourselves, about the Bible, about history, about doctrine and about God, had we, or as is more often the case, had those into whose labours we are entered, not employed the imagination. These things that we would not otherwise know are not fantasies, illusions, delusions, or hallucinations. These are facts about the real world which would remain otherwise beyond our ken. . . . Further, if imagination has thus a genuinely cognitive role, we have to revise our idea that it adds characteristics to reality which do not exist at all, or exist 'only in the mind of the beholder'. On the contrary, it is aware of dimensions of reality which are hidden from the unimaginative. In effect, reality is multi-dimensional and richly complex, and in our knowledge of it imagination plays a clearly definable part, one in fact without which much of reality would remain unknown.

Seven, up to this point we might be in danger of giving too intellectualist an account of imagination, and so we must at once draw attention to its *empathetic* function, the way in which it is able to project us not only intellectually into deeper understanding of the situation, but also affectively and emotionally into it, so that we identify with its components and with the persons involved in it. . . .

Eight, at this point we are beginning to pass over to another equally important function of the imagination, namely, its *communicative* role. It is the responsibility of the artist, the poet, the dramatist to make us feel as they do about a certain subject; and to achieve this end they must not only *have* the experience; they must also create the media for their interpretation and appreciation of it, media which place us where they are, enabling us to see with their eyes and hear with their ears. The difference between the genius and the commonplace lies at the point of communicative capacity. The one has it; the other does not. I wonder if I may go farther and say not only that communication is a role of imagination but also that imagination is the only means of effective communication. . . .

Nine, there are two other functions of imagination, which relate to time, the past and the present, which may now engage us. The first arises in relation to history, and to Christian faith, which is so firmly based upon history. We might call both of these the *contemporanising* function of imagination, and the first has to do with treating the past as present. . . .

But there is a second contemporanising to be found in the New Testament, that of the future with the present. Realised eschatology, which we examined earlier, is a good example of it, the idea that the Kingdom which in one sense is still future is now present, extended as we saw and applied to baptism, the eucharist, redemption and ethics. . . .

Ten, a not greatly dissimilar function of imagination can be defined in relation to space, which I call its *conspatialising* function. The role which the imagination here plays is to make the absent present. . . .

Eleven, there is a remark of Iris Murdoch that we may explore, namely, that imagination creates what she calls 'our-world', which we constitute by our system of values, our principles, but also by our prejudices, as well, we might add, by our religious commitments and subjects of faith, wherein appear all our hopes, ideals and ambitions, and also, if we are at all honest, our fantasies and delusions, not least of all about ourselves. Some of that world we obviously create for ourselves; some of it emerges from the pressures upon us; some we will wish to say comes through the grace of God; but on the human side the structure is formed and the tone set by our imagination. It is the framework within which our decisions are made, our ambitions defined, our emotional reactions stimulated, and in most general terms our lives are lived.

Twelve, I should like finally to nominate the *ecumenical* role which the imagination may play, in inter-church discussions. (Ch. 7, pp. 159–66)

Ecumenical conversation has been too often about arriving, about 'Here stand I; I can no other', and much too little about travelling hopefully, when we can still influence the directions we are severally taking. It is not too much to hope for, that we examine more than we do the thinking and the imaginative selection and construction which go into theology, the choice of images and models and the way they are extended and extrapolated; and pay less attention to the results of such processes, in regard to which we are so often obliged to make the choice of accept or reject, the choice of total absorption or mutually exclusive, if also courteously polite, pluralism.

Images The analytic of images will, not surprisingly, follow a similar pattern to that of the analytic of imagination, but it merits a separate treatment, insofar as there has grown up a body of thought about the role that images play in knowledge, communication, emotion and even logic. Moreover, it is necessary to reflect upon what exactly it is that imagination uses when it executes the functions which were described in the previous analytic. Let us then itemise the particulars as before:

One, we begin with the *epistemological* role of images . . . [W]e observe that the images we encounter in the Bible – of God as a rock, a strong tower, a shepherd, and most significantly of all as Father; or of the death of Christ as ransom, propitiation, sacrifice and redemption – are descriptive of God and of the cross, and are the subjects of knowledge. So close do they stand to the subject of knowledge, that we have no ground for saying that these images somehow represent a reality which in itself is ineffable, or transcends description. We may wish to say that some of these terms are used analogically when applied to God or to the death of Christ; but even so, the positive content in their analogy is sufficiently high to justify our claim that in knowing God thus in terms of these images or models, we have genuine knowledge and are not being deceived. . . .

Two, another way of describing the epistemological role of images is to say that they are mediative, the media whereby we know certain subjects of the faith and of theology. When their status is thus defined, while we do not rule out the possibility that in some cases there may be similarity between the image or model and the original, an analogical relationship which might even approximate to representation, nevertheless we are not obliged to hold that the relationship is that of one-to-one representation. . . .

Three, in a now famous statement, Paul Tillich once wrote that symbols participate in the reality which they symbolise, care being taken to differentiate signs and symbols in this respect – fatherhood in the reality of the God who is father of all, sonship in the reality of Christ who is Son to the Father, reconciliation in the reality of the death of Christ, and so on. So understood, symbols, images, and models acquire an *ontological* role and a status within reality. They form part of our-world, and when they integrate with value-systems, then their metaphysical character becomes clear. . . .

Four, thus construed the image will inevitably develop a *hermeneutic* role and become the means of interpreting sections of Scripture, or areas of theology other than that of its original setting. . . . The choice of adequate images, symbols or models by the imagination is of paramount importance in the translation of ancient doctrinal truth into the language of modern times.

Five, as a direct consequence of the hermeneutic role of the image comes its *constructive* role, as it is seen to be the means whereby systematic structures of theology are set up . . . .

Six, the image has a very interesting further function, namely that of *universalising* an experience or event which had a subjective character, or one which was very much bounded by its original historical origins. The essence of good art is that the artist should discover that image, that form, which will enable him by publicising his experience, to communicate to others what had up to that point been purely private. . . . It is the peculiar quality of the image at once to be particular, specific and private, and also to have the universalising function to which I refer, that of lifting an experience, or an aspect of the faith, out of the immediate consciousness of one person, and placing it at the disposal of all and sundry. . . .

Seven, partly in the communicational context, but also in others, the image may be said to have an *illuminative* role. In theological study, an image may suddenly throw light on other areas than those for which it was chosen or designed. . . .

Eight, sometimes this illuminative role is extended to the point where it hardens to become *regulative* and *prescriptive*. The image which was adopted for one part of the discipline acquires some kind of authority which is thought to empower it to prescribe the contents of other parts. . . .

Nine, it is then a short step to endowing the image with a *normative* character so that it becomes the criterion by which truth and falsity in theological statements are assessed. . . .

Ten, we have, therefore, to add to our growing list, that images have a logical function, which is both *methodic* and *argumental*. They are methodic in the sense that they are central to the method that we each of us employ in the construction of our theological views – even when we disclaim that we ever construct theological views, adding that we do not aspire to do other than understand them. Allowing for such proper modesty, we have to point out that understanding involves interpretation; and that is a process which is heavily laden with images of one kind or another. So, too, when we endeavour to argue our way through some theological issue, we shall find once again that we proceed with the use of images in the form of controlling categories and concepts, some of which will have clear visual connections, many with parabolic overtones and others with the modular character of classical theology. . . .

Eleven, it would be remiss of us to omit the singularly *evocative* role which images play. A great deal is made of this aspect of images in the arts: the use of a vividly pictorial phrase, a sharply sketched scene, even the phonic quality of the spoken word, will serve to induce some emotion or other. . . . We do not require to go far before we encounter massive evidence for the evocative role of religious images – in crucifixes, ikons, religious paintings and sculptures, in the whole architecture of a church, as well as in the acted imagery of the entire liturgy.

It is all designed, under and within the glory of God, to place us at the point where God will meet us and we him, and be renewed through this encounter with him. . . .

Twelve, the image must also be said then to have a *sustentative* role, insofar as it will often be the means whereby a flagging faith is sustained, a weak will is reinforced, and a fading conviction restored to full strength. No matter our denominational loyalty, we all depend heavily on the sustentative power of images, not because they have any power in themselves, but because they have been in our lives the means whereby God has so constantly refreshed and renewed us.

Thirteen, a final role of images is their *recreative* character. I am thinking first in general terms of the way in which the sight of a keepsake given by an almost forgotten friend of other times and other places, may give us a very immediate experience of him or of her as present-in-absence. . . .

So, in conclusion, the question is very often asked: how can we ensure that the role of imagination in religion and theology is not taken over by fantasy, and how, therefore, can we distinguish them from one another? It might seem that the appropriate response to give to these questions would be to enumerate a list of open-and-shut criteria. If we were to attempt that, my prediction is these criteria would reflect the differentiae of true images and of imagination which I have offered above, in the analytic of imagination and images. These different functions and roles are in practice the indicators by which we are able to detect the presence of imagination and images that are valid. But they establish themselves empirically, by leading us to repentance and renewal, by sustaining faith, by evoking in us the responses of thanksgiving and adoration, by enabling us to build up a theological structure which interprets to our generation the insights given to another age and no longer immediately accessible for our contemporaries, and so on through the two lists. Fantasy is the process which attempts to do that but fails, because it has used a false or a debased currency, the image that broke in its hands. What we dare not think is that somehow we have a choice – to use or not to use the imagination and its media, images, in religion and in theology. Whether we acknowledge it or not, we have been employing imagination in our religion and in our theology, ever since we first became involved in these practices. It is a question, then, not of whether we employ it or not, but of how good, how irreproachable we can, by the grace of God, make our employment of it. (Ch. 7, pp. 168–76)

Source: John McIntyre, *Faith, Theology and Imagination*, Edinburgh, The Handsel Press, 1987.

18.8 Garrett Green, from *Imagining God, Theology and the Religious Imagination*

Garrett Green (Connecticut College) has contributed several writings to theological aesthetics in recent years. In this passage he points out how in theology, as a hermeneutic discipline, and in the praxis of worship and proclamation of the Word, the imagination plays a central role.

The Faithful Imagination: The Task of Theology

The Theory and Practice of Imagination . . . Protestant theology has always seen the focus of divine-human encounter in the proclamation of the gospel, which takes place usually and typically in preaching. Proclamation, formulated in terms of the present argument, can be described as an appeal to the imagination of the hearers through the images of scripture. The preacher's task is to mediate and facilitate that encounter by engaging his or her own imagination, which becomes the link between scripture and congregation. The preacher must therefore pay particular attention to the imagery of the biblical text, seeking to present it with such clarity and force that it will be seen and heard by the congregation. To save sinners, God seizes them by the imagination: the preacher places himself at the service of this saving act by the obedient and lucid engagement of his own imagination. All of the preacher's technical preparation – biblical languages, exegetical method, sermon organisation, skilful use of language, oral delivery – will be in vain unless subordinated to this central purpose.

The Bible itself offers some images of imaginative proclamation. . . . The preacher can try to communicate the images so as to bring them to bear on our present situation, while leaving our response to the inspiration of the Holy Spirit.

The ambiguity of reality and illusion inherent in imaginative discourse takes on practical significance in proclamation, for the preacher must use imagination in order to call our usual assumptions about reality into question by means of imaginative forms that may initially appear illusory to the hearers – as did Nathan's to David. Understanding that the field of action is the imagination may help to clarify the preacher's task, especially in contemporary culture, where 'images' are created and manipulated by advertisers and politicians, and illusion is marketed as reality. Paul's observations about the divine 'foolishness' and 'weakness' (1 Cor 1.25) might reasonably be extended to the proposition that the illusions of God are more real than the realities of men.

But the practical theological consequences of the imaginative shape of revelation are not limited to the discursive level of homiletics. The importance and function of the other elements of worship are also implied, and they in turn serve to underscore the fact that imagination is not limited to the intellectual or moral level of human perception. Liturgical action, especially the sacraments, need not be justified indirectly as 'expressions' of theological truth, for they appeal directly to the imagination in their own right. The Lord's Supper is no mere illustration of the gospel but rather its embodied proclamation: 'For as often you eat this bread and drink the cup, you *proclaim* the Lord's death until 1 comes' (1 Cor 11.26). The function of music in Christian worship is no mere adornment but rather an imaginative 'language' of proclamation and faith. The musical imagination is a particularly apt analogy of revelation itself. . . .

These practical consequences of theological imagination show how the Word of God encounters and transforms the whole person. God does not appear, on this interpretation, to address the intellect, the feelings, or the conscience separately; and it does not require a subsequent theory to relate the various human faculties to each other and to revelation. Imagination is not so much a particular faculty as the integration in human experience of the various human abilities and potentialities. The integrative function of imagination in apprehending patterns of meaning externally also allows an integral response on the part of the imagining subject. To imagine myself, for example, as the random product of the forces of physical nature, or as a member of the master race, or as destined to fail at everything I attempt, or as a sinner redeemed from death and hell by the sacrifice of Christ – each of these images calls forth a total response, having intellectual, emotional, and volitional aspects. (Ch. 7, pp. 148–51)

Source: Garrett Green, *Imagining God, Theology and the Religious Imagination*, Grand Rapids, Michigan, Cambridge, UK, Eerdmans, 1989.

18.9 Enda McDonagh, from *The Gracing of Society*

In this passage the Irish moral theologian Enda McDonagh analyses the close relationship of prayer and poetry as they both respond to ultimate reality and are shaped by the creative imagination. In line with the Christian tradition, he refers to Christ as divine artist and emphasizes that the theologian must have not only a critical but also a creative faculty founded in prayer.

Prayer, Poetry and Politics

Poetry which trembles on the edge of prayer may be found in all languages and religious traditions. This occurs most obviously but not necessarily or exclusively in poems dealing directly with religious themes and in modern poets of such powerful religious sensibility as Hopkins, Eliot and R. S. Thomas. . . .

My concern is not so much with prayer that assumes clearly poetic form or with poetry that moves close to prayer because of its religious content, although these are important in themselves and to the completeness of my argument. I want to argue a deeper relationship of unity and distinction, challenge and convergence between prayer taken more generously as awareness of and response to ne ultimate reality we call God, and poetry more generally as the formal and concentrated and above all beautiful human expression of the reality, including the tragic reality of this world. I write mainly from within the Christian tradition and its Jewish foundations, but some of the argument will be clearly of wider relevance.

The prayer and the poetry are both response to reality, acknowledging that reality in its richness, even its mystery. Mystery is an element always associated with the ultimate reality, God, not as an excuse for ignorance or a cover for fraud, but as a signal to the unfathomable richness of the ultimate source and destiny of all being. Approaches to the ultimate are always inadequate and indirect. Acknowledgment of the ultimate is equally inadequate and indirect. The language of the relative, limited and created can only stumble over the reality of the absolute, unlimited and uncreated. What humanity says of God and to God is born of the relative and finite and stretched to reach the absolute. Human words and concepts in this context are true and not true. God is personal and loving but not just as humans are personal and loving. The words are used analogously, as the technical term beloved of Thomas and Thomists has it. The stretch in the words reaches back to our own activities in prayer as we praise God and thank God for his love, as we address God as 'Our Father', as we consider how 'The World is charged with the grandeur of God'. Human language in response to divine reality is charged with meaning it cannot quite contain or fully express. The 'instress' of God in humanity and cosmos has no adequate human 'inscape'. The mystery breaks through language and escapes our confining, dominating, domesticating pretensions. But it is the mystery, the reality, which seeks expression, moves and inspires human response in mind and heart and language. 'When we cry "Abba! Father!" it is the Spirit himself bearing witness' (Rom 8.16). Prayer is divine gift before it is human achievement. We can only speak of that which we have received (the Spirit), to him who has entrusted himself to us (God). Prayer is the halting human response to the divine initiative which seeks expression in the characteristic human gift of language. Such expression will always be inadequate but will at least seek to be less inadequate through the authenticity of the respondent and the beauty of its form. The psalmist was always conscious of this double responsibility.

The poet (and the musical composer or painter or sculptor) may seem (to the religious person) to be dealing with much less exalted reality and so have much less problem with adequacy of expression or form. At his best, in Shakespeare or Bach or Michelangelo, the artist is struggling with mysteries of humanity and cosmos, which are not readily accessible, comprehensible or expressible. Depth of experienced reality combines with beauty of expressed forms to mediate in artistic masterpiece the mysterious dimensions of the human and the cosmic. The interaction of reality as given, perhaps given within the self, and artist as creative recipient, is frequently described as inspiration. So the artist is spoken of as inspired or possessed or driven to write or to paint.

There are clear parallels between prayer as understood and practised in the

Christian tradition and poetry or other artistic activity. These may be sum-marised under the rubrics of mystery, inspiration and the search for adequate (beautiful) form. Yet all three may be no more than parallels moving on quite different planes of reality: divine and human mystery, divine and human inspira-tion, total inadequacy of human language in prayer, and beauty, even perfection of form, in poetry.

Granted these are very different levels of divine and human reality, it is still worth exploring how far prayer and poetry may illuminate or challenge one another. The third rubric of expression stresses the inadequacy of prayer-language and the beauty of poetry. This contrast might be sharpened by refer-ence to poet and prayer-master St John of the Cross. The high regard in which his poetry is held (and he himself did recognise its value) differs sharply from his necessarily more modest view of his composition as prayer. Hopkins was very confident that his poetry would survive but he refused to seek publication lest it interfere with his dedication to the religious life and its primary characteristic, prayer. Yet both these were creative artists whose poetry expressed their deepest responses to the mystery of God and humanity. For those responses only the most beautiful form believable would be tolerated, even if nothing would ever be adequate. The poet, the seeker after beauty of language and form, which is native to all but ignored or undeveloped in most, must be encouraged to provide the most adequate response to the divine mystery possible to each. (Ch. 10, pp. 126–8)

The climactic experience of liberating and re-creating prayer occurs in 'Jesus' own prayer in Gethsemane. In Matthew's account (26.38ff) we read: 'Then he said to them "My soul is very sorrowful, even to death; remain here, and watch with me." And going a little farther he fell on his face and prayed, "My Father, if it be possible, let this cup pass from me; nevertheless, not as I will but as thou wilt." '

This liberation of Christ was rehearsed and completed on Calvary in the same movement from the Eloi of 'My God, my God, why have you forsaken me?' (Mt 27.46, Mk 15.34) to the Abba of 'Father, into thy hands I commend my spirit' before 'he breathed his last' (Lk 23.46). On Golgotha, in the garden of Gethsemane as in the garden of Genesis, the creative, transforming, liberating 'artist' is God, the Spirit of God. Human prayer is the immediate field of the divine artist as poet who enables us 'in the ground of our beseeching' (Eliot) to say with Jesus, 'Abba, Father' (Romans). The suffering of the human artist in his work of transformation (Yeats's 'much labouring' after Adam's fall) connects with that of our redemption/transformation by the divine artist. . . .

Divine and human creativity in prayer and poetry share also a sense of cele-bration. The human and cosmic wonders, which poetry celebrates, must be recognised in their unique selfhood, 'All things counter, original, spare, strange' (Hopkins). Yet their 'enselving' reality and mystery cannot, except at the cost of final meaninglessness, be closed off from the ultimate reality and mystery who 'fathers forth whose beauty is past change. Praise him'. As Hopkins above all recognised, the very stuff of poetry and poetic celebration must self-transcend to the ultimate, or self-destruct. Poetry as celebration of the beauty and mystery of humanity and cosmos has this inbuilt final reference to prayer. But prayer in turn needs this attention to the human and cosmic, to 'original, spare, strange' creatures and to the words which worthily mediate their mystery, if it is to be a worthy response to the true, ultimate mystery, the creator and redeemer God. (Ch. 10, pp. 130–1)

The interactions of prayer, poetry and politics are not those of a static circle. Development or decline in mutual promotion or corruption are the options, with the inevitable historical mixture of both. It is the predominance of development and mutual promotion or decline and mutual corruption which determines at any stage the direction of a circle which can go spiralling up or spiralling down and at varying speeds. And it is partly the task of the theologian to examine the connections between these three *loci* of creative-redemptive activity and the directions of their spiralling movement.

To do that he must have access to the *loci*, to the worlds of prayer, poetry and politics. This does not mean that he must be a mystic in the sense that St John of the Cross was, a poet like Hopkins or Heaney, or be actively engaged in parliamentary politics. He must share these activities in sympathy and imagination by being open, effectively, to the achievement of mystic, poet and politician. The imagination and the skill must be developed through education and dedication. Submitting himself to the biblical awareness and response to God, to writings of the mystics and of other authorities on prayer, will be part of his brief. Entering into the world of the artist, allowing it to re-create him in some fashion, will be a further stage in his attempt to understand the symbolic expression of the mystery of humanity and so of divinity. Making his own the ambitions, frustrations and achievements of politicians in pursuit of justice and peace, liberation and reconciliation will ground the engagement with kingdom and neighbour which is essential to Christian faith in search of understanding.

Will all this be only at second hand? Is the theologian condemned forever to examining at a remove, however sympathetically and imaginatively, the attitudes and achievements of others? Obviously not in the case of prayer. Prayer is the concentrate of faith which is basic to theology. Without prayer he may do interesting scholarly work but not theology. Prayer is not a substitute for critical and creative intellectual reflection but is a basis to the intellectual reflection called theology. A person of prayer the theologian must be but scarcely a person of poetry, that is, a poet or artist himself. Without a sense of symbol and symbolic expression, faith-expression and theology become impossible. What the poet or artist accomplishes in concentrated beauty, every person can manage in some lumbering and loose way. To have no sense of the language of poetry or music or painting, primitive and undeveloped as it may be, is to lack a sense of mystery and of its proper, limited, human expression. Some criticism of the recent liturgical renewal and scriptural translation is pertinent here. A biblical scholar remarked of a colleague once, 'He is a scholar, but he has a tin ear for the English language!' It seems, if true, a serious handicap in attempting to understand the word of God as expressed in human words. . . . Without sensitivity and attention to symbol, image and word, in theological creation and criticism, the Word of God in both first- and second-order *theologia* will be reduced to banality. Creative as well as critical skills are demanded of the theologian.

Traditionally at least the theologian has worked with words. So perhaps he ought to pay more attention to them in their aptness, accuracy and beauty. But politics? What has the theologian to do with that secular pursuit? . . . A Christian theologian as member of society is engaged in politics, for good or ill, as supporter or opponent of systems and activities which serve or disserve fellow citizens and neighbours. Becoming conscious of this, he will be forced to take a stand for or against certain structures and practices as he explores the love of neighbour which expresses love of God, as he examines the historical and social dimensions of the prayer of faith. It is not possible to continue in society without an attitude, a stand and so an engagement. Disengagement is also an engagement. In accepting the political engagement he sees it in close interaction with the rest of his faith-commitment as challenge and critique. And so he is led to further theologising and from that to fuller and fuller engagement. This is the dynamic of the creative, developing spiral. The engagement of disengagement can only lead to the spiral of decline. (Ch. 10, pp. 136–8)

Source: Enda McDonagh, *The Gracing of Society*, Dublin, Gill and Macmillan, 1989.

18.10 Elisabeth Moltmann-Wendel, from *I Am My Body*

A theology of the body pertains to a theory of sense perception from a theological perspective, i.e. a theological aesthetics. It is appropriate therefore to include a theologian in this volume who has written on this theme. Having repeatedly addressed feminist-theological issues in her work, Moltmann-Wendel here radically emphasizes the need for a holistic theology, which properly integrates and appreciates our embodied existence as God Godself became incarnate.

Being Open to New Areas

Towards a theology of embodiment A theology of embodiment does not seek to outline a new theology, but it does seek to open up a forgotten place which is important today, from which there can be theological thought and action: the human body. It seeks to draw attention to our origin, to the fact that we are born from mothers, a fact which is constantly forgotten in a culture of fathers but which shapes us all our lives, whether we are women or men.

Stimulated by feminist praxis and theory and by feminist theology, it sees that the human body is repressed and misused in the Western Christian tradition. As woman's body it has been despised, feared, burned. Woman's full personhood has been denied her on the basis of her body. Even now it does not fit into the structures of churches and societies. The man's body has been glorified, made a norm, instrumentalized and also misused. Even now its alleged continuity shapes our ideal of the body and our understanding of achievement.

There have been signs of the return of the body for years. In the meantime experiences and investigations have shown how impressively the human body reproduces our experience, our history, our suffering, which remain stamped on it and are hard to heal. Torture, rape, incest and sexual abuse are at present the most striking examples. The body is the place where many contemporary social and psychological processes are articulated. It is striking for church and theology how much negation and thus loss of energy can be noted in the human body.

A theology of embodiment is leading to a new interest in the bodies and lives of the most varied marginalized groups: women, the old, lesbians, homosexuals, people of colour, who have to fight for recognition in a variety of forms, and who thus suffer a loss of energy and cannot contribute their positive powers to society, since young people and white males are still favoured not only in society but also in the church. A theological return to embodiment recalls the distinctive feature of Christianity, that God became body and in so doing has confirmed and healed all our bodily nature. This was a scandal in the religions of the ancient world – and is an unresolved challenge in the present world.

Reflection on embodiment as a central Christian topic prompts mistrust of a Western Augustinian theology which begins with the fall instead of creation and the pleasure which God took in this creation. It does not see sin as a general fate which is suffered as a matter of principle, and which for many theological traditions is still rooted in sinful human flesh, in the structure of its drives. It does not fail to recognize the potential for destruction in human beings, but sees this far more strongly as the problem of a lack of relationship, beginning in an earlier phase of life, a lack of relationship between human beings, between human beings and animals, between human beings and their environment. Sin must be made clear and identified in particular, different conflicts.

A theology of embodiment mistrusts all abstract spirituality which is dissociated from the body, life, earth and social relationships. It trusts all embodiment which speaks from a concrete, involved spirit, moved by eros and related to the cosmos. Disembodiment is lovelessness. Insecurity, coldness, power and weariness are hidden behind abstraction.

A theology of embodiment mistrusts all self-made fantasies of the beyond which are engaged in at the expense of the healing of people here and the realization of the kingdom of God on this earth. It is committed to a this-worldly expectation which here already looks for full, complete life, for wide spaces for women and men, and from this work derives the hope that nothing can separate us from the life and love of God.

It seeks to give people once again the courage to use their senses, which atrophy in a rational culture, to stand by themselves and their experiences and accept themselves with their bodies, to love them, to trust them and their understanding, and to see themselves as children of this earth, indissolubly bound up with it.

It prefers a concrete body language which also incorporates symbols, myths and fairy tales into theological discourse to a disembodied language. Instead of the traditional forensic language of salvation it seeks biblical images new and old, of being saved, becoming whole, ideas of the bodily world which correspond to the body and its rhythms and awaken healing energies in human beings which bind them to one another. It attempts to revive old rituals which affect the body and shape new ones which draw us into the cosmic dance.

However, a theology of embodiment is not in love with success. It looks at the cross as a symbol of failure, but also of a hope which is contained in the beams which point to the four corners of heaven, a hope that there is life in death, gain in failure, resurrection in passing away. For it the cross is not a symbol of Christ's sacrificial death, but a symbol of his death for a just cause.

It thinks in processes which correspond better to our life and its constant changes than linear patterns and the belief in unique and final experiences.

It is orientated on Jesus' humanity, his life, his love, his sacrifice, his passion. It regards his divinity as his deepest humanity. It discovers the God of the Bible in many images of the biblical and post-biblical tradition which are sometimes unknown even now: the woman giving birth, the beloved, the old woman, wisdom, source, tree, light.

It sees that God weeps with us and in us, for his ravaged creation and in it.

It recognizes God in many human experiences which remind us that life begins in the mother's body, that it begins as a twosome, not alone, and that our bodily life represents God's life on this earth.

'The end of all God's works is embodiment', wrote the Württemberg theologian Friedrich Christoph Oetinger in the eighteenth century. I would like to expand the sentence: The beginning and end of all God's works is embodiment. (Ch. 3, pp. 103–5)

Source: Elisabeth Moltmann-Wendel, *I Am My Body*, London, SCM Press, 1994.

18.11 David F. Ford, from *Self and Salvation, Being Transformed*

The central role of feasting in human and, especially, in Christian life is discussed by Irish systematic theologian David Ford (University of Cambridge) whereby he emphasizes its inclusive, transcending and transformative dimension.

The aesthetics of feasting All the senses are engaged in a good feast. We taste, touch, smell, see, hear. Salvation as health is here vividly physical. Anything that heals and enhances savouring the world through our senses may feed into a salvation that culminates in feasting. From prayer for healing, and all the skills of medicine, through the accumulated wisdom of traditions of cookery, wine-making and brewing, to the experiences and habits which refine our sensual discriminations and enjoyments, the requirements for full feasting draw us deeper into appreciation of our embodiment.

The arts are elaborate refinements of embodied perception. They are woven into feasts and festivals in many ways – Homeric bards; Bach cantatas; the murals and architecture of a banqueting hall; a sculpted monument to a victory; music and dancing at a party or wedding; bands at sports events; the concerts that celebrated South Africa's transition to majority rule. The intensity of feasting rejoices in the celebratory potential of the arts and their overflow of expression which configures and refigures reality. The relaxation of feasting gives time and space for leisure is the basis of culture.

Are there also possibilities of transformed sensing which see with 'the eyes of the heart', hear with 'the inner ear', smell 'the odour of holiness', savour 'the sweetness of the Lord' or feel 'the touch of the Spirit'? Are these 'only' metaphors? Or is there something in the rich traditions about 'the spiritual senses' within and beyond Christianity?

Much in this book's previous chapters is an invitation to see the face of Jesus Christ with the eyes of the heart. Those who know the teachings on the spiritual senses will recognise many points of contact. This seeing has involved ethical and intellectual disciplines, counsels of detachment from idols, meditation on scripture and other texts, learning from Jesus Christ and from saints, and above all the habit of prayer and worship. Insofar as seeing the face of Christ is concerned, all this points to the basic feature of the spiritual senses: they are about the whole self in relation to God, and are far from any technique enabling the curious to inspect spiritual truths without further involvement. The pure in heart see God, and it is a purity of love to the point of being crucified.

The aesthetics of Easter feasting therefore passes through Good Friday's death of Jesus's sensing, thinking and acting. Yet the thrust of the theology of the face of Christ has not been to single out sensing (or the visual arts) as a path of danger and idolatry. The suggested (though in this book only occasionally explicit) aesthetics of the face of the crucified and risen Jesus Christ allows, for example, for the Orthodox Christian tradition of iconography. That is rooted in a rich theological tradition about the spiritual senses, and in its icons the face of Christ is characteristically set at the centre of a cross.

This could be extended to all the other arts too. What does it mean in film, literature, music, dance, theatre and other media to be creative in ways which not only acknowledge (in however implicit ways) that the first audience is Jesus Christ, but also participate in the 'ecology of blessing' which he generates? How is there new perception of matter, life, death, time and people? How can the arts contribute to transformations of daily life, public life and worship?

The ethics of feasting Jesus went to meals, weddings and parties and had a feast-centred ethic. The images are vivid: water turned into wine; guests jockeying for places at table and being told to aim for the lower places; the invitation of a life-time refused because of being too busy with work or family; Jesus challenging conceptions of God's acceptance by eating with the outcast and marginalised; Dives feasting while Lazarus starves at his gate; children eating messily to the delight of the dogs; a woman sinner shocking the company by anointing Jesus and being forgiven by him; the reversal of expectations as the poor, handicapped and outsiders of all sorts are welcomed at the feast of the Kingdom of God while those who thought themselves sure of a place are left out; advice about not inviting to your banquet those who will invite you back; a master sitting a servant down and serving him; the Prodigal Son welcomed back unconditionally with the best robe, a ring, shoes, the fatted calf and a celebration; Jesus's last supper, which was probably also a celebration of Passover; Jesus washing his disciples' feet; and the mysterious meals of the risen Jesus.

Jesus was immersed in the religion, economics and politics of his time, and his teaching and practice about meals and feasting were sharply relevant to his particular situation. The challenge to those who want to learn from him today is to be involved in our situations with comparable perception and sharpness, in ways that testify to the abundant generosity of God, our acceptance of it, and our imitation of it.

As millions starve, ought anyone to be feasting? Ought there not to be a long detour of working to feed everyone, postponing the feasting till that has been achieved? Or should we keep alive the hope of food for all by working for justice and, if we have food, simultaneously celebrating the goodness of God? Can we even sustain work of compassion and justice in the right spirit if we are not also having some celebratory foretaste of the Kingdom of God? Or, looking at the story of the early church in the Acts of the Apostles, in the light of the explosion of joy and gratitude that followed the resurrection and Pentecost is it not the most obvious thing in the world both to share with those in need and also to celebrate with them?

That combination of sharing and celebrating is, perhaps, the most radical of all the implications of the teaching and practice of Jesus. Feeding the hungry is not a matter of the well-fed offering handouts and getting on with their private feasting: the vision is of everyone around the same table, face to face. Even to imagine sitting together like that gently but inexorably exposes injustice, exploitation, sexism, hard-heartedness, and the multiple ways of rejecting the appeal in the face of the other. Once we have started doing it in little ways, the implications for politics, economics and church life never cease ramifying. Remission of actual debt becomes inseparable from the forgiveness of sins, and idolatry of money is seen as an inhibitor of everyone's joy.

Finally, what about the ethics of exclusion? At many points in previous chapters I have tried to follow the gaze of Jesus across divisive boundaries and have interpreted his life, death and resurrection as his taking on of limitless responsibility towards other people. The feast of the Kingdom of God is described (and acted out) by him as generously inclusive beyond anyone's wildest dreams. That is the main point: the free, surprising love of a God who can be utterly trusted to judge truthfully and then decide far more compassionately than any of the rest of us. There is also a sharp note of exclusion, but it is one that follows from the inclusiveness. The excluded are those who cannot bear God's generosity and will not imitate it. The Prodigal Son's older brother is the archetype, complaining against his father welcoming his brother home with a party, and perhaps (the ending is significantly left open) refusing to join in the celebrations. He is matched by those who complain about Jesus eating with tax-collectors and sinners, by those who presume to know where God draws lines between the invited and uninvited or the acceptable and unacceptable, and by those who harden their hearts against the poor, sick, handicapped, hungry, prisoners, children, and others in need. These poor, sick and needy are at the centre of the feast as the honoured guests, and to reject them is to exclude oneself from their host's presence. The other side of this is that to seek them out is to relate to their host too, as the parable of the sheep and the goats says (Matthew chapter 25).

Of contemporary issues of exclusion, one of the most sensitive for Christians is that of other religions. It is not possible to do more than touch interrogatively on this vast, many-sided topic, but it is an appropriate conclusion for a meditation on the ethic of feasting before the face of Christ.

What does it mean to realise that those of other faiths (and none) are before the face of Christ? Christians have no overview of how the relationship with them is carried on, or what happens from either side. This ethic therefore begins in agnosticism. Yet Christians need to try to imagine what the implications might be of Jesus being guest as well as host in relation to Mohammed, the Buddha and other founders and their followers. What might be involved in hospitality between religious communities that might give substance to such imagining? What are appropriate anticipations of the feasting of the Kingdom of God? What ethic of communication of the gospel is in line with the face on the cross? How can conversations engaging with crucial matters of meaning, truth and practice be sustained? What new shapes of Christian and other communities might there be if imaginative hospitality helped to generate honest confrontations and new understanding? Where do Christians fall into the temptation of being less generously welcoming than God? How can they come to realise their Christian self 'as another' – Jew, Muslim, Hindu, Buddhist, atheist or whatever? And what happens when guests and hosts become friends?

The metaphysics of feasting It sounds pretentious or at least unacceptably anthropomorphic to talk of feasting as fundamental to the way reality is. But if a God of love and joy, communicated in Jesus Christ, is that than which none better or greater can be conceived then, recognising the analogical uses of 'feasting' (not at all grudgingly – analogy, as Ricoeur argues, is intrinsic to an adequate, multifaceted ontology), it is appropriate to speak like that. The metaphysics of feasting is first of all about the reality of that God who transcends all our categories; then about the 'logic of superabundance' which might be discerned in creation and history; and finally about the orientation of the divine economy that is appropriately described in, among other ways, the figure of feasting.

The resource and 'currency' for exchange in that economy is the life, truth and love of God. It is a trinitarian metaphysic, giving priority to the doctrine of God in conceiving 'being' or 'reality'. Yet it is never able to rest in its knowledge of God or of creation – there is infinite stretching of heart and mind in trying to do justice to a God who is complexly and interestingly involved in the whole of creation and history. The metaphysics of feasting is especially concerned with the abundance of the truth and wisdom of God and of creation. How can that be savoured more fully? What are the structures and dynamics of a universe which is created to culminate in feasting? How do the natural and human sciences, the scholarly disciplines, philosophy, the arts, and various cultures and religions testify to this? How can joy in truth and wisdom be fulfilled if we do not feed on such courses?

For this metaphysics the danger to which Levinas alerts us is that of a new totality. Feasting, however, allows for his ethical pluralism of being. There is no overview of all those encounters and conversations, but the feast can enact the union of substitutionary joy in the joy of others with substitutionary responsibility.

The hermeneutics of feasting To envisage the ultimate feasting is to imagine an endless overflow of communication between those who love and enjoy each other. It embraces body language, facial expressions, the ways we eat, drink, toast, dance and sing; and accompanying every course, encounter and artistic performance are conversations taken up into celebration. We can imagine a 'great feast of languages' (Shakespeare), with cultures and traditions in conversation. There can be a pluralism without divisiveness – there is only a limited number of exchanges any guest can take part in, and nobody needs to know what is going on in every conversation. Aesthetics, ethics and metaphysics converge in this performance that is 'infinitely communicative' (Traherne).

It is a '*fête du sens*', a feast of meaning, into which all aspects of hermeneutics feed: immersion in language, being shaped by it and shaping it; appreciation of many styles, figures, genres and contexts; labours in study and in debates over the sense, reference and application of texts and other communications; sensitivity to nuance, irony, humour and play. Pervading all is the significance of silence, reticence and mystery, in recognition of the inexhaustible abundance of meaning and an inexpressibility which yet continually invites further speech. (Ch. 11, pp. 267–72)

Source: David F. Ford, *Self and Salvation, Being Transformed*, Cambridge, Cambridge University Press, 1999.

19

Divine Revelation, Beauty, and the Vision of God

—-—

19.1 Friedrich von Hügel, from *The Reality of God*

The German Catholic theologian-philosopher von Hügel (1852–1925) held that the abiding dimensions in religion are the mystical, the intellectual and the institutional. Here he argues that the human being has not only a sense of existence, but also enjoys an aesthetic sense, which von Hügel understands in Platonist terms as the desire for beauty, harmony and proportion. Rare among theologians is his reference to plants and animals who also have an aesthetic sense.

Ethics and the theory of knowledge I hope soon to bring out clearly how, in Ethics also, there is involved a Reality different from our own lesser reality – in this case a Reality apprehended primarily not as Intelligence, but as Goodness. But here I want to add the following which we can find, and indeed have already found, interwoven with the sense of *what is*, as a sort of analogy of, and preparation for, the sense of *what ought to be*. We have seen that the external world, especially in so far as organic, not only responds to our need of Existence, but brings evidence, in the Existence thus offered to us, of Intelligence, of a Mind of immense knowledge and efficiency, and, at the same time, satisfies our aesthetic sense – our need and search for beauty, proportion, harmony. We found that this need for, attraction to, and apprehension of, beauty is like the need for, and attraction to, existence, not a quality exclusively possessed by man, since we find the animals, and indeed the plants, beautiful, and indeed, in some cases, exquisitely lovely, and this, not primarily to please us, but, in the first instance, for the male animal or plant to please and to attract the corresponding female. We have here one of the many strong reasons for believing in a dim consciousness of the plants, since only so can it make any difference to the female plant if the male plant, or flower, or part of a flower, is decked out in gorgeous colouring, or delicious scent, or not. And in the animals, even amongst the inferior animals, we note that their consciousness is thoroughly aware of these pleasures of sight and of smell. We have then, in the aesthetic sense, apart from all question of the moral sense, a sense distinct from the sense of Existence – and this aesthetic sense, together with the aesthetic qualities in the objects corresponding to it, is at work within the world, certainly of man and of the animals, and very probably in the world of plants also, so that men and animals and plants possess certain objectively beautiful qualities, and apprehend and enjoy these qualities in their fellow-men and fellow-animals and fellow-plants as beautiful. True, the aesthetic sense is directly awakened and satisfied by certain aesthetic objects – by certain aesthetic qualities in man, or in the animal, or in the plant. We have here still *what is*, not *what ought to be*. Yet we can also find an analogy for the *oughtness* of morals in a certain *Oughtness* everywhere largely constitutive of the objects we see and know in the external, organic world through our intellects alone. For we found that, in so far as evolution is true and operative, it is not so from any struggle for existence of the fittest, alone or even primarily. The lichen resists the wear and tear of life, as regards any struggle for bare existence going on, far better than the orchid, indeed better even than the rose; and so with animals and so especially with man. For every step taken by my body or my mind, especially every step I take myself, upwards in rich articulation and accurate response to existence and to truth, renders me more vulnerable to external nature around me, and, at every change in time and space, less easily adapted to it. What alone can explain evolution (if, and in so far as, it really exists) is a principle such as M. Fouillee's *idées forces*, ideals of the different plants and animals and man (and doubtless also of such other races of beings as inhabit the other planets and stars) which press, as so many forces, these various beings up and out into higher and wider ranges of beauty and significance. It is, doubtless, through such ideals of the several individual reals [sic], seen by us in these reals, that we attain to a genuine knowledge of significant reality at all. All this has already, and above all other thinkers, been magnificently taught us by Plato. (pp. 75–6)

Source: Baron Friedrich von Hügel, *The Reality of God* and *Religion and Agnosticism*, ed. Edmund G. Gardner, London, Toronto, J. M. Dent & Sons, 1931.

19.2 Gerardus van der Leeuw, from *Sacred and Profane Beauty, The Holy in Art*

In his seminal work on theological aesthetics, the Dutch Protestant theologian and leading proponent of the phenomenological interpretation of religion, van der Leeuw (1890–1950), examined the intersection of religion and art, especially in the Christian context. Here he writes that the nature of their relationship is both paradoxical and analogical; ultimately their unity is founded in the doctrine of the incarnation.

Theological Aesthetics

Independence and Interdependence Our time is full of yearning for the lost unity of life. Everywhere efforts are being made to replace the tangent planes with concentric circles. We have had our fill of limited 'realms', and justly so. But this yearning must not tempt us to try to revive the primitive, nor even to erase the boundaries; least of all should we anticipate all that only exists in the eschatological sense, that is, through the grace of God. 'Among primitive peoples, art and morality, as well as science, melt together with a confused and complex activity which one can call religious, but which in reality already contains the germ, the principle, of all the higher activities.' But we cannot restore this artificially. We can only recognize boundaries and points of access. The unity is a matter of faith. Art is not a province of life, still less, in the sense of the nineteenth century, a sub-division. Art participates in all of life, and all of life participates in it. Just as the whole of life, it has its origin elsewhere. This origin is hidden from our gaze. Therefore we need again and again the independence of art as a defence against the imperialism of scientific or dogmatic thought. The life stream of art does not flow into a fruitless and artificial seclusion: 'Thus art strives to return to an undivided total life, seeking a new, a conscious, an articulated interdependence in which it, like all other realms of life, can simultaneously preserve and surrender its own nature.' We must constantly be aware that this striving is only a direction of life, not a goal attained. The goal attained is only conceivable in the beyond.

The recognition of the creation of God in the creation of the arts is analogous to the Platonic recognition in the reverse sense: it is a recognition in hope, not in fact. A complete unity of religion and art would be neither conceivable nor desirable, for both would have to be absolute. We have repeatedly stood at this boundary. Absolute religion is mysticism; it is without shape and without sound. Absolute art can neither be seen nor heard. True art is eschatological art, 'music no longer tonal art', the invisible image, the word falling silent, the dissolving dance, the building which is lost in the stretches of the infinite landscape. In silence, religion and art meet and interpenetrate. Religion and art are parallel lines which intersect only at infinity, and meet in God. If in spite of this we continue to speak of a renewed unity, of influences by which holiness and beauty can meet, of a point at which religion and art meet in our world, we mean a direction, a striving, a recognition, which ultimately must destroy itself.

Points of Intersection This point of intersection of religion and art we shall find where art turns to the absolute; where the wholly other is. For that was our definition of the holy. We have already seen that the holy by its very nature cannot approach the beautiful; the beautiful must instead betake itself to the holy (which, of course, does not mean that beauty gives up its rights in favour of those of the holy). But it is also true that the holy, equally by its own nature, already bears the beautiful within itself. Its meaning abolishes any other 'meaning'. It only remains to find the places where beauty passes over into holiness.

Thus we must tune our ears and sharpen our eyes for the beauty which confronts us with an absolute claim, for the beauty which appears in absolute majesty. We must listen to the word which is the Last Word, to the note which strives for the absoluteness of inaudibility; we must keep a lookout for the image which reminds us of the image and likeness of him whom we cannot see, for the movement which is conveyed by the rhythm of the stars, for the building which is the house of God. But we must also search within ourselves, to see whether we experience the beauty which is thus revealed to us as the wholly other. This we shall only know when beauty not only attracts us, but also repels us; not only enchants us, but also disturbs us in a way we never knew before. We seek in beauty both the friendly countenance of God and the terror of the Lord; we seek the Comforter who calls to us when we are weary and heavy-laden, but also the terrible one who repels us from himself with, 'What have I to do with you?' At this point of intersection we seek, with the words of Rudolf Otto, that beauty which is both fascination and awe, which we approach with glad hope, but with trembling reverence.

The aesthetic form of life in itself, of course, brings edification and broadening, making us forget the ego for the sake of something different, something higher. But only religion seeks the absolute and the wholly other. Therefore only religious art is 'one which causes the ultimate sense of life to flow out into the play of richly related forms of phantasy.' . . .

Harmony as the Creation of God Upon the holy ground we found harmony. We ascertained that it was achieved by men. Art is nature and culture, and in both holiness is revealed. But it is also and even primarily creature, the creation of God. Whoever believes this cannot view art as a birth from the primal womb; he cannot view it as a conquest of man. Of course, it is this, but by nature it is something else. The holy will of God also stands behind art.

This belief also shows us the reverse side of harmony: holiness means distance. Between the holy God and his creation yawns a mighty chasm. The 'creation' of the artist is by no means a parallel to the creation of God. It is its dullest reflection, and is completely overwhelmed by the light of the life of God. Whoever truly serves beauty, serves God. But whoever serves God does not yet therefore serve beauty. God can destroy for his servant all beautiful words and sounds. The deepest, even the ultimate religious art, cannot exist before the face of God. In its highest forms of expression we feel a longing for a different image, a different song; for something which would be no longer 'art'. Whoever hears or uses many words feels an indescribable longing for the Word which is with God. Even in art, creator and creature confront each other as God confronts his image in man. Maritain expresses this clearly and beautifully when he says of God: 'His and only his love calls forth the beauty of that which he loves, while our love is called forth by the beauty of that which we love.' Thus God's love is also wholly other than that of the artist. All came from God's love, even beauty. Our love, even if it devotes itself to a work of art, is only love returned.

Nevertheless, this is not said in order that we should have misgivings. There is creation. There is distance. There is incarnation. And there is proximity. . . .

Through beauty we can share in his work of new creation. Perpendicular through nature and culture in its heathen holiness, the work of God's creation is erected, even in the work of art of men, which serves him. We may change the scholastic 'gratia naturam non tollit, sed perfecit' (grace does not abolish nature, but perfects it) as follows: grace does not abolish nature, but creates it anew.

Therefore there is no 'religious' art. Here Maritain warns us again: 'If you want to make Christian art, be Christians, and seek to make a beautiful work, in which your entire heart lies; do not try to make it Christian.' For genuine art is Christian: 'Everywhere where art – whether Egyptian, Greek, or Chinese – has attained a certain level and a certain degree of purity, it is in expectation already Christian, because all spiritual radiance is the promise and image of the divine weighing out of the Gospel.'. . .

Thus the soul of the artist, during the period of Christ's passion, undertakes a quiet pilgrimage to the holy place of God. Perhaps it hardly knows this. The builders of the great cathedrals did not think of 'holiness'; they hardly thought of beauty, but, above all, of doing good work. 'They believed, and, as they were, so they did. Their work revealed the truth of God, but without intention, and precisely because they did it without intention.' God's holiness would destroy all art were it not at the same time for his grace, which deigns to reveal itself in beauty. Before the face of God, art is nothing and less than nothing (*ut palea*, like straw, said Thomas Aquinas). But this is the great paradox of faith, that before the face of God and from God's hand art receives simultaneously its life and its glory.

A Metaphysics of Art? Is what has been said sufficient to arrive at a metaphysics of art? I hardly think so. We shall remain phenomenologists. We do not want to forget that we have spoken only of experiences and phenomena. We shall let it rest at that. Logically viewed, we can call everything of the essence of art which we have related to the essence of religion 'mere analogy'. Thereby it becomes useless for metaphysics. . . .

We can only repeat that every true work of art is in a sense religious. Every true work of art bears within itself the germ of self-abolishment. The lines yearn to be erased, the colours to pale. Every true art is experienced as the incarnation of what is further distant from us, and different.

A Worship of Beauty? We declined a metaphysics of art, because it is only a surrogate for something which art possesses in a world of the beyond. Here religion has its divine correlative in faith. But it does not coincide completely with faith, and it must not be confused with faith, though it is nevertheless rooted in faith. Religion as a human gesture derives its strength from faith, from the divine act. Still, there is nothing which could stand in the same relationship to art as faith does to religion. In other words: religion, in faith, becomes worship. Beauty, on the other hand, is served, but not worshipped. Wherever we find worship of beauty, we note at once that form and content are taken from the realm of religious belief. (pp. 332–7)

Incarnation . . . We found religious art, where in the creation of the artist we recognized the lines and contours of God's creation. But is that possible? . . .

It can and must be possible to recognize in the beautiful work of man the features of the work of God, since God himself gave to his earthly creation the features of his own image. It can and must be possible to praise the whole variety of the human world, the glorious multitude of forms of art and religion as revelation of the glory of God, if God himself gave himself to this human world, himself assumed form and moved as man among men. The Incarnation means our redemption also in the sense that the world and our works in it need not be without meaning, but can be bearers of a divine revelation.

Thus, as phenomenologists, as men of the science of art and religion, we find points of access and boundaries. Thus, as religious men, we experience again and again the miracle of the blending of religion and art. As theologians, who can neither separate artificially the revelation in Christ and that apparently different one given us as revelation, nor desire to lose ourselves in the generality of an idea of God, we find the unity of art and religion where alone we know unity: in the doctrine of the Incarnation. As believers, we find the possibility of complete beauty in him in whom we find everything, in the divine figure, in the son of Mary, in the Son of God, who is the most beautiful. And, with the old folk song, we say: All the beauty of heaven and earth is contained in Thee alone. (pp. 339–40)

Source: Gerardus van der Leeuw, *Sacred and Profane Beauty, The Holy in Art*, trans. David E. Green, London, Weidenfeld and Nicolson, no date (originally published 1932).

19.3 Karl Barth, from *Church Dogmatics, vol. 2, The Doctrine of God*

Barth (1886–1968), one of the foremost theologians of the twentieth century, emphasized the supremacy of God's revelation in Jesus Christ. Here he points out that God's beauty is primal and the standard of all beauty. The perfect divine being radiates outwards in God's perfect form and thereby attracts and brings about our joy in the divine. God is beautiful in the form of God's freedom and love, in God's works and essence. The form of the divine 'has and is itself divine beauty'.

The Perfections of the Divine Freedom

The Eternity and Glory of God . . . The concept which lies ready to our hand here, and which may serve legitimately to describe the element in the idea of glory that we still lack, is that of beauty. If we can and must say that God is beautiful, to say this is to say how He enlightens and convinces and persuades us. It is to describe not merely the naked fact of His revelation or its power, but the shape and form in which it is a fact and is power. It is to say that God has this superior force, this power of attraction, which speaks for itself, which wins and conquers, in the fact that He is beautiful, divinely beautiful, beautiful in His own way, in a way that is His alone, beautiful as the unattainable primal beauty, yet really beautiful. He does not have it, therefore, merely as a fact or a power. Or rather, He has it as a fact and a power in such a way that He acts as the One who gives pleasure, creates desire and rewards with enjoyment. And He does it because He is pleasant, desirable, full of enjoyment, because He is the One who is pleasant, desirable, full of enjoyment, because first and last He alone is that which is pleasant, desirable and full of enjoyment. God loves us as the One who is worthy of love as God. This is what we mean when we say that God is beautiful. . . .

Owing to its connexion with the ideas of pleasure, desire and enjoyment (quite apart from its historical connexion with Greek thought), the concept of the beautiful seems to be a particularly secular one, not at all adapted for introduction into the language of theology and indeed extremely dangerous. If we say now that God is beautiful, and make this statement the final explanation of the assertion that God is glorious, do we not jeopardise or even deny the majesty and holiness and righteousness of God's love? Do we not bring God in a sinister because in a sense intimate way into the sphere of man's oversight and control, into proximity to the ideal of all human striving? Do we not bring the contemplation of God into suspicious proximity to that contemplation of the world which in the last resort is the self-contemplation of an urge for life which does not recognise its limits? Certainly we have every reason to be cautious here. But the question is even more pressing whether we can hesitate indefinitely, whether we can avoid this step. Has our whole consideration of the matter not brought us inevitably to the place where what would otherwise remain a gap in our knowledge can be filled only in this way? Finally and above all, does biblical truth itself and as such permit us to stop at this point because of the danger, and not to say that God is beautiful? . . .

In our discussion of the leading concepts of the Christian knowledge of God, we have seen that no single one of them is this key, and that if anyone of them is claimed as such it inevitably becomes an idol. There can be no question, then, of finally allowing an aestheticism to speak which if it tried to have and keep the last word would inevitably be as false and unchristian as any dynamism or vitalism or logism or intellectualism or moralism which might try to slip into the doctrine of God in this role and with this dignity.

For all that, it is as well to realise that the aestheticism which threatens here is no worse than the other 'isms' or any 'ism'. They are all dangerous. Indeed, as we have more or less clearly encountered them all, we have seen that in their place they are all mortally dangerous. But we have also seen that there is a herb that is a match for them. There is no reason to take up a particularly tragic attitude to the danger that threatens from the side of aesthetics – which is what Protestantism has done according to our historical review. Nor is there any reason to shrink back at this point with particular uneasiness or prudery, suppressing or dismissing out of sheer terror a problem that is set us by the subject itself and its biblical attestation.

Attention should also be given to the fact that we cannot include the concept of beauty with the main concepts of the doctrine of God, with the divine perfections which are the divine essence itself. In view of what the biblical testimony says about God it would be an unjustified risk to try to bring the knowledge of God under the denominator of the idea of the beautiful even in the same way as we have done in our consideration of these leading concepts. It is not a leading concept. Not even in passing can we make it a primary motif in our understanding of the whole being of God as we necessarily did in the case of these other concepts.

To do this is an act of philosophical wilfulness of which Pseudo-Dionysius is guilty in the passage quoted and elsewhere, and which even lurks behind the passage in Augustine's Confessions. The Bible neither requires nor permits us, because God is beautiful, to expound the beauty of God as the ultimate cause producing and moving all things, in the way in which we can and must do this in regard to God's grace or holiness or eternity, or His omnipotent knowledge and will.

Our subject is still the glory of God. We speak of God's beauty only in explanation of His glory. It is, therefore, a subordinate and auxiliary idea which enables us to achieve a specific clarification and emphasis. With the help of it we are able to dissipate even the suggestion that God's glory is a mere fact, or a fact which is effective merely through God's power, a formless and shapeless fact. It is not this. It is effective because and as it is beautiful. This explanation as such is not merely legitimate. It is essential. It is certainly true that the idea of the beautiful as such and in *abstracto* does not play any outstanding or at least autonomous part in the Bible.

grasped, theology as a whole, in its parts and in their interconnexion, in its content and method, is, apart from anything else, a peculiarly beautiful science. Indeed, we can confidently say that it is the most beautiful of all the sciences. To find the sciences distasteful is the mark of the Philistine. It is an extreme form of philistinism to find, or to be able to find, theology distasteful. The theologian who has no joy in his work is not a theologian at all. Sulky faces, morose thoughts and boring ways of speaking are intolerable in this science. May God deliver us from what the Catholic Church reckons one of the seven sins of the monk – *taedium* – in respect of the great spiritual truths with which theology has to do. But we must know, of course, that it is only God who can keep us from it. The beauty of theology is an insight to which there is occasional allusion in Anselm of Canterbury. The *ratio* which *fides quaerens intellectum* has to seek is not only *utilitas*. It is also *pulchritudo*. When it is found, and as it is sought, it is *speciosa super intellectum hominum* (*Cur Deus homo* I, 1), a *delectabile quiddam* (*Monol.* 6). . . .

It belongs to the nature of the subject that the real proof of our statement that God is beautiful can be provided neither by few nor by many words about this beauty, but only by this beauty itself. God's being itself speaks for His beauty in His revelation. . . . The form of the perfect being of God is, as we have seen all along, the wonderful, constantly mysterious and no less constantly evident unity of identity and non-identity, simplicity and multiplicity, inward and outward, God Himself and the fullness of that which He is as God. . . . There can be no question of distinguishing between the content and the form of the divine being and therefore of seeking the beauty of God abstractly in the form of His being for us and in Himself. The beauty of God is not to be found in the unity of identity and non-identity, or movement and peace, as such. Here, too, our final recourse must be to God Himself. He is the perfect content of the divine being, which also makes His form perfect. Or, the perfection of His form is simply the radiating outwards of the perfection of His content and therefore of God Himself. But this content does actually make this form perfect, clearly because the form is necessary to the content, because it belongs to it. And in this form the perfect content, God Himself, shines out. The glory, the self-declaration of God, is based entirely on the fact that He Himself has His life in it both inwards and outwards. . . . Only the form of the divine being has divine beauty. But as the form of the divine being it has and is itself divine beauty. And where it is recognised as the form of the divine being it will necessarily be felt as beauty. Inevitably when the perfect divine being declares itself, it also radiates joy in the dignity and power of its divinity, and thus releases the pleasure, desire and enjoyment of which we have spoken, and is in this way, by means of this form, persuasive and convincing. And this persuasive and convincing form must necessarily be called the beauty of God. (para. 31, part 3, pp. 650–9)

Source: *Karl Barth, Church Dogmatics*, 2/1, eds G. W. Bromiley and T. F. Torrance, Edinburgh, T. & T. Clark, 1957.

19.4 Hans Urs von Balthasar, from *The Glory of the Lord, vol. 1, Seeing the Form*

The Swiss theologian von Balthasar (1905–88) conceived his entire oeuvre in terms of a theological aesthetics. In this section of his first volume of The Glory of the Lord, *he outlines his understanding of the relationship between form* (Gestalt) *and splendour* (Glanz). *He indicates how a theological aesthetics is to be developed in two stages: first, as a theory of vision, or fundamental theology and, second, as a theory of rapture, i.e. dogmatic theology.*

The task and the structure of a theological aesthetics

From everything we have reviewed, it now becomes possible to determine tentatively what the task and structure of a theological aesthetics should be. We now know in what direction its object is to be sought and in what way the investigation of this object is to be carried out. But we also know the ways in which such an inquiry may by no means be undertaken. We are, then, both spurred on and warned. Our point of departure was very much a layman's insight into the beautiful. For the present, however, it would be incorrect for us to go beyond this unreflected concept lest we should prejudice our inquiry either philosophically or theologically. We may, however, without prejudice distinguish and relate to each other, albeit in a very preliminary way, two elements in the beautiful which have traditionally controlled every aesthetic and which, with Thomas Aquinas, we could term *species (or forma)* and *lumen (or splendour)* – form (*Gestalt*) and splendour (*Glanz*). As form, the beautiful can be materially grasped and even subjected to numerical calculation as a relationship of numbers, harmony, and the laws of Being. Protestant aesthetics has wholly misunderstood this dimension and even denounced it as heretical, locating then the total essence of beauty in the event in which the light irrupts. Admittedly, form would not be beautiful unless it were fundamentally a sign and appearing of a depth and a fullness that, in themselves and in an abstract sense, remain beyond both our reach and our vision. In this way, the soul manifests itself in the body in various degrees of relationship which Kant and Schiller have described in a strict sense as beauty and as 'the sublime' in the sense of gracefulness and dignity. In this way, too, the Spirit appears in history in a concealed manner; and, in a manner still more concealed due to his infinite freedom and superiority to the world, God manifests himself in his creation and in the order of salvation.

Psychologically, the effect of beautiful forms on the soul may be described in a great variety of ways. But a true grasp of this effect will not be attained unless one brings to bear logical and ethical concepts, concepts of truth and value: in a word, concepts drawn from a comprehensive doctrine of Being.

The form as it appears to us is beautiful only because the delight that it arouses in us is founded upon the fact that, in it, the truth and goodness of the depths of reality itself are manifested and bestowed, and this manifestation and bestowal reveal themselves to us as being something infinitely and inexhaustibly valuable and fascinating. The appearance of the form, as revelation of the depths, is an indissoluble union of two things. It is the real presence of the depths, of the whole of reality, *and* it is a real pointing beyond itself to these depths. In different periods of intellectual history, to be sure, one or the other of these aspects may be emphasised: on the one hand, classical perfection (*Vollendung:* the form which contains the depths), on the other, Romantic boundlessness, infinity (*Unendlichkeit:* the form that transcends itself by pointing beyond to the depths). Be this as it may, however, both aspects are inseparable from one another, and together they constitute the fundamental configuration of Being. We 'behold' the form; but, if we really behold it, it is not as a detached form, rather in its unity with the depths that make their appearance in it. We see form as the splendour, as the glory of Being. We are 'enraptured' by our contemplation of these depths and are 'transported' to them. But, so long as we are dealing with the beautiful, this never happens in such a way that we leave the (horizontal) form behind us in order to plunge (vertically) into the naked depths. When it comes to confronting this structure (in which we encounter all Being both objectively and subjectively), with the contents of Christian theology, it should be clear from the outset that there can be no question of a univocal transposition and application of categories. This must be so because the living God is neither an 'existent' (subordinate to Being) nor 'Being' itself, as it manifests and reveals itself essentially in everything that makes its appearance in form. Protestant theology, therefore, has been wholly right consistently to reject the application to Biblical revelation of the schema inherited from pre-Christian, and especially Greek, philosophy, a schema that distinguished between a 'ground of Being'; and an 'appearance of Being'. But we have already shown elsewhere that this schema exhibits different analogical gradations even in the worldly realm, since the expressions of a free spirit (namely, as word and creative deed) are structured differently from those of organic and sub-spiritual nature, and yet they are not thereby excluded from the schema. But, again to use the analogy in a supereminent sense, what is the creation, reconciliation, and redemption effected by the triune God if not his revelation in and to the world and man? Not a deed that would leave its doer in the background unknown and untouched, but a genuine self-representation on his part, a genuine unfolding of himself in the worldly stuff of nature, man, and history – an event which in a supereminent sense may be called an 'appearance' or 'epiphany'. *Quia per incarnati Verbi mysterium nova mentis nostrae oculis lux tuae claritatis infulsit: ut dum visibiliter Deum cognoscimus, per hunc in invisibilium amorem rapiamur* (Christmas Preface). We should note that in this classical text there is no express reference to 'faith', but to the two things which implicitly contain it: 1. to the 'eyes of our mind' which are struck by a 'new light' from God which then enables them to know visibly – contemplatively (*visibiliter*): an object which is actually 'God', but God as 'mediated' (*per*) by the 'sacramental form of the mystery' (*mysterium*) of the 'enfleshed Word'. 2. to a 'mediating' (second *per*) vision which occasions a 'rapture' and a 'transport' (*rapiamur*) to an 'eros-love' (*amor*) for those 'things unseen' (*invisibilia*) which had announced themselves by appearing in the visibleness and revelation of the Incarnation. In the first point, the emphasis is given to a certain seeing, looking, or 'beholding', and not to any 'hearing' or 'believing'. 'Hearing' is present only implicitly in the reference to the 'Word' become man, just as 'believing' is implied in that what is seen is the mystery that points to the invisible God. But the all-encompassing act that contains within itself the hearing and the believing is a *perception* (*Wahrnehmung*), in the strong sense of a 'taking to oneself' (*nehmen*) of something true (*Wahres*) which is offering itself. For this particular perception of truth, of course, a 'new light' is expressly required which illumines this particular form, a light which at the same time breaks forth from within the form itself. In this way, the 'new light' will at the same time make seeing the form possible and be itself seen along with the form. The *splendour* of the mystery which offers itself in such a way cannot, for this reason, be equated with the other kinds of aesthetic radiance which we encounter in the world. This does not mean, however, that that mysterious *splendour* and this aesthetic radiance are beyond any and every comparison. That we are at all able to speak here of 'seeing' (and not exclusively and categorically of 'hearing') shows that, in spite of all concealment, there *is* nonetheless something to be seen and grasped (*cognoscimus*). It shows, therefore, that man is not merely addressed in a total mystery, as if he were compelled to accept obediently in blind and naked faith something hidden from him, but that something is 'offered' to man by God, indeed offered in such a way that man can see it, understand it, make it his own, and live from it in keeping with his human nature. It is only on this condition that man himself can truly real-ise [sic] what is described in the second point, rather than merely let it *be realized* in him in a passive way. For it is not said explicitly that the *mysterium Christi*, being the *lux tuae claritatis*, is the appearance of God's *amor invisibilis*. This is rather presupposed, while the text goes on straight away to speak of the event whereby man is transported because of having seen the *Deus invisibilis* in a human way. There is a good reason why the word used here is *amor* (*eros*) and not *caritas*. For what is at stake here is the movement effected by seeing what God has shown. This is a movement of the entire person, leading away from himself through the vision towards the invisible God, a movement, furthermore, which the word 'faith' describes only imperfectly, although it is in this movement that faith has its proper 'setting in life' (*Sitz im Leben*). The transport of the soul, however, must here again be understood in a strictly theological way. In other words, it must be understood not as a merely psychological response to something beautiful in a worldly sense which has been encountered through vision, but as the movement of man's whole being away from himself and towards God through Christ, a movement founded on the divine light of grace in the mystery of Christ. But the whole truth of this mystery is that the movement which God (who is the object that is seen in Christ and who enraptures man) effects in man (even in his unwillingness and recalcitrance, due to sin) is co-effected willingly by man through his Christian *eros* and, indeed, on account of the fact that the divine Spirit enthuses and in-spires [sic] man to collaboration. We ought at this point to recall the Areopagite's apology for employing the word *eros* in Christian theology, as well as his emphatic protestation that he is not using it 'in contradiction to Sacred Scripture'. In the opinion of Denys, *eros* captures the sense of the transport of man's being as such far better than does *agape*, and this constitutes for Denys an aesthetic as well as a soteriological statement. For man's transport to God does not stop at the Aristotelian and Neo-Platonic *kinoun hos eromenon* but grounds the latter in an antecedent and condescending divine *ekstasis* in which God is drawn out of himself by *eros* into creation, revelation and Incarnation. . . . Delete from this text [*The Divine Names*, IV, 13], if you will, everything which appears too Neo-Platonic. One will nonetheless have to acknowledge that its substance is genuinely Biblical and consistent with the most authentic covenant-theology of either Testament, a theology that sees the jealous and consuming love of the divine Bridegroom doing its work in his bride in order to raise her up, invite her, and bring her home to the very same answering love. All divine revelation is impregnated with an element of 'enthusiasm' (in the theological sense). . . .

Because God actually effects that which he reveals in the sign, and because in God's order of salvation Plato's idealistic imago-metaphysics and Aristotle's realistic *causa-et-finis* metaphysics actually come together on a higher plane, we can never approach Christian *eros* and Christian beauty from a merely Platonic tradition and expect to interpret them adequately. The enthusiasm which is inherent to the Christian faith is not merely idealistic; it is, rather, an enthusiasm which derives from and is appropriate to actual, realistic Being. This is why God's Word constantly brings the false kind of enthusiasm which hovers about suspended on aestheticist and idealistic proleptical illusions back down to the level of sobriety and truth (1 Thess 5.6–8; 1 Pet 1.13; 4.7; 2 Tim 4.5; Mt 24.42; 25.13; 26.41; Rev 3.2f.; 16.15; etc.). But the Word calls us no less persistently out of the profanity of a worldly life to a 'pneumatic' existence spent 'in spiritual psalms, hymns, odes, singing through grace to God in your hearts' (Col 3.16) – in a word, to that world of prayer in which the Colossians are admonished 'to be watchful in thanksgiving' (4.2). The 'glory' of Christian transfiguration is in no way less resplendent than the transfiguring glory of worldly beauty, but the fact is that the glory of Christ unites splendour and radiance with solid reality, as we see pre-eminently in the Resurrection and its anticipation through faith in Christian life. As Karl Barth has rightly seen, this law extends to the inclusion in Christian beauty of even the Cross and everything else which a worldly aesthetics (even of a realistic kind) discards as no longer bearable. This inclusiveness is not only of the type proposed by a Platonic theory of beauty, which knows how to employ the shadows and the contradictions as stylistic elements of art; it embraces the most abysmal ugliness of sin and hell by virtue of the condescension of divine love, which has brought even sin and hell into that divine art for which there is no human analogue. The conclusion to be drawn from all this is that, just as we can never attain to the living God in any way except through his Son become man, but in this Son we can really attain to God in himself, so, too, we ought never to speak of God's beauty without reference to the form and manner of appearing which he exhibits in salvation-history. The beauty and glory which are proper to God may be inferred and 'read' off from God's epiphany and its incomprehensible glory which is worthy of God himself. But in trying to perceive God's own beauty and glory from the beauty of his manner of appearing, we must neither simply *equate* the two – since we are to be transported *per hunc (Deum visibilem) in invisibilium amorem* – nor ought we to attempt to discover God's beauty by a mere causal inference from the beauty of God's epiphany, for such an inference would *leave this epiphany behind*. We must, rather, make good our *excessus* to God himself with a *theologia negativa* which never detaches itself from its basis in a *theologia positiva*: DUM *visibiliter cognoscimus*. When later on we analyse the Areopagite and John of the Cross – the two theologians who relied most consistently on the apophatic method – we will see that they never divorced it from the cataphatic approach. They could exalt the vertical to such a degree only because they never let go of the horizontal. For this reason they can be considered the two most decidedly aesthetic theologians of Christian history.

God's attribute of beauty can certainly also be examined in the context of a doctrine of the divine attributes. Besides examining God's beauty as manifested by God's actions in his creation, his beauty would also be deduced from the harmony of his essential attributes, and particularly from the Trinity. But such a doctrine of God and the Trinity really speaks to us only when and as long as the *theologia* does not become detached from the *oikonomia*, but rather lets its every formulation and stage of reflection be accompanied and supported by the latter's vivid discernibility.

If this is so, then theological aesthetics must properly be developed in two phases, which are:

1. *The theory of vision* (or fundamental theology): 'aesthetics' in the Kantian sense as a theory about the perception of the form of God's self-revelation.

2. *The theory of rapture* (or dogmatic theology): 'aesthetics' as a theory about the incarnation of God's glory and the consequent elevation of man to participate in that glory. Using the concept 'aesthetics' in this double sense might appear to be a playful fancy. But a little reflection will dispel such an impression, since no theological perception is possible outside the *lux tuae claritatis* and outside the grace that allows us to see, a grace which already belongs objectively to rapture and which subjectively may be said at least to initiate man's transport to God. In theology, there are no 'bare facts' which, in the name of an alleged objectivity of detachment, disinterestedness and impartiality, one could establish like any other worldly facts, without oneself being (both objectively and subjectively) gripped so as to participate in the divine nature (*participatio divinae naturae*). For the object with which we are concerned is man's participation in God which, from God's perspective, is actualised as 'revelation' (culminating in

Christ's Godmanhood) and which, from man's perspective, is actualised as 'faith' (culminating in participation in Christ's Godmanhood). This double and reciprocal *ekstasis* – God's 'venturing forth' to man and man's to God – constitutes the very content of dogmatics, which may thus rightly be presented as a theory of rapture: the *admirabile commercium et conubium* between God and man in Christ as Head and Body.

If this is correct, then it has far-reaching methodological implications. For it would follow that fundamental theology and dogmatic theology – the theory of vision and the theory of rapture – are, in the last analysis, inseparable. To be sure, there is a road which the human spirit takes as it seeks for the Christian truth (*intellectus quaerens fidem*), and this search may be fostered by variously showing and making visible in an appropriate way the form of God's revelation, which conceals itself from the eyes of the world and of history *sub contrario*, as Luther has it. As we have said, however, this road itself already stands in the rays of the divine light, a light which, in an objective sense, makes the form visible and which, in a subjective sense, clarifies and illumines the searching spirit, thus training it in an act and a *habitus* which will become perfect faith once the vision has itself been perfected. In 'dogmatics', moreover, this developing (*wachsende*) and now adult (*erwachsene*) faith continues to grow (*wächst*) as *a fides quaerens intellectum*. But this continued growth is not to be thought of as a leap from the *praeambula fidei* of fundamental theology and the evidence it provides, as from a springboard which is then left behind – a leap to pure fiducial faith. Rather, the facts of revelation are perceived initially in the light of grace, and faith grows in such a way that it allows the self-evidence of these facts – an evidence that itself was 'enrapturing' from the outset – to continue to unfold according to its own laws and principles. In this manner, through the growth of the mysteries of faith, for which I can provide no evidence of my own, the image in which God initially appeared and illumined me deepens and acquires traits that reveal new and even deeper aspects of its rightness. What I cannot verify in itself (*in propiis causis*) may nevertheless be verified indirectly in the understanding of faith by the manner in which it is reflected and echoed in the form of revelation. Although he can elsewhere distinguish very clearly between 'faith' and 'vision', Paul, in the *locus classicus* of his theological aesthetics, nevertheless speaks of a 'vision of the Lord's splendour with unveiled face', through which 'we are transformed into the same image' (2 Cor 3.18). Paul thus unites vision and rapture as a single process. We shall have to keep the unity constantly in mind as we deal separately in what follows with fundamental theology and dogmatic theology. (Ch. 1, para. 7, pp. 117–27)

Source: Hans Urs von Balthasar, *The Glory of the Lord, A Theological Aesthetics, vol. 1, Seeing the Form*, trans. Erasmo Leiva-Merikakis, ed. Joseph Fessio, SJ and John Riches, Edinburgh, T. & T. Clark, 1982.

19.5 Jacques Maritain, from *Art and Scholasticism*

French Neo-Thomist philosopher Maritain (1882–1973), who taught in Paris, Toronto and Princeton, sought to relate the philosophy of Aquinas to various strands in philosophy and also to art and poetry. In this extract this is clearly evident. He refers to Aquinas in expounding his view on beauty and on the beauty of the Christ. Like Thomas, he describes the work of the artist in terms of being analogous to, and continuing, divine creation.

Art and Beauty . . . If this is so, it is because the beautiful belongs to the order of the *transcendentals*, that is to say, objects of thought which transcend every limit of genus or category, and which do not allow themselves to be enclosed in any class, because they imbue everything and are to be found everywhere. Like the one, the true and the good, the beautiful is *being* itself considered from a certain aspect; it is a property of being. It is not an accident superadded to being, it adds to being only a relation of reason: it is being considered as delighting, by the mere intuition of it, an intellectual nature. Thus everything is beautiful, just as everything is good, at least in a certain relation. And as being is everywhere present and everywhere varied the beautiful likewise is diffused everywhere and is everywhere varied. Like being and the other transcendentals, it is essentially *analogous*, that is to say, it is predicated for diverse reasons, *sub diversa ratione*, of the diverse subjects of which it is predicated: each kind of being *is* in its own way, is *good* in its own way, is *beautiful* in its own way.

Analogous concepts are predicated of God pre-eminently; in Him the perfection they designate exists in a 'formal-eminent' manner, in the pure and infinite state. God is their 'sovereign analogue', and they are to be met with again in things only as a dispersed and prismatized reflection of the countenance of God. Thus Beauty is one of the divine names.

God is beautiful. He is the most beautiful of beings, because, as Denis the Areopagite and Saint Thomas explain, His beauty is without alteration or vicissitude, without increase or diminution; and because it is not as the beauty of things, all of which have a particularized beauty, *particulatam pulchritudinem, sicut et particulatam naturam*. He is beautiful through Himself and in Himself, beautiful absolutely.

He is beautiful to the extreme (*superpulcher*), because in the perfectly simple unity of His nature there pre-exists in a super-excellent manner the fountain of all beauty.

He is beauty itself, because He gives beauty to all created beings, according to the particular nature of each, and because He is the cause of all consonance and all brightness. Every form indeed, that is to say, every light, is 'a certain irradiation proceeding from the first brightness', 'a participation in the divine brightness'. And every consonance or every harmony, every concord, every friendship and every union whatsoever among beings proceeds from the divine beauty, the primordial and super-eminent type of all consonance, which gathers all things together and which calls them all to itself, meriting well in this 'the name *xalós* which derives from "to call" '. Thus 'the beauty of anything created is nothing else than a similitude of divine beauty participated in by things', and, on the other hand, as every form is a principle of being and as every consonance or every harmony is preservative of being, it must be said that divine beauty is the cause of the being of all that is. *Ex divina pulchritudine esse omnium derivatur.*

In the Trinity, Saint Thomas adds, the name Beauty is attributed most fittingly to the Son. As for integrity or perfection, He has truly and perfectly in Himself, without the least diminution, the nature of the Father. As for due proportion or consonance, He is the express and perfect image of the Father: and it is proportion which befits the image as such. As for radiance, finally, He is the Word, the light and the splendour of the intellect, 'perfect Word to Whom nothing is lacking, and, so to speak, art of Almighty God'.

Beauty, therefore, belongs to the transcendental and metaphysical order. This is why it tends of itself to draw the soul beyond the created. (Ch. 5, pp. 30–2)

The Purity of Art . . . Art, then, remains fundamentally inventive and creative. It is the faculty of producing, not of course *ex nihilo*, but from a pre-existing matter, a new creature, an original being, capable of stirring in turn a human soul. This new creature is the fruit of a spiritual marriage which joins the activity of the artist to the passivity of a given matter.

Hence in the artist the feeling of his peculiar dignity. He is as it were an associate of God in the making of beautiful works; by developing the powers placed in him by the Creator – for 'every perfect gift is from above, coming down from the Father of lights' – and by making use of created matter, he creates, so to speak, at second remove. *Operatio artis fundatur super operationem naturae, et haec super creationem.*

Artistic creation does not copy God's creation, it continues it. And just as the trace and the image of God appear in His creatures, so the human stamp is imprinted on the work of art – the full stamp, sensitive and spiritual, not only that of the hands, but of the whole soul. Before the work of art passes from art into the matter, by a transitive action, the very conception of the art has had to emerge from within the soul, by an immanent and vital action, like the emergence of the mental word. *Processus artis est duplex, scilicet artis a corde artificis, et artificiatorum ab arte.*

If the artist studies and cherishes nature as much as and a great deal more than the works of the masters, it is not in order to copy it, but in order to *base himself* on it; and it is because it is not enough for him to be the pupil of the masters: he must be the pupil of God, for God knows the rules governing the making of beautiful works. Nature is essentially of concern to the artist only because it is a derivation of the divine art in things, *ratio artis divinae indita rebus.* The artist, whether he knows it or not, consults God in looking at things. . . .

Nature is thus the first exciter and the first guide of the artist, and not an example to be copied slavishly. Ask the true painters what their need of nature is. They fear her and revere her, but with a chaste fear, not with a slavish one. They imitate her, but with an imitation that is truly filial, and according to the creative agility of the spirit, not with a literal and servile imitation. One day, after a walk in the wintertime, Rouault told me he had just discovered, by looking at snow-clad fields in the sunshine, how to paint the white trees of spring. 'The model,' said Renoir for his part, 'is there only to set me on fire, to enable me to dare things that I could not invent without it. . . . And it makes me come a cropper if I throw myself too much into it.' Such is the liberty of the sons of the Creator.

Art has not to defend itself only against the allurements of manual dexterity (or of that other cleverness which is *taste*) and against slavish imitation. Other foreign elements also threaten its purity. For example, the beauty to which it tends produces a delight, but it is the high delight of the spirit, which is the exact contrary of what is called pleasure, or the pleasant tickling of the sensibility; and if art seeks to please, it betrays, and becomes deceitful. Similarly, its *effect* is to produce emotion, but if it *aims* at emotion, at affecting the appetites or arousing the passions, it falsifies itself, and thus another element of lie enters into it.

This is as true of music as it is of the other arts. Music no doubt has this peculiarity that, signifying with its rhythms and its sounds the very movements of the soul – *cantare amantis est* – it produces, in producing emotion, precisely what it signifies. But this production is not what it aims at, any more than a representation or a description of the emotions is. The emotions which it makes present to the soul by sounds and by rhythms, are the *matter* through which it must give us the felt joy of a spiritual form, of a transcendent order, of the radiance of being. Thus music, like tragedy, purifies the passions, by developing them within the limits and in the order of beauty, by harmonizing them with the intellect, in a harmony that fallen nature experiences nowhere else. . . .

I willingly accept the ascendancy of the *object* which the artist has conceived and which he lays before my eyes; I then abandon myself unreservedly to the emotion which in him and in me springs from a same beauty, from a same transcendental in which we communicate. But I refuse to accept the ascendancy of an art which contrives suggestive means by which to seduce my subconscious, I resist an emotion which the will of a man seeks to impose upon me. The artist must be as objective as the man of science, in the sense that he must think of the spectator only in order to present him with the beautiful, or the *well-made*, just as the man of science thinks of his listener only in order to present him with the true. The cathedral builders did not harbour any sort of thesis. They were, in Dulac's fine phrase, 'men unaware of themselves'. They neither wished to demonstrate the propriety of Christian dogma nor to suggest by some artifice a *Christian emotion*. They even thought a great deal less of making a beautiful work than of doing good work. They were men of Faith, and as they were, so they worked. Their work revealed the truth of God, but without *doing it intentionally*, and because of not doing it intentionally. (Ch. 7, pp. 60–3)

Source: Jacques Maritain, *Art and Scholasticism* and *The Frontiers of Poetry*, trans. Joseph W. Evans, New York, Charles Scribner's Sons, 1962.

19.6 Charles Hartshorne, from *Man's Vision of God*

This North American theologian's idea of God, which includes process and change, is apparent in this section, too, when he argues that divine beauty is constituted by the fact that God in Godself is both unity and contrast. Moreover, he notes that God can feel more intensely than all other beings. Beauty is continuously emerging in the work of artists, absolute beauty can be understood as the 'abstract eternal principle of cosmic search for beauty' and as a concretely attained 'ever growing totality of beauty'.

God and the Beautiful . . . The denial of parts and of change to God not only deprives God of contrast within himself, and so of beauty, but it also robs him of unity, and so of beauty in his relation to the world. For if this relation is to be beautiful, then, in spite of the infinite contrast between creator and creature, there must also be a no less profound similarity. The creature must really be the image of God, and that in all his being, for man must be a variation on the cosmic theme, which is divinity. Here traditional theology tended to sacrifice unity to diversity. Within God the diversity of contingent things was lacking; but between God and things there was little but the sheer contrast between the un-created creator and the uncreative creature, the purely necessary and the contingent. Man changes; God simply does not. Man has a body; God has none. Man alters, but cannot, like God, create substance. Thus while God within was ugly by defect of variety, reality, as composed of God and the world, was ugly by defect of unity, and the two defects were clearly two sides of the same defect. For the only way to unify God with his creatures is to regard the unity of God's being (the supremacy of which lies in its inclusiveness) as the unity of reality as such. And the only way to give maximal diversity as well as unity to God is to allow that his unity genuinely embraces all that is, with all the variety which it really has. (Ch. 6, p. 219)

Aesthetics equally condemns the ideas of a merely perfect and of a merely imperfect deity (first- and third-type theisms). For in either case there is failure of contrast not only not compensated for by more adequate unity but – as we have seen already for first-type doctrine – aggravated by an equal failure of unity. In a wholly imperfect deity the contrast of perfect and perfectible would be lacking; and also such a deity by definition could not represent maximal (perfect) unity, or adequate unification of all that is. He must fall short somewhere in his unification of reality. His sympathy could not integrate all the riches of the world and could not parallel all of its variety.

On the other hand, in the 'pure actuality' of first-type theism all contrast vanishes. In God so defined there is either no contrast or, what comes to the same, all possible contrast. For to compose a pattern of all possible contrasts, rejecting none, is to compose no pattern and to lose all contrasts in the sheer continuity of the merely potential (not 'actual' at all). It is the possible (grounded in the primordial or abstract nature of God) that is above definite diversity and composition. We get definiteness by restricting the possible, and that restriction *is* definiteness. You may in a picture combine blue with yellow of some shade, but to combine all hues of yellow with all hues of blue is the same as to do nothing aesthetically. You may go on to other parts of your picture and use more and more hues in these additional parts, but the rejected possible combinations of hue and shape in the first-named parts are rejected once for all, since other parts are other parts because in some characters they fail to duplicate the given parts, either as they are or as they might have been had certain choices been made otherwise. . . . God may enjoy Shelley and Keats together in a manner quite impossible to Shelley or Keats; but what no aesthetic experience can do is to combine the Keats or Shelley that actually was with the Keats or Shelley that might have been, had choices of these men fallen otherwise. For the incompatibility of alternative possibilities is the meaning of possibility, and of all distinctions whatever. The poems Keats could have written no one else in all past or future cosmic history ever could write; for other individuals must, by the very meaning of individuality, lack the personality which is the theme expressed potentially in all the possible states of Keats. The once potential Keats is now forever impossible, and impossible even for God, in the same way as round squares are impossible for him, that is, because it is nonsense that something should be known by omniscience as both actual and not actual, or known as not actual, yet as yielding all the contrasts it would have exhibited had it been actual. That would merely be to say that the actualisation of the potential is aesthetically superfluous, and to really believe that would be to cease to actualise, to cease to live.

Thus aesthetics seems to be adequate to decide between the three types of doctrine, provided only one admits that a thoroughly or infinitely ugly view of the cosmos would be a more radical sacrifice of values – including intellectual values, for what is truth *as appealing* but intellectual beauty? – than anyone can really make except in words; so that we must regard atheism or first- or third-type theism as pretences, not real beliefs. One can admit ugly aspects of the world; but to make ugliness the essential pervasive feature, as atheism implicitly does – is that more than a gesture, in beings who continue to go about their business in the world? Or if they do not do so, then how is one to argue with them, if their business be philosophy?

But aesthetics throws yet other light upon theology. Theologians have often done some justice to the beauty of the world, so far as it was defined through structure as correlated with intellect. The world as relational is the satisfying object of mind as the sense for relations. Also, even simple qualities were sometimes admitted to have aesthetic value, as in their simplicity clearly apprehended and so satisfyingly accessible to our awareness. Thus Thomas says 'clarity' is a feature of the beautiful, including brilliance or vividness as an aspect of clarity. And God, as supreme knower, corresponds to the world as clear, as God as will does to the world as active. But knowing as sense for relations is distinguishable from knowing as mere having of qualities. There seems but one way to know a quality, and that is to feel it. There is nothing in it to think, if by thought is meant relating; for a simple quality is not a relationship, but the term without which relations would not be possible, as the complex presupposes the simple. God must equally know qualities and relations, and how he could know a quality except by having it as a feeling-tone, a quality of his experience itself, we have not the faintest clue in experience. There is no intellectual content whatever to the blueness of blue except such as presupposes the non-intellectual, the purely sensory content. A God who knows but never feels, who has no feeling-tones, but only superintellection, or superintuition entirely above the contrast between terms and relations, is an aesthetically hideous or empty conception.

Aesthetics is the study which has finally brought philosophy to take feeling and quality seriously as positive excellences, not defects. It is time that we incorporated this insight into our speculations about God. Either feeling is or it is not reducible to a special case of thinking or willing (or to mere matter in motion); and if it is not, then being as such involves it. For being as such is simply the irreducibles in their unity. Only the idea of God exhibits the unity plainly and vividly, and this only if God be conceived not as without feeling but as more rich in feeling-tones than any other being, not as without the experience of potency but as equally supreme in achieved actuality and in potency of actuality to come. We must preserve contrasts, all of them (except those between something and nothing, e.g., knowledge and ignorance, and even such contrasts as vicariously enjoyed), in God, while ascribing to him a matchless power to hold these contrasts together (so far as intrinsically compatible) in one experience.

It is sometimes said that aesthetics is concerned with essences, not existences, as though possibility were enough for beauty. But I have yet to meet a man who enjoyed merely possible symphonies as much as actual ones. . . .

It may be held that to a strong enough imagination possibles would be as beautiful as actuals. But this raises the question whether or not the completely imagined would be any different from the completely perceived, that is, the actual. It is not to be assumed that 'imagination' is in essence a dealing with the 'possible' but only accidentally a dealing with it as more or less indefinite, and hence aesthetically unsatisfactory. If the possible is not distinguished from the actual by deficient definiteness, how is it distinguished? And if the possible is as good as the actual, then why actualise? . . .

The contrasts which give life its value need not be sacrificed in forming the conception of the highest value; rather, we must give to 'highest' just such meaning as will express and preserve, not annul, these contrasts, so that the unity of the highest will be a unity of something – not just bare unity. As Fechner so well said, the God of traditional theology (A) is empty unity, as the world of traditional theology is ununified plurality. The 'form of forms' lacked content, the content lacked an inclusive form. The cosmic art is the content-with-the-form, the form-with-the-content. It is the one living experience, sublime in its infinite past and present, sublime in its potencies for the future, sublime in the contrast between these, sublime in its multiplicity and variety of parts, sublime in the wholeness to which their partiality is relative. God is neither a poem containing all possible poems – a hideous nightmare of the incompossible [sic] – nor is he the mere sum of all actual poems, nor yet merely one poem among others, nor finally is he sheerly above all definite patterns and forms. He is rather the never ending poem of which all actual poems are phrases, all cosmic epochs yet elapsed are verses, and whose 'to be continued' is the promise of infinite poetic creation to come. He is the poet as enjoying this poem, the poem as the life of the poet down to the given present. But the phrases of the cosmic poem are themselves poets enjoying their poems. In this respect many aesthetic analogies are false. Thus in poetry words are mere carriers of meaning, they do not possess, enjoy, meanings. Much human art manipulates materials similarly regarded as not themselves enjoying any of the aesthetic experience they make possible. The chorus director or stage manager is in a way closer to God than the poet or painter, who is not an artist dealing, as God does, with lesser artists, recognised as such. (The molecules of pigment or of ink may indeed be sentient, and enjoy rudimentary harmony as well as suffer from rudimentary discord, but this is of no interest to the human artist.) God's art is superior to man's not because he 'controls' his materials more absolutely, but almost the contrary, because he knows how to set the limits within which the living units of his work are to control themselves, to do as they happen to please, not precisely as even he could foresee. Of course this means that the resulting art work cannot exhibit 'perfect' harmony (whatever that would be), and certainly discord, evil, hatred, suffering exist in God's world if anything exists there. The play of the world is a tragic as well as comic play, for players and for playwright. The social nature of existence makes tragedy in principle, though not in particular, inevitable.

God is the cosmic 'adventure' (Whitehead) integrating all real adventures as they occur, without ever failing in readiness to realise new states out of the divine potency, which is indeed 'beyond number' and definite form, yet is of value only because number and form come out of it. God is not the super-staleness of the never new, the never young, the monomania-like poverty – vainly called super-richness – of the merely absolute (just as he is not the blind chaos of the merely relative). As Fechner said, every child that comes into the world and brings a new note of freshness, every youth for whom the world looks young, contributes this freshness – this slightly novel beauty of feeling as well as this feeling of novelty – to God, who is literally the youngest and the oldest of all beings, the richest in accumulated experiences, and consequently the most equipped with suitable background for diverse new ones, as the man with a varied past is apt to have the most capacity to assimilate further variety.

If such a cosmic adventurer did not exist, we should from an aesthetic point of view be compelled, in Voltaire's phrase, to invent him. The ideal by which the artist is inspired is not any notion of 'absolute beauty' as either a supreme sample or a fixed total of possible beauty. The artist wishes, taking the past of culture as given, to add something new which is both intrinsically valuable or enjoyable, and is appropriate to, enjoyable together with, that past, though by no means deducible from it. He wishes in a small way to simulate the cosmic adventure, to create a note in the next phase of that adventure as visible from his corner of the world. The reformer seeking new beauties of social relationship is essentially in the same attitude, but his 'corner' is somewhat different. The only static 'beauty as such' or timeless absolute which the artist ever contemplates, even subconsciously, is purely abstract, such as the principle of unity in contrast; not any definite unity in contrast or any absolute sum of such unities (which would have neither unity nor contrast since it would be nothing), but the purely general requirement. Let there be as much unity in contrast as possible, both within the new pattern and between it and the old patterns – so that the pattern of ongoing life shall be unified and diversified. (I have adapted this thought in part from Van Meter Ames.) This is the aesthetic imperative which the artist feels laid upon him by the scheme of things, and it is the voice of God as truly as any other imperative. As Berdyaev says, the service of God consists, not in rule-conforming correctness of behaviour, but in that creativeness of new values together with respect for old ones by which man can most truly imitate the ever-lasting creator. But the artist has also a concrete ideal, which is by no means timeless. This is his glimpse of the concrete, ever newly enriched beauty of the present actual world; for of what avail would it be to contribute beautiful parts to a whole which was mere chaos or monotony or nothingness in terms of value? Indeed, if the beauty of experience which the artist creates for men is to really 'exist' in the universe, this universe must as a whole possess a value which exactly provides for his contribution. Thus an abstract eternal principle of cosmic search for beauty, and a concrete ever growing totality of beauty actually achieved, provide the two senses in which 'absolute beauty' can rightly be spoken of. Neither one sense nor the other nor both together constitutes an entity absolute or perfect in every sense which these words have sometimes been supposed to bear, but they represent so much of perfection as can really be conceived. (Ch. 6, pp. 221–9)

Source: Charles Hartshorne, *Man's Vision of God and the Logic of Theism*, Hamden, CT, Archon Books, 1964.

19.7 Jürgen Moltmann, from *Theology and Joy*

Moltmann (b. 1926), emeritus of Tübingen University, has been highly influential in the latter three decades of the twentieth century, especially through his contributions on the theology of the Cross, on hope and the Trinity. In this extract he emphasizes the need for joy in Christian life, as otherwise faith declines into legalism and moralism. The vision of God's glory and splendour is revealed in the Crucified, which leads to hope and transformation of self and of the world.

Is God beautiful? . . . The concept which in biblical usage complements that of God's dominion is the *glory of God*. It is God's display of splendour, his beauty and his kindness or loveliness. On man's side, the corresponding terms are amazement, adoration and praise; that is, freedom which expresses itself in gratitude, enjoyment and pleasure in the presence of beauty. Another corresponding term is love, a love which does not merely manifest itself ethically in love to the neighbour but also aesthetically in festive play before God.

The one-sided emphasis on the dominion of God in the Western church, especially in Protestantism, has subjected Christian existence to judicial and moral categories. Theology describes Christ as prophet, priest and king, but of doxology and the 'transfiguration of Christ', which is of central importance to the Eastern church, little has remained. The aesthetic categories of the new freedom have given way to the moral categories of the new law and the new obedience. There are many who argue all too hastily that if faith liberates us from the law, from guilt and godless bonds, then *freedom from* is not enough; we must discover the *for what of freedom* as well. So they are searching for new laws and goals of action. But Paul has said in Galatians 5.1, 'For freedom Christ has set us free', and not for a new set of laws. This liberation for freedom is not just a liberation from an old law to a new one, but also a liberation from the compulsion and coercion to act in the first place. We are not merely set free from an old, alien law, but we are, so to speak, set free even from the law of our own liberty. This freedom from the coercion to act manifests itself as festive *rejoicing in freedom*.

In the Old Testament tradition the term 'glory of God' is used in association with special theophanies and has a specific meaning. It describes an awareness both of the *fear of Yahweh* and the *glory of Yahweh*. Hence the *kabod* of Yahweh has pronounced mystic traits. Psalm 97 tells of the glory of God in thunder, lightning and all-consuming fire. In the prophet Ezekiel it appears as storm, cloud, lightning and the roar of water. The redacted priestly tradition takes it to be a glowing fiery substance. In each case it is something men cannot bear. 'For man shall not see me and live' (Exod 33.20). Therefore Moses is asked to hide in the cleft of a rock, when he is chosen to behold the back of the passing *beauty of Yahweh* and to remain alive (Exod 33). After his encounter with God on the mountain, his face reveals an unbearable brightness which frightens the people of Israel so that he has to cover it with a veil. If in the Old Testament the 'glory of God' can be called beautiful, then it is only in the sense of the religious poet Rilke's *Duineser Elegien*: 'For the beautiful is nothing but the beginning of the terrible, which we are just barely able to endure; and we admire it so because it calmly refuses to destroy us.' The Hebrew traditions never attached special importance to events of this kind. After all, they cannot be repeated. The records of these encounters with God consistently stressed the 'word of God' rather than the visible circumstances in which they 'happened'. But when the prophets proclaimed the coming dominion of God in words of judgment and promise, all these words of God, which destroy history and announce future, were in the last analysis taken by them as signs of a visible theophany of God, that is of the glory of God with which all the earth shall be filled. The historical words declaring God's will as law and comfort point to God's ultimate and universal glorification, when he himself shall dwell among us in the new creation. Hearing the word of God then points to the final vision of his glory which is to come. The *hope for a vision of God* has its roots not only in the Greek tradition but – in this eschatological sense – in the Hebrew tradition as well. Then no man will have to teach another. For they shall all see him as he is, face to face, says Jeremiah 31.34. In the New Testament also, *doxa* signifies divine honour, divine splendour, divine power and visible divine brightness. The term *'doxa'* describes both the divinity of the father and the divinity of the son. By the *doxa* of the father Jesus is resurrected from shameful death (Rom 6.4). God has raised him from the dead and given him the glory (1 Peter 1.21). While in the Old Testament the glory of God is the epitome of the anticipated future of God, the resurrection of the crucified from the dead signifies his resurrection into that very future. The pronouncements about God's glory may therefore be applied to Jesus as well. Since he has been raised into the glory of the coming God, that glory has already entered the sufferings of this time through him and through his fate. Since he has been raised into God's future, that future in turn has already come into the present through him. Therefore the 'lord of glory' (1 Cor 2.8) also stands for the 'God of glory' (Acts 7.2). The brightness of divine glory is reflected in the face of Christ and illuminates the hearts of men through him, just as on the first day of creation the creator 'let light shine out of darkness' (2 Cor 4.6).

In the Synoptic Gospels divine brightness appears at the birth and transfiguration of Jesus. In other passages dealing with the earthly life of Jesus the Synoptics rarely use the term, reserving it rather for the manifestations of the risen Christ. Only John identifies the exalted Christ completely with the earthly Jesus and speaks of the *doxa* of the earthly Jesus as well. While he too regards awareness of the glory of Jesus as a matter of faith and not of direct sight, still such faith paradoxically sees the glory of Christ in his suffering and death: The crucifixion of Jesus in shame is his glory. His degradation is his exaltation. This means that God has glorified himself in him who has become the servant of all; he has revealed his unbearable brightness in him who died the death of the forsaken for the forsaken; he has shown his honour by making the shame of Jesus on the cross his own shame. This implies a radical shift in our understanding of the glory of God. Masters surround themselves with the splendour of their riches, kings with the honour of their authority, even nations with their glory. But God reveals his strength in the weak, his honour, in lowliness and his splendour in the cross of Christ. His glory is not the splendour of otherworldly superior power but the beauty of love which empties itself without losing itself and forgives without giving itself away. If then the glory of God manifests its brightness on this earth in the face of him who was crucified by its laws and powers, it follows that this law and these powers no longer are glorious and need no longer be feared or adored. He who in the world's view has been disgraced by death on the gallows as a common criminal has then been changed into the one who is most highly exalted. The *glory of the crucified God* leads of necessity to a transformation of all values and takes away the glory from those who have proclaimed themselves divine.

Faith owes its liberty to the awareness of this *crucified God*. In the crucified Christ it recognises the divine right of grace which justifies those who have no rights. In him it also becomes aware of the creative love of God which makes the ugly lovable. Hence, it recognises in him also the beauty of God which gives joy to those who mourn. So the hope of faith points to full participation in the glory of God. Just as the believer is justified by 'faith for faith' (Rom 1.17), he is also being changed 'from glory to glory' (2 Cor 3.18). When by faith he lifts his head from the dust because salvation is near, he also reflects the glory of God 'with unveiled face' (2 Cor 3.18) and need no longer cover himself for fear or shame. He is filled with the 'hope of glory' (Col 1.27). Dogmatic tradition denotes the justification of the godless as the beginning of their glorification and their glorification as the fulfilment of their justification.

But what do we mean by the *glorification of man*? The First Epistle of John has pointed out that 'it does not yet appear what we shall be, but we know that when he' – namely God himself – 'appears we shall be like him' (1 John 3.2). Being a child of God by faith then means being equal with God. This does not imply an apotheosis of man, where man puts himself into God's place, but it does mean man's ultimate transformation to complete conformity with the visible God by seeing him face to face. It is the hope of the Christian faith that the *eritis sicut Deus* of the serpent in the Garden of Eden will actually be fulfilled – but on God's initiative. What is meant here is not just a restoration of man's pure creature-hood, but beyond this a much closer fellowship with God of which we have a foretaste on earth in the fellowship with Christ. Paul states emphatically that he is not merely speaking in a spiritual sense when he talks about the transformation of our 'lowly body' into the new 'glorious body' (Phil 3.21).

If after this brief excursion into the biblical use of the language about *glory* we now return to the problem of the *relation between ethics and aesthetics*, we must note that these are inseparable both in our awareness of God and in the life of faith. We experience God's dominion equally as his glory and as his beauty and as his sovereignty. His glory cannot be reduced to his dominion and his dominion cannot be reduced to his glory. One interprets the other and protects it from misunderstandings. The beautiful in God is what makes us rejoice in him. So, in corresponding to him and answering him, man's obedience is joined together with his 'new son'. Without the free play of imagination and songs of praise the new obedience deteriorates into *legalism*. Christian living would become a matter of watching out for things one is not allowed to do. But with-out concrete obedience – which means without physical, social and political changes – the lovely songs and celebrations of freedom become empty phrases. 'We have no right to chant in the Gregorian mode if we fail to cry out for the Jews,' Bonhoeffer justifiably reproached the church at a time when the Hitler regime was persecuting the Jews and the church had inwardly emigrated into liturgy. Yet Bonhoeffer himself was very fond of chanting in the Gregorian mode. Perhaps he was so outraged and cried out against the plight of the silenced Jews because he wanted to sing with them in freedom.

But it is said, 'Man shall not see me [God] and live' (Exod 33.20). 'It is a fearful thing to fall into the hands of the living God' (Heb 10.31). So we can 'see' God only by dying to him and being born out of him to new life. Where the believing fellowship with Christ means being baptised into his death, it carries out that dying. Where the believing fellowship with Christ means living with him, the rebirth of hope anticipates that seeing. The glorification of man begins with his awareness of God's justifying love. So the believer is already seeing God, but he is seeing him in the mode of hope and return. Taking part in Christ's visible suffering in the world, the believer shares in Christ's invisible glory. When a man so 'dies' and loses his life, he is seeing God. From the Christian point of view it may therefore be justified to turn Rilke's verse around, awful though this may sound: 'For the terrible is but the beginning of beauty.' The *vision of God* comes to life by following the crucified with permanent *repentance* and through constant *changing* of existing conditions. It cannot be obtained apart from this. Permanent repentance is the daily dying of the old man and the renewal of the inner, the new man. This is painful but constitutes only the reverse side of rejoic-ing in hope. Transfiguration cannot be demonstrated on a mountain away from the world. Even the transfiguration of Jesus took place on the road to Jerusalem and the cross. The transfiguration of the unveiled face must be demonstrated in a suffering and struggling transformation which involves changing oneself and existing conditions so that man, together with other men, may be conformed to his future.

Even if the practice of transfiguration and of the vision of God is repentance and change in the footsteps of Christ, they are not painful efforts which we must force ourselves to endure. *Repentance is joy*, as Julius Schniewind has exegeti-cally shown us. Man is not liberated from his old nature by imperatives to be new and to change, but he rejoices in the new which makes him free and lifts him beyond himself. Where repentance is understood as a spiritual return to the evil and rejected past, it deals in self-accusation, contrition, sackcloth and ashes. But when repentance is a return to the future, it becomes concrete in rejoicing, in new self-confidence and in love. Even then we may happen to be mourning, but we can accept the past without loss of identity since we can be another person and have moved beyond ourselves. The journey of Henry IV to Canossa was no repentance. The Occidental tradition of repentance placed too much emphasis on the dying of the old man and thus became legalistic – and not only in the church. It has been unable to demonstrate either practically or theoretically the gospel of the joy of God and the liberation of man. But if repentance as return to the future already is rejoicing in freedom, then out of that joy it should also be possible to bring about changes of unjust and oppressive social and political conditions. We must only see beyond the moral necessity of repentance and learn to rejoice in it. The rule of law spoils everything, even the revolution of freedom. (pp. 58–64)

Source: Jürgen Moltmann, *Theology and Joy*, London, SCM Press, 1973.

19.8 Bernard Häring, from *Free and Faithful in Christ*

In the development of a contemporary Catholic moral theology, the German theologian and Redemptorist Häring (1911–98) has played a major role. He proposed a non-legalist ethics. Here he emphasizes the essential connection between the good, the true and the beautiful. Like von Balthasar, he argues morality without beauty declines into dull rules, coldness and pettiness.

Beauty as a Dimension of God's Revelation

The mystery that binds and liberates To dismiss the beautiful as something superfluous is to make life miserable, mean, barren. For a Christian who knows and adores God's glory and majesty, disparagement of the beautiful is betrayal of the Spirit, for beauty is a splendour of the true and the good. In it man senses the attractive power of all that is good and true. One who, in all his being, knows truth and knows goodness is already caught by the love of the beautiful.

Beauty does not unfold itself to cold reasoning or to calculations of utility; it communicates its reality only through loving contemplation. Its radiance fills us with delight and lifts our spirits. The believer regards it as reflection of the Spirit in whom the human mind and heart repose, a blessed repose in truth and goodness beyond every purposiveness.

We do not know how angels might grasp the beautiful, but we do know that the human person experiences it most vitally and vividly in the totality of his or her being. Visible, audible, embodied beauty is in perfect harmony with the nature of the human person. The divine Artist expresses his message in sound, colour, figure. He shares the knowledge of the true and the good in such a way that their splendour speaks to the human heart and spirit, filling them with rapture.

We do not experience beauty as an addition to truth and goodness. The beautiful is as extensive as being. 'The true and the good – being – is beautiful, that is, joy and bliss of spirit.' As the true and the good, so also the beautiful is a basis for fellowship and community of heart and mind. The new heaven and the new earth which we are expecting is the community in truth, in goodness, in love and joy, basking in God's beauty. The human community, insofar as it is on the way to the blessed community of love, cannot dispense with the beautiful and its gentle power to unite people in true and loving fellowship. . . .

All the created beauty and the glory of salvation history come from the mystery of the triune God and turn our eyes and our hearts to it. The primordial source of all beauty and all honour in heaven and on earth is the glory which God possesses in his own intimate life. In his eternal Word the Father communicates all his love, his truth, his glory to the Son. In his Son he sees reflected his own infinite beauty and majesty. And the Son, with equal love, communicates himself entirely to the Father in the love-glow of the Holy Spirit. The Holy Spirit, self-giving love, is the Spirit of glory. From all eternity before the seraphim chanted their 'Holy, holy, holy', God in his intimate triune life and love celebrates the holy Word and response of glory. The Father honours the Son, reflection of his splendour; the Son honours the Father in the Holy Spirit. Father and Son glorify the Spirit of love.

Since the triune love of God is fullness of being and beauty itself, where there is life in mutual love there is mutual honour, beauty, the splendour of truth and love. The contemplation of the eternal beauty of God stirred Augustine to exclaim in ecstasy, 'How beautiful is everything, since you have made it, but how ineffably more beautiful are you, the Creator of all this.'

Uncreated beauty becomes fully visible in human form in the Word incarnate. 'We saw his glory, such glory as befits the Father's only Son, full of grace and truth' (Jn 1.14). This goes far beyond the cloud of light which the people of the Old Testament saw over the Ark of the Covenant in the temple. The greatest beauty is that which shines forth in the countenance of Jesus Christ. Eternal beauty has become man. 'It was there from the beginning; we have heard it; we have seen it with our own eyes; we looked upon it and felt it with our own hands; and it is of this we tell' (1 Jn 1.1).

Here again we are faced with the contrast harmony of concealment and unconcealment. The life of Jesus, and especially the Paschal Mystery, speaks also of the hiddenness of the divine glory. Only those who follow the lowliness, the *kenosis* of the Son of God will see his glory and share in it. 'Let your bearing towards one another arise out of your life in Christ Jesus. For the divine nature was his from the first; yet he did not prize his equality with God, but made himself nothing, assuming the nature of a slave. Bearing the human likeness, revealed in human shape, he humbled himself and, in obedience, accepted death – death on a cross. Therefore God raised him to the heights' (Phil 2.5–10).

A morality of beauty and glory does not overlook the fulfilment of the prophecy: 'He had no beauty, no majesty to draw our eyes, no grace to make us delight in him; his form disfigured, lost all the likeness of a man, his beauty changed beyond human semblance' (Is 53.2). He whose name is Beauty took upon himself our misery. For such was the consequence of sin that man no longer possessed the glory, the beauty and the right to honour which God had originally designed for him. Hence he who is the brightness of the Father's glory humbled himself to the ignominy of the cross in order to restore grace to all, and to grant a share in the Father's glory to all those who confess him as the Lord, 'to the glory of God the Father' (Phil 2.11).

We cannot separate beauty and honour from its source, the divine glory. Only by joining Christ in the glorification of the Father can we live in the truth and rejoice in its glory. This work of glorification so significant in salvation history, is effective in and through the Holy Spirit who is self-giving love. Jesus Christ, receiving everything from the Father and returning it to him in unlimited love, becomes for us the source of the living water, of the Spirit. The Spirit of truth whom he sends to those who follow him on the road of humility is 'the Spirit of glory' (1 Pet 4.14).

The divine refulgence, radiating from the humanity of the risen Lord in his full glory is the prerequisite and source of the transfiguration that gives the saints, the 'just', a share in God's splendour in a glorious resurrection. The Christian expects not merely bliss of soul. He looks forward hopefully to the resurrection of his body in glory, in participation with the reflective splendour of Christ's own beauty. Therefore he not only reveres his own bodily reality as 'a shrine of the indwelling Holy Spirit' but also understands the command '. . . then glorify God in your body' (1 Cor 6.20).

We honour Christ as 'the light of the world' (Jn 8.12), as 'the image of the invisible God' (Col 1.15), as 'the bright morning star' (Rev 22.16). Giving to him, and with him to the Father, all glory in the Holy Spirit, we come to understand the good news that we, too, are light, 'a light for the world'. Those who serve the Lord in purity of heart understand their great vocation and mission, 'And you, like the lamp, must shed light among your fellows, so that when they see the good you do, they may give praise to your Father in heaven' (Mt 5: 16).

Our mission in the world and our final hope are presented in terms of beauty and glory. Until his glorious coming, Christ bestows the Spirit of truth. The Spirit of love, upon his disciples to make them sharers of his beauty and glory. He does the same for his Church, 'so that he might present her to himself all-glorious, with no stain or wrinkle or anything of the sort, but holy and without blemish' (Eph 5.27).

The community of those who are totally consecrated to the glory of the Father will be glorious at the coming of the Lord, more so than any 'bride adorned for her husband' (Rev 21.2). . . .

One of the basic symbols of Christian faith and life is the woman 'robed with the sun, beneath her feet the moon, and on her head a crown of twelve stars' (Rev

12.1). It is Mary, the mother of the Lord, the most beautiful of women, and the Church insofar as she joins Mary in the discipleship of Christ the Servant.

Some ask, 'May the Christian love beauty?' But how is it possible not to love it, since beauty is surely the Christian's home, his hope! The whole life of the believers is turned to 'the glory of God revealed in the face of Jesus Christ' (2 Cor 4.6), 'until they will be taken up into his eternal glory'.

For those who have contemplated God in the Word incarnate, and made the glorification of the Father their life's main purpose, Christ's high priestly prayer will be fulfilled: 'The glory which thou gavest me I have given to them, that they may be one as we are one . . ., so that they may look upon my glory which thou hast given me because thou didst love me before the world began' (Jn 17.22–24).

God's own beauty is itself the primordial source of our joy, our strength, our love and our fellowship with all of his children. It will be our eternal bliss in the praise of God, the reflection of his truth and love in our final absorption in the very glory of his truth and love.

Moral-psychological relevance of the beautiful Gratitude for beauty and openness to its message are of utmost importance in a sacramental vision of Christian life. Ralph Waldo Emerson warns, 'Never lose an opportunity of seeing anything that is beautiful. For beauty is God's handwriting – a quasi-sacrament.' The New Testament writers have chosen the word *charis*, which means the charm of beauty, to blend the message of God's grace and graciousness.

For each person, the experience of the beautiful opens the way, in a singular and inescapable manner, to value-experience, to the good as a gracious gift, the good and the truth in their own attractive splendour. In the right encounter with the beautiful, we transcend the realm of profit or utility. We also leave behind a morality that speaks with an unattractive 'must'. Those who know beauty will never choose a morals [sic] of 'must', detached from value. Rather, in wonderment, gratitude and joy, they sense the beautiful in all its delicacy and refinement, and soon discover that the beauty in nature and art opens new vistas to the stream of beauty that waters the earth through the moral sensibilities of its people.

The graced nature of moral value will never be captured by anyone who cannot repose and rejoice before all the beauty that God has communicated to us. One might object that the experience of the beautiful has nothing to do with morality, since the value response to beauty re-echoes spontaneously, and as soon as one approaches it too purposefully and with imperatives, he is not on the right wave-length. Besides, it could be said that while morality cannot be severed from the majestic call to commitment, the beautiful grants and requests nothing else than delight.

To this objection we say that the focus is too much on naked duty and does not take seriously enough the sphere of the beautiful. It also tends to deprive the good of its attractive power and of its giftedness which generate gratitude, the very energy-source of a morality under the law of grace. While we can admire a person who does the good even though it might cost him great pain, we cannot at all appreciate a morality based on emotional starvation. Christ proclaims Gospel morality of graciousness and blessedness, and he promises his disciples his peace and the art of rejoicing even in the midst of difficulties.

The morality of beauty is something much deeper than that of 'must' and 'ought'. Its experience is inescapably personal, a loving and grateful approach to life itself. The fullness of being is experienced as a beautifying gift, an attractive appeal that solicits a loving response. Anyone who allows the beautiful, in all its dimensions, to bring its message home, knows that life is meaningful, a wonderful gift and opportunity. Who, for instance, can be moved by the majestic beauty of the works of Mozart, Beethoven and Bach, and not experience wholeness, and not trust that life is worthwhile? The fragrance and beauty of a single flower, absorbed in gratitude, brings us closer to the giver of all good gifts.

A morality totally imprisoned in the question, 'What have I to do?' ignores the moral implications of our response to the beautiful. But as soon as our basic moral question is, 'What kind of person am I meant to be?' a new vista opens. Then we know the relevance of the beautiful for all of our lives. It will be a dimension in all our responsibilities, in our care for a healthy environment and for beautiful relationships with others.

Because beauty is simply and wholly a gift, our relation to it is unrestrained. But the very gratitude that makes us able to rejoice in it will motivate us to cultivate the beautiful in our lives. It needs space and time in the ordering of our life, not merely alongside other dimensions but as a formative force of all the facets of existence.

The genuine experience of the beautiful is holistic; it brings our whole being into contact with the all-embracing reality. The transcendental qualities of being – the good, the true and the beautiful – are inseparable; therefore, to neglect one of them has disastrous consequences for the others. Take their splendour away from the good and the true, and you have condemned them to concealment. Make aesthetics a thoroughly separate sphere, and you destroy art itself. Block the access through the beautiful and you impoverish the good and the true. Take beauty away, for example, from the life and spirituality of St Francis of Assisi, and you can no longer understand him or rejoice with him.

Once we have understood that beauty is as much a transcendental dimension as oneness, truth and goodness, then we will see it clearly in God and all his works, in creation, in history, in the incarnation of the divine Word. Then it will be easier to overcome the split between the sphere of love and that of knowledge, 'through the contemplation of the Divine Beauty where the Spirit of Truth is the shining splendour of the Divine Beauty'.

If, in education and theology, the value of the beautiful is neglected, nothing is left finally but the moral of despots or of hucksters, a purposive reckoning of man-the-maker who, like a beast of burden, no longer knows how to be an artist and to rejoice while he is producing and consuming things. Alienation from the beautiful among moralists and educators has made of biblical morality, with its gratitude, joy and wholeness, a fretful groaning under incomprehensive imperatives, laws and controls, a chilling encounter with duties, or a petty computation of merits for the other world. A morality that has no concern for the beautiful knows nothing of the blessedness that dwells within the good, which is the voice of the all-holy God. (pp. 102–9)

Source: Bernard Häring, CSsR, *Free and Faithful in Christ, vol. 2, The Truth Will Set You Free*, Slough, St Paul Publications, 1979.

19.9 Leonid Ouspensky, Vladimir Lossky, from
The Meaning of Icons

Ouspensky, one of the leading contemporary Russian Orthodox theologians, presents in this passage the theology of the icon, which essentially has not changed since the 7th Ecumenical Council. The official recognition of the equal status of image and word, emphasized here, is unique to the Orthodox Church.

Thus the Church gradually creates an art new both in form and content, which uses images and forms drawn from the material world to transmit the revelation of the Divine world, making this world accessible to understanding and contemplation. This art develops side by side with the Divine services and, like the latter, expresses the teaching of the Church in conformity with the word of the Scriptures. This conformity between word and image was particularly clearly expressed by the ordinance of the VIIth Oecumenical Council, which re-established the veneration of icons. Through the voice of the fathers of this Council the Church rejected the compromise proposal to place their veneration of icons on a level with that of sacred vessels, and ordained that it be on a level with the Cross and the Gospels: – with the Cross as the distinctive symbol of Christianity, with the Gospels, as representing a complete correspondence between verbal image and visible image. The formulation of the Holy Council says: 'We preserve, without innovations, all the Church traditions established for us, whether written or not written, one of which is icon-painting as corresponding to what the Gospels preach and relate . . . For if the one is shown by the other, the one is incontestably made clear by the other.' This formulation shows that the Church sees in the icon not a simple art, serving to illustrate the Holy Scriptures, but a complete correspondence of the one to the other, and therefore attributes to the icon the same dogmatic, liturgic and educational significance as it does to the Holy Scriptures. As the word of the Holy Scriptures is an image, so the image is also a word. 'What the word transmits through the ear, that painting silently shows through the image, says St Basil the Great', and 'by these two means, mutually accompanying one another . . . we receive knowledge of one and the same thing.' In other words, the icon contains and professes the same truth as the Gospels and therefore, like the Gospels, is based on exact concrete data, and in no way on invention, for otherwise it could not explain the Gospels nor correspond to them. . . .

Through the Divine service and through the icon, revelation becomes for believers their property and precept for life. For this reason Church art acquires from the very beginning a form in keeping with what it expresses. The Church evolves an entirely special category of image, in accordance with its nature, and this special character is conditioned by the purpose it serves. The Church is a 'kingdom not of this world' (John 18.36) existing in the world and for the world, for its salvation. Its nature is peculiarly its own, distinct from the world, and it serves the world precisely by being thus different from it. Consequently the manifestations of the Church, through which it fulfills this service, be they word, image, singing or some other, differ from analogous manifestations of the world. They all bear the seal of their transcendental nature, which externally distinguishes them from the world.

Architecture, painting, music, poetry cease to be forms of art, each following its own way, independently of the others, in search of appropriate effects, and become parts of a single liturgic whole which by no means diminishes their significance, but implies in each case renunciation of an individual role, of self-assertion. From forms of art with separate aims, they all become transformed into varied means for expressing, each in its own domain, one and the same thing – the essence of the Church. In other words, they become various instruments of the knowledge of God. It follows that from its very nature Church art is a liturgic art. Its liturgic character is not due to the fact that the image serves as a framework and addition to the Divine service, but to their complete mutual correspondence. The mystery enacted and the mystery depicted are one, both inwardly in their meaning and outwardly in the symbolism which expresses this meaning. This is why the image of the Orthodox Church, the icon, does not define itself as an art belonging to one or another historical epoch, nor as the expression of the national peculiarities of one or another people, but only by its function which is as universal as Orthodoxy itself, being determined by the very essence of the image and its role in the Church. Since in its essence the icon, like the word, is a liturgic art, it never served religion but, like the word, has always been and is an integral part of religion, one of the instruments for the knowledge of God, one of the means of communion with Him. This explains the importance which the Church attributes to the image – an importance such that of all victories over a multitude of various heresies, it was only the victory over iconoclasm and the reestablishment of the veneration of icons that was proclaimed as the Triumph of Orthodoxy, celebrated on the first Sunday of Lent. (pp. 30–1)

As we have said, Christianity is the revelation not only of the Word of God but also of the Image of God, in which His Likeness is revealed. This godlike image is the distinctive feature of the New Testament, being the visible witness of the deification of man. The ways of iconography, as means of expressing what regards the Deity, are here the same as the ways of theology. The task of both alike is to express that which cannot be expressed by human means, since such expression will always be imperfect and insufficient. There are no words, nor colours nor lines, which could represent the Kingdom of God as we represent and describe our world. Both theology and iconography are faced with a problem which is absolutely insoluble – to express by means belonging to the created world that which is infinitely above the creature. On this plane, there are no successes, for the subject itself is beyond comprehension and no matter how lofty in content and beautiful an icon may be it cannot be perfect, just as no word image can be perfect. In this sense both theology and iconography are always a failure. Precisely in this failure lies the value of both alike; for this value results from the fact that both theology and iconography reach the limit of human possibilities and prove insufficient. Therefore the methods used by iconography for pointing to the Kingdom of God can only be figurative, symbolical, like the language of the parables in the Holy Scriptures. But the content expressed in this symbolical language is immutable, both in the Scriptures and in the liturgic image.

Just as the teaching concerning the purpose of Christian life – the deification of man – continues to exist, so the dogmatic teaching concerning the icon continues to exist and live in the Divine services of the Orthodox Church, thanks to which the right attitude to the icon is preserved. For an Orthodox man of our times an icon, whether ancient or modern, is not an object of aesthetic admiration or an object of study; it is living, grace-inspired art which feeds him. In our times, as of old, not only does the icon continue to be painted according to the Canon, but the consciousness of its content and significance is again awakening; for now, as before, it corresponds to a definite concrete reality, a definite living experience, which is at all times alive in the Church. For example, one of our contemporaries, a staretz of Mount Athos who died in 1938, describes his personal experience in the following words: 'There is a great difference', he says, 'between merely believing that God is, knowing Him from nature or from the Scriptures, and knowing the Lord by the Holy Spirit.' 'The Lord is known in the Holy Spirit, and the Holy Spirit is in the whole of man – in his soul, his mind and his body.' 'He who has come to know the Lord by the Holy Spirit assumes the likeness of the Lord; as St John the Evangelist said, "We shall be like him; for we shall see him as he is" (1 John 3.2), "and we shall behold his glory".' Thus as the living experience of the deification of man continues to exist, so, too, lives the iconographic Tradition, and with it even its technique; since as long as this experience is alive, its expression, whether in word or image, cannot disappear. In other words, being the outer expression of the likeness of God in man, the icon cannot disappear just as the likeness of man to God itself cannot disappear. (pp. 48–9)

Source: Leonid Ouspensky, Vladimir Lossky, *The Meaning of Icons*, trans. G. E. H. Palmer and E. Kadloubovsky, Crestwood, NY, St Vladimir's Seminary Press, 1983.

19.10 Sallie McFague, from *Models of God, Theology for an Ecological, Nuclear Age*

A concern with theological aesthetics includes awareness of the meaning and application of metaphors and imagery for God in each age. North American feminist theologian Sallie McFague presents in this passage the idea of God as lover, the erotic dimension in God, and the human and divine desire for union. She is one among few theologians who use both the female and male pronoun for God.

God as Lover

The Love of God as Lover: Eros . . . We speak of God as love but are afraid to call God lover. But a God who relates to all that is, not distantly and bloodlessly but intimately and passionately, is appropriately called lover. God as lover is the one who loves the world not with the fingertips but totally and passionately, taking pleasure in its variety and richness, finding it attractive and valuable, delighting in its fulfillment. God as lover is the moving power of love in the universe, the desire for unity with all the beloved, the passionate embrace that spins the 'living pulsing earth' around, sends the blood through our veins, and 'draws us into one another's arms'.

This is a poetic way of saying what many others have said of eros, from Plato (love is the 'everlasting possession of the good') to Tillich (love is the desire for union with the valuable). This is the love that finds goodness and beauty in the world and desires to be united with it. By itself, unqualified by other kinds of love, it can become aesthetic and elitist, but its importance, as we have seen, is that it expresses better than any other kind of love the *valuableness* of the beloved. In a time such as ours, when the intrinsic value of our world must be stressed, eros as the love of the valuable is a necessary aspect of both divine and human love. This is a critical dimension of our model and will figure prominently in our understanding of the work of God as lover, for we shall understand salvation to be the making whole or uniting with what is attractive and valuable, rather than the rescuing of what is sinful and worthless.

The assumption that eros is the desire for union with, or possession of, the valuable suggests, however, that it lacks what it would have. It assumes a situation of separation, a situation of alienation in contrast to a situation of original unity. And it is this lack or need – what Tillich calls the 'urge toward the reunion of the separated' – that is the point of identity in all forms of love, from epithymia (desire, including sexual desire), to agape, eros, and philia. In fact, one sees it most clearly in sexual desire: the act that both brings new life into being and gives the most intense pleasure to all living creatures is a powerful symbol of the desire for unity with others that is shared by all forms of life. Agape, the love that gives with no thought of return; eros, the love that finds the beloved valuable; and philia, the love that shares and works for the vision of the good – none of these can be reduced to sexual desire, but all of them in different ways attest to the oneness of love, so evident in sexual union, as 'that which drives everything that is towards everything else that is'. Sex is the most basic physical symbol for unity, and therefore, in a theology concerned to express the Christian vision as an inclusive one of fulfillment for all creation, it must be allowed its hallowed place as the one act that up and down the ladder of creation signifies the desire to be united with others. As with birth, eating, and other basic physical acts, we use sex in a vast multitude of ways to communicate all manner of complex human emotions, but they all depend for their meaning on the power of the original base. Love cannot be reduced to sex, but it cannot escape it either, or if it tries, it becomes bloodless, cold, and sterile, no longer the embrace that spins our pulsing earth, sending blood through our veins and drawing us into each other's arms.

This description of eros – that it is a passionate attraction to the valuable and a desire to be united with it – may initially mark it as a strange candidate, from a traditional Christian perspective, for expressing God's saving love. It implies that the world is valuable, that God needs it, and that salvation is the reunification of the beloved world with its lover, God. (Ch. 5, pp. 130–1)

The second implication of our model of God as lover is that God needs the world. Lovers need each other, and in fact, the classic treatment of eros in Plato's *Symposium* describes it as the love that would complete us and make us whole. Plato says that love (eros) is the child of Plenty and Poverty and hence has a dual nature that drives it from finite and transitory embodiments of the good and beautiful up the ladder until it reaches the Forms of absolute goodness and beauty. So lovers start with their beautiful bodies and proceed to the beauty of the mind. This view of eros as using valuable objects and persons as stepping-stones to intellectual self-fulfillment is certainly part of the reason eros has received such negative treatment in Christian circles. However, the model of God as lover of the world who needs the world does not have the utilitarian, dualistic, and self-centered characteristics of Plato's view. . . .

The response that God as lover needs is from us not as individuals but as parts of the beloved world; God as lover is interested not in rescuing certain individuals from the world but in saving, making whole, the entire beloved cosmos that has become estranged and fragmented, sickened by unhealthy practices, and threatened by death and extinction. God as lover finds all species of flora and fauna valuable and attractive, she finds the entire, intricate evolutionary complex infinitely precious and wondrous; God as lover finds himself needing the help of those very ones among the beloved – of us human beings – who have been largely responsible for much of the estrangement that has occurred. We are needed lest the lover lose her beloved; we are needed so that the lover may be reunited with his beloved. The model of God as lover, then, implies that God needs us to help save the world! This is, as we shall see, a different view of salvation from the traditional one, where God does the entire work of salvation and we can do nothing but accept God's gift with gratitude. (Ch. 5, pp. 133–5)

Source: Sallie McFague, *Models of God, Theology for an Ecological, Nuclear Age*, Philadelphia, Fortress Press, 1987.

19.11 Patrick Sherry, from *Spirit and Beauty*

Patrick Sherry has concerned himself with theological aesthetics in his recent writings. In his important study on the trinitarian and, especially, on the pneumatological dimension of beauty, he argues that natural and artistic beauty are signs of grace and of eschatological anticipation. The spirit is the source of all beauty, and ugliness is thus a sin against the Spirit.

Conclusion . . . The thesis I have looked at is that the divine beauty is to be explained in Trinitarian terms, for the Father's glory is reflected in the Son, his perfect image, and diffused through the Holy Spirit; that the Spirit has the mission of communicating God's beauty to the world, both through Creation, in the case of natural beauty, and through inspiration, in that of artistic beauty; that earthly beauty is thus a reflection of divine glory and a sign of the way in which the Spirit is perfecting creation; and that beauty has an eschatological significance, in that it is an anticipation of the restored and transfigured world which will be the fullness of God's kingdom. It remains for me to say a little more about some particular difficulties we have encountered, and to point a few morals.

Retrospect Clearly I have assumed that a concern with natural beauty and art is a serious one. It is not merely a luxury; still less is it to be dismissed with the derogatory term 'aestheticism' (it would be interesting to speculate on how both 'theological' and 'aesthetic' have tended to become derogatory terms, especially considering that their parents, religion and art, are both supposed to be concerned with what is profound and moving in human life). Theologically, such a concern arises both out of one's own experience and out of an acceptance of the doctrine of Creation. John W. Dixon points out that an artist cannot hate his material, and that for a Christian artist physical material is glorified both through Creation and through the new creation which proceeds from the Incarnation. If indeed the world has been created by God, then the qualities in it which delight us (or disturb us too, sometimes) have been put there by Him, perhaps with this purpose – which is not to say that they must affect everyone in the same way at the same time. Likewise, our creative powers and faculties of appreciation are gifts of God; and although they may be abused (for a lack of grace can contaminate them as much as any other human powers), they may also be infused and guided by His spirit. Thus both worldly beauty and our creative powers may be described as a 'grace'. Indeed, there are some grounds for going still further, if we accept that our creative powers are part of the image and likeness of God with which we are endowed, and if we accept also that God's glory shines through His creation. In exercising their creative powers in the production of things of worth, men and women may become channels of God's creativity; and the beauty of what they create may, like natural beauty, have a sacramental significance, in that by it the material may convey the spiritual and indeed, some would say, serve as a sign of God's presence and activity.

Here we are approaching one of the most difficult subjects discussed in this work, the divine beauty and the way it is reflected in the world. Although it is true that a lot of Christian thinking on the matter is much influenced by Plato and his successors, especially Pseudo-Dionysius, there is nevertheless good biblical warrant for ascribing beauty to God and for treating worldly beauty as a reflection of His glory. In any case, it is hardly likely that He would choose to disguise this particular attribute, though most theologians may have given this impression by their neglect of the topic. . . . Many Protestant theologians (though not Jonathan Edwards) are unhappy with what they regard as speculations about God's beauty, and are content to claim simply that natural beauty and artistic talents are divine gifts, particularly associated with the Holy Spirit. This position is not one which I accept, because I think that it disregards much Christian tradition and fails to do justice to the religious character of beauty and other aesthetic properties . . . but it must be treated seriously. . . .

Philosophically, the main problems in this work are suggested by the commonly quoted remark that 'beauty is in the eye of the beholder' and by the claim that beauty is no longer a central concept in aesthetics. It is indeed true that many of the ideas which we have considered were set out originally in an intellectual milieu very different from today's. . . .

The intellectual difficulties are reinforced by the confusion occasioned in many people's minds by some modern artistic movements, especially in painting and music. But perhaps the difficulties are not quite as severe as they appear at first sight. Beauty is indeed subjective, in the sense that it is a matter of our reactions to the perceived properties of things, and people may disagree about this as about so many other matters. But it does not follow that these properties are unreal or our perceptions illusory. Likewise, although it is true that beauty is not as central a concept in modern aesthetics as it was in much ancient and medieval aesthetics, and also, more generally, that critical evaluation is regarded today as only one part of aesthetics, it is still an important concept and one which attracts a lot of attention. What is true is that modern aesthetics tries to 'place' the concept of beauty logically by elucidating the relationship between it and other aesthetic concepts, showing that it is part of a network of such concepts. But this development is all to the good, since there is no reason why we should confine our treatment to a single concept; and other aspects of nature and of works of art may have a pneumatological significance besides beauty. Modern aesthetics offers us all sorts of possibilities here, and not just with regard to aesthetic evaluation. There is also the nature of symbolic systems in art to be considered, and the analogy which they suggest with languages; and there is the investigation of the social and economic factors which influence artists. The latter investigation is often suspect to religious people and regarded as materialistic, perhaps because of its connection with Marxism. But if God can work through secondary causes (as I have argued in my discussion of inspiration), there is no good reason for excluding the factors which I have mentioned from a theological aesthetics. Modern aesthetics may well make a positive contribution to our investigation, rather than blocking it off or hindering it.

Openness to the Spirit The argument which we have examined has a disturbing consequence: those who destroy the beauty of God's creation or who create ugliness may be sinning against the Holy Spirit. Such a conclusion is likely to seem unwelcome and strange to most people, because we have got used to the ideas that beauty is a luxury, that a concern with natural beauty or with art is only one among many things which may occupy people's leisure hours, and that such a concern has little to do with religion. Occasionally such assumptions are shattered, as in the scene in Heinrich Böll's powerful novella, *And where were you, Adam?*, in which the concentration-camp commandant shoots the Christian Jewess, Ilona, because he cannot bear the beauty of her singing of a Latin motet, when she is being auditioned for the choir which is his great pride and which he subsequently orders to be destroyed; the commandant's action is depicted by Böll as something like a sin against the Holy Spirit. But perhaps these assumptions are themselves a sign of the disastrous divorce between religion and a sense of beauty in our time, a divorce which is a far more serious problem than the pagan nature of much modern art, and which is manifested in many different ways, for instance in the toleration of drab or makeshift liturgies and in the failure to follow up Ruskin's denunciation of the squalor of industrial towns and cities (often the squalid has simply been replaced by the dreary). But if indeed the argument of this book is correct, then a failure to create beauty, and a lack of appreciation of it, are both signs of an absence of the Holy Spirit. Either the Spirit has not been given, or else there has been what St Paul calls a quenching or suppression of the Spirit (1 Thess 5.19). If the Spirit has not been given, we have to ask whether this is simply a matter of divine freedom ('The wind/spirit blows where it wills'), resulting in the lack of inspiration so familiar to artists in their dry periods, or whether there has also been a lack of openness to the Spirit, and a failure to pray for and to eagerly await his promptings.

All this, however, sounds rather grim and condemnatory (though it has to be said). Let us be more positive and turn the argument round. Aquinas, as we have seen, said that all truth is from the Holy Spirit, and Calvin followed him in saying that the Spirit of God is the only fountain of truth, even that of profane writers. Now, again, if the argument of this book is correct, it would seem that the Holy Spirit is the source of all real beauty and aesthetic merit, both because of his work in Creation and because of his freedom to inspire whomsoever he wills, often, it seems, without much regard to the recipient's moral character or religious orthodoxy. So the argument has also a more tolerant and wide-embracing aspect.

Even this more positive note, however, is still too solemn and moralistic to end on. The Book of Proverbs describes wisdom as delighting God at Creation and playing joyfully in His presence, and as at play everywhere in the world, delighting to be with the sons of men (8.30f.); and the Book of Job describes all the stars of the morning as singing with joy at the Creation (38.7). . . . The important thing is that we look (or listen), rejoice, and give thanks. (Ch. 8, pp. 176–82)

Source: Patrick Sherry, *Spirit and Beauty, An Introduction to Theological Aesthetics*, Oxford, Clarendon Press, 1992, 2nd edn, SCM Press, 2002.

19.12 Richard Harries, from *Art and the Beauty of God*

Harries, Bishop of Oxford and writer on faith and culture, examines the nature of, and essential connection between, beauty, truth and goodness as well as beauty's distortion, i.e. kitsch. He asserts – in line with early church and medieval theologians – that glory is manifested in the confluence of the three transcendentals.

At its least adequate the word beauty is close to conveying the notion of what is only decorative. This is a fine feature, not to be disparaged in its proper place. But there is also the searing, disturbing, haunting element which is present in many of the greatest works of art. . . . Beauty, properly understood, needs to be seen in conjunction with truth and goodness. It is because beauty is, quite properly, associated with these other qualities that it can sometimes seem wracking and awesome. . . .

Like Tillich I believe that genuine art catches, conveys and participates in some aspect of reality, even ultimate reality, to use his phrase. This is the truth content of art, which Tillich also refers to as its depths or import. There is, however, also the form, without which no work of art would exist and which is also included in Tillich's analysis. Beauty has to do with this form. To be beautiful as opposed to merely pretty, it needs to be associated with other values like truth or integrity. But the two values of beauty and truth are distinct, if in the end inseparable. It muddies the water to subsume one into the other. . . .

All forms of art are in the business of truth: truth of eye and ear and mind. True beauty is inseparable from the quest for truth. When the attempt to produce something beautiful is separated from truth the result is sentimentality. . . .

The attempt to get at the truth of things . . . is inseparable from certain moral qualities. Artistic integrity is the most obvious quality that is required. Here we come across the fact that sometimes an artist may be all over the place in their personal life whilst still producing works of great quality. This is because, whatever the mess in the rest of their life, they are still totally committed to their work, brooking no compromises. . . .

One of the problems of bringing morality into a discussion on beauty or art is that the word sets up such misleading associations. People immediately tend to think that sex or violence is being referred to. But all works of art inevitably express a feeling for life and convey certain moral values. There is no morally neutral realm in art or elsewhere. Nothing in this life is value-free. And some works of art which are bitterly attacked as being immoral are in fact the product of a profoundly moral view of existence.

Another quality that is necessary for great art is love. Truth without love leads in the end to bitterness and cynicism. An artist who is always disdainful, who can only see the worst, who hates what they are working on, cannot produce great art. Love means, first, an act of self-transcendence, in order to see truly what is being depicted whether in words or paint or stone or any other medium. Secondly, the artist needs a sense of the value of what is portrayed. The person depicted might be truly awful, even utterly cruel but, unless they are to be a cardboard cutout or a piece of propaganda, it will be necessary even so to retain a sense of the pity and tragedy of their life. *Sunt lacrimae rerum*, as the Roman poet Virgil put it: 'There are tears in things.' Art needs all that Simone Weil meant by 'attention'. And attention, she argued, means putting aside the illusion that 'my eye' is the centre of the world and focusing on things as they are. To focus on things as they are, in this way, is to share in God's act of self-renunciation, his love. (Ch. 4, pp. 47–51)

When goodness, truth and beauty are combined we have glory. When boundless goodness, total truth and sublime beauty are combined in supreme degree, we have divine glory. The word glory has come to mean honour and renown. In church we often repeat the *Gloria*: 'Glory to the Father and to the Son and to the Holy Spirit.' But the ascription of glory to God should be seen as a response to the glory that is inherent in his being. Before our recognition and praise, God is in himself all glory in a sublime conjunction of beauty, truth and love. This glory is majestic. It brings wonder and awe and worship.

The divine glory was disclosed first of all to the people of Israel. In the Hebrew Scriptures the word glory and its cognates glorious, glorify, etc. are used many times in relation to God. The glory of God shines out in the beauty and order of creation. 'The heavens declare the glory of God' (Psalm 19.1). This all-glorious God sometimes gives a glimpse of his glory to particular people. When Moses received the Ten Commandments on Mount Horeb, he was both in awe and as one speaking to God as a friend: 'The skin of his face shone because he had been talking with God' (Exodus 34.29). Sometimes in the Scriptures God is depicted as one who makes himself known by his superior power, his sheer might. He can do what other gods cannot do and break the bodies as well as the wills of recalcitrant people. This would be intolerable tyranny except that it was linked to his loving kindness, his undeviating goodwill towards his people and the luminous beauty of his holiness. What stops the God of Israel being experienced as sheer terror is his being as love and beauty. He is not just power but glory. Power can browbeat us but glory lures and entices us by stirring what we most deeply desire.

It is the Christian conviction that this glory is fully known in Jesus Christ. He is 'the Lord of glory' (1 Corinthians 2.8). The glory of God in Jesus Christ is a theme that runs throughout the New Testament. 'He reflects the glory of God and bears the very stamp of his nature' (Hebrews 1.3). But it is in John's Gospel where the theme receives most sustained and consistent treatment. When the Word became flesh, 'We beheld his glory, glory as of the only Son from the Father' (John 1.14). This glory was revealed in the signs, starting at Cana of Galilee (John 2.11). Above all, however, the glory of God shines out in the Cross and Resurrection. Jesus prays that in his life and the coming climax of his death God might be glorified. But this glorification of the Father is also a glorification of the Son. For Jesus has given himself over totally to do his Father's will. His Father's work is what he came to accomplish. Because his being is one with the Father, through all temptations and suffering, it is his glory that is revealed as well as that of the Father (John 12.27–33; 17.1–5). John looks at Jesus through the eyes of one who believes in him; in the light of the Resurrection and coming of the Spirit. He had come 'to see' and believe.

The picture painted by Mark's Gospel is very different. It stresses the failure of the disciples, the betrayal by Judas, the denial by Peter and the abandonment by the disciples. Everyone falls away and in the end Jesus is left on the Cross uttering the agonized words 'My God, my God, why hast thou forsaken me?' (Mark 15.34). The glory of God in Christ, except at the Transfiguration, is hidden.

In Mark and John we have the two poles of Christian truth. To generalize the truth revealed in Christ, God's glory is revealed in humble, self-effacing lives of faith and love. It can be fully present in failure and ignominy. It is almost entirely a glory that is veiled. Yet, however hidden, lives of sacrificial love lived in response to the Father manifest the glory of God and the glory of Christ. For Christ has been raised and his Spirit is with us, unveiling Christ's journey to the Cross as a movement to the Father and revealing the divine glory. In the light of this many of our standard notions of success and failure are radically reversed. Christ, the King of Glory, reigns from the tree. . . .

Christ reveals the divine glory because he is the truth of God and the love of God, in human terms. But what about the beauty of God? Gerard Manley Hopkins said in a sermon: 'There met in Jesus Christ all things that can make man lovely and lovable. In his body he was most beautiful.' . . . Earlier writers fight shy of extolling Christ's physical beauty, indeed there is discussion about whether we should think only of his spiritual beauty or of both spiritual and physical beauty.

All writers, however, are agreed in applying the words of Isaiah 53.2 to Christ on the Cross: 'He had no form or comeliness that we should look at him, and no beauty that we should desire him.' For our sake the beauty of God takes on ugliness. As Augustine put it in a sermon: 'His deformity is our beauty.'

In his description of the physical build of Christ, Gerard Manley Hopkins is in grave danger of slipping into kitsch. Kitsch is the enemy of all that is true, good and beautiful. . . . In art kitsch takes the form of the pretty, the sentimental and fashionable. It excludes all that is truly disturbing and harrowing. In morality kitsch takes the form of totalitarianism, the exclusion of all that is individual and distinctive. (Ch. 4, pp. 54–8)

The two points I wish to make here are that first, kitsch, in whatever form, is an enemy of the Christian faith and must be exposed as such. Secondly, kitsch reveals to us that the aesthetic, the moral and the spiritual realms are inseparably interconnected. The failure of kitsch is a moral and spiritual failure as much as an aesthetic one. The success of a work of art is a moral and spiritual success as much as it is an aesthetic triumph. The beauty of Christ is not a sentimental prettiness, however much nineteenth-century kitsch religious souvenirs have shaped people to think of him in that way. We do not know the extent of Christ's physical beauty. We do, however, in faith, believe that there is in him a spiritual loveliness which permeates his whole being, breaks down our resistance and wins us to him. (Ch. 4, p. 60)

True beauty is inseparable from the quest for truth and those moral qualities which make for a true quest. In the world of art this means integrity, a refusal to go for easy popularity, for cheap truth; the willingness to transcend the clamant ego, to attend to what is there, in its own terms, however painful. This is why works of art, in whatever medium, as well as having a form which pleases will convey truth which may disturb. The conjunction of beauty with truth and goodness has its origin in God and is what we mean by his glory.

The Bible does not dwell long on beauty in isolation but it has much to say on the subject of glory. The God who is revealed is a God of glory and his glory is destined to illuminate and shine in us. For a Christian this glory is above all revealed in Jesus Christ. This was, for the most part, hidden glory. Only at the Transfiguration and in the light of his Resurrection is Christ's life of self-offering to the Father revealed in all its splendour as the life of God made Man and the destiny of humanity to become like God. This means that as human beings we will always stand in a profound, puzzling, tensionful relationship to all forms of human beauty. For the full glory of the world about us will be largely hidden in lives of secret self-sacrifice, of unceasing inner prayer, of profound artistic achievement that goes unrecognized in its own time. On the other hand, all that is fine and flourishing, all that is beautiful and radiant as God intends it to be, has its place in that transformed world which belongs first and foremost and finally to the poor and humble. (Ch. 4, p. 62)

Source: Richard Harries, *Art and the Beauty of God, A Christian Understanding*, London, Mowbray, 1993.

19.13 John Navone, from *Toward a Theology of Beauty*

John Navone of the Gregorian University, Rome, has written, in particular, on narrative theology. In this extract he puts forward a Neo-Thomist theology of beauty with the revelation of the triune God and the transcendentals at its centre.

Theology of Beauty: Résumé of Presuppositions

The triune God is the One, True, Good, and Beautiful. These four transcendentals are conceptually distinct but ontologically identical and interchangeable with Being Itself/God.

The four transcendentals are aspects of Happiness Itself.

Happiness Itself is an interpersonal unity of communion, community, and communications consisting of knowing its truth, loving its goodness, and delighting in the beauty of its truth and goodness.

The triune God, Happiness Itself, delights in its unity, truth, and goodness; it knows the truth of its unity, goodness, and beauty; it loves the goodness of its unity, truth, and beauty.

The triune God, Happiness Itself, is Spirit: the One, the True, the Good, and the Beautiful. All created/human happiness, unity, truth, goodness, and beauty is a limited participation in Happiness/Truth/Goodness/Beauty Itself or Spirit. Transcendentals are rooted in spirit (divine/human) as aspects of Being Itself.

The triune God, Happiness Itself, is the Common Good of the universe/all creation. There is no happiness, unity, truth, goodness or beauty apart from its origin-ground-fulfillment in the Triune God, Happiness Itself, the Common Good of all creation.

The triune God, Goodness Itself, is the Common Good that originates, sustains, perfects, and fulfills all created/finite/human happiness, unity, truth, goodness, and beauty. All created goodness participates in the Common Good/ Goodness Itself/Triune God. God is one, good, true, and beautiful by God's essence; creatures are so by participation. God alone exists by God's essence; creatures exist by participation. God is Being Itself; creatures receive or have it by participation.

God sees (knows) all that God has made, and it is good because God sees it and sees it as good. God's vision is not a response to created beauty/goodness; it is the cause of created beauty/goodness.

God creates all in God's likeness. The unity, truth, goodness, and beauty of creation reflects the Creator as the One, the True, the Good, and the Beautiful. The One creates a cosmos/universe rather than chaos, within which there is an order of interrelated, interacting, interdependent, parts enabling our affirmation of the unity, truth, goodness, and beauty of things.

The Spirit/God is where the Spirit/God acts. The Spirit/God acts as the principle of unity, truth, goodness, and beauty of all the universe/creation; as the

Creator, Sustainer, Director, and Fulfillment of the universe/creation. The unity, truth, goodness, and beauty of things are, therefore, evidence of the presence and activity of the Spirit/God. The Spirit/God reveals something of Itself in creation.

Because God acts freely, both God's creation and revelation are gifts or forms of God's self-giving. God is in God's gifts, giving them existence, unity, truth, goodness, and beauty, as well as meaning, direction, and purpose. All creation is, therefore, a motive for gratitude. Nothing exists that we have not been freely/lovingly given. All creation irradiates the splendour of the Creator's self-giving love.

God is not an object to be known among other objects. No object/creature is self-explanatory. God is known as the transcendent explanation for all objects/creatures. Similarly, nothing makes sense out of context. God is the Ultimate Context in and from which all objects/creation make sense or has sense/meaning/purpose. Being Itself, the One/True/Good/Beautiful Itself, is the measure of all created reality which possesses existence and its transcendental qualities by participation. Apart from its Ultimate Context, all creation is ultimately absurd or meaningless.

The faith whereby we apprehend the splendour/beauty of transcendent Love-Wisdom has a relative as well as an absolute aspect; for it apprehends all things in the light and shadow of that Love-Wisdom. In the shadow, for transcendent Love-Wisdom is supreme and incomparable. In the light, for transcendent Love-Wisdom transforms, magnifies, and glorifies all things within its all-encompassing goodness. The triune God, Truth/Goodness/Beauty Itself, is not a part of creation; rather, God transforms, magnifies, and glorifies it.

God created the universe, as Thomas affirms (*In Div. Nom.*, c. 4, lect. 5, n. 349), to make it beautiful for himself by reflecting his own beauty. Out of love for the beauty of his own true goodness, God gives existence to everything, and moves and conserves everything. Beauty Itself intends everything to become beautiful within the fullness of its own true goodness.

We reflect Beauty Itself to the extent that we conform to it. We become beautiful in conforming to the grace and call of God's will/love/truth for us. Self-will, in opposition to God, deforms our God-given beauty; for we are true in God's truth, good in God's goodness, and beautiful in the beauty of God's true goodness.

Just as there is a distinction between our true good and an apparent good, there is a distinction between true beauty and seductive beauty. True beauty, like our true good, is whatever attracts us to our true fulfillment and happiness. Seductive beauty entails whatever allures us to our self-destruction (morally or spiritually). The same distinction holds between the prudent and the clever person. Although both have a talent for knowing the means to achieve their ends, the former is moral (virtuous) and the latter is immoral. Similarly, there are true solutions and pseudo-solutions to problems. There are true friends and apparent friends.

True beauty entails our true joy/delight in knowing and loving things as they truly are: God above all, and everything else as limited. There is no true joy/delight in loving God for less than what God is or in loving a creature above all. True love and joy entail loving things as they truly are. Our true happiness is always related to our true knowledge and love of true beauty and goodness. Self-deception can never ground such joy or happiness.

As the perfect image of God, Jesus Christ is perfectly conformed to God as the Incarnate Word/Light/Love/Beauty of the triune God's Eternal Word/Light/Love/Beauty. He is the transfigured and transfiguring Son of Man and Son of God, transforming/transfiguring the deformed image and likeness of God in self-willed humankind. He is the communion of the divine and human creating communion/community/communications between God and humankind. He is the sacrament of God, the efficacious sign, making all things beautiful in the beauty of God's true love and goodness. Jesus Christ and his Church are the sacrament for the triune God's making all things beautiful, for reforming/transforming/conforming/transfiguring the deformed/disfigured/distorted human image of God in order that all humankind might have life fully in communion/community/communications with Truth/Goodness/Beauty Itself.

Our Christian faith apprehension of the glory/beauty of God in Jesus Christ, the beauty of the Incarnate Word/Light/Love, results from the Triune God's gift of God's Holy Spirit. It is our loving knowing and knowing loving that results from God's showing his love for us by the gift of God's Spirit to our hearts (Rom 5: 5). It is the knowledge-born-of-love, of the mutual love that unites Father, Son, and Christian. Without faith, without the eye of love, we cannot joy in the beauty of love visible in Christ, who 'reflects the glory of God' (Heb 1.3). Such faith enables Paul to see God working in all things for the good of those who love him (Rom 8.28). It enables us to see the beauty of God's loving kindness in all things. Hearts can, however, grow cold; we can lose sight of God's loving kindness. God gives God's self to us in all our experience, whether or not we have the eye of love to see the beauty of God's self-giving love.

God's creating the universe to be beautiful implies that God creates it to be delightful; for the beautiful is delightful. Because God is Happiness/Beauty Itself, our conformity to God entails our participation in Happiness/Beauty Itself. 'Thy will be done' implies our welcoming Happiness/Beauty Itself. God's will for us is always God's true love and happiness for us. The triune God, Happiness/Beauty Itself, is eternally and essentially self-giving. Our happiness and beauty, therefore, consist in accepting/welcoming/participating in God's self-giving Spirit. We can contemplate Beauty Itself in persons manifesting the splendour of God's self-giving Spirit. God's beauty is manifested wherever God's will is done because God's will for us is always God's love for us. Beauty is the splendour of God's love. It is the radiant joy of Happiness/Love/Truth Itself.

Salvation in Jesus Christ means freedom *from* and freedom *for*. Jesus is God's servant Messiah sent to free us from *all* the obstacles to our having communion, community, and communication with Happiness/Truth/Love/Beauty Itself. Jesus Christ and his Church are the triune God's saving sacrament (efficacious sign) freeing humankind *for* communion, community, and communication with Happiness/Truth/Love/Beauty Itself. Jesus Christ and his Church are the sacrament Happiness/Truth/Love/Beauty Itself for the beauty and joy of all creation. The triune God is operative in the sacramental liturgy of the Church for the beauty and joy of humankind under the sovereignty of God's eternal and invincible love.

Catholic doctrines of the universal Church ground a Catholic theology of beauty.

Creation. All creation reflects the beauty of its knowing and loving Creator; therefore, we can contemplate something of Beauty Itself in all creation.

Providence. Having created all things to be beautiful, the Creator draws them to the ultimate perfection of their beauty in eternal communion-community-communication with Beauty Itself.

Eschatology. The beatific vision of Beauty Itself is the destiny and eternal happiness of all who love God. 'Eye has not seen, nor ear heard . . . what God has prepared for those who love him.'

Incarnation and *Revelation.* Jesus Christ is the incarnate Son and revelation of God/Beauty Itself.

Christology. Jesus Christ is the perfect image/form of God because he is perfectly conformed to the mind and heart of God.

Soteriology. Christ, the perfect form of God, transforms/transfigures/beautifies/divinizes/saves/redeems a sinful/deformed humankind as the Good/Beautiful Shepherd who, when lifted up in the mystery of the Cross, draws all humankind to himself/Beauty Itself incarnate. The self-giving power of Beauty/Love Itself saves the world.

Pneumatology. God's love poured into our hearts through the gift of the Spirit transforms us, enabling us to see with the eye of love/faith all things in the light of Beauty Itself. We rejoice even now in our faith/love vision that is a prelude to the beatific vision and eternal happiness. (Ch. 7, pp. 77–82)

Source: John Navone, SJ, *Toward a Theology of Beauty*, Collegeville, MN, The Liturgical Press, 1996.

19.14 Alejandro García-Rivera, from *The Community of the Beautiful, A Theological Aesthetics*

García-Rivera, associate professor at the Jesuit School of Theology at Berkeley, has worked specifically on the dialogue of theology and the arts. In this extract from his groundbreaking book, he explains that the task of theological aesthetics is to point once again to the origin of beauty in the divine and its reception by 'the human heart'. He emphasizes that the experience and language of beauty are essential to the life of the Church, to its faith and witness in the world.

Pied Beauty

What is Theological Aesthetics? It may surprise that the term 'aesthetics' did not appear in its contemporary meaning, i.e., the philosophy and science of the beautiful, until the eighteenth century. Alexander G. Baumgarten coined the term in 1735 to describe what he called the new 'science of sensory cognition'. Let me propose, however, that aesthetics may be recast as the science which asks a more profound question: *what moves the human heart?* Put in this way, aesthetics has existed since the first human heart was moved by the influence of the beautiful. The cave paintings of Lascaux or Altamira, for example, still manage to affect the modern heart after thousands and thousands of years. As Jean Clottes, France's foremost expert on prehistoric rock art, confessed: 'I remember standing in front of the paintings of the horses facing the rhinos and being profoundly moved by the artistry. Tears were running down my cheeks. I was witnessing one of the world's great masterpieces.' Asking the question, *what moves the human heart?*, I believe, brings us closer to the mysterious experience of the truly beautiful, an experience that transcends geological space and prehistoric time, an experience that holds the most persuasive claim to being what has become an *aporia* in our day, the real universal. Moreover, the tears of Msr Clottes, like the tears shed by St Ignatius in his mystical trances, speak as well of a religious experience. Indeed, recasting the question of aesthetics as the question of what moves the human heart is nothing more than following St Augustine's approach in his *Confessions*. As such, it allows aesthetics a philosophical approach while leaving open the possibility of a theological contribution, i.e., a theological aesthetics.

Theological aesthetics recognizes in the experience of the truly beautiful a religious dimension. This religious dimension is evident in the Lascaux and Altamira paintings. Most anthropologists, for example, believe the paintings to be religious in nature. Somehow Beauty and religious sentiment go hand in hand. As Jean Anouilh (1910–87), the French playwright, asserts in his play on Thomas à Becket, 'Beauty is one of the rare things that do not lead to doubt of God.' Beauty's trace reveals a divine starting point. Indeed, Beauty's religious dimension is found in its origins. It is little wonder then that throughout the history of theology, Beauty has played a major role, both implicit and explicit, in theological reflection. Why, then, not simply speak of a theology of Beauty rather than a 'theological aesthetics'?

It is true that until very recently, i.e., the eighteenth century, the long history of theological reflection emphasized Beauty rather than its experience. A theology of Beauty alone clearly does justice to the absolute origins of God's Beauty. God is not simply beautiful. Beauty originates in God's Own Self. There is, however, another dimension of divine Beauty that must be considered. What is Beauty if it is not received? A theology of Beauty alone leaves open the question of the inner dynamism of the human spirit. How can the finite human creature name the nameless, perceive the imperceptible, make visible the invisible? For Pseudo-Dionysius, however, it was not so much a matter of 'can' but of 'how'. Denys never questioned whether the human creature can experience the divine. His question simply was: *how*? Dionysius' 'how' is also the question of theological aesthetics. Its answer must account both for Beauty's divine origins as well as its reception by the finite human heart. If the grand tradition of the theology of Beauty never spoke of an 'aesthetics', it is because it never questioned the human creature's capacity to receive divine Beauty.

The assumption of receptivity, however, began to be questioned in the eighteenth century. Alexander Baumgarten asked the question not about Beauty but about the beautiful. How, exactly, is the beautiful experienced? In asking the question, Baumgarten reversed the assumptions of the Theology of Beauty. If the pre-modern reflection of the beautiful had assumed the human capacity to receive Beauty, Baumgarten's aesthetics begins with such capacity as problematic. And if the classical and medieval tradition speculated on Beauty's divine origins, Baumgarten's aesthetics essentially assumed them by methodically ignoring the issue. In disengaging Beauty from the beautiful, Baumgarten revealed a trend that has reached its apex in our day. We have lost confidence, perhaps belief, in the human capacity to know and love God as Beauty. Thus, while some may still believe that God is the source of Beauty, and many that the beautiful can be experienced, few would be willing to say that these two are connected in a profound and organic way.

The theological stakes are enormous. Do we believe in a God who wishes to be known and loved by his human creation? Does the human creature, in turn, have the capacity to know and love this God? At the heart of these questions, this brewing theological hurricane, is the doctrine of the Incarnation. Indeed, Beauty's transcendental nature, which nevertheless emerges into the human heart's experience of the beautiful, is a parallel of the Incarnation. Divine and human merge mysteriously in an act of divine initiation and human response, an act which is both knowledge and love. Irenaeus, the great theologian of the second century, exquisitely phrased it: 'the Glory of the Lord is living human being and human being lives for the vision of God.'

Theological aesthetics addresses this modern theological crisis by doing justice to these twin aspects of Beauty: its absolute origins in the transcendent God who nonetheless wishes to be known and loved by his human creation. Theological aesthetics attempts to make clear once again the connection between Beauty and the beautiful, between Beauty's divine origins and its appropriation by the human heart. In doing so, theological aesthetics discloses the importance of restoring the connection between Beauty and the beautiful which, in our day, has been severed. Human life has a worth and a dignity which only Beauty can reveal through the beautiful. Without the language and experience of Beauty and the beautiful, the Church will find difficult the expression of her faith, much less her conviction of the dignity of the human person, and, even less, be a sacrament to the world. There is, however, a more personal and concrete reason for a reconsideration of the organic connection between Beauty and the beautiful. It is the experience of a particular living ecclesial tradition, the Latin Church of the Americas, whose voice may add a guiding light in the present darkness of the Church's pilgrimage. As the Church faces the dissolution of Modernity, Beauty's call as experienced by the Latin Church of the Americas may serve as guiding buoy in the tempest ahead. (Ch. 1, pp. 9–12)

Source: Alejandro García-Rivera, *The Community of the Beautiful, A Theological Aesthetics*, Collegeville, MN, The Liturgical Press, 1999.

19.15 Richard Viladesau, from *Theological Aesthetics, God in Imagination, Beauty, and Art*

This book by North American theologian Richard Viladesau, of Fordham University, is one of the most important contributions to theological aesthetics at the turn of the millennium. Here he outlines what constitutes an aesthetic theology and a theological aesthetics. He furthermore discusses beauty as a means of approaching the divine, and the essential link between the true, the good and the beautiful.

Theology and Aesthetics

Theological Aesthetics as Theory 'Theological aesthetics,' then, as I conceive it, includes both narrative/metaphorical and metaphysical approaches. It comprises both an 'aesthetic theology' that interprets the objects of theology – God, faith, and theology itself – through the methods of aesthetic studies, and a more narrowly defined 'theological aesthetics' that interprets the objects of aesthetics – sensation, the beautiful, and art – from the properly theological starting point of religious conversion and in the light of theological methods. Hence 'theological aesthetics' in the second, narrower sense will include the following elements:

1. A theological account of human knowledge on the level of feeling and imagination ('aesthetics' in the sense of Schiller and Kant). The treatment of God and imagination involves the question of metaphor and analogy mentioned briefly above: how can the transcendent God be thought by a human mind that is tied to sensation? A related area is the theology of revelation and its relation to symbolic consciousness. Finally, there is a reflection on theological method: the development of a theological theory of interpretation (both of the Scriptures and of religious experience) that appeals to imagination and art, and the relationship of this hermeneutical task to systematic thought. This 'epistemological' form of theological aesthetics explores the relations of symbolic and theoretical consciousness, of hermeneutics to metaphysics, of religious experience to secular reason, of feeling to logical discourse, of beauty to truth.

2. A theology of beauty. This will reflect on the nature of the beautiful in relationship to God and to the 'transcendental'; the way in which beauty is a quality of revelation; and the place of 'beauty' as a criterion of theological judgment.

3. A theological reflection on art and on the individual arts. This reflection will attempt to understand how the arts can communicate concerning the divine; how they can mediate revelation and conversion; and what formal similarities they show to the practice of theology. (Ch. 1, pp. 23–4)

God in Thought and Imagination: Representing the Unimaginable

The Task of Fundamental Theological Aesthetics . . . In the light of the foregoing, we may conceive three interconnected divisions of the task of a 'fundamental' theological aesthetics as a study of the perception of revelation in sensible form. It will attempt through 'transcendental deduction' to discern the anthropological 'conditions of possibility' of:

1. Knowing God through a mind intrinsically tied to sensibility – in particular in the light of the Kantian critique of knowing. This involves the recognition of the radical openness of the personal subject to the transcendent; in traditional theological language, the doctrine of the human person as 'image' of God.

2. Receiving (or embodying) a historical revelation from God in personal and symbolic form. This involves understanding the notion of the 'image' of God as extending to interpersonal relations, so that materially and linguistically located human history can be the embodiment of revelation.

3. Using 'word' or language (in the widest sense, including verbal, pictorial, musical, and gestural symbols and images) to embody, formulate, interpret, and communicate the knowledge of God and of historical revelation. This implies the possibility of 'analogous' discourse, on the level of both concept and image. This means the analogous use of concepts, imaginative paradigms, and symbols to represent: (a) the divine transcendence; (b) the human mind itself; (c) human revelatory events in their historical particularity and universal relevance. (Ch. 2, pp. 70–1)

God and the Beautiful: Beauty as a Way to God

The Transcendental Condition of Beauty . . . I propose that the condition of possibility for the experience of beauty – in the sense of the joyous affirmation of the 'form' or desirable intelligibility of existence, even in its finite limitation – is the implicit and unavoidable co-affirmation of ultimate Beauty, a reality the apprehension of which would be unmixed and unlimited joy in existence, and which in itself – that is, as self-apprehending – is self-conscious Beauty or infinite Bliss.

The idea that God is infinite bliss is, of course, a part of the classical Western tradition, yet it seems sometimes to be lost both in theology and in our imaginative representations of the Deity. Perhaps this is in part because, in order to underline its ethical imperative, Western religion has frequently emphasized God's justice and anger with the sinful world (an angry person is by definition not happy). This in turn is a natural result of the idea that God is engaged in a historical 'dialogue' with the world, in which our responses 'make a difference' to God. It would seem to follow (at least to projective imaginative thinking) that God, like us, cannot finally be happy until the eschaton. Thus God's 'bliss' appears accidental: a state of being that God must attain, rather than an essential element in the meaning of the word 'God'. But my contention is that beauty points to the fact that being is in essence joyous: self-presence with delight. And the condition of possibility for finite beauty is the existence of the Beautiful as such.

This conclusion is revealed in the dialectic of fullness and longing in the spiritual experience of beauty: being is seen as capable of being apprehended with joy, worthy of giving oneself over to in affirmation and love. Yet this same being – both the being that is apprehended and the being of the one apprehending – is always limited, finite, marked with nonbeing and bearing the memory of death. In itself it appears incapable of supporting a total affirmation of the joy of existence. But the aesthetic act is possible and real because finite being in its apprehension by spirit is borne by its source and goal, which is 'co-apprehended' with it – not in a separate act, alongside it, but rather as what is interior to categorical being and to the apprehending mind.

As in other forms of the 'transcendental' argument, the critical point is that this ultimate reality is not conceived or projected as a transcendental idea, but is co-affirmed as actual in the very act of aesthetic joy. The act of commitment to the reality of finite beauty is at the same time given implicitly and unavoidably to the reality of the Absolute. That reality may subsequently be explicated by reason as the condition of the reality of our factual experience, or it may be explicitly denied. In the latter case, the reality of our experience itself is undermined, and our joy becomes groundless and (to that extent) illusory. (It must be recalled at this point that the 'joy' in question is distinct from simple sensible aesthetic 'pleasure', which may as such remain unaffected by the existence of an ultimate 'Ground' of beauty. On another level, the very existence of sensation –

as of any being or act at all – calls for metaphysical explanation. This, however, involves a different set of categories than the aesthetic.) To phrase the argument in terms parallel to Hans Küng's: just as the affirmation of the existence of God is the only possible final ground for a fully rational act of fundamental trust in existence, so it is likewise essential to an ultimately 'grounded' apprehension of beauty, insofar as this implies the joy of existence.

It will be noted that each 'transcendental' line of thinking arrives at God precisely as the fullness of the spiritual quality with which it begins and for which it seeks the condition of possibility. Thus Lonergan argues 'that if the real is completely intelligible, then God exists; he therefore arrives at God as the totally unconditioned act of intelligibility, or the 'Idea of Being'. Kant argues (in the sphere of 'practical reason') that if the good is an absolute 'ought' – if there is a categorical imperative – then there exists an absolute Will. Similarly, the line of thinking I have pursued here argues that if finite existence can be apprehended with joy, it is because reality in its wholeness – in its various degrees of realization – can be and is to be apprehended with joy; and that this is possible only on the condition that there exists the absolute Act of such apprehension. It thus arrives at God as subsistent, self-conscious Beauty.

The reasoning in the last step of this process is similar, on the one hand, to Lonergan's argument leading to the subsistent Idea of Being, and, on the other hand, to the Platonic-Augustinian ascent of the mind. In higher aesthetic experience we pre-apprehend an unconditional beauty, a complete ground for joy in existence. But the finite beautiful cannot be unconditioned. Material beauty is merely potential, since it must be apprehended by mind. Spiritual beauty – the beauty of the apprehending mind itself, in the aesthetic act – cannot be total or unconditional: first, because it is (and feels itself) incomplete; second, because it depends upon material conditions outside itself; third, because, being spatio-temporal, it is impermanent and is concretely threatened by change and ultimately by death. The only possibility of a complete grounding of the reality of beauty is a subsistent act of apprehension of form that is at once subsistent Being, subsistent Consciousness, and subsistent Joy. These three constitute the Hindu philosophical name for God, *Sat - Cit - Ananda;* and they are the supreme personal form of the three traditional transcendentals. (Ch. 4, pp. 138–9)

The Beautiful and the Good

Beauty and Goodness: Art as the Mediator of Virtue . . . In other spheres of life, beauty may be introduced purposely through art in order to facilitate learning. Despite the dangers that we have spoken of, in the light of what has been said concerning the need for conversion we may recognize that art, especially insofar as it seeks and mediates beauty, has a place in the pursuit of the good. Indeed, when aesthetic conversion is achieved in art, it becomes particularly relevant to moral conversion. Like morality, art can transcend the realm of pure immediacy. . . .

Art is an effective moral educator in that it portrays vice and virtue rather than legislating about them or explaining them in theoretical terms. Narrative art is particularly apt at teaching about human fallibility. The fundamental moral evil of 'seeing the worse for the better,' for example, 'is more informatively (though of course less systematically) carried out by poets, playwrights, and novelists' than by moral philosophers and theologians. Likewise, virtue is more convincing and imitable when it is embodied concretely in art than when it is commanded or expounded theoretically. 'Perhaps in general art *proves* more than philosophy can.' Art need not be didactic in order to serve the good – although there is clearly also a place for beauty and art in preaching and teaching, as in every form of communication. Art as communication can have a transformative effect on the person because it can literally give us a new way of seeing, hearing, feeling, and so on. Moreover, the kind of art that serves beauty, as Balthasar says, 'brings with it a self-evidence that enlightens without mediation.'

This self-evidence of beauty is the ultimate connection between art and good-ness, and is a fitting point on which to end these considerations. The good, in order to be morally effective, must also appear good; that is, its connection with our final end, with our deepest desire, must be perceivable. The good must be seen as beautiful, as joy-filled and fulfilling. God's self-revealing love in our hearts is necessary for this perception to occur at its deepest level: for us to recognize beauty in the drama of the Christ event and to be attracted to its imi-tation. But God's self-gift is always also a human achievement. Human collabo-ration is no less called for in the revelation of beauty than in the transmission of truth and the teaching of virtue. Michelangelo tells us (in a poem!) that art can be an idol; but it can also be the means by which the heart's terror is overcome, and it opens to the nearness of the transcendent: to 'that divine love which opened its arms on the cross to take us.'

There always remains for the Christian the need to make prudent decisions about the use of the world and its goods. The poor are always with us (Mark 14.7; Matt 26.11; John 12.8); and it is not always clear in the concrete whether the more 'beautiful work' of love (Mark 14.6, Matt 26.10) is in meeting their material needs or in nourishing the spirit's hunger. We do not live by bread alone; and the inspiration of hope through artistic beauty can also be a 'word from the mouth of God' (cf. Matt 4.4). Finally, as Barth says, it 'belongs to the essence of the glory of God not to be *gloria* alone but to become *glorificatio*.' The glorifying of God demands from us above all the spiritual beauty of agapic love; but it includes as well the integration of human creativity and sensitivity in the praise of God through art.

The need for art in conjunction with religion is perhaps especially crucial today, when the world has been transformed by human intervention and so many of the earth's inhabitants live in an environment far removed from any natural beauty. St Thomas quotes with approval the passages in Aristotle's *Ethics* in which he says that 'no one can remain long without delectation,' and that 'those who cannot rejoice in spiritual pleasures will turn to corporeal ones.'

'Sadness' about the spiritual realm – a lack of experience of the beauty of what is truly good, a lack of 'taste' for the holy – turns people away from the value of communion with others and toward the pursuit of material pleasure. Humankind is more and more responsible for our environment and our relations with each other. Crucial decisions that affect the future of our species – and of large parts of the nonhuman world as well – increasingly depend upon human insight and virtue. But our ability to be intelligent and responsible will depend largely on our having a vision of the good that touches and convinces us. A form of art is needed to produce such a vision. (Ch. 6, pp. 210–13)

Source: Richard Viladesau, *Theological Aesthetics, God in Imagination, Beauty, and Art*, New York, Oxford, Oxford University Press, 1999.

19.16 Joan Chittister, from 'Monastic Wisdom for Seekers of Light'

Joan Chittister, a North American Benedictine theologian has written on feminist and liberation theological themes. Here she makes an urgent plea for the presence of beauty in our lives as it is transformative, transcends the banal, and takes us into the realm of the mystical and of truth.

Beauty . . . What may be most missing in this highly technological world of ours is beauty. We value efficiency instead. We want functionalism over art. We create trash. We bask in kitsch. But beauty, right proportion in all things, harmony in the universe of our lives, truth in appearances, eludes us. We paint over good wood. We prefer plastic flowers to wild flowers. We reproduce the Pietà in plastic. We forgo the natural and the real for the gaudy and the pretentious. We are, as a people, awash in the banal. A loss of commitment to beauty may be the clearest sign we have that we have lost our way to God. Without beauty we miss the glory of the face of God in the here and now.

Beauty is the most provocative promise we have of the Beautiful. It lures us and calls us and leads us on. Souls thirst for beauty and thrive on it and by it nourish hope. It is Beauty that magnetizes the contemplative and it is the duty of the contemplative to give beauty away so that the rest of the world may, in the midst of squalor, ugliness and pain, remember that beauty is possible.

Beauty feeds contemplation and Beauty is its end. A sense of Beauty evokes in us consciousness of the eternal in the temporal. It calls us beyond both the present and the past to that everlasting Now where Beauty dwells in perpetuity.

Beauty, in other words, lifts life out of the anesthetizing clichés of the pedestrian. An encounter with the beautiful lifts our eyes beyond the commonplace and gives us a reason for going on, for ranging beyond the mundane, for endeavouring ourselves always to become more than we are. In the midst of struggle, in the depths of darkness, in the throes of ugliness, beauty brings with it a realization that the best in life is, whatever the cost, really possible.

Beauty takes us beyond the visible to the height of consciousness, past the ordinary to the mystical, away from the expedient to the endlessly true. Beauty sustains the human heart in the midst of pain and despair. Whatever the dullness of a world stupefied by the mediocre, in the end beauty is able, by penetrating our own souls, to penetrate the ugliness of a world awash in the cheap, the tawdry, the imitative, the excessive and the cruel. To have seen a bit of the Beauty out of which beauty comes is a deeply spiritual experience. It shouts to us always, 'More. There is yet more.'

Beauty is not a matter of having enough money to buy anything in sight. It is a matter of having enough taste to recognize quality, depth, truth, harmony when we see it. 'Beauty is truth and truth beauty/ That's all we know and all we need to know,' the poet John Keats wrote. A thing is beautiful, in other words, when it really is what it purports to be. There are cures, of course, for a deprivation of spirit. We could take down the billboards that turn the landscape into a junkyard of old ideas. We could clear away the clash of colours and things that saturate space and make seeing into the soul of a thing impossible. We could refuse to allow people to turn marble statues into plastic replicas. We could study the order, the harmony, the proportion of a flower. We could strain our eyes to look for what is beneath the obvious in the wrinkles of age, the misshapened knuckles of a worker's hands, the meaning in every moment, the ultimate in every possibility, the essence of every encounter. Or, we could simply own one soul-shattering piece of art ourselves, put it up in a solitary place over and against the commonplace which normally surrounds us. We could let it seep into the centre of the self until we find that we can never be satisfied again, anesthetized again, by the visual platitudes of the world in which we live.

What we do not nourish within ourselves cannot exist in the world around us because we are its microcosm. We cannot moan the loss of quality in our world and not ourselves seed the beautiful in our wake. We cannot decry the loss of the spiritual and continue ourselves to function only on the level of the vulgar. We cannot hope for fullness of life without nurturing fullness of soul. We must seek beauty, study beauty, surround ourselves with beauty. To revivify the soul of the world, we ourselves must become beauty. Where we are must be more beautiful because we have been there than it was before our coming.

To be contemplative we must remove the clutter from our lives, surround ourselves with beauty and consciously, relentlessly, persistently, give it away until the tiny world for which we ourselves are responsible begins to reflect the raw beauty that is God. (pp. 178–80)

Source: Joan Chittister, OSB, 'Monastic Wisdom for Seekers of Light', *Religious Life Review*, vol. 40, May/June, 2001.

Further Reading

In addition to the text extracts included in this Reader and their sources listed in the Acknowledgements, this bibliography is intended for further reading in the field of theological aesthetics.

Agnew, Una, *The Mystical Imagination of Patrick Kavanagh: A Buttonhole in Heaven?*, Dublin, Columba Press, 1998

Apostolos-Cappadona, Diane and Adams, Doug (eds), *Art as Religious Studies*, New York Crossroad, 1990

Ballinger, Philip, *The Poem as Sacrament: The Theological Aesthetic of Gerard Manley Hopkins*, Leuven, Peeters, 2000

Beckett, Wendy, *Art and the Sacred*, London, Rider, 1992

Begbie, Jeremy, *Voicing Creation's Praise, Towards a Theology of the Arts*, Edinburgh, T. & T. Clark, 1991

Begbie, Jeremy, *Theology, Music and Time*, Cambridge, Cambridge University Press, 2000

Begbie, Jeremy, (ed.), *Sounding the Depths: Theology through the Arts*, London, SCM Press, 2002

Bond, Fiona, *The Arts in Your Church: A Practical Guide*, Piquant Press, 2001

de Borchgrave, Helen, *A Journey Into Christian Art*, Oxford, Lion Publishing, 1999

Bredin, Hugh and Santoro-Brienza, Liberato, *Philosophies of Art and Beauty: Introducing Aesthetics*, Edinburgh, Edinburgh University Press, 2000

Burch Brown, Frank, *Good Taste, Bad Taste, and Christian Taste: Aesthetics in Religious Life*, London, New York, Oxford University Press, 2003

Bustard, Ned, *It Was Good, Making Art to the Glory of God*, Baltimore, MD, Square Halo Books, 2000

Cartlidge, David R. and Elliot, J. Keith, *Art and Christian Apocrypha*, London, Routledge, 2001

Chipp, Hershel B., *Theories of Modern Art*, Berkeley, CA, London, University of California Press, 1968

Coates, Paul, *Cinema, Religion and the Romantic Legacy*, Aldershot, Ashgate, 2002

Corby Finney, Paul, *The Invisible God – The Earliest Christians on Art*, London, New York, Oxford University Press, 1994

Corby Finney, Paul (ed.), *Seeing Beyond the Word: Visual Arts and the Calvinist Tradition*, Eerdmans, 1999

Cork, Richard, *Jacob Epstein*, London, Tate Gallery Publishing, 1999

Coulson, John, *Religion and Imagination*, Oxford, Clarendon Press, 1981

de Cruchy, John, *Christianity, Art and Transformation: Theological Aesthetics in the Struggle for Justice*, Cambridge, Cambridge University Press, 2001

Dagget Dillenberger, Jane, *Style and Content in Christian Art*, New York, Crossroad, 1965 (1986)

Dagget Dillenberger, Jane, *Image & Spirit in Sacred & Secular Art*, New York, Crossroad, 1990

Dagget Dillenberger, Jane, *The Religious Art of Andy Warhol*, London, New York, Continuum, 1998

Dawtry, Anne and Irvine, Christopher, *Art and Worship*, London, SPCK, 2002

Deacy, Christopher, *Screen Christologies – Redemption and the Medium of Film*, Cardiff, University of Wales Press, 2001

Dillenberger, John, *Images and Relics – Theological Perceptions and Visual Images in Sixteenth Century Europe*, Oxford, Oxford University Press, 1999

Drury, John, *Painting the Word: Christian Pictures and Their Meanings*, Yale, Yale University Press, 1998

Dryness, William, *Visual Faith: Art, Theology and Worship in Dialogue*, Grand Rapids, MI, Baker Academic, 2001

Eco, Umberto, *Art and Beauty in the Middle Ages*, trans. Hugh Bredin, New Haven, London, Yale University Press, 1959 (1986)

Eliner, Robert, *Buddha and Christ: Images of Wholeness*, Cambridge, Lutterworth Press, 2000

Farley, Edward, *Faith and Beauty, A Theological Aesthetic*, Aldershot, Ashgate, 2001

Fiddes, Paul, *The Novel, Spirituality and Modern Culture*, Cardiff, University of Wales Press, 2000

Fiddes, Paul, *The Promised End: Eschatology in Theology and Literature*, Oxford, Blackwell, 2000

Finaldi, G., MacGregor, N., et al, *The Image of Christ*, London, National Gallery, 2000

Fuller, Peter, *Images of God – The Consolation of Lost Illusions*, London, The Hogarth Press, 1992

Gadamer, Hans-Georg, *Truth and Method*, New York, Crossroad, 1984

Gadamer, Hans-Georg, *The Relevance of the Beautiful and Other Essays*, ed. Robert Bernasconi, Cambridge, Cambridge University Press, 1986

Golding, John, *Paths to the Absolute*, London, Thames and Hudson, 2002

Hall, James, *Hall's Dictionary of Subjects and Symbols in Art*, revised edition, London, John Murray, 1974 (1984)

Hederman, Mark Patrick, *Anchoring the Altar, Christianity and the Work of Art*, Dublin, Veritas, 2002

Heidegger, Martin, *Basic Writings*, ed. D. Farrell Krell, London, Henley, Routledge & Kegan Paul, 1978

Hurley, Richard, *Irish Architecture in the Era of Vatican II*, Dublin, Dominican Publications, 2001

Jasper, David and Prickett, Stephen, *The Bible and Literature*, Oxford, Blackwell, 1999

Jensen, Robin Margaret, *Understanding Early Christian Art*, London, Routledge, 2000

Kandinsky, Wassily, *Concerning the Spiritual in Art*, New York, Dover Publications, 1977

Kearney, Richard, *The Wake of Imagination*, London, Routledge, 1994

Kessler, Herbert L., *Spiritual Seeing: Picturing God's Invisibility in Medieval Art*, Philadelphia, University of Pennsylvania Press, 2000

Kuschel, Karl-Josef, *Poet as Mirror: Human Nature, God and Jesus in Twentieth Century Literature*, London, SCM Press, 1999

Latour, Bruno and Weibel, Peter, *Iconoclash: Beyond the Image Wars in Science, Religion and Art*, Cambridge, MA, MIT Press, 2002

Mackey, James P. (ed.), *Religious Imagination*, Edinburgh, Edinburgh University Press, 1986

Martin Jr, James Alfred, *Beauty and Holiness, The Dialogue Between Aesthetics and Religion*, Princeton, Princeton University Press, 1990

May, John R., *Nourishing Faith through Fiction, Reflections on the Apostles' Creed in Literature and Film*, Franklin, Wisconsin, Sheed and Ward, 2001

McGrath, Alistair E., *Christian Literature – An Anthology*, Oxford, Blackwell, 2000

Millbank, John, Pickstock, Catherine and Ward, Graham (eds), *Radical Orthodoxy*, London, New York, Routledge, 1999

Murphy, Daniel, *Christianity and Modern European Literature*, Dublin, Four Courts Press, 1997

Murphy, Francesca Aran, *Christ the Form of Beauty: A Study of Theology and Literature*, Edinburgh, T. & T. Clark, 1995

O'Donohue, John, *Divine Beauty, The Invisible Embrace*, London, New York, Bantam, 2003

Otto, Rudolf, *The Idea of the Holy*, Oxford, Oxford University Press, 1958

Pattison, George, *Kierkegaard: The Aesthetic and the Religious*, London, SCM Press, 1992

Pelikan, Jaroslav, *Jesus through the Centuries*, Yale, Yale University Press, 1997

Power Erikson, Kathleen, *At Eternity's Gate: The Spiritual Vision of Vincent van Gogh*, Grand Rapids, MI, Eerdmans, 1999

Roskill, Mark (ed.), *The Letters of Vincent van Gogh*, London, Fontana, 1983

Safran, Linda (ed.), *Heaven and Earth: Art and the Church in Byzantium*, Philadelphia, Pennsylvania State University Press, 1998

Sheldrake, Philip, *Love Took My Hand – The Spirituality of George Herbert*, London, Darton, Longman and Todd, 2000

Viladesau, Richard, *Theology and the Arts, Encountering God through Music, Art and Rhetoric*, New York, Mahwah, NJ, Paulist Press, 2000

Walker, Keith, *Images or Idols? The Place of Sacred Art in Churches Today*, Norwich, The Canterbury Press, 1996

Weir, Anthony and Jerman, James, *Images of Lust – Sexual Carvings on Medieval Churches*, London, Routledge, 1993

Wessels, Anton, *A Kind of Bible: Vincent van Gogh as Evangelist*, London, SCM Press, 2000

Wind, Edgar, et al, *The Religious Symbolism of Michelangelo: The Sistine Ceiling*, Oxford, Oxford University Press, 2000

Wuthnow, Robert, *Creative Spirituality: The Way of the Artist*, Berkeley, University of California Press, 2001

Yates, Nigel, *Buildings, Faith & Worship, The Liturgical Arrangement of Anglican Churches 1600–1900*, Oxford, Oxford University Press, 2000

Acknowledgements

We wish to express our gratitude to the following publishers and authors for permission to reproduce copyright material:

Alba House, The Society of St Paul, for extracts from pp. 361–2 from *The Christian Faith in the Doctrinal Documents of the Catholic Church*, by J. Neuner and J. Dupuis, 2001.

Augsburg Fortress for extracts from pp. 84–5, 90–1, 96, 99–100 from *Luther's Works, vol. 40, Church and Ministry II*, edited by Conrad Bergendoff, general editor Helmut T. Lehmann, 1958. Used by permission of Augsburg Fortress.

Augsburg Fortress for extracts from pp. 258–60 from *Luther's Works, vol. 36, Word and Sacrament II*, edited by Abdel Ross Wentz, general editor Helmut T. Lehmann, 1959. Used by permission of Augsburg Fortress.

Augsburg Fortress for extracts from pp. 315–16 from *Luther's Works, vol. 53, Liturgy and Hymns*, edited by Ulrich S. Leupold, general editor Helmut T. Lehmann, 1965. Used by permission of Augsburg Fortress.

Augsburg Fortress for extracts from pp. 130–1, 133–5 from *Models of God, Theology for an Ecological, Nuclear Age*, 1987, reprinted by permission from *Models of God* by Sallie McFague, copyright © 1987 Fortress Press. Used by permission of Augsburg Fortress.

Augsburg Fortress for extracts from pp. 150–3 from *Against the Wind, Memoir of a Radical Christian*, translated by Barbara and Martin Rumscheidt, 1999, reprinted by permission from *Against the Wind* by Dorothee Sölle, copyright © 1999 Augsburg Fortress. Used by permission of Augsburg Fortress.

Jeremy Begbie for extracts from pp. 147–53 from *Beholding the Glory, Incarnation through the Arts*, London, Darton, Longman and Todd, 2000 © Jeremy Begbie.

Blackfriars for extracts from pp. 71, 73 from *Summa Theologiae, vol. 2, Existence and Nature of God (Ia. 2–11)*, translated and edited by Timothy McDermott, 1964.

Blackfriars for extracts from pp. 43, 45, 47, 49, 129, 133, 135 from *Summa Theologiae, vol. 7, Father, Son and Holy Ghost (Ia. 33–43)*, translated and edited by T. C. O'Brien, 1976.

Blackfriars for extracts from pp. 75, 77 from *Summa Theologiae, vol. 19, The Emotions (Ia2æ. 22–30)*, edited by Eric D'Arcy, 1967.

Blackfriars for extracts from pp. 245, 247, 249, 251 from *Summa Theologiae, vol. 39, Religion and Worship (2a2æ. 80–91)*, translated and edited by Kevin D. O'Rourke, 1964.

Blackfriars for extracts from pp. 73, 75, 77 from *Summa Theologiae, vol. 43, Temperance (2a2æ. 141–54)*, translated and edited by Thomas Gilby, 1968.

Blackfriars for extracts from pp. 149, 151, 153, 155 from *Summa Theologiae, vol.*

53, *The Life of Christ (3a. 38–45)*, translated and edited by Samuel Parsons, Albert Pinheiro, 1971.

Geoffrey Bles for extracts from pp. 207–14, 218–21 from *Dream and Reality, An Essay in Autobiography*, by Nicolas Berdyaev, 1950.

The Catholic University of America Press for extracts from pp. 41–3, 346–7 from *Saint Justin Martyr*, edited by Thomas B. Falls, 1948, The Fathers of the Church series; reprinted with permission from The Catholic University of America Press.

The Catholic University of America Press for extracts from pp. 150–1, 180–3, 185–7, 193–4, 200–1, 217, 231, 249 from *Clement of Alexandria, Christ the Educator*, translated by Simon P. Wood, CP, 1954, The Fathers of the Church series; reprinted with permission from The Catholic University of America Press.

The Catholic University of America Press for extracts from pp. 214–18, 220–3 from *Tertullian, Apologetical Works and Minucius Felix, Octavius*, translated by R. Arbesmann, E. J. Daly and E. A. Quain, 1950, The Fathers of the Church series; reprinted with permission from The Catholic University of America Press.

The Catholic University of America Press for extracts from pp. 98–101, 161–2 from *Lactantius, The Divine Institutes*, translated by Mary F. McDonald, 1964, The Fathers of the Church series; reprinted with permission from The Catholic University of America Press.

The Catholic University of America Press for extracts from pp. 313, 499–500 from *Saint Hilary of Poitiers, The Trinity*, translated by Stephen McKenna, 1954, The Fathers of the Church series; reprinted with permission from The Catholic University of America Press.

The Catholic University of America Press for extracts from pp. 338–40 from *Ephrem the Syrian, Selected Prose Works,* edited by Kathleen McVey, translated by Edward G. Mathews and Joseph P. Amar, 1994, The Fathers of the Church series; reprinted with permission from The Catholic University of America Press.

The Catholic University of America Press for extracts from pp. 11–13, 220–2 from *Saint Basil – Exegetic Homilies,* translated by Agnes Clare Way, 1963, The Fathers of the Church series; reprinted with permission from The Catholic University of America Press.

The Catholic University of America Press for extracts from pp. 36–40, 42–4, 110–11 from *Gregory of Nyssa, Ascetical Works*, translated by Virginia Woods Callahan, 1967, The Fathers of the Church series; reprinted with permission from The Catholic University of America Press.

The Catholic University of America Press for extracts from pp. 259–60, 293–4 from *Saint Ambrose, Hexameron, Paradise, and Cain and Abel*, translated by John J. Savage, 1961, The Fathers of the Church series; reprinted with permission from The Catholic University of America Press.

The Catholic University of America Press for extracts from pp. 72–3, 86–8, from *Saint Ambrose, Theological and Dogmatic Works*, translated by Roy J. Deferrari, 1963, The Fathers of the Church series; reprinted with permission from The Catholic University of America Press.

The Catholic University of America Press for extracts from pp. 220, 290 from *Saint Augustine, The City of God, Books 8–16*, translated by Gerald G. Walsh and Grace Monahan, 1952, The Fathers of the Church series; reprinted with permission from The Catholic University of America Press.

The Catholic University of America Press for extracts from pp. 216–17 from *Saint*

Augustine, Letters, vol. 3, translated by Wilfrid Parsons, 1953, The Fathers of the Church series; reprinted with permission from The Catholic University of America Press.

The Catholic University of America Press for extracts from pp. 90–1, 269–70, 297, 447–8 from *Saint Augustine, Confessions,* translated by Vernon Burke, 1953, The Fathers of the Church series; reprinted with permission from The Catholic University of America Press.

The Catholic University of America Press for extracts from pp. 328, 344–5 from *Saint Augustine, The Divine Providence and the Problem of Evil, etc.,* translated by Robert P. Russell and Thomas F. Gilligan, CIMA Publishing Co., Inc., 1948, The Fathers of the Church series; reprinted with permission from The Catholic University of America Press.

The Catholic University of America Press for extracts from pp. 306–7 from *St John Chrysostom, On the Incomprehensible Nature of God,* translated by Paul W. Harkins, 1984, The Fathers of the Church series; reprinted with permission from The Catholic University of America Press.

The Catholic University of America Press for extracts from pp. 241–4, 370–3 from *Saint John of Damascus, Writings,* translated by Frederic H. Chase Jr, 1958, The Fathers of the Church series; reprinted with permission from The Catholic University of America Press.

Cistercian Publications for extracts from pp. 232–4, 236–9 from *The Works of Bernard of Clairvaux, vol. 3, On the Song of Songs,* translated by Kilian Walsh, Cistercian Fathers Series, no. 7, 1976.

The Continuum Publishing Group for extracts from pp. 650–9 from *Church Dogmatics, 2/1,* by Karl Barth, edited by G. W. Bromiley and T. F. Torrance ©1957, T. & T. Clark Ltd, Edinburgh, reprinted by permission of The Continuum International Publishing Group.

The Continuum Publishing Group for extracts from pp. 117–27 from *The Glory of the Lord, A Theological Aesthetics, vol. 1, Seeing the Form,* by Hans Urs von Balthasar, edited by Joseph Fessio, SJ and John Riches, translated by Erasmo Leiva-Merikakis © T. & T. Clark, 1982; reprinted by permission of The Continuum International Publishing Group.

The Continuum Publishing Group for extracts from pp. 188–92, 214–16 from *Art, Creativity, and the Sacred, An Anthology in Religion and Art,* edited by Diane Apostolos-Cappadona, Copyright © 1984 by The Crossroad Publishing Group, reprinted by permission of The Continuum International Publishing Group.

The Continuum Publishing Group for extracts from pp. 135–7 from *Decrees of the Ecumenical Councils, vol. 1,* edited by Norman P. Tanner, SJ, Sheed & Ward and Georgetown University Press, 1990; reprinted by permission of The Continuum International Publishing Group.

The Continuum Publishing Group for extracts from pp. 47–51, 54–8, 60, 62 from *Art and the Beauty of God, A Christian Understanding,* by Richard Harries, Mowbray © Richard Harries 1993, reprinted by permission of The Continuum International Publishing Group.

Copibec for extracts from pp. 255–6, 633–4 from *Periphyseon (The Division of Nature),* by John Scotus Eriugena, translated by I. P. Sheldon-Williams, revised by John J. O'Meara, Washington, Dumbarton Oaks, and Montreal, Bellarmin, Éditions Fides, 1987.

J. M. Dent & Sons and to E. P. Dutton & Co. Inc. for extracts from pp. 167, 173–4 from *Biographia Literaria*, by Samuel Taylor Coleridge, edited by George Watson, London, 1975.

Dimension Books for extracts from pp. 191–3, from *Symeon the New Theologian, Hymns of Divine Love*, translated by George A. Moloney, Denville, NJ, no date.

Dominican Publications for extracts from pp. 152–9 from *Documents Vatican Council II, Constitutions, Decrees, Declarations*, edited by Austin Flannery, OP, revised edition, 1996.

Dominican Publications for extracts from pp. 178–180 from 'Monastic Wisdom for Seekers of Light', by Joan Chittister, *Religious Life Review*, vol. 40, 2001.

Eerdmans for extracts from pp. 14, 22 from *The Writings of the Fathers down to AD 325, Tertullian et al*, edited by James Donaldson and Alexander Roberts, The Ante-Nicene Fathers, vol. 4, 1965.

Eerdmans for extracts from pp. 193–9 from *Art in Action, Toward a Christian Aesthetic*, by Nicholas Wolterstorff, 1980.

Eerdmans for extracts from pp. 148–51 from *Imagining God, Theology and the Religious Imagination*, by Garrett Green, 1989.

Element Books for extracts from pp. 153–61 from *Meister Eckhart, Sermons & Treatises, vol. 1*, translated and edited by Maurice O'Connell Walshe, 1989.

David Ford and Cambridge University Press for extracts from pp. 267–72 from *Self and Salvation, Being Transformed*, by David F. Ford © Cambridge University Press 1999, by permission of the author and Cambridge University Press.

Fordham University Press for extracts from pp. 24–9 from 'Theology and the Arts', by Karl Rahner in *Thought*, vol. 57, no. 224, 1982.

Gill and Macmillan for extracts from pp. 126–8, 130–1, 136–8 from *The Gracing of Society*, by Enda McDonagh, 1989.

Grace Publications Trust for extracts from pp. 57–62 from *John Owen, The Glory of Christ*, edited by Hervey Mockford, general editor J. K. Davies, 1987.

Greenwood Press and Yale University Press for extracts from pp. 135–7 from *Images or Shadows of Divine Things*, by Jonathan Edwards, edited by Perry Miller, 1948.

Greenwood Press and the University of Oregon for extracts from pp. 254–7 from *The Philosophy of Jonathan Edwards, From His Private Notebooks*, edited by Harvey G. Townsend, Westport, CT, Greenwood Press, 1972, (University of Oregon Monographs, 1955)

Walter de Gruyter GMBH & Co. KG for extracts from pp. 317–29 from *Paul Tillich: Writings in the Philosophy of Culture, Kulturphilosophische Schriften, vol. 2*, edited by Michael Palmer, 1990.

Hackett Publishing Company, Inc. for extracts from pp. 119–23 from *The Critique of Judgement* (1790), by Immanuel Kant, translated by Werner S. Pluhar, copyright © 1987 by Werner S. Pluhar, reprinted by permission of Hackett Publishing Company, Inc. All rights reserved.

The Handsel Press for extracts from pp. 159–66, 168–76 from *Faith, Theology and Imagination*, by John McIntyre, 1987, reprinted by kind permission of The Handsel Press, 62 Toll Road, Kincardine, Alloa, Scotland.

Herder and Herder for extracts from pp. 177–9, 182–90 from *Religious Art in the Twentieth Century*, by Pie-Raymond Régamey, 1963.

Hodder and Stoughton for extracts from pp. 76, 95–6, 120 from *A Rapture of Praise*,

Hymns of John and Charles Wesley, edited by H. A. Hodges and A. M. Allchin, 1966.

Indiana University Press for extracts from pp. 55, 368, 371, 373, 376, 378, 379, 380 from *Journals and Papers, vol. 1*, by Søren Kierkegaard, translated and edited by Howard V. Hong and Edna H. Hong, 1967.

The Institute of Carmelite Publications for extracts from pp. 155–9, 717–18 from *The Collected Works of St John of the Cross*, translated by Kieran Kavanagh, OCD and Otilio Rodriguez, OCD, 1973.

The Institute of Carmelite Publications for extracts from pp. 237–44 from *The Collected Works of St Teresa of Avila, vol. 1*, translated by Kieran Kavanagh, OCD and Otilio Rodriguez, OCD, 1987.

The Liturgical Press for extracts from pp. 77–82 from *Toward a Theology of Beauty*, by John Navone, 1996.

The Liturgical Press for extracts from pp. 9–12 from *The Community of the Beautiful, A Theological Aesthetics*, by Alejandro García-Rivera, 1999.

Lutterworth Press for extracts from pp. 499–503 from *The Divine Imperative, A Study in Christian Ethics*, by Emil Brunner, translated by Olive Wyon, 1937.

Macmillan Publishers for extracts from pp. 130–2, 153–4 from George Pattison, *Art, Modernity and Faith, Restoring the Image*, 1991, Macmillan Academic and Professional, reproduced with permission of Palgrave Macmillan.

The Medieval Academy of America for extracts from pp. 95, 472–3 from *Hugh of Saint Victor, On the Sacraments of the Christian Faith (De Sacramentis)*, translated by Roy J. Deferrari, 1951.

New City Press for extracts from pp. 109, 113–14 from *Francis of Assisi, Early Documents, vol. 1, The Saint*, edited by Regis J. Armstrong, J. A. Wayne Hellmann and William J. Short, 1999.

Aidan Nichols, OP, for extracts from pp. 91–4, 98–100, 112–13, 115–16 from *The Art of God Incarnate, Theology and Image in Christian Tradition*, Darton, Longman and Todd, 1980.

The Open Court Publishing Company for extracts from pp. 22–3, 58–9 from *St Anselm, Proslogium; Monologium; an Appendix In Behalf of the Fool by Gaunilon; and Cur Deus Homo*, translated by Sidney Norton Deane, 1903, reprinted by permission of Open Court Publishing Company, a division of Carus Publishing Company, Peru, IL, from *St Anselm, Proslogium; Monologium; an Appendix In Behalf of the Fool by Gaunilon; and Cur Deus Homo*, copyright © 1903 by the Open Court Publishing Company.

Orbis Books, Maryknoll, for extracts from pp. 95–7 from *Liberating Grace*, by Leonardo Boff, 1979.

Oxford University Press for extracts from pp. 9–11, 534–9 from *Aesthetics – Lectures on Fine Art*, by Georg F. W. Hegel, translated by T. M. Knox, vol. 1, 1975; reprinted by permission of Oxford University Press.

Oxford University Press for extracts from pp. 23–4, 70–1, 138–9, 210–13 from *Theological Aesthetics, God in Imagination, Beauty, and Art*, by Richard Viladesau, copyright © 1999 by Richard Viladesau. Used by permission of Oxford University Press, Inc.

Oxford University Press for extracts from pp. 204–7 from *Faith and Reason*, Oxford Readers, edited by Paul Helm, 1999; reprinted by permission of Oxford University Press.

Paulist Press for excerpts from pp. 272–4 from *The Poems of St. Paulinus of Nola*, translated and annotated by P. G. Walsh, from the Ancient Christian Writers, No. 40, Copyright © 1975 by Rev. Johannes Quasten and Rev. Walter J. Burghardt, SJ and Thomas Comerford Lawler, Paulist Press, Inc., New York/Mahwah, NJ. Used with permission of Paulist Press. www.paulistpress.com.

Paulist Press for excerpts from pp. 37, 64 from *Maximus Confessor: Selected Writings*, translation and notes by George C. Berthold, from The Classics of Western Spirituality, Copyright © 1985 by George Berthold, Paulist Press, Inc., New York/Mahwah, NJ. Used with permission of Paulist Press. www.paulistpress.com.

Paulist Press for excerpts from pp. 161–5 from *Richard St Victor: The Book of the Patriarchs, The Mystical Ark, Book Three of the Trinity*, translation and introduction by Grover A. Zinn, from The Classics of Western Spirituality, copyright © 1979 by Paulist Press, Inc., New York/Mahwah, NJ. Used with permission of Paulist Press. www.paulistpress.com.

Paulist Press for excerpts from pp. 442, 444, 445–8 from *Hildegard of Bingen: Scivias*, translated by Mother Columba Hart and Jane Bishop, from The Classics of Western Spirituality, copyright © 1990 by the Abbey of Regina Laudis: Benedictine Congregation Regina Laudis of the Strict Observance, Inc., Paulist Press, Inc., New York/Mahwah, NJ. Used with permission of Paulist Press. www.paulistpress.com.

Paulist Press for excerpts from pp. 69, 71–3, 75–8, 160–1 from *Bonaventure: The Soul's Journey Into God, The Tree of Life, The Life of St Francis*, translation and introduction by Ewert Cousins; preface by Ignatius Brady, from The Classics of Western Spirituality, copyright © 1978 by Paulist Press, Inc., New York/Mahwah, NJ. Used with permission of Paulist Press. www.paulistpress.com.

Paulist Press for excerpts from pp. 166–8, 241, 242–4, 249, 253, 256, 278, 279–80, 281 from *Nicholas of Cusa: Selected Spiritual Writings*, translated and introduced by H. Lawrence Bond, preface by Morimichi Watanabe, from The Classics of Western Spirituality, Copyright © 1997 by H. Lawrence Bond, Paulist Press, Inc., New York/Mahwah, NJ. Used with permission of Paulist Press. www.paulistpress.com.

Paulist Press for excerpts from pp. 114, 129 from *Angelus Silesius: The Cherubinic Wanderer*, translation and foreword by Maria Shrady, from The Classics of Western Spirituality, copyright © 1986 by Maria Shrady, Paulist Press, Inc., New York/Mahwah, NJ. Used with permission of Paulist Press. www.paulistpress.com.

Paulist Press for excerpts from pp. 76–80, 82–3 from *Pseudo Dionysius: The Complete Works*, translated by Colm Luibheid; foreword, notes, and translation collaboration by Paul Rorem; preface by René Roques; introduction by Jaroslav Pelikan, Jean Leclercq, and Karlfried Froehlich; from The Classics of Western Spirituality, Copyright © 1987 by Colm Luibheid; Paulist Press, Inc., New York/Mahwah, NJ. Used with permission of Paulist Press. www.paulistpress.com.

Paulist Press for excerpts from pp. 286–9, 293–5 from *Julian of Norwich: Showings*, translated from the critical text with an introduction by Edmund Colledge, OSA and James Walsh, SJ from The Classics of Western Spirituality, Copyright © 1978 by Paulist Press, Inc., New York/Mahwah, NJ. Used with permission of Paulist Press. www.paulistpress.com.

Paulist Press for excerpts from pp. 59–61, 80, 106 from *Gregory Palamas: The*

Triads, edited with an introduction by John Meyendorff, translation by Nicholas Gendle, preface by Jaroslav Pelikan, from The Classics of Western Spirituality, Copyright © 1983 by Paulist Press, Inc., New York/Mahwah, NJ. Used with permission of Paulist Press. www.paulistpress.com.

Pickwick Publications for extracts from pp. 68–70 from *Huldrych Zwingli, Writings, vol. 2, In Search of True Religion: Reformation, Pastoral and Eucharistic Writings*, translated by H. Wayne Pipkin, Allison Park, 1984.

Princeton University Press for extracts from pp. 47, 49, 61, 63, 65, 67 from Abbot Suger, *On the Abbey Church of St. Denis and Its Art Treasures*, edited and translated by Erwin Panofsky, 2nd edition by Gerda Panofsky-Soergel. Copyright © 1979 by Princeton University Press; reprinted by permission of Princeton University Press.

Princeton University Press for extracts from pp. 166–9, 258–62 from Søren Kierkegaard, *Either/Or, part 2*, translated and edited by Howard V. Hong and Edna H. Hong. Copyright © 1987 by Howard V. Hong; reprinted by permission of Princeton University Press.

Princeton University Press for extracts from pp. 109–11, 165–8 from Frank Burch Brown, *Religious Aesthetics, A Theological Study of Making and Meaning*, copyright © 1989, by Princeton University Press, reprinted by permission of Princeton University Press.

Helga Robinson-Hammerstein for extracts from pp. 41–2 from Helga Robinson-Hammerstein, *Faith, Force and Freedom, Translation of the Fourth Invocavit Sermon & Introduction*, A Navicula Publication, Dublin, Trinity College, School of History, 2001

Routledge for extracts from pp. 94, 109, 121, 152 from *Irenaeus of Lyons*, The Early Church Fathers, edited by Robert M. Grant, 1997.

SCM Press for extracts from pp. 99–100, 105–7, 109–15 from *Calvin: Institutes of the Christian Religion*, The Library of Christian Classics, vol. 20, edited by John T. McNeill, Ford Lewis Battles, 1961; in USA and Canada: Westminster John Knox Press.

SCM Press (USA: Simon & Schuster) for extracts from pp. 162–3, *Letters and Papers from Prison*, Dietrich Bonhoeffer, edited by Eberhard Bethge, translated by Reginald Fuller © SCM Press Ltd, 1953, 1967.

SCM Press (USA and Canada: Harper Collins) for extracts from pp. 58–64 from *Theology of Joy*, by Jürgen Moltmann © SCM Press Ltd, 1973.

SCM Press (USA and Canada: Crossroad) for extracts from pp. 37–9, 41–7 from *Art and the Question of Meaning*, by Hans Küng, translated by Edward Quinn, 1981.

SCM Press (USA and Canada: Crossroad) for extracts from pp. 107–15 from *The Analogical Imagination*, by David Tracy, London, 1981.

SCM Press (USA and Canada: Crossroad) for extracts from pp. 241–2, 244–9 from *A Theology of Artistic Sensibilities, The Visual Arts and the Church,* by John Dillenberger, 1986.

SCM Press (USA: Continuum) for extracts from pp. 103–5 from *I Am My Body, New Ways of Embodiment*, by Elisabeth Moltmann-Wendel, translated by © John Bowden, 1994.

Charles Scribner's Sons for extracts from pp. 30–2, 60–3 from *Art and Scholasticism and The Frontiers of Poetry*, by Jacques Maritain, translated by Joseph W. Evans, 1962.

Patrick Sherry for extracts from pp. 176–82 from *Spirit and Beauty, An Introduction to Theological Aesthetics*, Clarendon Press, 1992 (2nd edition SCM Press 2002) © Patrick Sherry.

Shoe String Press and Harper Collins for extracts from pp. 219, 221–9 from *Man's Vision of God and the Logic of Theism*, by Charles Hartshorne, Archon Books, 1964.

SLL/Sterling Lord Literistic and Harvey Cox for extracts from pp. 275–9 from *The Seduction of the Spirit*, by Harvey Cox, Simon and Schuster, 1973; reprinted by permission of SLL/Sterling Lord Literistic, Inc., copyright by Harvey Cox.

St Paul Publications for extracts from pp. 102–9 from *Free and Faithful in Christ, vol. 2*, by Bernard Häring, 1979.

St Vladimir's Seminary Press for extracts from pp. 20–2, 81, 100–3 from *St Theodore the Studite, On the Holy Icons*, translated by Catharine P. Roth, 1981; used by permission of St Vladimir's Seminary Press, 575 Scardale Rd, Crestwood, NY 10701; 1-800-204-2665.

St Vladimir's Seminary Press for extracts from pp. 30–1, 48–9 from *The Meaning of Icons*, by Leonid Ouspensky, Vladimir Lossky, translated by G. E. H. Palmer, E. Kadloubovsky, 1983; used by permission of St Vladimir's Seminary Press, 575 Scardale Rd, Crestwood, NY 10701; 1-800-204-2665.

The University of Chicago Press for extracts from pp. 316–19 from *Disfiguring: Art, Architecture, Religion*, by Mark C. Taylor © by the University of Chicago, 1992.

The University of Notre Dame Press for extracts from pp. 60–3 from *Images of Faith, An Exploration of the Ironic Imagination*, by William F. Lynch, 1973.

Weidenfeld and Nicolson for extracts from pp. 332–7, 339–40 from *Sacred and Profane Beauty, The Holy in Art*, by Gerardus van der Leeuw, translated by David E. Green, no date (orig. 1932).

Zondervan for extracts taken from pp. 29–31 from *Experiencing God, Jonathan Edwards, Selected Readings from His Spiritual Classics*, by Robert Backhouse, copyright © 1995 in this compilation HarperCollins Publishers. Used by permission of The Zondervan Corporation.

Public domain:

Expositions on The Book of Psalms by Augustine, Bishop of Hippo, vol. 2, translated by members of the English Church, A Library of Fathers of the Holy Catholic Church, Oxford, John H. Parker, F. and J. Rivington, 1848, extracts from p. 230.

The Poetical Works of George Herbert, by George Herbert, New York, D. Appleton and Co., 1857, extracts from pp. 65–7, 81, 83–4.

Translations of the Writings of the Fathers, vol. 9, Irenaeus et al, edited by Alexander Roberts and James Donaldson, The Ante-Nicene Christian Library, Edinburgh, T. & T. Clark, 1869, extracts from p. 544.

The Writings of Origen, The Ante-Nicene Christian Library, vol. 10, edited by J. Donaldson and A. Roberts, Edinburgh, T. & T. Clark, 1869, extracts from pp. 22, 24–6.

Modern Painters, by John Ruskin, extracts from vol. 2, part 3, sections 1 and 2, New York, John Wiley & Sons, 1889, extracts from pp. 138–41.

Gregory the Great, Part 2, Selected Epistles, A Select Library of the Nicene and Post-Nicene Fathers of the Christian Church, Second Series, vol. 13, Oxford, James

Parker and Company/New York, The Christian Literature Company, 1898, pp. 297–8.

An Essay in Aid of A Grammar of Assent, by John Henry Newman, London, New York, Bombay, Calcutta, Longmans, Green, and Co., 1909, extracts from pp. 82–3, 106–10.

The Reality of God and *Religion and Agnosticism*, by Friedrich von Hügel, edited by Edmund G. Gardner, London, Toronto, J. M. Dent & Sons, 1931, extracts from pp. 75–6.

Every effort has been made to correctly identify and acknowledge the copyright holders of the selected extracts included in this volume. If there are any inadvertent omissions or errors, we apologize and will undertake to rectify these in any future edition.

Subject Index

Name Index

Note: *Biblical figures are in italics*

Abraham 15, 68, 116
Adam 17, 58, 70
Ambrose 10, 11, 12, 26, 28, 41, 42,
    58, 109, 207
Angelus Silesius 162–3
Anouilh, J. 5, 359
Anselm of Canterbury 61, 63, 74,
    103, 109
Aquinas, T. 59, 63, 88, 105–6,
    123–4, 205, 208, 219, 298, 320,
    326–7, 331, 350, 356, 365
Areopagite, Denys the 323–4, 326
Aristotle 5, 16, 124, 196, 323, 365
Auden, W.H. 288
Augustine 9, 10, 12, 13, 29, 33, 42,
    61, 72, 90, 95, 105–6, 109, 124,
    137, 139, 207–8, 219, 316, 339,
    359

Bach, J.S 219, 304, 342
Baggley, J. 242
Balthasar H.U. v. 204, 207, 219,
    230, 320, 325, 338, 365
Barth, K. 3, 204, 207, 315, 323, 365
Basil 9, 23–24, 39–40, 68, 98, 343
Baumgarten, A. G. 3, 156, 159,
    359–60
Beckmann, M. 256
Bede 91
Beethoven, L.v. 342
Begbie, J. 249, 252
Berdyaev, N.A. 206, 276, 281, 333
Berkeley, G. 179

Bernard of Clairvaux 59, 61, 95,
    118, 121
Blake, W. 158
Böll, H. 350
Boff, L., 3, 284–5
Bonaventure 59, 61, 63, 84, 88
Bonhoeffer, D. 282, 337
Bonnard, P. 223
Braque, G. 212
Bruckner, J.A. 218
Brunner, E. 3, 206, 273, 276
Büchner, G. 245
Burch Brown, F. 3, 204, 206, 266,
    270
Burke, E. 156, 158–9

Caesar 133
Cage, J. 287
Calvin, J. 125, 127, 136, 142, 350
Caravaggio, M.M.d. 156
Celan, P. 245
Cézanne, P. 203, 212, 215
Chagall, M. 212
Charlemagne 141
Charles the Bald 115
Chirico, G. de 212
Chittister, J. 208, 366–7
Chopin, F. 158
Cicero 89–90
Clement of Alexandria 10, 49, 53
Clottes, J. 359
Coleridge, S.T. 179, 181
Collingwood, R.G. 231